Blue Coat
or Powdered Wig

Blue Coat or Powdered Wig

FREE PEOPLE OF COLOR

IN PRE-REVOLUTIONARY

SAINT DOMINGUE

Stewart R. King

THE UNIVERSITY OF GEORGIA PRESS

ATHENS AND LONDON

© 2001 by the University of Georgia Press
Athens, Georgia 30602
All rights reserved
Designed by Betty Palmer McDaniel
Set in 10/13 Caslon
by G&S Typesetters, Inc.
Printed Digitally
Library of Congress Cataloging-in-Publication Data
King, Stewart R., 1960–
Blue coat or powdered wig : free people of color in pre-
revolutionary Saint Domingue / Stewart R. King.
p. cm.
Includes bibliographical references and index.
ISBN 0-8203-2233-4 (alk. paper)
1. Saint-Domingue—History—18th century. 2. Free Blacks—
Saint-Domingue—History. 3. Free Blacks—Saint-Domingue—
Economic conditions—18th century. 4. Free Blacks—Saint-
Domingue—Social conditions—18th century.
F1911 .K56 2001
972.94'00496—dc21   00-056782

British Library Cataloging-in-Publication Data available

Paperback ISBN-13: 978-0-8203-3029-7

2017 Hardcover Reissue ISBN-13: 978-0-8203-5213-8

Contents

Contents

Acknowledgments

The research on which this book was based was made possible primarily by funding from the Department of History at the Johns Hopkins University. Research in France was generously supported by the Milton S. Eisenhower Library of the Johns Hopkins University, through its Collections Division; I am especially grateful to Thomas Izbicki, director of that division, for his assistance with this project. The staff of Clackamas Community College, particularly its interlibrary loan division, were very helpful during the writing.

My editor, David Des Jardines, was very supportive and encouraging during the long process of turning the dissertation that was into the book that is. Jane Curran did signal service as copyeditor, greatly improving some rather rough prose. This work would not have been possible without the guidance, suggestions, detailed comments, and careful editing, throughout the process of research and writing, of my adviser at Johns Hopkins, Franklin Knight. In addition to Dr. Knight, Robert Forster, Philip Curtin, Dominique Rogers, Anne King, and John Garrigus read sections of the work, and their commentary was invaluable. David Geggus, Michel-Rolph Trouillot, and Carolyn Fick all gave me exceptionally useful advice about preparing for my research trip to France. The staff of the Archives d'Outremer in Aix-en-Provence were most welcoming and professional to me during my stay there. The photographic staff in particular was especially helpful. My warm thanks to the director and staff of the archives for their very welcoming attitude toward foreign scholars working in their facility. Jean and Anne Durand-Rival were my hosts during my stay in Aix-en-Provence. Without their kind hospitality, my stay there would have been much less pleasant as well as less productive. They have been hosts to the American student population of Aix-en-Provence for three decades, and I join their other "adoptive children" in thanking them and wishing them well on the occasion of their retirement.

The staff of the United States Information Service in France provided very useful logistical support to my mission. USIS Marseilles Public Affairs Specialist Danielle Gallo was especially helpful and lived up to the best traditions of the Foreign Service in assisting this American student. I regret very much the closure of the United States Consulate in Marseilles and hope that the State Department and Congress will reverse this penny-wise, pound-foolish decision. The staff of USIS Paris and Deputy Public Affairs Officer James Hogan provided important assistance and access to records during the first days of my mission in Paris. Jean-Luc Bechennec, my host in Paris, went far out of his way, motivated entirely by friendship, to help me get my feet on the ground in a strange city.

My parents, Anne and Donald King, are to a greater extent than anybody else responsible for what I am intellectually. Their support—emotional, personal, intellectual, and financial—was crucial to the production of this book. Finally, no part of this work would have ever seen the light of day without the assistance of my microfilm photographer, mistress of the darkroom, and darling wife, Kadijatou, to whom I owe everything.

Introduction

On 9 August 1780, in the bustling colonial city of Cap Français, a young free black couple, Sergeant Pierre Augustin and his wife, Marie Janvier Augustin née Benjamin, visited a notary. They had come to offer a house in the town as security to one of their neighbors, a woman of mixed race, for a loan of 9,000 *livres*.[1] (All amounts of money in this book are denominated in *livres colonial* unless otherwise stated. The colonial *livre* was worth two-thirds of a *livre Tournois*. Each *livre* was subdivided into 20 *sols,* and in turn each sol was worth 12 *deniers.* It was apparently a money of account rather than an actual coin, with a dizzying variety of Spanish, English, and French currency actually circulating in the colony, helpfully translated by the notaries into *livres colonial* in almost all notarial acts.) The amount of the loan to the Augustins was about four times what a newly arrived African male slave cost at the time. The loan was the price, apparently, of a small coffee farm in the countryside of Saint Domingue, for it is from this date forward that Augustin began to style himself *habitant,* or gentleman farmer, instead of *perruquier,* or wigmaker. He also changed his official residence from the city to the outlying district of La Souffrière in the parish of Limbé.

He was born, apparently, in Africa and brought to the colony as a slave while very young. He was freed by an unknown master, who had trained him as a wigmaker—it is possible that he purchased his freedom out of the proceeds of this very lucrative trade. He married a free black woman with some resources and parlayed military service, valuable trade, rural and urban landholdings, and apparently considerable personal gifts into a position of some importance in free colored society of Cap Français in 1780. Racially, he was a black and, worse yet, probably a *bossale,* or African-born black, and thus he was at the bottom of the racial hierarchy of the colony. He started as a slave laborer but by the 1780s was clearly in the upper reaches of the free colored aristocracy. The house he pawned in 1780 adjoined another one, of more or less equivalent value, owned by him and leased to a white man. The 1776 cadastral survey of Cap shows him or his wife as proprietors of four lots in Cap Français. The one apparently described as rented to a white in this act was evaluated at that time as having a potential rental income of 1,500 *livres* per year (somewhere in the vicinity of what Pierre Augustin himself must have cost upon his arrival in Saint Domingue).[2] Status as an *habitant* marked him as a cut above the common herd, to say nothing of his ability to raise 9,000 *livres* and still have significant capital uninvolved in the transaction.

Augustin was socially as well as financially successful. He stood as godfather to numerous, apparently unrelated, young free coloreds, was a regular witness at the marriages of unrelated fellow militiamen and their daughters, was executor for wills and guardian of children for the community, and exhibited many of the other characteristics of a important person in that society.[3]

Augustin was not the only successful free person of African ancestry in the colony. A few miles away from his new rural seat was the home of the Laporte family. Louis Laporte, a young Frenchman who arrived sometime in the 1720s, first brought the family name to the colony. In those days, racial lines were not so clearly drawn. Therefore, nobody thought much of it when, after his white wife died, leaving him one child, he married a free black woman. She gave him four more surviving children, and over the next four generations this family, mingled with other mixed-race families, became one of the most successful groups of planters in the mountains south of Cap Français. Quietly circumventing an increasingly discriminatory legal regime, they owned plantations and slaves in several parishes, rode fine horses and dressed in imported fabrics, sent their children to be educated in France, and in most other ways lived like their white neighbors and fellow planters. Nobody would have been in any doubt by 1780 that any member of the Laporte clan deserved the label of *habitant*.[4]

A high point for the Laporte family was the signing of the marriage contract, on 24 January 1785, between the patriarch's young granddaughter, Elizabeth Sophie, and a young (white) man from Tulle, in France, named Jean Madelmon.[5] The wife brought her personal articles, two slaves, her bed and dresser, and a horse to the marriage. The groom must have been a young man with a future, but his possessions at the time of the marriage did not rate any description in the contract. The one thing the groom did possess, though, was a white skin—the racial climate had harshened considerably since the easy-going days of the 1720s, and Louis Laporte's *quarteron* granddaughter must have found it harder to land a white husband than her mother and grandmother had. She did not surrender all for a racially advantageous match, though. In a pattern common in free colored marriage contracts, she retained the right to 5,000 *livres* of the community property in case of dissolution of the marriage by divorce or death, in addition to the personal effects she brought with her.

This book explores the lives of the free coloreds of Saint Domingue, the modern Haiti, in the years before the great Revolution of 1791. It focuses on the two groups represented by Pierre Augustin and Elizabeth Sophie Laporte. This study, based as it is on colonial documents, cannot pretend to explain the complex events of the 1790s in the colony. However, an understanding of those events must proceed from a solid grounding in the social and economic conditions of the preceding decades.

In addition, an understanding of the role of free people of color is vital in order to comprehend the society of Saint Domingue. Free coloreds in slave societies functioned as an intermediate class, standing between slave and free and between black and white. Sharing characteristics of both groups, they served as a bridge or buffer between them. Recent scholarship on slave societies has underlined the importance of this class to the smooth functioning of the plantation system.[6]

Free people of color in the colonial Caribbean filled a number of niches in different places. Much of the literature on free people of color in the Caribbean has drawn a strict border between the "rural" and "urban." In Jamaica, as in the other British colonies, the free coloreds tended to concentrate in towns and worked principally in service jobs. Legal and social restrictions kept them, for the most part, from a role as a slave-owning farmer producing for the export market.[7] Maroon slaves in Jamaica formed a nascent peasantry, but there were few links between these de facto freedmen and their fellows in the towns. Similarly, in St. Kitts, a limited number of free coloreds were able to obtain land in rural areas, but most seem to have concentrated in the towns. In Grenada, a substantially greater number of free coloreds lived in the countryside than in the city. Whites outnumbered free coloreds in the towns, but the rural free coloreds of Grenada were small farmers, almost peasants for the most part. Although described as plantation owners, they operated typically on places of fewer than 25 acres.[8] In Brazil, laws and customs restricted free colored advancement in urban business, especially in the mining areas where many of them lived during the colonial period. Nonetheless, there seems to have been a fairly vibrant urban free colored population with a strong role in the lower reaches of the retail and skilled trades. Free coloreds do not seem to have been involved in mining or farming or other rural occupations to anything like this degree—free coloreds had a "small" place as plantation managers, and there were "exceptional" cases of free colored mining entrepreneurship. In the sugar-producing areas of Brazil, substantial numbers of free coloreds owned land and grew small amounts of sugar as *lavradores de cana*, but the larger plantations with the mills that permitted control of the trade were almost exclusively in the hands of whites. As in the case of Jamaica, the most notable group of free coloreds in the countryside in Brazil was the quasi-free of the *quilombos*.[9] Taking Cuba before the sugar revolution as an example of a place outside the plantation complex, we find that there was a strong community of rural free coloreds. In the early days, their role seems to have been that of a free peasantry. As the plantation system expanded across the island, however, free coloreds became agro-industrial workers, and the land in the countryside fell into the hands of large white sugar farmers.[10] As the plantation complex strengthened, legal or customary strictures limited free colored land- and slaveholding.

While free coloreds found it difficult in general to form alliances with slaves until the time of emancipation, the fear of such an alliance often affected governmental policy.[11] African-descended populations grew rapidly in colonies that were experiencing the agricultural transformation of the sugar and coffee revolutions. Colonial governments and leaders of white society, in these colonies with growing populations of people of African ancestry, seemed to be determined to limit the frequency with which free coloreds had unsupervised control over slaves. As a result, the free colored populations of those colonies became more homogenous as the plantations grew, drifting toward the role of urban worker, small craftsperson, or minor and peripheral agricultural entrepreneur, at best.

In Saint Domingue, on the other hand, free coloreds served as a small landholding class, filled the ranks of the peasantry, dominated urban small commerce and trades, and filled important roles in the colony's administration, especially in the area of security. They produced two distinct internal leadership groups.

On the one hand, Elizabeth Laporte and her relatives come from the planter elite. These were families who were mostly rural landholders with substantial slave workforces. The free colored planters were generally, although not always, people of mixed African and European ancestry. The one thing that was most characteristic of them as a group was that they had strong personal and business ties to whites, their own relatives and others. They were mostly successful managers of their property—indeed, sometimes more effective than most whites. They were not dependent on whites for financial support, but their contacts with whites were an important part of their self-image. Even those who were of pure African ancestry had close personal relationships with whites. Many from this group found that their social and financial contacts with white relatives gave them important advantages. They were conservative users of their capital, for the most part. Holding onto and developing their land for the long term, these planter elites had values and attitudes similar to those of white landholders in France.

On the other hand, Pierre Augustin represents a group who did not owe their status to white relatives (if any). The differences between these groups were twofold. The second group had many fewer important contacts with whites, both personal or familial and economic. In addition, there was a difference in mentality. These people owned plantations but used their land and slaves much more entrepreneurially than the planter elites. In place of the conservative attitude of the *seigneur* of the *ancien régime,* they exhibited that of the modern capitalist agricultural businessman. They bought and sold land much more freely and managed it for profit rather than long-term stability. In addition, although some planter elites had important urban interests, the second group dominated the urban business community.

This group is referred to as the "military" leadership, since almost all families had members who were leaders in the colonial military. They used their contacts with other military members, both whites and free coloreds, as their "network" in place of the planter elites' kin groups. Therefore, study of the colonial military, and free coloreds' role in that institution, is an important part of this work.

THE FREE COLORED IN THE MILITARY

Study of the free colored colonial military is important for several reasons. First, military service was a significant route for social advancement and financial gain in colored society, at all levels from slavery to the plantocracy. Men of African ancestry who did not possess some of the usual requirements for upward social and economic mobility could get ahead through building networks of fellow servicemen, both free coloreds and white officers. Access to credit, technology, and markets was enhanced through these networks. In addition, military service could give direct financial advantage. Although whites could and did serve in the colonial military, established white families in the colony would not have found the financial incentives for military service sufficiently important to be attractive. New white immigrants, who perhaps were in a position to need these benefits, had come to the island in the hopes of becoming wealthy planters and had little time or patience for military service. The free colored planter elites occasionally volunteered for overseas expeditionary corps for patriotic reasons or to confront racist stereotypes. However, they frequently had more important opportunities awaiting them in civilian life and did not make military service in peacetime a priority. The military leadership group of free coloreds, though, often began their careers in an economic position to find the financial rewards of military service attractive. As natives of the colony (for the most part) who intended to remain, they did not share the whites' distracting dream of quick wealth and a return to France.

Study of the free colored military is also important because the white ruling class depended on free coloreds for their security. In fact, this may have been the most important function of the class, from the point of view of the colony's leaders. Free coloreds were disproportionately likely to serve in the colony's armed forces, and they were much more effective soldiers than their white colleagues. Free blacks or persons of mixed race made up more than half of the colony's militia companies by the end of this period, although free coloreds were considerably less than half of the colony's free male population. The rank and file and noncommissioned officers of the rural police, the *maréchaussée,* were exclusively colored after midcentury. Free coloreds made significant contributions to three major expeditionary forces raised in Saint Domingue. Two of these fall outside the time period of this study, the force that went to Cartagena in 1697 and a force raised during the Seven Years' War that never went overseas, but many of the veterans of these expeditions were still active in the period covered. The third expeditionary force, which attacked Savannah during the American Revolution, was raised during the period covered by this work and was an important event in the self-definition of free coloreds, especially the military group. The French government considered raising a regular free colored regiment, the Chasseurs-Royaux de Saint-Domingue, after the success of the free colored contingent in the Savannah expedition, but coloreds resisted recruitment to this regiment, and the government dropped the idea at the end of the War of American Independence. Nevertheless, many free people of color served in regular French Army units, both in Saint Domingue and abroad, as well as on French Navy ships.

In addition, participation in the military, and especially in the high-profile overseas expeditionary forces recruited from among Saint Domingue's colored population during France's many colonial wars, provided free coloreds with a way to lay claim to equal status with whites and to refute white racist stereotypes. Coloreds proved their patriotism and civic virtue, values that were to resonate in the public mind of Republican France in later years, through their energetic contributions to Saint Domingue's defense. After the anti-militia unrest of the mid 1760s, when it became clear to the authorities that whites were unwilling to serve in the colony's armed forces, the free colored role became especially important.

Opinion makers urged service in the free colored part of the expeditionary corps that went to Savannah in 1779, the Chasseurs-Volontaires de Saint-Domingue, on the colored population as a way of enhancing their collective as well as individual position in society. The majority of troops enlisted in Haiti for this expedition were colored, and the Chasseurs-Volontaires made up almost one-third of the total ground strength of the expedition. During the period when the government was raising and training this force, officials, the leadership of the expedition, and veterans of former free colored expeditions all repeatedly stressed the value of service to the free colored community as a whole and the potential advantage accruing to the individual volunteer. These arguments were especially attractive to the educated sons of the planter elite, and many members of this group served in the Chasseurs-Volontaires.

However, after the defeat at Savannah, the French high command distributed the Chasseurs around the Caribbean in small groups as garrisons. Some members remained on active duty for more than three years. Free coloreds at home in Saint Domingue resented this seeming mistreatment and feared possible conscription.

On the other hand, free colored military participation provided the African-descended population of Saint Domingue with an important pool of experienced leaders when the time came in 1791 to resolve their differences with colonial society by violence. Previous studies of the Haitian Revolution have laid great stress on the importance of the Chasseurs-Volontaires as a training ground for the cadre of the revolutionary armies of 1791–1804.[12] Originally an investigation of this connection was to be an important part of this study. However, the names of only five Chasseurs-Volontaires who were certainly participants in the revolutionary wars have come to light: mulatto rebel Jean-Baptiste Chavanne; Pierre Augustin, who served as an officer in Toussaint Louverture's army; black general and later president of independent Haiti Jean-François L'Eveille; mulatto Limonade innkeeper and revolutionary captain Fabien Gentil; and a mulatto lieutenant colonel in the Santo Domingo garrison in 1803 named Gautier. None of the other famous names often cited—Christophe, Pétion, Rigaud—turned up in the notarial records as Chasseurs-Volontaires. However, several pre-revolutionary militiamen who did not serve in the Savannah expedition but who later served in the revolutionary armies appear in the records. Unfortunately, the personnel records of Toussaint's Armée de Saint-Domingue are not in the archives, if indeed Toussaint's forces kept any records. Leclerc's expedition incorporated some Armée de Saint-Domingue units after some of Toussaint's chiefs surrendered in 1801, and the names of a few hundred soldiers have survived, from which the few names that are a part of this study come.[13] However, many prewar free coloreds served in the revolutionary armies, and nothing here contradicts the assumption that their often extensive prewar military experience was an important asset to those armies, as well as to the locally recruited Spanish, English, French Royalist, and Bonapartist forces that opposed them.

This book, however, stops in 1791, when its sources run out. It presents parallels and analogies to the revolutionary period without alleging or attempting to prove any causal connection. *Post hoc, ergo propter hoc,* the reader may say, perhaps with some justice. This work is merely a social history of the pre-revolutionary free coloreds. The attention devoted here to the military role of this group is in proportion to the importance of service to the group as a whole.

FREE COLORED SOCIETY

In 1788, on the eve of the great slave insurrection that was to bring the colony of Saint Domingue to independence, there were at least 21,813 free persons of color in the colony, compared with 27,723 whites.[14] These figures come from the official census and most likely understate the free colored population because more free coloreds than whites, proportionally, lived in remote areas of the colony where they were difficult to count. In addition, free coloreds with irregular liberty papers might have had good reason to avoid the census taker.[15] Thus, we can assume that the free coloreds of Saint Domingue made up at least half of the total free population by 1791, the start of the Revolution.

Free coloreds were important to the colony's economy. A few white planters controlled the great wealth of the colony.[16] Many of the top-level planters were absentee landlords, businesspeople, or nobles from the *metropole* investing in Caribbean sugar. However, the second rank of planters contained a large proportion of free coloreds, and some of these were among the wealthiest planters actually living on their plantations. Many free colored families, like the Laportes, made their first economic strides in the 1720s and 1730s, as sugar transformed the colony's economy. These old mulatto families then pursued marriage for their daughters with promising newly arrived whites, taking advantage of the gender imbalance of the white immigrant pool and the attraction of large dowries to build relations with whites. This long-term family strategy resulted in the powerful and wealthy group here referred to as the planter elites, who were well-installed in Saint Domingue society by the middle of the century. In the 1760s and 1770s, these families came under increasing pressure from a new and much larger wave of fortune-hunting white immigrants. These new arrivals, unlike free coloreds of all social levels, had very weak roots in the colony.

Many whites came to Saint Domingue in the 1760s and 1770s to seek their fortune.[17] Some found it, others did not; all dreamed of returning wealthy to France. Alongside the few rags-to-riches success stories were dozens of poor whites. For example, the *maréchausée* cavaliers (free colored rural policemen) Etienne Maubonne and Bernard Despines found an "unknown white man, aged 14 to 15, without a beard," lying beside the road in a pool of fecal matter near the town of Mirebalais early in the morning of 2 January 1779. The policemen called a surgeon, who determined that the young fellow had died of *misère* (poverty). He was buried anonymously in the local churchyard.[18]

Out of hundreds of free colored burials enumerated for this study, not one was anonymous. Coloreds were a much better integrated part of the society in which they lived than were poor whites. Colored residents of the colony were officially discouraged, by the Police des Noirs regulations in France, from thinking of ever living in the *metropole*, and most had deep roots as well as substantial investments in the colony.[19] Even the poor free colored had a place in the society, connections with other Creoles, white as well as black, and at least some prospects.

Many free coloreds in this society who succeeded in advancing from misery to the powdered wig of the gentleman farmer began their careers with slave and land acquisition, either through purchase or donation by a patron. Then, they typically began to use what little resources they had more entrepreneurially. They planted cash crops and began to participate more fully in the market. The next step could be a move to the city and investment in land and a business there.

As the Saint Domingue free colored family gained success in the city, in many cases they reinvested their profits in rural land. The entrepreneur who had succeeded by this route, however, was typically a member of what I call the military leadership group.

The planter group achieved success by other means that were less dependent on urban entrepreneurship and safer, but slower. The people who joined this group during the time under study got their startup capital—land and slaves—through donation or inheritance from a white relative or patron. This would permit them to begin to operate a small but economically viable farm producing for the export market with a number of slaves. Further success would be a process of slow accretion rather than the aggressive entrepreneurship of the military group.

Both planter and military group proprietors were much more likely than whites to personally take charge of the management of their estates, even at the top of the economic scale. Direct oversight meant that they were more efficient, both by reducing the cost of management services and by limiting losses to fraud or mismanagement. Not being eligible for nobility, important officeholding, or even (officially) residence in France, they had less to attract them away from the land. In addition, among the planter group especially, conservative economic behaviors paid off for them during periods of downturn, such as the War of American Independence (in which the French participation extended from 1778 to 1783). Perhaps as a result, the military leaders, and to an even greater extent the planter elites, were much more willing to look to the long-term value of their property and consequently were less easily distracted by short-term profits. Because of these generally successful investment strategies, there was a steady flow of capital—land and slaves—into the hands of the free coloreds.

This flow of capital was a social development of the greatest importance, since it held the seeds of profound change in the balance of power among the races. The white administration of the colony imposed a dizzying variety of discriminatory regulations in an attempt to discourage or punish free colored social advancement. Regulations included limitations on what sort of clothing free coloreds could wear, what sort of carriages they could buy, what sort of weapons they could own or display, and which professions they could practice. The colony's government never restricted the right of free coloreds to own land and slaves, though. There was, however, an attempt to restrict the right of white patrons to give or will land and slaves to free coloreds.[20] This was always a dead letter because the white planter class needed free colored intermediaries and often trusted their free colored relatives more than white hirelings as plantation managers. In any case, the discriminatory legislation would have been least galling in rural areas, especially outside the core sugar-growing areas in the colony. This is where free colored planters tended to congregate, taking advantage of the growth of coffee cultivation in the colony starting in the 1750s. Coffee required less capital and fewer slaves to produce economically, making it even more attractive to free colored planters.

Alongside the rural entrepreneurs, free coloreds formed most of the urban small business and artisan class. Almost all wholesale businesspeople were white. Most large retail traders were also white, but the smaller retail market was predominantly free colored. Free and quasi-free coloreds, mostly women, predominated in the open-air markets where most people, regardless of color, shopped for their daily needs. Meanwhile, free coloreds typically operated the small shops (although sometimes they had white partners).

Some poor whites came to the colony with qualifications in the skilled trades, but many of them were hoping to live a life of leisure as planters and had no interest in working as boatmen or carpenters or masons in the colony. The few white master craftsmen who were active in the colony seemed to be in business principally in order to train colored journeymen, for a substantial fee in cash or in years of free labor. Sometimes their apprentices were slaves, whose masters paid for their training, but a slave with such a valuable skill found it easier to become free. Thus, free coloreds also dominated the skilled trades.

In the countryside, although poor whites occasionally struggled on useless worn-out pieces of land, they always identified themselves as *habitants*, or planters, and at least pretended to produce a cash crop. Peasants identified as such in the records were all free coloreds. Dominating these three crucial areas of the economy helped make free coloreds an essential part of the colony.

INTERNAL DIVISIONS WITHIN THE CLASS OF FREE COLOREDS

In Saint Domingue, then, free coloreds were as often rural agriculturists as urban artisans. As farmers, some were planters producing for the export market, while others filled the ranks of the peasantry in areas that had not yet experienced the full force of the agricultural transformations related to sugar and coffee production.

Many of the soldiers who appear in this study came from subsistence farming backgrounds. Some of these families were getting by on less than a hectare of land, which was real *misère* (poverty) if there were any number of children or older relatives to support. Poor free coloreds typically did not use the notarial system much, as its price was out of their reach, with the significant exception of manumissions. On occasion, though, wealthier free coloreds or whites would notarize a transaction with poorer neighbors. Sometimes, especially in the case of the military leaders, this would be part of a patronage strategy. It is difficult, then, because of the constraints of the sources used, to say much about this lower stratum of the free people of color.

However, there was also a substantial middle class of free coloreds. Some were domestic employees or dependents of wealthy whites. Some were professional employees—plantation managers for absentee white proprietors, often their relatives. Others, however, were ambitious independent tradesmen or small planters. Many were slave owners. About these, the book has a good deal to say, especially since free coloreds were more likely to use the notarial system than whites, all other things being equal. In particular, people whose title to property was questionable would nail down their claims beyond all doubt by notarizing deeds and sales contracts—and the free colored middle class often had the weakest of titles both due to racial prejudice and poverty.

Of course, some had realized their ambitions and acquired plenty of land and slaves. Families at the top of the free colored landholding hierarchy approached the living standard of the wealthiest white planters and far surpassed the mass of whites. Some of these free colored planter elites felt themselves the equals of the white planters, and representatives of this class fought during the Revolution, not for the general equality of people of African descent, but for their right as property owners to be a part of the plantocracy.

Studies of the colony's society have often treated the Saint Domingue free coloreds as a unitary group. Certainly French official regulations considered them a more or less homogenous social caste, separate from whites and also from slaves. A *tache ineffaçable* (indelible stain) of slavery was attached, in public prejudice, to their color, as many observers noted.[21] The legal regime related to the free people of color was very complicated and, like many a legal regime of racial division in other times and places, was twisted beyond recognition in actual practice.

The famous *Code Noir* of 1685 represents the first codification of the race and color system in the French colonies.[22] When it was published, French colonization in the Caribbean was already more than 50 years old. In Saint Domingue, although the main island of Hispaniola was still not officially French, the French colony was beginning to grow economically. The other French colonies in the Lesser Antilles were even more highly developed. The number of slaves and free coloreds in

French possessions was growing, and French colonial administrators felt a need to define their place in the status-obsessed society of *ancien régime* France through written laws.

The *Code Noir* was actually quite liberal in its treatment of both slaves and free coloreds. Observers have often cited it to demonstrate supposed better treatment of blacks in the French colonies as opposed to the English ones.[23] However, the liberal provisions of the *Code* were superseded in many cases by harsher laws as the eighteenth century proceeded; in other cases, they were simply ignored by slave masters and government officials alike.

The French legal system treated free persons of color as a special caste, separate in type from the wholly white and the slave, and imposed special legal restrictions on them. A few legal provisions made special distinctions between those of wholly African ancestry and those of mixed background, but mostly the free coloreds were a unitary caste under the law. The intent of the laws was to keep free coloreds subordinate to whites.

Many observers of the colony's society, both at the time and later, have accepted this relatively unitary view of a society polarized along racial caste lines.[24] Others have posited the existence of a sharp division between free black and free mulatto—with some documentary support—and have gone on to treat each subgroup as an undifferentiated whole. It is tempting to see the distinction in racial terms, especially as this was the almost-universal practice of observers, both white and colored, at the time.[25] However, many families, wealthy and poor, included both wholly African and mixed-race individuals. Even some people of entirely African ancestry, such as Toussaint Louverture, still had close relationships with white patrons, like Toussaint's former master Bayon de Libertat. Some people of mixed race were poor and cut off from any white relatives. A racial calculus based purely on ancestry also fails to deal with the real complexity of the society.

Another method of analysis divides the free colored group along class lines. Most mulattos were wealthy, as the reasoning goes, while most free blacks were poor; hence, what is really a social class division looks like a racial split. The problem with this answer is that it is very difficult to classify individuals or families as to their social class in colonial Saint Domingue. Social and economic mobility within the racially designated caste of free people of color was very high. What would be the social class identity of a Pierre Augustin? He was, as we have seen, wealthy and well connected, but he was born in Africa and was thus at the bottom of the colonial racial hierarchy. He certainly started on the socioeconomic ladder at the bottom and yet rose and achieved.

This work divides the free coloreds, or those who appear in the notarial archives, into the two groups discussed above, the planter elite and the military group. Augustin belonged to the military leadership. He was a noncommissioned officer in the city's militia and a veteran of the Savannah expedition. In addition, he exhibited many of the other characteristics of this group: few identifiable personal or economic ties with whites, an entrepreneurial attitude toward capital, and the strong urban component of his assets. However, he clearly owned property in rural areas as well, valuing it for its social cachet as well as its ability to produce profits, thereby demonstrating characteristics that are more conservative as well.

This group confounds both class and color analysis of colonial Saint Domingue society. Their social influence was undeniable. Their economic power was significant, although not quite up to the standards of the planter elite group in most cases. They were not really a middle class in the conventional sense. That is, individuals or families did not advance from poverty through an entrepreneurial middle class to finally arrive as members of the respectable aristocratic planter elite. Persons rising to join the planter elite group did not exhibit the characteristics of the military group on their way to the top in most cases. Military group members who achieved the greatest economic and social success, like Augustin, exhibited few of the characteristics of planter elites. Distance from slavery does not seem to explain the differences: military group families who had had their money for a long time and who were far in time and generational status from slavery did not mutate into planters. At the same time, planter families included many individuals who had been born slaves but who did not exhibit the characteristic behaviors of the military group. Color is also not a reliable guide to group membership. Most planter families had white relatives, but many also had pure black members. Although a majority of those in the military group were pure black, there were significant numbers of persons of mixed race.

Members of both groups manipulated similar markers of social class in order to advance socially and economically. The primary difference in behavior on the economic plane was aggressiveness in trading the basic capital goods: land and slaves. Free colored planter elites tended to acquire capital goods and then hang onto them, using them to legitimize a claim to the social status of *habitant*. For them, it was better to be a small, stable *habitant* than to take a risk of failing in order to become enormously wealthy. Free colored military leaders were not nearly as reckless as many white entrepreneurs. However, they were more willing to acquire slaves with a view to reselling them. They would speculate in land with much greater freedom than the planters. They were more willing to engage in trade and were more entrepreneurial when doing so.

There were also many non-economic markers of social class status. Members of these two leadership groups had different relationships to these markers. Literacy, or at least the ability and willingness to sign one's name to an official document, is a very good guide to the observer attempting to ascertain an individual's status. Real literacy skills need not correspond with public use of those skills, of course. Toussaint Louverture, for example, almost certainly could at least write his own name in the 1770s. However, as a farmer barely meriting the title of *habitant,* he never signed any of the notarial acts in which he appeared in the 1770s and 1780s. When he became a high-ranking public official—"Governor-General for Life"— in the 1790s, he signed official acts. Public literacy, though, was a mark of status that could be claimed by an upwardly mobile free colored.

Travel to France was another way to climb socially, and free coloreds who had made the trip, often in the face of restrictive legislation, were quick to make sure everybody else knew about it.

Possession of status goods—such as imported clothing, wigs, military uniforms, fine weapons, and expensive horses—was also a useful way of proclaiming one's status. Observers at the time were united in describing the wealthy free coloreds as knowledgeable and skilled horsemen.

Petty officeholding, both civilian and military, was also important. The free colored public, and even many whites, had a special respect for free colored men who had held actual officers' commissions in the colored militia units before a royal decree made the officer corps white only. They were community leaders even when their wealth and other indicators placed them below the top of the economic scale. Free colored society even respected noncommissioned officers, and officeholding helped hold together the military leadership group.

What one called the structure one lived in (*case, magasin,* or *maison*), occupational identification, and many other subtle distinctions were also important ways of defining one's status.

Overt adherence to moral codes of the dominant group was one very important marker defining status within the group. Marriage was a crucial part of any free colored family's strategy for social promotion, and legitimacy of children was an important marker of status. These two groups differ sharply in the way they used marriage and family structure to achieve family goals.

Religious piety was an important component of "respectability" as defined by white society. Free coloreds, particularly members of the planter elite, also used this tool, as we can see by their use of religious formulas and boilerplate in notarial acts and through their assumption of minor church offices. All these factors help us to explore the mentality of the free coloreds and the way in which this mentality changed as one crossed the line between subgroups.

An important variable in the mentality and group identification of free coloreds, and the most striking difference between the two leadership groups, was their level of personal relationships with whites. Members of the military leadership group tended to have no active family or other close personal relationships with whites. Free blacks as well as mulattos who had strong patronage or family relationships with whites seem to have found themselves more likely to share the values of the planter group, regardless of skin color or economic status.

A remarkable example of this phenomenon was the *menagères*, or free colored housekeepers (and frequently lovers), of white planters. These women were often free blacks and generally came from the lower social and economic ranks of free colored society. Many were freedwomen who gained their freedom thanks to their contact with their white masters. Nonetheless, these women, and their children, often achieved remarkable economic success, and when they did, they very often adopted the values and behavior of the planter elite group.

Even free coloreds who were not family members of whites, but who had significant personal and business relationships with them, fall among the planter elite class. The future Toussaint Louverture provides a noteworthy example of the generalization that personal contact with whites was key to group identification among free coloreds. Toussaint was a beneficiary of a solid patronage relationship with powerful white plantation manager Bayon de Libertat. He demonstrated the conservative values of the planter elite even as he rose to command the slave rebel forces and led the colony to near-autonomy within the French Empire. His role in 1791 was contradictory, suggesting that his behavior was influenced by the same factors as other free coloreds with important associations with whites. Although Toussaint sat out the Ogé-Chavanne fiasco, the first violent intervention of the free colored planter elite class, his first reaction to the August 1791 slave uprising was to escort Bayon de Libertat and his family to safety in Cap Français. Toussaint's relationship with the slave rebels was an arm's-length one for some time in the early days of the rising. However, he was secretary to one of the rebel leaders by the end of September (thus demonstrating a literacy that he did not admit in notarial acts made only a few years before), but he did not begin to lead troops in the field until 1792. Throughout the revolutionary wars and during his short tenure as ruler of an undivided Saint Domingue, Toussaint revealed himself as a half-hearted revolutionary at best. He never wavered on the elimination of slavery but sought to preserve forced labor on the plantations in a different form. He fought Napoleon's attempt to reimpose direct metropolitan rule on the colony but always rejected an out-and-out declaration of independence. His title alone demonstrates his objectives; instead of *president* or *emperor,* he styled himself "Governor-General for Life." It was only after his arrest and the radicalization of many Haitians under the boots of Leclerc that the *purs et durs,* Dessalines and Christophe and their supporters, springing from a very different social class than Toussaint, tore the white out of the *tricouleur,* acquiesced in the destruction of the plantation system (although even they tried to save it in the national period in an altered form), and created an explicit independence movement.

Before beginning this examination, a cautionary note is in order. This work deals to a considerable extent with social mobility. The people who appear in this work are those who were mobile, those who were or could have been leaders in the upheavals to come. Most of the mobility in question was upward; African people so often had no place to go but up, and in any case declining economic status frequently (but not always) meant that the individual ceased to appear in the economic records that form the principal source of this work. The general trend of the economy was upward in the time under study (temporary dislocations caused by the War of American Independence aside); rising tides lift many boats. The reader of the Horatio-Algeresque stories that follow must keep in mind that most individuals of color in this society did *not* experience any significant social or economic mobility. The colony of Saint Domingue imported roughly 850,000 slaves between 1629 and 1791.[26] Importations in the period under study averaged roughly 26,400 a year, even taking into account the years of low importations during the War of American Independence.[27] The African-descended population in 1788 was about 450,000 slaves and approximately 27,000 free persons of color. Such a negative rate of natural growth means that mind-numbing numbers of those imported from Africa died without issue, frequently in the first year or two. For every African Pierre Augustin or Jean-Baptiste Bambara, who appears in the record as having accumulated some wealth and prestige, there were thousands of unknown "Pierres" and "Jean-Baptistes" who died of mysterious diseases in a land far from home, or if they were "lucky," they sweated out their natural lives in the cane fields.

Chapter 1 of this work is a discussion of the sources. The principal source is the notarial archives of Saint Domingue, now held in the Section Outremer of the National Archives of France in Aix-en-Provence. Notarials are a very useful social-historical source in the French system, as the notary must not only witness oaths, as in the English system, but must also attest to the veracity of statements made in notarized documents and ensure that contracts are framed in accordance with the law. The notarial archives contain everything from marriage contracts to death inventories, sales of slaves to the incorporation papers and accounts of important businesses. In addition, some important evidence, especially on family structures, came from parish registers maintained rather haphazardly by the *curés* of the colony. Other documents from the Section Outremer illuminated other aspects of the world of Saint Domingue's free coloreds, especially the Collection Moreau de St. Méry and the personnel records of the colonial administration.

The purpose of chapters 2, 3, and 4 is to give the reader the basic facts about the places and actors needed to understand the analysis of free colored economic and social behavior that follows. Chapter 2 considers physical and economic geography, in the latter case focusing on agriculture as the colony's principal economic activity. Chapter 3 takes up demography of free coloreds on the island.

Chapter 4 describes the forms of military service open to free coloreds in Saint Domingue. It analyzes the military as an institution in which served free coloreds of all shades and classes (as well as whites). This chapter appears here, under general information, since the military as an institution was so important to the colony's free coloreds. In a sense, the chapter parallels the extensive description of agriculture, the principal business of the planter elite, in chapter 2. The group of free colored military leaders is taken up in chapter 11.

With chapter 5, the work becomes a study of economic and social activity of free coloreds in the colony as a whole as revealed by the sample of notarial documents. The four chapters that follow provide a context for the discussion of free colored leadership groups, which concludes the work. Chapter 5 focuses on slaveholding and the economic and non-economic value of slaves to free coloreds. An important consideration of this chapter is the attitudes of free coloreds toward their slaves.

Chapter 6 concentrates on the free colored as a landholder and a businessman. The principal business of the colony was plantation agriculture, and along with slaves, who are examined in chapter 5, land was required for this business. Besides this economic value, land had a non-economic value, especially strong for free coloreds. In order to understand how the free colored community related to the world of colonial Saint Domingue, we must understand both the economic and non-economic value land had to them and the ways they manipulated these values.

Chapter 7 concentrates on entrepreneurship. One of the marked characteristics of the free colored upper class was their success as businessmen. However, some were successful through patient, conservative, accretion of resources, while others were aggressively entrepreneurial and sought high-risk, high-gain strategies.

Thus chapters 5, 6, and 7 study the way free coloreds manipulated the economic and non-economic values of the basic elements of capitalist enterprise on the island: slaves and land. The continuing theme of this entire part of the work has been the complex interrelationships between free coloreds' twin quests for social advancement and economic security. Chapters 8 and 9 turn to areas where the social value is more marked, although, of course, social and economic value can never be completely divorced. These chapters have a broader focus than the preceding three because they consider a range of ways in which free coloreds manipulated non-economic markers of social status. Chapter 8 looks at a broad range of markers of social status, including literacy, piety, officeholding, material culture, clothing, and color and its official description. Chapter 9 focuses on the family as a component of social advancement and on free coloreds' family strategies for social advancement. The chapter also covers the free colored family as an institution and looks at internal relationships, as far as they are illuminated by the sources used here.

We then come to part three, the new analytical framework that this book proposes, in the form of a comparison of the two leadership groups identified in Saint-Dominguan free colored society. The first of those groups, the planter elite, including Elizabeth Sophie Laporte and her peers, is the subject of chapter 10.

Chapter 11 explores the other half of the ruling classes of free colored society, the military leadership group of Pierre Augustin and his comrades. Many free colored men participated in the military at some point in their lives. Only a few, though, made military service an important part of their strategy for financial and social advancement.

The military was a means to profit and advancement that was not so intimately tied to patronage by whites as was the traditional route to the top favored by the planter elites. Those in the military leadership were markedly less likely to perform business or family notarial acts with whites than were the planter elites. Aside from their relative independence from whites, though, these leaders had different attitudes toward capital and different relationships with other free coloreds than did the planter elites.

Although almost all families in this group had one or more members who were military leaders, obviously not everyone in this group served. However, they were all intimately tied into a cohesive social group by family and pseudo-kin ties and shared the same set of attitudes toward capital and toward other groups in the society.

This work concludes with chapter 12, which summarizes the major findings of this investigation of the two principal leadership groups, the military in their blue coats and the planters in their powdered wigs.

PART ONE

The Colony and Its People

CHAPTER ONE

The Notarial Record and Free Coloreds

To understand this book, it is important to understand the data on which it is based. In addition, the nature and function of the notarial system illustrates some important facts about both the colonial society of Saint Domingue and the place of free people of color in that society. Therefore, this first chapter considers the notarial system of the colony, primarily by examining notarial documents.

Notaries in the French system, both pre-revolutionary and modern, were important government officials who ensured that contracts were framed in accordance with the law, which helped to guarantee the legally binding nature of those contracts. The notary had to be prepared to testify to facts that he had been called upon to witness in the performance of his duties. In practice, the law courts of the colony generally accepted notarized statements as factual without needing to call upon the notary in person.

Notaries have existed in the French legal system since the Middle Ages, but administrative reforms of the 1770s made their rich archives available to colonial historians. Starting in 1776, notaries were required to make a duplicate copy of all their registers and to file them with the royal archives. Some duplicate copies exist of notarial acts from before this period. However, making these copies was a special service executed by the notary for an additional fee. Thus, the pre-1776 notarial archives contain only those acts executed by people with extra money to spend on preserving a duplicate record of their transactions. This makes the few notarial records surviving in the North and West provinces from before 1776 somewhat suspect in terms of their representativeness. After the 1776 edict, all notarial acts were, in theory, preserved, and all persons executing such acts were subject to the fee for the second copy. Some notaries were better than others at obeying the 1776 law, and so some lacunae exist in the documentary series. Nonetheless, it seems that almost all of the post-1776 files of these, the front line of royal government in the colony, have survived.

The sample consists of 3,520 notarial acts and 719 other primary documents. This represents all notarial acts in the registers of eight notaries from six parishes in which a free person of color was either a principal actor or a major participant. This sample includes about 4 percent of all notarial acts preserved in the archives for this period. The parishes are:

1. Cap Français, the colony's principal port and the center of the most highly developed sugar-growing area (the notaries Jean-François Doré and Jean-François Bordier *jeune*)

2. Fort Dauphin, a smaller port and commercial center also in the northern sugar-growing area (the notary André Leprestre)

3. Limonade, a parish divided into a coastal sugar-growing area and a highland coffee-growing area. The highlands were the home of many people of color (the notary Jean-Louis Michel)

4. Port-au-Prince, the colony's capital and market center for the newer and less highly developed West province (another notary surnamed Michel, who did not use his personal name in his records)

5. Croix des Bouquets, also known as Cul de Sac, an area containing both sugar and coffee plantations (the notary Renaudot)

6. Mirebalais, an isolated rural community in the central mountains, producing livestock and indigo as well as some coffee, which was a stronghold for people of color during the Haitian Revolution (the notaries Lamauve and Beaudoulx).

Some free coloreds were frequent users of the notarial system, such as the militia leader Jean-Baptiste Magny *dit* Malic, who appears forty-eight times in the sample. Most free coloreds had only a few items to notarize, and the average frequency of appearance is under three. Remembering that each notarial document had at least two, and usually more, main actors, approximately 4,000 distinct free individuals, almost 75 percent of them free coloreds, appear in the sample along with 4,197 slaves.

Of the 4,239 documents, 958 included at least one participant from a family that was among the "economic elite" of free coloreds, those individuals or families with three acts in the sample evaluated at over 10,000 *livres*. Members of the military leadership group executed 493 of the documents, and members of the planter elite group figured in 539. Quite a few military leaders and a few planter families were not part of the economic elite. Free blacks participated in 2,072 of these documents, free persons of mixed race in 2,639, and whites in 2,132 (many documents had participants from at least two racial groups).

The notaries selected preserved a complete series of records from 1776 to 1789 in each of these parishes—either one notary who was active throughout or, in the case of Cap Français and Mirebalais, two notaries, where one seems to have succeeded to the other's practice sometime during the period. Each notary did a lot of business with people of color—the three in the two rural parishes were the only ones active throughout the period under study in areas that were dominated by people of color. The urban notaries were chosen because of the high proportion of their business that was done with people of color (ranging from 10–50 percent depending on the notary and year).

Notaries in the urban centers seem to have specialized in certain types of business. One notary in Port-au-Prince, for example, had another official position as the colonial administrator of vacant successions, administering the goods of persons who died intestate and without natural heirs in the colony. His notarial business was dominated by the affairs of those estates, which were almost exclusively those of young, single white men. For this reason, his records did not form a portion of the sample. Another worked in the port district of Cap Français and did most of his business with merchants trading with French ports. The only person of color among his regular clients was the future revolutionary leader Vincent Ogé. Both of these notaries had incidental and secondary contact with free people of color, as sellers and buyers from their principal clients. The notaries in both of those cities who worked the most closely with the free colored communities were selected instead.

This choice has the potential to unnaturally skew the sample. As a check on this possibility, a colleague contributed records of her research in the notarial archives. The documents from her sample were acts performed by free coloreds before notaries not generally associated with the free colored community. Comparing this group with the sample used in this work showed that the people who appear here are broadly representative of the free colored population as a whole.

THE NOTARY AS BUSINESSMAN

Although the holder of a public commission, the notary in Saint Domingue was financially supported by the fees paid by his clients. A notarial office resembled an eighteenth-century law office, with two notaries, a senior (*notaire général*) and junior (*son confrère*) partner, in attendance, and a number of clerks to make out copies of the documents as needed. Since the senior partner always signed the document, and they are indexed in the archives under his name, notaries are here referred to in the singular, and individual firms are referred to by the name of the senior partner.

Clients would come to the notary's office, or send for him to come to their residences, whenever they had a contract or other factual matter for him to witness. The notary would charge a basic fee plus travel, waiting time, and other expenses, in much the same way as an attorney in the colony.

The basic fee for executing a notarial act averaged about 20 *livres* for the period under study. To this was generally added the notary's travel expenses, if the act was executed outside the notary's office. This frequently occurred in the case of wills executed or updated on the testator's deathbed. Notaries also frequently traveled when inheritances were to be divided up. In addition, some acts took hours or days to execute, especially in the case of disputed inheritances. Notaries charged a per diem, which varied widely depending on the economic climate and perhaps the ability of the actors to pay. The total cost of some notarial acts approached 300 *livres*, and complicated inheritances might render the notary who handled them more than 1,000 *livres*, taking into account a deathbed will, an inventory of the deceased's possessions, perhaps in several locations, and one or more acts of division of the property among the heirs. Fees might escalate even more if the division was contentious in some way—if, for example, the white heirs in France fought provisions of a deceased planter's will giving significant possessions to his colored housekeeper and children, as the notary would then be able to charge for his time to appear in court as a witness.[1]

To give an understanding of the purchasing power represented by these fees, private soldiers in the Chasseurs-Volontaires were paid 105 *livres* per year plus 22 *sols* 6 *deniers* a day subsistence allowance; a new male slave cost between 1,800 and 2,500 *livres*, depending on the market; a *carreau* of good farmland in Limonade cost about 300 *livres*.[2] Thus, executing a notarial act was not a trivial expense.

Free coloreds used the notarial system for a wider range of economic transactions than did whites, it is argued, in order to gain greater security for their possessions in the face of growing discrimination and to enhance the social value of their property.[3] Whatever the explanation, the free coloreds were enthusiastic users of the notarial system, for a wide range of different kinds of acts, with varying economic and social objectives.

THE NOTARIAL DOCUMENT

The modern French notarial act is a very formulaic document, with all the information about subjects and objects recorded in a set manner. These formulas date to the eighteenth century, when they were already laid out in legal manuals with boilerplate and blanks to fill in.[4] Textbooks notwithstanding, the formulas were considerably less well established in colonial Saint Domingue than in today's French legal practice. The ideal act, in 1780 or today, would include the name, place of birth, parents' names, and residence for each actor, and, in the case of free persons of color in the colony, mention of their color and proof of free status. A full description of the object sold should also appear. In the case of land, this would include a summary of the report of the *arpenteur*, or public surveyor, describing the boundaries, a description of the buildings on the land, and a summary of land under cultivation and crops that were planted. Finally, the recent ownership history of the piece of land should appear, to prove that the seller has valid title. Similar information, perhaps in somewhat less detail, would describe movable property such as slaves or personal property. The total effect seems to have been to provide a guarantee to the purchaser. In reality, no single act contained all these features. (A representative example *in extenso*, giving the reader an idea about the contents of this notarial document, is contained in appendix 4.)

CLASSIFICATION OF NOTARIAL ACTS

Jean-Paul Poisson, in his epochal study of the French *ancien régime* notariat, considered the types of acts recorded by notaries. He made a subtle and perhaps overly twentieth-century distinction between family matters and economic issues in his typology of notarial acts made in Paris.[5] Making a sharp distinction between, say, a marriage contract and the establishment of a limited partnership to manage an indigo plantation creates a false dichotomy that probably did not exist in the minds of the people of the time. The marriage contract was an economic transaction, more permanent and expensive, but no different in kind from the sale of an undeveloped plot of urban land. Similarly, the sale of land touched the family in a personal way; though the social implications of landholding were perhaps less profound, they were certainly like in kind to the giving of a daughter in marriage. Thus, a notary lived in both personal and cold economic space at the same time, and the documents in the registers illuminate many facets of the lives of their actors.

The majority of documents to be notarized were transactions or, in other words, acts of sale, rental, or donation. In Saint Domingue, about 60 percent of these transactions included land, while almost 45 percent included slaves (with many, of course, featuring both sorts of capital goods), a few included livestock, with an occasional movable property sale being notarized. Table 1 gives a general idea of the types of documents in the sample of archival documents which forms the basic source for this book.

The family acts or, in other words, marriage contracts and resolutions of dis-

TABLE 1

Documents in Sample of Notarial Acts Used in Research for This Book, by Type

TYPE OF DOCUMENT	NUMBER OF DOCUMENTS	PERCENTAGE OF ALL DOCUMENTS
Notarial Acts	3,520	83
Transactions (sales, rentals, and donations)[a]	2,122	50
Sales Transactions	1,406 (67%)	
Rental Transactions	459 (22%)	
Donations	257 (12%)	
Family Acts (marriages, wills, etc.)	777	18
Parish Register Entries (baptisms, marriages, funerals)	522	12
Census Enumerations	182	4
Military/Criminal Reports	5	0
Total	4,229	

Source: Sample of 4,229 notarial acts and other documents selected from the six target parishes. All documents preserved by the one or two notaries from each parish who handled the notarial business of the free persons of color in that parish were selected. In addition, parish registry entries and other documents related to persons identified through the notarial archives were included in the sample.

[a]Of these, 1,212 (57%) included transfer of land and 907 (43%) included transfer of slaves.

puted inheritances and the like are among the most informative notarized documents; both often contain detailed inventories of an individual's property and records of expenditures over a long period of time. Other common types of notarized documents in the sample were acts of manumission, business partnerships, notarized sets of orders to business agents, and police reports or criminal complaints.

FREE COLOREDS IN THE NOTARIAL DOCUMENTS

No official rule ever required it, but Saint Domingue notaries generally referred to people of color as *le nommé* or *la nommée* ("the so-called"), a term used by notaries in France to refer to anyone of lower social class or to those accused of crimes. The term was rarely used for whites in this sense in Saint Domingue (and it always produces maximum confusion in the reader when it was used in this sense). Almost all whites in Saint Domingue were called *sieur* (or *dame* or *demoiselle*) so-and-so in notarial acts, although in France these titles were reserved for the gentry. A number of colonial and royal government directives required that people of color be described by their racial status (*mulâtre* or *negre* or some other color-based label) in all acts.

Only free persons could execute notarial acts. A change in official practice (dictated by the local authorities) in 1778 required that all free persons of color executing notarial or parish acts present proof of their free status (baptismal records or patent of manumission), which was then to be taken note of in the act.

Some notaries were more punctilious than others in the performance of all of these requirements. The wealthier and more powerful the colored person, the less likely it was that his or her status and dates of liberty or baptism would appear in the register. Sometimes, the only clue for the modern reader is to construct a family tree—the son of a *mulatresse libre* and a man born in France was most likely a *quarteron libre* even though he never appeared in the records as anything but, say, "Sieur Louis Laporte, *habitant* of Limonade."

Free people of color were more likely than their white neighbors to execute notarial acts, and some acts were for very small transactions. Some free people of color executed notarial acts for sales of land worth a few hundred *livres*—a sign of their poverty but also of their desire to legitimate their ownership beyond all doubt. Of 1,404 acts of sale, 102 were for less than 500 *livres*, and 238 were for less than 1000 *livres*. The record for lowest-valued sale to be notarized belongs to Chasseurs-Volontaires veteran Julien dit Evian of Mirebalais, who bought a wedge of land 21 feet wide at its widest point in the town of Mirebalais from Jacques Jaquet *dit* Bambara on 7 August 1787 for 63 *livres*. The notary's fee in this case is not stated, but it must have been at least 15 *livres*.[6] While all land sales were, in principle, to be the subject of a notarial act, small sales of moveable property and slaves, at least among whites, were rarely notarized. Not so for the free colored community. There are dozens of acts of sale of slaves and even livestock or other moveable property, which were notarized at a cost of as much as 10 or 20 percent of the basic sale price. For this reason, transactions with or among people of color may be overrepresented in the notarial archives. At the same time, this means that the notarial archives give broader information about the lives of humbler people among the free colored community than they would if whites alone were to be considered.

Acts that were not notarized at the time of sale (*actes de vente privée*) were often regularized after the fact—usually when the object in question was to be resold or willed. Of course, to use this procedure, at least one participant had to be literate —although grammar and spelling in these private acts tend to be idiosyncratic. Such ex post facto notarizations were the cheapest way to obtain a notarial act, since the notary had only to make a copy of the private act in his register. Fees for this service were often below the standard rate for in-office acts of sale. Occasionally, the date on the act of private sale is the same as the date of deposition of the act into the notary's files, suggesting that the actors were simply bypassing the notary's scribes and reducing their expenses by writing out the bill of sale themselves.

Much of the analysis of these documents depends on being able to identify individuals and family relationships over a number of documents. Many individuals, especially freedmen, were identified in notarial acts only by first names. Sometimes, these names were spelled differently from act to act. Others were identified by different surnames or appellations in different acts. A colonial government regulation of 1773 required that all persons of color, when freed, be given a surname "drawn from the African idiom."[7] Free persons of color were forbidden from bearing the family name of a white. In the case of legitimate offspring of white people, this edict was almost universally ignored, although Garrigus suggests that the colored Raimonds of Aquin changed the spelling of their family name in response to the edict; their white, legitimate father spelled his name Raymond.[8] In the case of an illegitimate white father, notaries would sometimes use a modified form of the last name. They would also occasionally use the father's last name with a notation that the person was "known as" or "formerly called" by that name. This was apparently the case with Luce Rasteau in the above document.

All this confusion with names makes it difficult to follow the career of individuals. However, parish of residence was almost universally included. Often, the notary specified the actor's residence in a subunit within the parish. Census records indicate the number of free adults of color in each parish and frequently by subunit. A detailed discussion of the demography of free coloreds appears in chapter 3, but a couple of examples suffice to show how an individual's career can be traced in the notarial record despite this problem. In rural Haut du Cap, it seems safe to assume that the free black referred to as "Toussaint Breda" was in fact Toussaint Louverture of later fame. We know that Louverture was known as "Breda" before the Revolution and that he came from the Breda plantation at Haut du Cap. The census of 1775 shows five free black adult males living in the *dépendances du Cap*, which would include Haut du Cap.[9] Although the census does not give their names, at least one other of these men appeared in notarial acts as *"dit* Breda," which would suggest that he too was a former slave on the Breda sugar plantation at Haut du Cap. However, his personal name was Blaise. Toussaint, although a common personal name today in Haiti, was not particularly common before 1791. Although some, particularly those whose liberties had not been officially registered, may have escaped the census takers, we would have to presume that the de facto free outnumbered the de jure free by an overwhelming majority to make it statistically likely that there was another Toussaint *dit* Breda.

By similar logic, it is reasonably certain that Marie Zabeth, sister of Marie Therese, free black, living in the Savane district of Limonade, who bought a slave from her sister in 1780, is the same as Marie Elizabeth, wife of Andre Poupart, free black, living in Savane, who sold a half-carreau field to her sister Marie in 1778.[10] A detailed breakdown of Limonade's census figures by subparish has not survived, so we cannot be sure of the figure for the Savane, but the whole of Limonade together with the neighboring parish of l'Acul du Nord counted only 277 free persons of color in 1780.[11]

Names could often become confused in families by the habit of giving the same personal name to more than one individual. The Laportes of Limonade, linchpins of the planter elite of Limonade, whose family tree appears in appendix 1, are an outstanding example. One of the challenges of working with this family was the fact that there were six separate individuals, ranging in racial classification from white to *mulâtre* and spread across four generations, all of whom bore the name Louis Laporte. The notaries helpfully but inconsistently referred to different individuals as "father," "son," the "younger," or the "elder," and some can be identified by the names of their wives, or their color, if stated. But there are a few acts referring to Louis Laporte whose precise identity remains unclear. The white patriarch, who had two (legal, sequential) families (and at least one concubine), was named Louis, and must have liked the name.

Family relationships were often stated, but just as often they were left open to question. The widow Daugin's precise relationship to the seller, Louis Daguin, in the act quoted in its entirety in appendix 4, was clearly stated. This was a mercy on the part of this notary, who often left the reader to guess what the relationship was between, for example, the nine persons surnamed Fagneau who sold a piece of land divided into seven pieces.[12] In the case of the Fagneaus, reference was made to an act of division of their inheritance that was performed before the 1776 edict and that is therefore not in the archives. Other acts performed by various Fagneaus at other times, however, permitted the identification of three of the nine individuals in this case as nieces and nephews of the other six, who were all brothers and sisters and principal heirs of their deceased parents, the former owners of the land in question. The mother of the three nieces and nephews was dead, and they were acting as her heirs. The notary in the first act did not make the precise relationships clear.

Family relationships to whites are even harder to pin down. When the white parent was married to the parent of African descent, things are no harder than usual—although sometimes the African ancestry of the mother gets obfuscated. "Natural" fathers could recognize their children under French law, and sometimes they did in the case of illegitimate children of African ancestry. This was seen occasionally in wills where the white testator had no close legitimate relatives in France. Often, acts executed by the children after the death of a white father, especially marriage contracts and wills, would baldly state the family relationship even though the father made no such admission, at least officially, during his lifetime. In the most common case, however, the father remained officially unknown even after his death. In these cases, where possible, fathers have been identified by other means. Notaries in the North province used a formula phrase in acts of donation: "to take the place of a *pension viagère,*" or living expense allowance. By French common law, fathers of illegitimate colored children were supposed to provide an annual allowance to their children. The *Code Noir* required such child support on pain of a fine.[13] Wherever a white man performed an act of donation in which he gave a free colored woman and her natural children some capital goods —land or slaves—"in lieu of *pension viagère,*" or in the rarer cases where an actual annual allowance was pledged, that donor has been provisionally identified as the father of those children. All donations by men, even white men, to colored women were not so directly instrumental—there are several cases in which the colored family was almost certainly not the direct offspring of the white donor. These cases are most likely attributable to patrons, relatives, or friends of the poverty-stricken, dead, or neglectful white father taking care of his offspring for him. In the questionable cases, the number of acts in which the mother and possible father appeared together and the intimacy of their economic relationship has served as a guide to presumptive identification of illegitimate fathers.

In some cases, of course, the family relationship between individuals cannot be definitely established. Persons coming from the same parish and bearing the same surname are more likely than not related, but the relationships are often unclear from the notarial record. If the relationship is unclear, the term "relative" or "presumed relative" appears.

PARISH REGISTERS

One method of clarifying family relationships is the parish registers. A selection of the parish registers for the six parishes in the sample has been consulted. The "new social history" technique of family reconstruction through the parish registers, common in *ancien régime* French social history, was not possible for Saint Domingue free coloreds because of the lack of vital identifying information in many of the parish register acts. As with the notarial acts, the parish registers often failed to include the parents' names, date and place of baptism, and other information on a free colored person that a metropolitan French parish priest would have considered essential in any parish register entry. In the notarial acts, the researcher can use other clues to connect an actor with a known family, but the parish register acts are generally fairly terse. The parish registers do not permit the production of any sort of general census or demographic study, so this book simply notes acts in which a person already identified from the notarial records was an actor. Thus, the parish register acts served to demonstrate family and pseudo-kin relationships among free coloreds already part of the study.

Acts in the parish registers are one of three types: baptism, burial, and marriage. All acts contained at a minimum the following elements:

Baptisms: The names of the child, the mother, the father, if known or admitted, and at least two godparents. Residences were noted for the primary actors in most cases. In any case, unless a special exemption was granted by the bishop and noted in the act, nobody could be baptized outside their parish of residence. This restriction seems to have been intended to make it harder for parents to "pass" a light-skinned baby as white, but it also made it easier to determine the home parish of some itinerant free coloreds. Illegitimate fathers were more likely to acknowledge parenthood in the baptismal record than in notarial acts. Godparenthood was also very important for establishing patron-client relationships for both child and parent. Wills of wealthy persons often contained sizable bequests for their godchildren, and godparents often made significant gifts to their godchildren upon marriage or majority. Godparenthood was a sort of glue that held the community of people of color together, especially in the case of members of the military leadership group, who lacked strong blood kinship ties in many cases. In the case of the planter group, godparenthood helped reinforce its links to white society as white grandparents and other kin turned out at the baptisms of their free colored relatives. Godfatherhood can also serve as a cloak for illegitimate fatherhood, and this was one of the signposts used to determine who the father of a child was.

Marriages: Marriage was part of the bourgeois morality that Julien Raimond and other defenders of the free coloreds claimed they upheld. The data show that free coloreds married in the colony at a much higher rate than whites. Of course, there were few white women, and some of the colony's white men were married to women who remained in France. Marriage acts in the parish registers contained at least the names of the bride and groom and of several witnesses. Often, the parents of the couple were named, even if not present. Prenuptial children were common, especially among poorer free coloreds. Marriage celebrations were expensive. They were always listed, with a reference to the date of their baptism, so that their new legitimate status could be recorded. The presence of witnesses was also an important marker of patron-client relationships and perhaps suggestive of covert white fatherhood. Many white fathers attended the weddings of their mulatto sons and daughters and gave liberal gifts to the couple. A dead giveaway to the relationship is when the gift was explicitly described as "an advance on inheritance." Even if not stated so baldly, the presence of whites in the wedding party demonstrated links with white society.

Burials: Often, only the name of the deceased and a witness appeared. However, if the deceased was a prominent person in the community, much more information about him or her would be included. Place and date of baptism, names of parents, children, and spouses, and even a list of official mourners, with signatures, were all common ingredients at elite funerals. Usually, the priest would note whether the deceased had received extreme unction, which measured how close he or she lived to a church and also indicated something about the piety of the individual or of his or her family.

Church Offices: The parish registers also include the names of the petty officials of the church—the *margouilleurs,* or ushers, and *syndics,* or vestrymen. In several cases, free people of color held these offices. Although barred from civil office-holding and military commissions by various royal decrees of the mid-eighteenth century, lower church offices remained, like military noncommissioned ranks, a way in which prominent free colored men could demonstrate and reaffirm social status.[14] This was particularly true of the rural parishes in the sample, which were dominated by free people of color. The chapel or subparish of Sainte-Suzanne, in the mountains of Limonade, had a large population of free coloreds, and some of the vestrymen were coloreds.

OTHER DOCUMENTARY SOURCES

There are a number of other collections of official papers in the Archives Nationales Françaises d'Outremer in Aix-en-Provence that illuminate in some way the lives of free people of color during this period. The *Greffe,* or court clerk's office papers, are available for all the jurisdictions. These include pleadings, depositions of witnesses, and decisions in cases, both civil and criminal, that came before the various courts of the colony. Unfortunately, they are poorly indexed and offer only a very fragmentary view of the court cases to which they refer. Sometimes, a notarial act would refer to a *Greffe* document.[15] Criminal court depositions by *maréchausée* officers describing police activities were especially useful in understanding the role and structure of that force. A few examples of free colored resistance to military service appear in the criminal court registers.

Several cadastral, or land-ownership, surveys of Cap Français have survived. One, especially useful, identified the properties by street location and estimated rental value. From these, land owned by individual persons of color could be identified and evaluated. This survey was particularly helpful since it described owners and often occupants of properties by racial category, permitting the mapping of free colored and white neighborhoods.

Finally, Moreau de St. Méry, who was both archivist of France toward the end of his career and an inveterate collector of French colonial documents, included a good deal of items related to the question of people of color in his voluminous personal archives. Although it would perhaps be too much to suggest that an archivist of France would actually steal documents from the archives for his personal library, there are a lot of government documents in the Moreau de St. Méry papers that are not in their correct locations in the regular archives. For example, there are reports from the Savannah expedition that are not in the military records, commentary and correspondence from various colonial officials throughout the years, and cases from his own legal firm's files. Plenty of useful snippets of information can be culled from the Collection Moreau de St. Méry by the diligent and unhurried researcher.

CONCLUSION

The material preserved in the colonial archives offers a wealth of evidence on the lives of free people of color in the colony. Because of the propensity of the caste to use the notarial system, even free coloreds of relatively humble means are represented. The issue of the mutability of free coloreds' names and the sometimes slipshod habits of Saint Domingue's notaries have deterred many researchers from trying to use this resource in the past, due to the difficulty in identifying individuals from document to document. However, with care and observation of other identifying details, it has been possible to track particular individuals through a series of notarial and other documents. The spareness of information in parish registers, however, defeated attempts to use them extensively in this study. A certain amount of "anecdotal" evidence, such as reports from government officials and policemen, travel books written at the time, and the fascinating variety of material that Moreau de St. Méry collected, help the reader grasp the *mentalité* of whites and to some extent that of free coloreds as well.

It is through their behavior that we best appreciate the *mentalité* of the free coloreds. That behavior is revealed in detail in the notarial acts they performed on every conceivable occasion. It is in this way that the system itself becomes an important clue to the functioning of the society. The trust that free coloreds placed in legalisms—a trust that was not misplaced, as their property was often protected by the system against white aggressors—illustrates the role of law and the importance of lawfully framed and issued paperwork in the society.

CHAPTER TWO

The Land

Geography, on Hispaniola, was the mother of history. This chapter looks at the
places that are the stage on which the actors in this book play out their parts. First,
it explores briefly the geography of the island as a whole. Next, it turns to the geography of each of the parishes selected for special consideration, beginning with
a brief history of French settlement in the area. This is supplemented in the two
units dealing with the major cities by a look at economic developments in that city's
hinterland during the eighteenth century. Then, each unit considers the cities,
towns, or villages in the parish both in terms of physical geography—public and
private buildings, streets, utilities—and in terms of the services—governmental,
cultural, and commercial—offered there. The notaries come under the heading of
governmental services. Thus, at this point the reader meets the notary (or notaries) from that parish whose papers were selected for study. Last is a consideration,
for each parish in turn, of the economic geography of that parish during the period 1776–1791, focusing, especially in the case of the rural parishes, on agriculture.

The purpose of this organization is to look at each parish in terms of its place
in the economy of the larger colony. Places in this colony can be looked at hierar-
chically, with those offering more complex services at the top and those offering
merely basic production at the bottom. The six parishes selected for study contain
two large cities, Cap Français, the economic center of the colony, and Port-au-
Prince, its administrative capital. There are two flourishing agricultural areas with
small market towns, Fort Dauphin in the northeast and Croix des Bouquets just
north of Port-au-Prince. Finally, there are two rather remote rural areas, Mirebalais in the West province and Limonade in the north. Limonade was a very
profitable sugar-growing area, but the notary dealt primarily with the free coloreds

living in the southern part of the parish, a remote mountainous area without significant sugar cultivation.

These three parishes from the north and three from the West province were selected to control for regional differences. The South province is not covered here because its free coloreds are the subjects of John Garrigus's dissertation.[1] There has been some discussion of regional differentiation within the colony, and certainly the picture drawn in this book differs to some extent from what Garrigus found. The sample contains geographically and economically comparable parishes from both regions.

THE ISLAND

Hispaniola is located in the Greater Antilles between Cuba and Puerto Rico. The portion controlled by France until the Revolution of 1791–1804 takes up the western third of this island. Spain controlled the remainder of the island. Hispaniola, part of the Greater Antilles, is toward the leeward end of the Antilles island chain and thus downwind of the Lesser Antilles. A voyage by sailing ship from Europe to Hispaniola must, therefore, first pass the smaller islands and run the risk of naval interception. In peacetime, Saint Domingue's location toward the downwind end of the Caribbean meant that moving cargoes to and from Europe or Africa was somewhat more time-consuming and expensive than for the smaller colonies in the Lesser Antilles—Guadeloupe, Martinique, and their English-controlled neighbors.

The landscape of Saint Domingue is characterized by several small plains divided by ranges of mountains that reach up to 2,000 meters. There are five main areas of plains. First, in economic importance anyway, is the Plaine du Nord between Cap Français and Fort Dauphin, which is on the northern coast. Next are the valley of the Artibonite River, the Plaine du Cul de Sac around Croix des Bouquets with an arm extending north along the coast to Archaye, and the area around Léogane, all on the central bay of the colony. Finally, the southern plain extending from Saint-Louis to Les Cayes and Torbeck lies along the southern coast.

The French side of the island, like many of the larger islands of the Caribbean, is divided into a large number of microclimates. Small areas might get annual rainfalls of over two meters, while only a few kilometers away cactus and scrub signal semi-desert conditions. Some of the drier flat land also has saline soil, and in one area, at the eastern end of the Cul de Sac, large salt lakes render the surrounding soil unfit for agriculture. The plains that received heavy and regular rains were the first to be hit by the sugar revolution, whereas those regions with less water required considerable investment in irrigation infrastructure before they could be

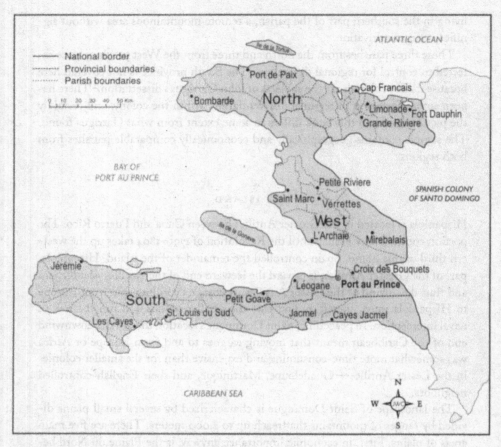

MAP 1. *The Colony of Saint Domingue*

exploited. They lagged behind somewhat in the race to join the plantation complex, but as the eighteenth century advanced, irrigation supplied the water where it was lacking.

The Atlantic slave trade supplied the labor, making the plains ideal for the cultivation of sugar. The great agricultural transformation referred to as the sugar revolution, which affected almost all of the island colonies of the Caribbean, hit Saint Domingue during the first half of the eighteenth century. Production climbed from 7,000 tons in 1714 to 43,000 tons in 1743, 77,000 tons in 1767, and 86,000 tons at its peak in 1786.[2]

Dense tropical forests covered the mountains that surrounded and divided the sugar-producing plains up until the middle of the eighteenth century. Sharp relief and shallow soils made them unsuitable for sugar cultivation. In addition, runaway slaves made their homes in the mountains, and although they presented no serious security threat to the defended plains, they were a hindrance to settlement in the mountains. Around midcentury though, with the introduction of large-scale coffee cultivation, settling the mountains became economically attractive, so the colony's government dealt with the threat from the *marons,* the maroon slaves. In most cases, the authorities liquidated them or drove them across the border to the Spanish colony by military force, but in some cases, government officials made treaties with the slaves that remained in force until the Revolution.

In the coffee boom, a second period of great economic growth that followed and supplemented the sugar boom, the plantation complex occupied the highlands between 1750 and 1780. This coffee boom was the great economic event of the middle of the century; its effects are discussed in Michel-Rolph Trouillot's article "Motion in the System."[3] For example, in the Sainte-Suzanne district of Limonade, by the 1770s whole regions that had been beyond the civilized frontier a few decades before became heavily populated and exceptionally wealthy.

The coffee boom was important to free coloreds for two reasons. First, land, which in some cases they already occupied, suddenly became much more valuable. Even if they were not landholders in the mountains, they had an advantage over the hordes of ambitious young white men who came to the colony to cash in on the coffee boom. They were already on the scene, with local contacts and knowledge, and thus had an easier time starting coffee farms. Secondly, coffee farming had a lower startup cost than did sugar cultivation, requiring fewer slaves and less work of preparation of the land, as well as less sophisticated machinery. Thus, free coloreds, with less capital than the white planters, were not necessarily barred from participation in the new boom. Consequently, the mountainous coffee areas came to be heavily populated by a newly wealthy class of free coloreds.

Although, as noted, rainfall can vary widely from place to place within the island, in general, the high mountains received sufficient rain for coffee. Another climatological feature of note was the relative absence of destructive hurricanes in the heavily populated areas of the colony. The storm track generally heads northwestward in this area, and the southeastern coast of the colony, and of modern Haiti, is lightly settled and mountainous. The mountains of the southern peninsula, and of the Spanish portion of the island, break up storms before they reach the populated central and northern plains. The Bay of Port-au-Prince, between the northern and southern peninsulas of the island and shielded by the Isle de la Gonâve, is an enormous protected anchorage. Only a few storms in recorded history have had a strong effect on the heavily populated West and North provinces. This is in sharp contrast to the experience of neighboring, and competing, Santo

Domingo and Jamaica, each of which suffered severe and repeated damage from hurricanes during the colonial period.

The colony of Saint Domingue was divided administratively into three provinces: North, with its capital at Cap Français, West, headquartered at Port-au-Prince, which was also the capital of the colony as a whole, and South, with its center at Les Cayes. Each province was subdivided into *quartiers*, which were then further subdivided into a varying number of parishes, most with a small market town at its center. The provincial capitals, with the exception of Les Cayes, are described below. They offered a wide range of services and greatly outweighed the other towns around them both from an economic and an administrative point of view. The parishes designated as central places for their *quartiers* hosted a court (*sénéchausée*) and were usually more important towns than their subordinate parishes. Some parish towns, like Limonade, had little more than a church and a market square, whereas others, like Mirebalais, were locally important centers that drew business from surrounding parishes.

The business of the colony was plantation agriculture, and the business of the towns and cities was supplying the needs of the farmers and getting their produce to the world market. Thus, the most important characteristic of a town was its port or market. Small amounts of manufacturing also took place in towns, especially the larger ones. However, labor was generally more profitably employed in agriculture. Only the most pressing needs were satisfied by the colony's own manufactures, and many manufactured goods were imported from France or elsewhere. There were some (illegal) exports to non-French colonies, but most of the colony's agricultural produce flowed to the *metropole*. There was an active (and barely tolerated) trade across the border with Spanish Santo Domingo, with Spanish ranchers trading their cattle and horses for Dominguan produce and cash.

The colony's administrators and their metropolitan masters desired control over the economy and sought to exclude smugglers by concentrating trade at a couple of major ports in each region. This effort was partially successful and contributed to the overwhelming economic presence of the major cities. However, geography conspired against these efforts, as the coast of the island is lined with protected anchorages. The northern and southern coasts have extensive reefs offshore, but there are many places that a skilled pilot can bring a ship through the reefs. At each such place, there is a landing that was occupied in colonial times by a small village. As well as serving as the sites for clandestine trade with English or Dutch freighters, these *embarquadaires* were important for the intra-island shipping trade, carrying the bulky hogsheads of sugar and other cargoes to and from the major ports. This local shipping trade was another avenue for free coloreds to break into business, for it required a small initial investment, but it was not an activity for the risk-averse.

Land transportation within the colony, on the other hand, was quite difficult, increasing the importance of the intra-island shipping trade. The colony's government made various attempts to build roads and bridges. Within the plains, these roads were at risk from floods, whereas in the mountains, they were often little more than rough tracks.

This isolation of regions within the colony permitted each region to develop a very distinct geographic personality. For this reason, each parish will be considered separately.

CAP FRANÇAIS

Located on the fertile northern coast of the island of Hispaniola, Cap Français was the largest urban area in the colony at the time under study. It was, says Moreau de St. Méry, the colony's "capital in fact, the principal seat of its wealth, its luxury, the greatest commercial city, and finally, that place which geography will always make the most important in the colony."[4] Moreau de St. Méry was, it must be remembered, a lawyer in practice in Cap and a member of various local institutions, and his analysis might be suspected of boosterism. However, he does not exaggerate the importance of the city to the colony.

French settlement at Cap dates back to before 1676, twenty years before the Treaty of Ryswick made peace between France and Spain and granted Spanish toleration to the French inhabitants of the island.[5] Treaties notwithstanding, French people and their African subordinates lived on the main island, and it was in 1676 that the Catholic Church established a parish at what was then called Bas du Cap. The center of French settlement on Hispaniola at the time was Port-de-Paix, 70 kilometers to the west and directly across the Tortuga Channel from the important French port and buccaneer base on the Isle de la Tortue. Port-de-Paix and Tortuga supported each other against Spanish attacks, and both were well-protected harbors suited to the small, maneuverable vessels favored by the pirates of the seventeenth century.

Cap's harbor, while not so easily defended by forts and cannon, is considerably larger than that of Port-de-Paix and thus more suited to the needs of larger merchant vessels needed to haul agricultural cargoes. In addition, the hinterland beyond Port-de-Paix is not particularly suitable for agriculture, being mountainous and not particularly well watered. Cap, on the other hand, is located in the middle of the large Plaine du Nord that stretches 70 kilometers from Limbé to the Spanish frontier and varies from 15 to 25 kilometers wide between the ocean and the mountains. This plain, the largest unbroken stretch of good agricultural land on the French side of the island, is watered by many streams and receives seasonal heavy rains. Its soil at the beginning of the eighteenth century was very fertile, as much of the flat land was a seasonally replenished flood plain.

At the end of the seventeenth century, France gained international recognition of its colony on the mainland of Hispaniola. The role of the colony in the French Empire began to change. Governors as far back as Bertrand d'Ogeron (1665–1676) had attempted to encourage the development of market agriculture on the island.[6] A brief tobacco boom in the 1660s lost out to Chesapeake Bay production. Indigo and other crops were tried, with varying degrees of success. The enormous success of the colony was due to the introduction of sugar. The sugar boom in the North province of Saint Domingue dates from the beginning of the eighteenth century. By midcentury, most of the suitable land in the North was under sugar cultivation, and by the late eighteenth century, the flat country around Cap Français was a fully mature sugar-producing area. Thus, Cap Français, in addition to being the colony's commercial capital, is a good example of an important market town in a well-developed sugar region. In this, it provides a good contrast with Port-au-Prince, where sugar production was important but had still not reached its apogee by the 1770s.

The mountains of the North province were unsuitable for sugar cultivation, having too sharp relief and lacking the deep fertile soils of the plains. Therefore, they remained more or less uninhabited by "civilized" colonial society until midcentury, being left to a scattered population of herders, hunters of wild cattle, peasants scratching out a living on the margins of society, and runaway slaves. Many of these people were free, or quasi-free, coloreds and thus fall within the purview of this work. The reader will see, in Mirebalais, a parish where this stage of development had not yet completely been surpassed in the 1770s and 1780s.

Because of the coffee boom in the northern mountains, the former marginal users of this land were mostly forced south, into the Spanish part of the colony, or west, into the northern peninsula where agriculture was not so strong. By the third quarter of the century, the vicinity of Cap, highland and lowland, had become a settled plantation colony, well within the borders of "civilization," with all that implies. This is again unlike the West province, in which substantial pockets existed outside the "plantation complex," potentially home to maroon slaves or poor but independent free coloreds.

This flourishing agricultural hinterland would have made Cap Français an important city in any case. A good deal of its urban activity was connected directly to the sugar and coffee business. Beyond this, though, Cap Français was well situated to be the major metropolis of the colony. Located on the northern side of the island, it was the closest major port to the place where ships coming from France would make landfall in the colony. Ships traveling to Port-au-Prince or the older

port towns of Léogane or Petit Goâve would have to round the northern peninsula and traverse the Bay of La Gonâve in often-fluky winds. Ships returning to
Europe from Cap Français could make their way to open ocean north of the Turks
and Caicos Islands. Alternatively, they could strike up the coast of Cuba to catch
the Gulf Stream more or less directly. In either case, they would not have to run the
risk of a voyage across the Bay of La Gonâve. Moreau de St. Méry's description of
the voyage to the colony makes clear that Cap Français was on the direct route to
and from Europe.[7] The trade winds were generally more reliable in the open Atlantic than they were in the constricted waters to the west or south of the island.
Thus, Cap Français served as a transshipment port for the entire colony, where
goods would be unloaded from the large ocean-crossing ships from France and
placed aboard smaller, more nimble intra-island boats for carriage to more southerly ports.

The city of Cap has often been described as "the Paris of the Antilles" for its
urban amenities and cosmopolitan spirit, and not just by the booster Moreau de
St. Méry. The Baron de Wimpffen comments that "Cap-Français is built in stone
. . . relative to the other towns [of the colony] there is, in the spirit that reigns there,
the same difference that one observes in their architecture; that is, that the spirit
of the one is to the other as a solid house [*maison*] is to a ruinous shack [*barraque*]."[8]
Colonial commentator and diarist (and fellow member with Moreau de St. Méry
of the Cercle des Philadelphes of Cap) Baudry des Lozières called the city "the
Paris of our island."[9]

These observers commented in part on the solidity of construction of both public and private buildings in the city. A decree imposed after a devastating fire in
1753 required all new construction to be in stone, and this edict seems to have been
widely respected, even in poorer neighborhoods. The notarial record supports this
impression: for samples of approximately the same size, 64 transactions of urban
real estate in Cap involved masonry buildings, whereas only 13 in Port-au-Prince
did. The streets, at least in the wealthier neighborhoods near the waterfront, appear to have been paved, as certain notarial acts refer to pavement stones. Moreau
de St. Méry said that those streets "consecrated to commerce" were paved down
the middle to provide a gutter and passage for carts, while the sides of the street
were covered in gravel.[10] This was not true of Port-au-Prince or any of the other
cities of the colony. When it rained in Port-au-Prince, mud was everywhere, and
when it was dry, choking clouds of dust arose at every step.

While not the official colonial capital, the city of Cap nonetheless was the site
of many important public buildings. The Conseil Supérieur had a nice building,
which the administrators of the colony took over on the frequent occasions when
they took up residence in the town. Especially in times of war, it was most efficient

for the colony's leaders to congregate in Cap. The best port and most impressive fortifications in the island, as well as the barracks of the Régiment du Cap, one of the two colonial infantry regiments permanently stationed on the island, were located at the foot of the mountain, at the western end of town.

Also on the western hills was the convent of the Sisters of Charity, which is what passed for a hospital in the North province. Courts often forwarded fines to the Maison de Charité, and the house was also a frequent recipient of bequests. It was a fairly large hospital; it rates its own volume in the colony's vital statistics (burials) records.

The parish church of Cap was a large and reasonably impressive edifice, at least from the outside. It had a fine masonry facade, decorated with statues, built in 1774, but the money raised for its construction was insufficient to build entirely in stone, so a goodly portion of the interior was still wooden in 1788.[11] Like many things in the colony, the facade was the important part, and the underpinnings could wait.

Cap did not have a cathedral. The colony was never assigned a bishop, probably to the relief of colonial officials and elites. The parishes of the colony were mission churches, served for the most part by regular clergy—Jesuits until 1763, then Capuchins and Dominicans. The presence of a parish church validated the existence of a community. Quite a few of the white colonists were Protestants, whereas others were fashionably anti-clerical. Still others belonged to a small but active Jewish community. Mission outreach to the slaves was minimal, especially after the Jesuits were thrown out. Nonetheless, both colored and white communities spent considerable time and money improving their (Catholic) churches.

The solidity of both public and private construction in Cap was in part a result of the fact that the city was an important administrative center. While never the titular capital of the colony, Cap Français nonetheless was the residence of the chief officers of government, the governor and intendant, from 1761 onward.[12] The Conseil Supérieur of Cap was one of two courts of appeal in the colony until it was suppressed in 1787. The two Conseils Supérieurs were seen by the colony's elite as having the status of *parlements* in the metropolitan system. The *parlements* were instruments of noble opposition to royal absolutism in the eighteenth century. The white plantocracy of Saint Domingue saw the Conseils as their defenders against the government. The Conseils registered edicts and laws with all the pomp of a provincial *parlement* in France. Moreau de St. Méry points out that the members of the Conseil Supérieur de Port-au-Prince were given the right to wear the same insignia of rank as were metropolitan *parlements* by royal decree in 1788.[13] (This was a mark of respect, perhaps intended to make up for the suppression of the colonial courts in 1787 and the belated restoration by the 1788 act, which reestablished only the Conseil of Port-au-Prince, giving it responsibility for the entire island under the close supervision of the governor.) The doings of the Conseil Supérieur du Cap figure prominently in the reports of Moreau de St. Méry. He was an attorney who argued many cases before this body, so it is necessarily overrepresented in his collection, but it seems to have been a very active court. Cap produced only a few less notarial registers than the official capital, Port-au-Prince, for this period.[14]

The Cap notaries whose records were the principal source for what we know about free colored society in the area, Jean-François Doré and Jean-François Bordier *jeune*, both had offices in the central business district. They attracted much more than their share of Cap's free colored population to their studies. Doré, interestingly, was an absentee planter in the mountain canton of Sainte-Suzanne, Limonade, an area dominated by free coloreds from which many of the Limonade representatives in this book come. After his death, his widow returned to the homestead in the mountains and became a prominent local *grande dame.* She was socially important since she was one of the very few white women of the planter class among all the colored planter elite ladies of this coffee-growing area. Bordier *jeune* was the younger of two brothers who served as notaries in Cap. The elder brother died shortly after careful record keeping began, so there is little from his archives in the sample. Doré's death at about the same time seems to have brought more business to the younger Bordier, as he inherited a large proportion of the Cap free colored population as his client base.

Cap provided a full range of urban services. There was a theater, with performances three times a week, where the cream of the colony's society would gather to see and be seen. Free coloreds were present, but only on the floor or the third rank of *loges.* The theater was supported by fifty stockholders and had a (paper) capital of 150,000 *livres* and an annual budget of 235,752 *livres* in 1771. Season tickets for a couple were 550 *livres,* exclusive of box rental.[15] The theater seems to have been the heart of Cap's social and business life.

Associated with the theater was a library, with eighty subscribing members who paid 42 *piastres* annually.[16] The library was also the home of the Cercle des Philadelphes de Cap, of which Moreau de St. Méry was a member. It was this organization that hatched the idea of writing a general encyclopedia of the island. Moreau de St. Méry took on the task, which resulted in his *Loix et constitutions des colonies d'amérique, Description . . . de la partie espagnole,* and *Description . . . de la partie française,* invaluable tools to the modern researcher studying the colony.

The intellectual life of the colony was centered in Cap and was energetic by colonial standards.[17] Cap had a print shop, and some works were printed in the city, but given the economic difficulties of finding and retaining skilled workers in the colony, it generally was cheaper to print in France anything not needed at once. Newspapers, of course, were topical, and the city was the home of the oldest and most frequently published newspaper in the colony, the *Affiches américaines*. The *Affiches* began publication in Cap in 1764 and was officially headquartered in Port-au-Prince starting in 1768, but it published its largest format and most frequent editions in Cap throughout the colonial period.

Presumably, free coloreds read the announcements of local interest—runaway slaves, estate sales, and the like. Certainly, they were advertisers in the *Affiches,* as reported by Jean Fouchard in his study of runaway slaves as seen through the eyes of the newspaper advertisers.[18] The rest of the intellectual life of Cap seems to have been a whites-only proposition. At any rate, there is no record of any free colored participating at the Cercle des Philadelphes. Certainly, the members of the influential and scientific Chambre de l'Agriculture were among the most prominent white planters in the colony; the African-descended need not apply. The "intellectual" professions, medicine and the law, had been closed to free coloreds by the 1760s. Many free coloreds had been educated in France, but racial prejudice by the 1770s would have made it difficult for them to work alongside whites in an intellectual sphere.

The free coloreds of Cap also tended not to live alongside the most powerful whites. Free coloreds lived in outlying areas of the city for the most part. The attractive, and valuable, properties were closest to the waterfront and toward the northern end of the town. Analysis of the cadastral survey of 1776 and notarial records suggest that as one got further south and west, the occupants of buildings grew darker.[19] The neighborhoods of Petite Guinée, le Carénage, and the area outside the city gates proper leading south toward the plain were popular areas for free colored settlement. This is not to say that free coloreds did not own downtown property—in fact, both survey and notarial records show that investment in commercial property was a common strategy of ambitious coloreds. But it would be unlikely to find a free colored proprietor actually *occupying* one of his properties east and north of an unmarked boundary line. This line was both unmarked and semi-permeable. Vincent Ogé and his mother lived in the midst of the wealthiest and whitest neighborhood on the Place de Clugny. Free colored mistresses of white men certainly made their residence inside predominantly white neighborhoods. No strict housing discrimination appears to have been practiced by the government in Cap.

Houses in the free colored area, as one might suspect, were more modest than those in the neighborhood inhabited by the wealthy whites. However, some of the houses in this dark-complexioned neighborhood were still quite substantial. For example, the house occupied by Pierre Medor *dit* Ange, at 22 rue St. Simon, near the center of town but in a mixed neighborhood, was built completely in masonry

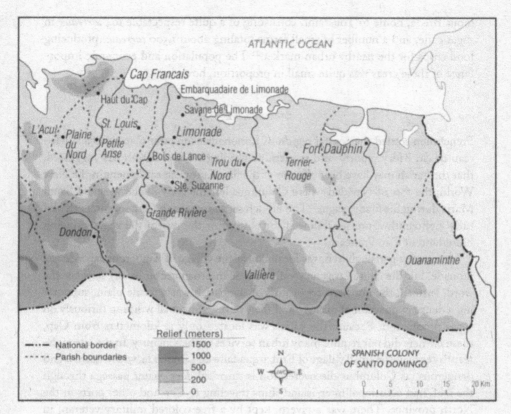

MAP 2. *The North Province*

and was estimated for tax purposes in 1776 as being worth 1,800 *livres* a year.[20] Many free coloreds were fearful of spending on what might have been seen as ostentation or luxury—especially given the plethora of sumptuary laws passed in the 1760s and 1770s—but were nonetheless interested in adopting a comfortable lifestyle and enjoying the fruits of their economic success. This was possible, within limits, and especially in the "appropriate" neighborhoods of the port cities. It was also possible in rural areas like Limonade, where prominent free coloreds enjoyed somewhat greater license to indulge themselves than their urban fellows.

The parish of Cap included a small part of the hinterland. The mountain that overlooks the city was under its administration, as was the small village and farming area of Haut du Cap, home of Toussaint *dit* Breda, the future Louverture. The *dépendances* (rural dependencies) of Cap contained one sugar plantation, the famous Breda, home to Toussaint, consisting of a quite respectable 104 *carreaux* in sugar cane, and a number of small farms totaling about 1,500 *carreaux* producing food crops for the nearby urban market.[21] The population and economic importance of these areas was quite small in proportion, however.

LIMONADE

Frenchmen settled the coastal region of Limonade soon after Cap Français. Moreau de St. Méry reports, and modern archaeological exploration has suggested, that the parish may have been the site of the first European settlement in the New World, the fort of Navidad where Columbus left the crew of the wrecked Santa Maria during his first voyage.[22] The French settlement in the late seventeenth and early eighteenth centuries followed the pattern of the rest of the sugar-growing hinterland of Cap Français.

Limonade's parish church was located near the village of Embarquadaire de Limonade, but the church was not really part of an urban center in any sense of the word. Instead, the northern two-thirds of the parish was a fertile plain, supporting a dense population of masters and their slaves, almost all working furiously on sugar production. Because the parish was located only 12 kilometers from Cap, these farmers did not require many urban services in their vicinity. In the late eighteenth century, the small village of Embarquadaire de Limonade, with a narrow and dangerous (as Columbus discovered to his surprise) deep-water passage through the reef, had occasional inter-island ships traveling to Cap and other ports in the North province. There was a tavern, kept by a free colored military veteran, in which labored the future ruler of the northern part of Haiti, Henry Christophe. None of the structures impressed the local notary enough to rate the honorific description *maison* in any notarial act.

Along the road to Cap, there was a small district or village of free coloreds called the Savane de Limonade. Haitian peasant communities today are widely scattered, hardly rating the description of "village." French peasants at the time, however, lived close together and walked to their fields. It is unclear which pattern the Savane followed. In any case, the settlement was a poor community; Moreau de St. Méry noted that it "required an active police presence."[23] These were peasant proprietors, living on land that was relatively flat but for some reason—perhaps soil salinity—unsuitable for sugar cultivation. Most pieces of land seem to have been around one *carreau*, or about two hectares. The sugar plantations all around them furnished a market for any excess food production, and the notarial records occasionally contain the traces of someone climbing from the poverty of the Savane. An example would be Marie Zabeth, the widow Poupart, who appears several times in this work, although her rise was followed by an equally spectacular fall.

The southern third of the parish, which stretched to the Spanish frontier, is mountainous and was not economically important until coffee arrived. The coffee boom of the 1760s turned the southerly canton of Sainte-Suzanne into another central community, seemingly at least as important as the coastal villages. The establishment of a chapel, subordinate to that at Limonade proper, in 1783 marked this new status.

Both chapel and church provided the opportunity for weekly markets where *habitant* and merchant could meet and make deals for future harvests while smaller farmers and peddlers sold their produce retail in dozens or hundreds of small stalls. This is the sort of rural market that can still be seen in most of the developing world, including Haiti. It is an essential urban service, one of the few that was provided in the parish.

Limonade's small towns did not offer much in the way of urban services. The Limonade notary, Jean-Louis Michel, seems to have been resident on his *habitation.* He provided legal services to those members of the Limonade community who did not travel regularly to Cap, including the humble free coloreds of the northern part of the parish. The affairs of the (mostly free colored) coffee planters of the southern mountainous area made up the largest part of his records. This population, while wealthier, had farther to go to get to the big city and thus did most of their notarial business locally. Aside from notarial services, it is unclear how much other legal or governmental business took place in the parish. It was the center of a *quartier,* which was the administrative division between parish and province, and thus at least in theory the seat of a *sénéchaussée,* or local court. The records of this court are not in the archives in Aix-en-Provence, and it does not appear to have been active during the period under study. Many purely local matters from Limonade seem to have been argued before the courts at Cap in the first instance. The *quartier* was also a military division, and the commander of the militia battalion formed by the companies from Grand Rivière, Quartier Morin, Dondon, Marmelade, and Limonade was resident here.

Agriculture, though, was the major business of the parish. A census recapitulation that combines data on the parishes of Limonade and l'Acul du Nord, a parish much like Limonade and directly adjacent to it, gives some idea of how the land was used in this area in the time under study.

The majority of the land under cultivation in the two parishes, 10,600 *carreaux,* was in coffee. There were 212 distinct coffee plantations, for an average of 50 *carreaux* per operation. This picture of numerous, small operations is consistent with what we know of the coffee business in St. Domingue as a whole. There were 59 sugar plantations in the lowland areas of the two parishes, with an average of 80 *carreaux* per plantation, a high average indicating the strong position of sugar plantations in the North province. Indigo, livestock, and food crops were minor sectors in this parish.[24]

The figure for *carreaux* used for the cash crops of sugar, indigo, and coffee represents only land actually planted with that crop, and not the entire extent of plantations (which would include fallow, pasturage, provision grounds, buildings, and other noncrop uses). The reported figure of *carreaux* in food crops and pasture apparently reflects only cash-crop farms (*habitations*) in which food or livestock was the primary product. Thus, small subsistence farms in the mountains as well as provision grounds and pasture land on sugar or coffee plantations are probably not reported accurately.

Nonetheless, these data demonstrate the great importance of the parish coffee and sugar crops. There were very few large operations producing food crops for the market, and there was effectively no pastoral industry. The commitment of the parish to cash cropping in tropical staples is clear.

FORT DAUPHIN

A little bit farther from Cap Français than Limonade, and a little more independent, was the small port city and farming area of Fort Dauphin. Now called Fort Liberté, the town lies 46 kilometers from Cap along a road that even today is of doubtful quality. Fort Dauphin boasts a large harbor in which oceangoing ships can easily find refuge. Moreau de St. Méry described the repair of a substantial French naval vessel in 1778 in this harbor.[25] The harbor is well protected against storms from almost any direction and was protected from enemy attack at the time by two batteries of artillery. However, a number of patches of reef across the harbor mouth made it risky for oceangoing ships to enter, and the difficulty of overland travel between Fort Dauphin and the rest of the colony meant that a large urban center never had the chance to grow here.

Instead, the town of Fort Dauphin in the 1780s was a small settlement serving the needs of the surrounding sugar- and coffee-growing areas, as well as playing a role in the defense of the colony against any military threat from the Spanish side of the island. The proximity to the Spanish colony meant that Fort Dauphin was also a reasonably energetic trading center.

The town of Fort Dauphin was relatively substantial. In 1788, there were 390 urban lots.[26] The free population in 1780 was 560.[27] In general, when urban land was sold, the lots were often subdivided. They were originally conceded by the government to individuals and were taxed as units, but in fact urban lots usually served as the site of several separate structures, owned by the same or different persons. Therefore, there must have been at least five hundred buildings in the town. The streets were wide, and the *Grand Rue* was said to be tree-lined, but none were paved. The central marketplace was large: 50 *toises,* or 300 feet, on a side. On the square was one of the "finest parish churches of Saint Domingue," according to Moreau de St. Méry.[28]

The town lies between the ocean and the river and is surrounded by wetlands. It was known for its hostile disease environment from the earliest days, and this may have served to slow settlement. Moreau de St. Méry gave an example of the unhealthful nature of the "air" around Fort Dauphin: in 1782, the Spanish Léon regiment lost 17 officers, 3 cadets, and 647 soldiers out of a total strength of 1,440 men while in garrison there.[29] To this day, Fort Liberté, as it is now called, remains one of the most persistent malarial areas on the island.

A border town means a border market. The market of Fort Dauphin boasted more than its share of wandering peddlers stocking up on small manufactured goods to sell over on the Spanish side, Spanish (often free colored) horse and cattle traders with their stock, and the occasional Spanish military or colonial official purchasing for his men. The large Spanish garrison on the other side of the border seems to have been less than perfectly supplied.

The town's market, while enlivened by cross-border trade, was primarily devoted to serving the adjacent farming regions. The people doing business at the local notary were, for the most part, farmers who lived within two dozen kilometers of the center. Since agriculture in the region was developing rapidly during the late eighteenth century, business was brisk in the local market. The prosperity of the market was at the root of the prosperity of the town.

Additionally, the town's economy benefited from a sizable French military presence. The presence of the Spanish garrison on the other side of the frontier and the fact that Fort Dauphin's harbor could hold oceangoing ships meant that the colonial government had to defend the city with an important force. A goodly part of Moreau de St. Méry's chapter on the parish is taken up with descriptions of the military architecture. Plans and drawings of these installations have a prominent place in the Dépot des Fortifications des Colonies papers in Aix-en-Provence. The mouth of the harbor was protected, as described, by two batteries with naval artillery pieces. In addition, there was the fort that gave the town its name. Built in 1735, this was a substantial piece of military architecture, with low but thick stone walls and powerful cannons, built according to the best principles of eighteenth-century fortress engineering. Given a sufficient garrison, no army in the world could have taken Fort Dauphin without a time-consuming siege, which would probably have been very expensive in lives given the challenging disease environment in the parish. The outlying areas also were peppered with fortifications: a few kilometers down the coast, there was a small battery at a break in the reef, and right at the frontier, at the mouth of the Massacre River, there was another small battery of four guns. A few artillerymen were the only regular garrison of these forts, but the local militia could provide the mass of men necessary to secure them in an emergency, and the Régiment du Cap was only two days' march away. When the government sent more troops to the colony and raised local regulars during the crisis of the Seven Years' War, their base was built in Trou du Nord, a rural area in the *quartier* of Fort Dauphin.

The town of Fort Dauphin also boasted a Government House, in which the *quartier*'s militia commander and the *sénéchausée* held court. The court of Fort Dauphin was quite active, and its records have survived. Because the harbor was suitable for oceangoing vessels, the town occasionally traded directly with France. In addition, as a frontier town, there was considerable trade (mostly illicit) with the neighboring colony. Therefore, there was an admiralty court, a royal treasurer, and other royal accountants and managers. The notaries of Fort Dauphin were busy. The one whose registers served as the principal source for this parish, André Leprestre, was one among many. He was chosen because he had the most contact with free coloreds, a full sequence of his records from 1777 to 1788 has survived, and he was the most active notary in town.

Outside of the town lies the eastern end of the great Plaine du Nord sugar-growing area. This end of the plain is not so well served by the rain as the area around Cap, and agriculture is somewhat more difficult. Investors with plenty of capital built irrigation systems to use the water from several rivers to make sugar cultivation possible; other planters stuck to dry cultivation of indigo as their primary crop. The mountains were experiencing the beginnings of the coffee boom in the 1770s, and many simple food-producing farms or livestock ranches still competed with the coffee planters for access to the best land.

The census compilation illustrates the wider variety of agriculture practiced in Fort Dauphin as opposed to Limonade. Fort Dauphin sported a larger proportion of its arable land in food crops, a smaller proportion of land in coffee, and lots more herding than found in the more settled landscape of Limonade. Specifically, 31 sugar plantations averaged 70 *carreaux* apiece, while 118 coffee plantations averaged a mere 21. There were 748 *carreaux* in food crops and over 3,000 *carreaux* in pasturage.[30]

A frontier town, a central place for a peripheral agricultural area where the tropical cash crops had not yet completely established their dominance—Fort Dauphin shared in some ways the frontier atmosphere of the West province, which is the subject of the next set of sketches.

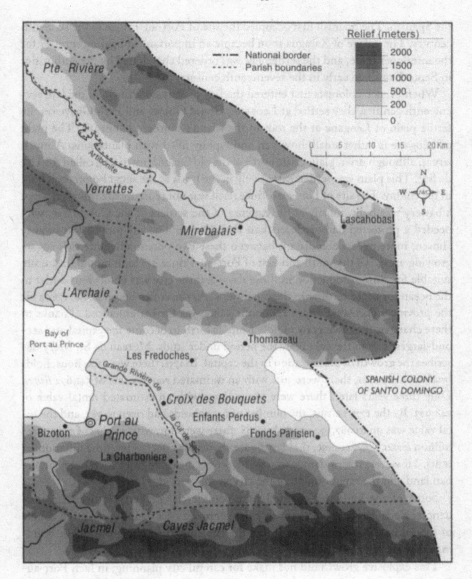

MAP 3. *The West Province*

PORT-AU-PRINCE

Port-au-Prince was the titular capital of the entire colony of Saint Domingue at the time of this study and was the central place of the West province. The West province actually contained the most easterly point in the colony—the name *West* comes from the fact that it is the most westerly area on the island ever settled by the Spanish. The Spanish first occupied the site of Port-au-Prince in the sixteenth century. The village of Xaragua soon became an important smuggling *entrepôt* for the interloper trade, and the settlement was ordered abandoned by the authorities in Santo Domingo early in the seventeenth century.

When French colonists first entered the Bay of Port-au-Prince, in the late seventeenth century, they settled at Léogane, Grand Goave, and Petit Goave on the fertile plain of Léogane at the root of the island's southern peninsula. The plain of Léogane is rather small, however, and rapidly filled with plantations. A much larger, although drier, plain exists north of the old Spanish town site, called the Cul de Sac. This plain was settled extensively in the 1730s as the sugar boom took hold in the colony. The site of Port-au-Prince itself was not reoccupied until 1742, when a battery was built, mostly at the expense of the settlers of the Cul de Sac, who needed a protected harbor closer than Petit Goave. The site proved fortuitously chosen, more or less equidistant between these two potentially quite rich sugar-growing areas. To the south and east of Port-au-Prince are high mountains, quite suitable for coffee production in those days, and the city was an obvious outlet to the ocean for those settling in the mountains. As the coffee boom of the 1760s hit the province, Port-au-Prince's economic value was further enhanced. Thanks to these changes, the town grew rapidly from its birth to become the capital and second-largest city in the colony by the period under study. Moreau de St. Méry describes the growth of urbanization in the capital. In 1751, there were 100 households [*maisons*]. By 1761, there were 392, with an estimated rental value of 541,672 *livres*. Only three years later, there were 683 *maisons* with an estimated rental value of 748,983. By the 1776 census, the number of households had risen to 787, and the total value was up to 987,390 *livres;* by 1788, there were 895, with a value of over three million *livres*. [31] Of course, that last figure shows the effect of wartime inflation on rents. However, it also demonstrates the profits available from investment in urban land and the rapid growth of the city in this period.

Some of the buildings counted were commercial property rather than residences. Each *maison* would probably be composed of a main house and a couple of subordinate structures. In addition, the city contained numerous public buildings that are not counted here.

This explosive growth did not make for careful city planning; in fact, Port-au-Prince was a rude frontier town whereas Cap Français was a cultured and solid city. The aristocratic observer Baron de Wimpffen described the city as a "vast Tartar camp." [32] However, there was some effort at planning, contrary to what the good baron suggested. The streets were laid out in a precise grid, which they follow, in the downtown area at least, to this day. They were 60 to 70 feet wide and had been paved in the 1750s when the city was first laid out, except for a sewer down the middle. Moreau de St. Méry notes that the pavement was not maintained, how-ever, and mud filled the streets when the rains came, while dust plagued passersby in the dry season.[33] Most buildings in the town were damaged in the earthquake of 1770, and a city ordinance forbade reconstruction in stone, so most private houses were one-story wooden structures. Builders who were more prosperous used wood frame construction with stone foundations. Wood was a cheap and plentiful com-modity in Saint Domingue at the end of the eighteenth century, but its extensive use as a building material in Port-au-Prince doubtless contributed to the appear-ance of impermanence that struck all observers.

Architectural beauty aside, Port-au-Prince had some pretensions to culture, al-though it was not so advanced in this area as was Cap. There was a theater in Port-au-Prince, located in the old section of town, which gave biweekly performances in the 1760s. However, in 1765, the director of the theater absconded to Jamaica with the props and costumes, and it appears that the institution fell on hard times. The commander of the military garrison was made responsible for policing the actors and administrators, and performances were cut back to once a week. The *Comédie* rented out its hall for public balls; apparently, the three days of Carnival were especially remunerative.[34] There seems to have been no restrictions on Port-au-Prince's free colored population who might have wanted, and could afford, to attend the theater, as there were in Cap.

Michel, the notary who did not use his personal name in his notarial acts and whose records form this book's principal source on Port-au-Prince, was the most active of the city's notaries in dealing with the free colored community. He was one of a very large contingent of notaries, many of whom were government employees notarizing official documents and transactions for the most part. Port-au-Prince has the largest number of notarial registers surviving in the archives.

Much of this legal activity is due to the fact that Port-au-Prince was the colony's capital beginning in 1751, although Cap booster Moreau de St. Méry did his best to make the case for Cap as the "real" capital because of its economic importance. However, the administrators of the colony were resident in Port-au-Prince, and it was to their court that the most serious issues were referred. It was from here that they represented the king and upheld his authority against colonial autonomism as represented by, in their view, fractious local militia commanders, insolent plant-ers, pretentious judges and councilors, surly and uncooperative poor whites, up-pity free coloreds, and the sleeping giant, the slave population. A considerable proportion of the city's population was involved with serving the various institu-tions of royal government. The demands of the various governmental institutions supported two print shops during the period under study. Two regiments of sol-diers, recruited in France for colonial service, inhabited Port-au-Prince at times during the period under study: the Légion de Saint-Domingue and the Régiment de Port-au-Prince. Interspersed with the barracks were the prisons, Admiralty (maintained by the Ministry of Marine) and civil. The civil prison of Port-au-Prince still stands on the same site, just west of the old Place d'Armes, now the Champs de Mars, and still houses Haiti's state prisoners. Port-au-Prince was also home to two large hospitals, one military and one civilian, which received patients from all over the island. The hospital was, in fact, the oldest institution in the city, as the buccaneers operating out of the neighboring town of Petit Goave originally founded it overlooking the site of the city from the foothills to the south.

It was also in these foothills that Port-au-Prince found its water. The downtown area had no water source other than intermittently flowing streams. Apparently, digging wells in the stony soil was impracticable. The city administrators built aqueducts that transported water from two springs in the hills south of town, setting aside the woodland overlooking the springs in order to protect their flow, in an early example of anti-deforestation legislation on the island. These forest reserves still had some trees left in the 1980s, another example of the continuing colonial legacy in modern Haiti.

Port-au-Prince's free coloreds were numerous and active, both as planters and urban landlords. When the city was established, says Moreau de St. Méry, some lots behind the seafront quarters of the powerful *negociants* were reserved for free coloreds "of good moral character."[35] Whatever their moral character, they seem to have snapped up the lots offered to them, to develop and rent or sell as the expanding city made their once-peripheral land part of the city's core. The astounding profits some of them gained from these early concessions can often be seen in the notarial record.

Unlike Cap, the parish of Port-au-Prince did contain significant agricultural and wild land outside the city. The parish extended northward to the Grand Rivière de la Cul de Sac, about 10 kilometers north of town, and south about 15 kilometers. Along the coast in both directions is flat and relatively fertile land, well suited to sugar cultivation. In particular, the south bank of the Grand Rivière held several large sugar plantations. A considerable district to the southeast of town was included in the limits of the parish. In fact, in this direction, the parish borders extended more than halfway to the southern coast of the island where they met the parish of Cayes Jacmel. This land is extremely mountainous—Montagne Noir overlooking Port-au-Prince is more than 1,700 meters high, and the peaks of the Chaine de la Selle, which form the border between the parishes of Port-au-Prince and Cayes Jacmel, exceed 2,500 meters. Early in the colony's history, this mountainous area was home to peasant farmers, hunters, and runaway slaves. The *marons* of the Chaine de la Selle were a significant threat to the colony's security in the 1750s, and numerous expeditions, all futile, were launched against them. Finally, in the 1760s and 1770s, coffee growing began to tame the highlands, and the *marons* were wiped out or made their peace with the colony. Coffee had not, however, conquered the mountains of the West nearly as thoroughly as it had the mountains of the North province, and small peasant holdings, stock raising, and wilderness still had a share of the land.

Although Moreau de St. Méry says, and geographical sense would dictate, that Port-au-Prince was a significant agricultural area, the data in the census compilations combine Port-au-Prince and Croix des Bouquets, which is the next parish considered. The census compilation gives some idea of the farming business in the two parishes. There were 68 sugar plantations, but they were rather small by the standards of the northern plain, at 54 *carreaux* each. There were only 27 coffee plantations, with an average of 60 *carreaux* each. Cotton appears as the principal business of five plantations, interesting in view of the labor-intensive nature of that crop without cotton gins. Food crops were very important, with more than 2,600 *carreaux*, while pasture took up 2,500 acres of land.[36]

Thus, the focus was on sugar, with coffee coming in a distant second even in terms of land under cultivation. The coffee sector was, nonetheless, vibrant with 27 large producers. The large amounts of land devoted to food gardens and pasture, when compared to Fort Dauphin and especially Limonade, demonstrate the transitional nature of the rural economy in these areas, though. Subsistence and small-market garden farming had not yet given way completely to production for an export market.

CROIX DES BOUQUETS

Originally created in 1687 under the name of Cul de Sac, after the valley in which it lies, the parish Croix des Bouquets was subsumed in that of Port-au-Prince upon the founding of the city. The parish reappeared under its modern name in 1750, with the parish center relocated from the coast to a point about 10 kilometers inland. In order to ensure the rapid development of the city of Port-au-Prince, the inhabitants of the parish of Croix des Bouquets were forbidden to establish any other installations near their church. This regulation was generally ignored, however, and the village of Croix des Bouquets grew into a respectable small urban center about 12 kilometers from Port-au-Prince on the banks of the Grande Rivière.

As in many provincial towns in the Americas, the urban amenities were not strikingly present in Croix des Bouquets. The town boasted a half-finished church, a considerable marketplace, and a few hundred private residences and other buildings. Official services, other than the religious, were all supposed to be delivered at Port-au-Prince, and so only one notary remained in residence for the whole period under study, Mâitre Renaudot. He apparently resided in town but owned some farmland in the valley nearby. Like Mâitre Michel in Limonade, Renaudot served principally those whose business did not take them regularly to the nearby large city, and so the more humble inhabitants of the parish and especially the free coloreds dominate his records.

The valley of the Cul de Sac is about 25 kilometers wide, considerably wider than the flat lands around Léogane or Archaye, the coastal parishes to the north and south. The valley runs all the way across the island to meet the sea at Barahona in the Spanish colony. The Cul de Sac valley is considerably drier, however, than either of the neighboring coastal parishes, and agriculture, especially sugar cultivation, is possible only with irrigation. There are three large lakes in the middle of the valley, but the water in them is salty, and even the soil around these lakes is quite sterile and useful only for pastureland. The hills on the northern side of the valley get very little rainfall, and that whole side of the valley is very dry. The streams running from the high mountains to the south, especially the Grande Rivière, provide the water necessary to agriculture in the valley. It was only when the security situation and level of investment permitted extensive irrigation works in the 1750s and 1760s that sugar growing really conquered the Cul de Sac. During the time under study, then, the sugar boom was new to this region, and the region's society was still in the grip of boom times.

Some of the free coloreds of Croix des Bouquets participated in the sugar boom, whereas others still struggled to survive in the economy of near-subsistence farming and stock raising that preceded it. Croix des Bouquets contains the single most valuable piece of land owned by free coloreds, a sugar plantation owned by the Daugé family, as well as some of the poorer farms. Social tensions were high, and at least one notarial act makes specific reference to wealthy free coloreds' desire to make their residences defensible.[37]

Of course, the ferocious maroons of the Pic de la Selle were not far away, and other, less famous maroon bands made Croix des Bouquets a very insecure place for planters. Besides the maroons, however, there were a number of free colored farmers in the hills and on the less-suitable flat land away from the river, keeping their *places à vivres* or herding their cattle. These people might have looked with some envy on the great planters and their success as plantation owners.

This social tension gave rise to the need for alternate leadership groups, devaluing the traditional status markers that reflected association with whites; it is no surprise that several of the most notable free colored military leaders come from Croix des Bouquets. At the same time, of course, the military was a useful tool for the planters to protect themselves from both maroons and surly underlings.

MIREBALAIS

Beyond the mountains to the north of Croix des Bouquets lies the parish of Mirebalais, where these small free colored herders and scratch farmers held even greater sway. The French settled this parish at the same time as the Cul de Sac for strategic reasons having to do with its proximity to the Spanish border. However, as the Spanish threat faded in the eighteenth century, the garrison was withdrawn, and the small farmers, hunters, and herdsmen became the parish's only economic support.

Mirebalais was one of the most remote parishes in the colony, not only distant from the population centers of the colony but also isolated from the sea. The parish is located at the headwaters of the Artibonite River, the largest in the colony. The valley of Mirebalais is fertile and well watered. Access to the Spanish part of the island through Hinche and Lascahobas is relatively easy, but travel to the rest of the French colony is quite difficult.

The town of Mirebalais was small, with free populations never exceeding 250 during the 1780s. However, because of the difficulty of access, it offered a wide range of urban services. Mirebalais was its own *quartier*, with a *sénéchaussée* court, a fine church in masonry, and a number of homes and other buildings that seem to have measured up to other provincial towns in terms of construction. That is, few houses were in stone, most of the better houses having stone foundations and ovens and wooden plank construction, while the average building was made out of logs or earth bricks between wooden structural beams. Buildings were almost universally described as *cases* (huts) or *magasins* (warehouses or shops), rather than by the big-city term *maison*.

Like Fort Dauphin, Mirebalais benefited from its location on the border with the Spanish colony. Its market attracted Spanish traders. Some Spanish colonists decided to stay longer, and several married local women. The border appears to have been more porous both to people and goods here in the wilderness than it was at Fort Dauphin in the settled north.

One important city service was notarial, and the notaries of Mirebalais were unusually busy for such a small urban population. Mirebalais produced more notarial acts than any of the other three predominantly rural parishes—Limonade, Croix des Bouquets, and Fort Dauphin. The notaries chosen, Beaudoulx and Lamauve, present a full series of records across the time period. Given the size of Mirebalais' free colored population—comprising 1,156 persons in 1788, or 63 percent of the free population—would have had a large proportion of acts by free people of color.[38]

All of these sources of income made the town more prosperous than it otherwise would have been, far as it was from the center of things. As a market for locally produced agricultural products, it was certainly second-rate. The parish had not yet experienced the sugar and coffee booms that had washed over the other parishes. The major problem was communication links with the outside. The easiest town to reach from Mirebalais was Lascahobas in the Spanish part of the island. The roads to the neighboring French urban centers of Croix des Bouquets, Port-au-Prince, and Saint Marc were exceptionally poor, and the Artibonite River was not used for transport to any significant extent at this time. Thanks to its isolation, Mirebalais was not suited to the production of sugar, a bulky crop. Even coffee was difficult to extract commercially across the awful roads of the interior of the colony, and as a result, there were only eight producers with an average of 28 *carreaux*. The easily transportable crop of indigo made some inroads here, with 250 small producers growing a total of 1,984 *carreaux*. This is comparable to what is found in similarly isolated areas in the South province, but without access to the sea and possible interloper traders, indigo was not highly profitable.[39] Livestock can move itself to market and requires lots of space for grazing; it was here that Mirebalais found its competitive advantage. As a result, pasturage consumed 4,831 *carreaux* of arable land in the parish.[40]

Farms in Mirebalais averaged much larger in area than in any other parish studied—as one would expect given the large proportion of land given over to grazing. It was not unusual to find parcels of over 100 *carreaux*, and even 200 was not unknown. Government concessions of unsettled land, which in the north averaged 50 *carreaux* and were occasionally much smaller, were no smaller than 100 *carreaux* in Mirebalais. A planter who accumulated land could build an enormous ranch. Free coloreds certainly participated in some very large land deals: the *habitation* purchased by Jean Joly *dit* la Grande Raque in 1781 was the largest land sale by free coloreds, in terms of acreage, in the sample. La Raque was a resident of the parish of Verrettes, down the valley from Mirebalais, and the *habitation* lay near the Mirebalais border but in the parish of Petite Rivière de l'Artibonite. However, La Raque did his notarial business in Mirebalais—suggesting Mirebalais's importance as a regional market. The combined holdings of the *habitation* included 432 *carreaux* in six pieces ranging from 28 *carreaux*, in cotton, to 180 *carreaux*, mostly undeveloped, as well as 82 slaves.[41] For a small island colony in the Caribbean, and for the free colored population, whose rights to own land were often restricted in other colonies, this was a huge collection of land.

CONCLUSION

Access to the sea and to a convenient sea route to Europe and access to major cities, rainfall, relief, soils, and other geographical considerations determined the economic role that any locality within the colony would play at any given stage of the colony's development. This, in turn, helped determine the role that free people of color would play within the society of that locality at that time. We have seen this process at work in the six parishes that were selected for special study in this book.

The big cities of Cap Français and Port-au-Prince were principally mercantile centers. In addition, Port-au-Prince, as colonial capital, had an extensive governmental community. Both cities offered urban services ranging from port facilities to hospitals to amusements virtuous and vicious. Both cities also functioned as the center of a galaxy of smaller centers, such as Fort Dauphin and Croix des Bouquets.

These two towns differed in strategic position, with Fort Dauphin remote from the centers of the colony and close to the Spanish border, while Croix des Bouquets, not far from the Spanish border, was also only a short distance from the colonial capital. Both towns, however, were at the center of developing agricultural areas and were experiencing the last stages of the sugar revolution at the time under study.

The canton of Sainte-Suzanne in Limonade was physically close to Cap Français, closer, in fact, than Fort Dauphin. However, in economic terms it had been very far away until the coffee boom of midcentury. With the discovery of coffee as a profitable crop, the mountains of southern Limonade suddenly became valuable property indeed, and the free coloreds who owned a sizeable percentage of that property often became quite rich as a result. Alongside the wealthy planters, though, there were still poor peasants and small farmers trying to make a living in the way they had been doing before coffee transformed the area.

Mirebalais, farther from the big cities and the ocean in terms of travel time than any other parish in the colony, was a place where the booms had yet to arrive during the period under study. Free coloreds, and the few whites who lived here, lived off livestock raising, provision grounds, and a little cash cropping that was not very profitable. In Mirebalais, the reader can see what the whole island must have been like once, before sugar and then coffee restructured its society.

CHAPTER THREE

The People

After examining the physical geography of Saint Domingue in the last chapter, we now turn to human geography: the demography of free people of color on the island. The chapter begins with a general analysis of fertility, gender ratios, age distribution, and mortality among free coloreds in the colony as a whole. Then, a separate subunit is devoted to each of the six selected parishes. The gender and age distribution of each parish is related to the general trends exposed earlier.

The demographic analysis will serve to place the people of color of this colony in the context of other free colored populations in the tropical Americas. For the reader familiar with the literature on this subject, the facts presented here will not come as much of a surprise. Again, though, the analysis serves to provide a basis for understanding social and economic behavior of this population as demonstrated through their notarial acts.

GENERAL

The free colored population of the colony was growing rapidly during the time under study, as reported by the colonial census. In 1775, there were 6,897 free persons of color counted by the general census.[1] In 1780, five years later, there were 10,427.[2] By 1788, this figure had increased to 21,813.[3] The white population during this period remained relatively steady, moving from 20,438 in 1775 to 20,543 in 1780 to 27,723 in 1788, a growth rate of about 2.25 percent per annum. The explosive population growth reported among free coloreds, amounting to a rate of a little under 11 percent per year, was fueled by a number of factors.

The first was reporting; as the colonial government got more efficient and as more highland and remote regions of the colony were brought under effective central administration, more people who had slipped through the cracks in earlier years were counted. It has been reported, for example, that the census of 1753 undercounted the free colored population of the remote southern parish of Nippes by as much as a third.[4] It is impossible, of course, to estimate the effect of this factor on total population numbers; the observer can only resolve to take with a grain of salt phenomenal population growth figures registered in "borderland" areas where extensive mountainous areas came under cultivation during the time studied.

A second source of free colored population increase was natural growth. The free colored population of the colony experienced relatively high fertility rates, as demonstrated in the census figures. The number of births per year per 1,000 adult women varied from 118 (in 1775) to 176 (in 1788), while the figure for whites was 114 (recorded in 1780, when free coloreds experienced a birth rate of 162).[5]

This evidence is corroborated by the high number of baptisms recorded in the parishes where baptismal registers survive. In Cap Français, annual baptisms of free coloreds between 1777 and 1784 ranged between 84 and 156, with a mean of 111.75 for a population averaging 431 free colored women over that period. This yields an estimated fertility rate of 257 children per 1,000 women per year. Some women from rural areas might have brought their children to Cap to be baptized. This would have been a violation of church regulations. Nonetheless, to do so was an obvious and probably not overly difficult attempt to enhance the children's status and connect them with urban opportunities through godparents and other relatives.

In addition, children would be more likely than adults to be undercounted. Modern Haitian babies are often not taken outdoors or even, in some areas, called by their names outside the family circle, until they are 30 to 90 days old, in order to avoid *mauvais yeux*, or the evil eye. Census takers, who performed their duties at the market or militia reviews, would certainly miss the youngest of children. Striking an unscientific but probably close to accurate balance between the two sets of figures, this work presumes that reported numbers of free colored children were more than 30 percent off, so estimated fertility numbers for their population have been modified to take these factors into account.

Free colored women's fertility rates seem to have remained consistently higher than those of their white sisters throughout the period under study. One very important reason for this phenomenon is that free coloreds were the only group on the island to have a normal gender ratio. In 1775, there were 44 adult white women per 100 adult white men, 112 adult free colored women per 100 adult free colored men, and 79 adult female slaves per 100 adult male slaves. In 1780, the figure for females falls to 41 for whites and 104 for free coloreds and remains unchanged for slaves. In 1788, the figure for whites fell again to 39, while for free coloreds there were equal numbers of both sexes. No gender breakdown for slaves is available in 1788.[6]

This normal gender balance was in part the result of a large number of adult females joining the free colored population through manumission. Of the 984 persons receiving manumission between 1776 and 1789 in acts in the sample, 455 were adult females (over 12 years of age), 145 were adult males, and 384 were children. Of the adult females, only 144, or 31 percent, were mothers being freed with their children. However, in an undetermined number of cases, the children may have already been free.

The free colored population was also much more likely to be native-born. There were exceptions, like Pierre Augustin, but only 23 percent of all newly manumitted slaves for whom a birthplace can be established were born outside the colony. Many free colored families had been free for generations and indeed were often among the oldest families in the colony. A native population would, of course, tend to have a normal gender ratio.

On the other side of the demographic balance, mortality rates for free coloreds were relatively low for the period under study, which also contributed to a high rate of natural growth. Demography is necessarily an inexact science in those times of poor records, but based on parish registers, annual free colored death rates in Cap Français varied between 13 and 71 per 1,000, with an average of 44.5, while white death rates were almost double, ranging from 30 to more than 145 per 1,000, with an average of 84.[7]

The white population consisted largely of migrants, mostly young men in relatively good health. Their high-mortality subgroups, children and older people, generally were left behind in France. White persons who grew old in the colony, even the native-born, often emigrated to France. The free colored population remained in the colony, for the most part, throughout their lives, yet they had a much lower overall mortality than whites. The explanation for this riddle lies in the very challenging tropical disease environment that Saint Domingue represented for white immigrants. Tropical diseases such as malaria, typhoid, and yellow fever, to which the native-born inherited some resistance and developed more during relatively mild childhood bouts of these illnesses, hit newly arrived adults very hard.

There was a "seasoning" period in the first few years after a new immigrant, from any source, arrived in the colony, in which he or she ran a very significant risk of death from disease. The importance of this seasoning period can be seen in slave prices: sales contracts for slaves described as "newly arrived" were evaluated at 45 percent of the average value of all sales contracts for slaves. Of course, this does not mean that 55 percent of the slaves died in the seasoning period; their value also increased as they acquired skills, language ability, and local knowledge. Slaves, of course, were challenged by the disease environment in somewhat different ways than whites: they had encountered tropical diseases before, albeit different strains than those present in the Caribbean, but had no previous experience with European or American diseases. The general point is that the encounter between African, American, and European disease environments in Saint Domingue was dangerous to all newcomers to the environment. As native-born made up the largest part of the free colored population, they were the least harmed by disease and thus the longest-lived population in the colony.

It should be no surprise to the student of the period that free colored populations were increasing rapidly through natural growth in Saint Domingue. This was true of almost all slave colonies in the Americas.[8] In British North America, the slave and white populations were also increasing naturally, while in the tropical Americas, on the whole, they required extensive immigration to keep up with natural declines. Virtually everywhere, though, the free colored populations showed considerable biological vitality.

One other important variable was the proportion that free coloreds comprised of the free population in the colony as a whole, and in each parish, during the period under study. Parishes where free coloreds predominated might have different social environments than those where whites predominated. The rapid free colored population growth can be seen in table 2.

TABLE 2

Free Coloreds in Saint Domingue as a Percentage
of Free Population, by Parish, 1775 and 1788

	1775		1788	
PARISH	FREE COLOREDS	AS % OF FREE POPULATION	FREE COLOREDS	AS % OF FREE POPULATION
Cap Français	487	24	1,231	30
Fort Dauphin	244	37	655	53
Limonade[a]	111	18	561	45
Port-au-Prince and				
Croix des Bouquets[b]	546	29	2,499	56
Mirebalais	327	24	1,156	63
Colony Total	5,897	22	21,813	44

Source: AN SOM G1 509 31, 38.

[a]The figures for Limonade and l'Acul were combined in the census compilation tables in 1788.

[b]The figures for Port-au-Prince and Croix des Bouquets were combined in the sources.

CAP FRANÇAIS

Cap's free coloreds, although small in proportion to the total free population, were nonetheless numerous and vital during the period under study. The census compilations give some idea of the composition of this population. Adult women always outnumbered men. In 1775, there were 750 adult women for every 100 adult males. Children comprised a mere 4 percent of the population. In 1780, the population statistics were somewhat more normal, with a gender ratio among adults of 119 to 100 and with 29 percent of the population being children. By 1788, the abnormal population distribution had reasserted itself, with a gender ratio of 197 to 100 and with children comprising only 11 percent of the population.[9]

It's unclear, of course, exactly how many free colored people escaped from this census, either because their liberty papers were incomplete or simply as a result of inefficiency of the census takers. At the time, maroons or *libres de fait* were assumed to concentrate in the countryside, especially in remote areas where plantation agriculture was not fully established. The distribution of *maréchaussée* personnel, the law enforcement group responsible for policing the laws on liberties and chasing runaway slaves, certainly reflected this estimate: Mirebalais and Fort Dauphin had twice as many *maréchaussée* men as Cap Français for free populations a fraction as large. However, recent scholarship has suggested that a goodly number of runaway or unofficially freed slaves made their way to the cities, where they blended in with the officially free.[10] Certainly, although the de facto free appeared rarely in the notarial record, of the few manifestations of their presence in the notarial archives, about half were from the big cities of Cap and Port-au-Prince. Fouchard noted in his exhaustive survey of the notices of runaways and slave recaptures printed in the *Affiches américaines* in Cap that many runaway slaves seem to have spent time in the cities.[11] Although the census clearly did not count every individual, it seems reasonable to assume that because of these factors, the big cities sheltered their share of those missed.

There were relatively few free colored children in Cap. This demonstrates the role of the colonial city as a destination for young, single, rural outmigrants, with the urban free colored population principally natives of somewhere else. In 1777, for example, Cap, with an estimated free colored population of 1,027, had 36 baptisms of free colored babies, while Limonade, with a free colored population of about 338 had 19.[12]

LIMONADE

Limonade was a rural parish, with a free colored population divided into two distinct geographic areas. Before the foundation of the chapel at Sainte-Suzanne in the mountains, the *Etat Civil* records for this parish are dubious. On several occasions, burials were recorded in the parish register of Limonade proper although they were performed "on the deceased's *habitation* in Sainte-Suzanne."[13] Interestingly, these funerals so recorded are all those of socially prominent free coloreds. It remains, of course, unclear how many burials of more humble persons took place without benefit of clergy and were never recorded. It was not only the dubiously free who escaped from official notice in frontier regions.

The chapel of Sainte-Suzanne was established in 1783. Priests performed 143 acts (marriages, burials, and baptisms) for free coloreds there between 1783 and 1788, while 15 acts relating to free colored residents of this area appeared in the main parish's registers from 1777 to 1782.[14]

However, Limonade's census figures miss even some of the individuals who made it into the parish register, giving the researcher a needed object lesson in the uncertainty of census tables, especially in rural areas.

The parish registers, for Limonade alone, reported 24 baptisms in the parish in 1777, 19 in 1778, 15 in 1779, and 24 in 1780, which would represent a quite impressive fertility rate for the 70 women the census reported in 1780 (292 per 1,000 per year). Some baptisms were of persons born earlier—7 of the 24 persons baptized in 1777 were over a year old. However, it is clear that the census must have missed significant numbers of free colored women. It is also possible that some babies were baptized as free although their mothers were unfree or, at least, their liberty was questionable: numerous and repeated government regulations forbade this practice, suggesting by their very repetition how common it must have been. Some of these children's mothers may have been resident in nearby towns and left their babies with relatives in the countryside, as is a common practice today. Church regulations required that a baby be baptized in the parish of his parents' residence, but nothing would have been simpler than for an urban migrant to send her children to a sister or mother in the village.

The number of free colored children must also have been under-counted in the census figures, however. They made up 21.4 percent of the parish's reported free colored population in the three census tables studied, while for the entire colony, children represented between 25 percent and 33 percent of the free colored population. The census noted an increase of 71 children between 1775 and 1780, which seems small given that there were 82 baptisms in 1777–80 alone. Some children must have grown to adulthood during that time, and while many others may have died, the mortality rate would have had to have been many times higher than reported in the parish registers to account for the relatively low reported numbers of children in the 1780 census.

Clearly, as with the runaways and notionally free in the cities, the countryside must have harbored a significant population of free coloreds who did not appear in the census records. The gradual incorporation of these marginal elements into officially recorded society must have been an important component in the very sharp increases in reported free colored population throughout the colony. Limonade was undergoing economic change, with the coffee boom, which would make it likely that later censuses would be more likely to count the underreported sectors.

FORT DAUPHIN

This trend was especially noticeable when an area moved from frontier to settled status. An even better example than Limonade is Fort Dauphin, which moved from "borderland" to economic centrality during the period. The reported free colored population of the parish went from 242 in 1775 to 395 in 1780 to 1,102 in 1788.[15] This represents a quite robust 12.5 percent annual growth rate. Certainly, some immigration must have occurred from the remainder of the colony, but a good deal of this increase must also have been the result of more settled administrators catching up with marginal mountain dwellers.

The population distribution by age and gender, especially in the 1788 census, showed a pattern consistent with other fully developed rural areas, such as Croix des Bouquets.

The figure for adult males in 1780, 232 compared to only 115 adult females, appears anomalous and may represent a number of transients drawn to the area by the military during the War of American Independence. Certainly, Moreau de St. Méry and the census records concur in placing the greatest portion of the economic boom in the parish after the end of that war.

Fort Dauphin contained a small city, and as in the big cities, urban free colored populations differed sharply from rural ones. One can get an idea of the urban-rural division of population in the parish from the one census year in which separate figures are given for the town of Fort Dauphin as opposed to its "*dépendances*" (a term suggesting *rural* dependencies) in 1775. The town reported 31 adult males, 60 adult females, and 19 children, while the rural areas had 50 men, 44 women, and 40 children.

Children made up 25 percent of the free colored population of the parish, again disregarding the 1780 figures. In rural areas, this climbs to 30 percent. Presumably, in the case of Fort Dauphin, as in Limonade, free colored women were undercounted, especially in rural areas, which were likely to be areas of weak governmental control. It would be men who would be more likely to encounter officialdom. As heads of household, they owed any taxes due, they were the militiamen, the *corvée*, or forced, laborers, and, occasionally, the potential *mauvais sujets* suspected by the rural police of consorting with maroons or contemplating other wrongdoing. On the other hand, the urban female population would be more likely than their brothers to come in contact with officials and be counted in a census, as they would be in the majority among the market vendors and would provide other services to whites.

PORT-AU-PRINCE AND CROIX DES BOUQUETS

Like Fort Dauphin, though on a larger scale, the parish of Port-au-Prince was divided between city and rural *dépendances*. Unfortunately, the census tables do not divide out for us the urban and rural population of the parish, rolling it together with its neighbor, Croix des Bouquets. The total figures for the two parishes were somewhat unbalanced as to gender and age, with 108 women per 100 men in 1788. This suggests a mixture dominated by the characteristically urban free colored population, who were more likely to be childless and women. However, there seems to be a strong admixture from the characteristically rural free colored population with a reported surplus of males and plenty of children.

Children made up 27 percent of the free colored population in 1775, declining to 21 percent by 1788. Total numbers of men approached those of women by the 1788 census. However, it is clear that the overwhelming tide of manumissions of childless women was having its effect on the population of Port-au-Prince as well. In fact, of 202 slaves manumitted in the sample of records from the parish, 99 (49 percent) were adult women, of whom only 31 were mothers, 30 (15 percent) were adult men, and the remaining 73 (36 percent) were children. Thus, Port-au-Prince manumissions were somewhat more likely to be of childless women than in the colony as a whole.

MIREBALAIS

Leaving Port-au-Prince and its relatively settled hinterland for Mirebalais, we arrive in the most rural of the parishes studied in this work. It is here that one expects to find the most evidence of the rural demographic pattern of undercounted women and plenty of children. This turns out to be the case, with men making up 34 percent of the reported free colored population across the three census reports, children 40 percent, and women a mere 26 percent.

It is interesting to note, however, that in the earlier two census years, women outnumbered men in the parish, with reported gender ratios of 118 in 1775 and 131 in 1780. These are the years when, one would think, the parish was the most "frontier-like" in its population makeup, and one would expect the 1788 census to record an increasing percentage of women. Given the small numbers in those earlier samples, this result can be explained away by sheer statistical variation.

That these earlier figures are questionable is also suggested by the reported population decrease between 1775 and 1780, from 327 to 276. Although this was a time of war and economic hardship, free colored populations elsewhere were not dropping during this period. Certainly, the economic hardships of the export sector would have been moderated in their impact upon this remote area whose economy was based on supplying a relatively inelastic demand for food and livestock within the colony. One presumes that the 1780 decrease is a creature of reporting errors only, as free coloreds, perhaps marginalized by such economic troubles that did make their way up the Artibonite River, slipped below the radar screen of the officials taking the census. It is significant that children, the most easily marginalized and undercounted individuals, were the population group with the largest decline.

CONCLUSION

The general pattern that this brief demographic survey shows us permits some generalizations. Discounting explicable undercounts of rural women and the confounding variable of the War of American Independence in the 1780 census, the following pattern emerges: young, childless people dominated the free colored populations of the cities, whereas children were more common in the countryside. It appears that this dichotomy represents not a difference in culture between rural and urban free coloreds but simply a life-course pattern. Significant numbers of free coloreds went to the cities while young and single, worked at urban trades, and speculated in urban real estate. Upon marriage or beginning of childbearing, many began to invest in rural land and moved to the countryside.

Those who wished to remain in the cities might very well send their children to live with relatives in the countryside, where they could easily disappear from both urban and rural censuses. The cities were dangerous disease environments everywhere in the world of the eighteenth century, and no parent would want to expose children to such risks needlessly.

Routine undercounting of children would increase the already dramatic apparent free colored fertility rate and might go a long way toward explaining the observed high population growth rate. In addition, some of the growth rate represents improvements in reporting, as more and more of the colony (including some of the areas sampled for this book) came under effective control of the colony's government. However, free colored populations were growing in the time under study. In contrast to slave and white populations, they were growing rapidly. Mortality was relatively low and fertility high, and few free coloreds emigrated to France or elsewhere.

The routine gender- and age-biased undercounting of free colored populations offers an interesting perspective on white officialdom's view of the utility of free coloreds. Rural women were not especially important, whereas women were more valuable in the cities because of the services they provided to whites. Free colored children were easy to overlook.

This rapidly growing population of free coloreds needed a way to support itself. The succeeding chapters discuss the methods free coloreds used to make themselves useful to the rulers of the colony and make their way in the colony's economy.

CHAPTER FOUR

Free Coloreds in
the Colonial Armed Forces

"The mulattos do all the military service of the colony; it is only they who can destroy the maroons." So said Governor de Fayet of Saint Domingue in 1733.[1] Two generations later, the situation was basically unchanged. This chapter explores the role of military service in the life of the colony and the lives of the free colored men who served.

On 3 November 1785, a Sr. Jean Louis Martin Theron, a (white) militia officer who was described by the local notary in his report as an *habitant* and thus was an important personage in Terrier Rouge, appeared before notary Jean-Louis Michel of Limonade. He was there to report a crime, thereby firing the first shot in a potential lawsuit. Some weeks before, Sr. Theron's horse disappeared from his *habitation* in Terrier Rouge, near the frontier with Limonade. While searching the region, he came to the plantation of a (white) Sr. Sicard. There, he saw a horse that he identified as his own being ridden by a black man. He called for the rider to stop, but the rider sped away, spurring the horse and crying out "until tomorrow." Theron pursued his horse and the mysterious rider to the vicinity of the plantation of Sr. Adhenet, who was the *exempt,* or local commander, of the *maréchaussée,* or rural police, of Limonade. There, Sr. Theron stopped to seek help. Adhenet was not present, but three of his men were: Michel and Louis Lamotte, mulattos and brothers who were *cavaliers* of the *maréchausée* (Michel may have been a *brigadier,* but in any case they were official members of the force), and a mulatto identified as Caquoin, who may have been a volunteer, a bystander conscripted ad hoc, or a slave of the *exempt.* The three gave chase after being promised a reward of two *por-*

52

tugaises (132 *livres*) for the recapture of the horse. They caught up with the rider and arrested him. He proved to be a slave named Louis, a Creole, aged 23, belonging to Sr. Sicard. Louis argued that the horse belonged to Sicard for it had been captured running free on the plantation's land. Louis was in possession of letters from Sr. Sicard to his brother in Limonade and a pass from the manager of the Sicard plantation. The *maréchaussée* men gave the horse to Theron, and Louis was allowed to proceed on his errand on foot.[2]

This story illustrates what may have been the most important way that free coloreds could make themselves useful to the power structure of the colony: as its armed defenders. This chapter examines the armed forces of the colony as an institution and looks at the participation of free coloreds in that institution. A detailed discussion of the social group within free colored society—the military leadership group—is taken up in chapter 11.

People of color played an important role in the colonial defense forces of most exploitation colonies within the plantation complex. They proved to be particularly important to the metropolitan governments because they were an effective and inexpensive alternative to sending out troops recruited in the home country. Stationing regular metropolitan troops in these colonies was expensive because of the long distances involved, because of the high cost of disease, and because white metropolitan soldiers and officers who survived the initial "seasoning" process often found more lucrative opportunities awaiting them in civilian life in the colonies.

Local whites in every colony were more or less reluctant to serve in the militia, the more so on those occasions when it became a time-consuming and possibly dangerous combat force instead of a ceremonial and somewhat status-enhancing social club. Colonial officials found it easier to coerce or convince free coloreds to serve, as they were of lower social status.

Persons from all levels of free colored society served in the military for different reasons. This chapter begins by considering the role of the slave in the military in Saint Domingue and especially the role of the military as a route to manumission or to regularization of informal manumissions. This was the first benefit conferred upon free coloreds by the military and, for many, was the most important. Following this is a look at each branch of service in turn, exploring the special conditions of that branch of service as they affected its free colored members. The chapter concludes by considering the effects of free colored military service on attitudes. Some whites, especially government leaders, were quite impressed by the free coloreds' willingness to serve the state as soldiers.

Saint Domingue was not the only colony in the Caribbean to call upon its free coloreds for defense and policing. In Cuba, free coloreds made up the majority of the colony's locally raised troops from very early in the colony's history up into the nineteenth century.[3] In the British Caribbean, they formed significant minorities of the armed forces, especially after colored populations in these colonies grew markedly at the end of the eighteenth century. Britain even raised several regular regiments of West Indian blacks and coloreds, something the French were unable to do despite occasional efforts in that direction.[4]

British free coloreds also played an important role in law enforcement, especially among the slave population. Apparently, free coloreds were respected by white administrators and local military commanders in the British colonies for their ability to make forced marches and penetrate remote areas in pursuit of runaway or insurrectionary slaves and maroon bands. Therefore, they came to be an important part of the colony's defense against these threats. Saint Domingue faced a similar threat and, even more than in Jamaica, turned to the free coloreds in an attempt to address it.

Free people of color served in the Saint Domingue colonial military under three broad rubrics: the *maréchaussée,* or rural police, the militia, and the regular armed forces, especially ad hoc formations raised for overseas expeditions. The last part of this chapter examines each of those institutions in turn to better illuminate the role free coloreds played within them.

SLAVES IN THE ARMED FORCES

Although this chapter deals with the role of the military in free colored society, it looks first at the role of slaves in that institution. This is appropriate since the military served as one very important way that slaves could achieve freedom or that the quasi-free could regularize their status, and thus it was an important contributor to the population explosion among free coloreds in the colony during the period under study.

Slaves had a place in the military of the colony from the earliest days of its existence. There were no military units composed primarily of slaves, but slaves owned by the government or by individual officers often filled certain positions within units composed primarily of free people of whatever race. Slaves followed their masters to war. Sometimes they were combatants in buccaneering expeditions, as, for example, when Vincent Olivier, future commander of all colored troops in the North province, followed his master to Cartagena in 1697.[5] Sometimes they were purely servants, as in the case of Antoine *dit* Sorlier, servant of M. le Baron de Lestrade, who was commander of that portion of the Régiment de Gatinois that went on the Savannah expedition. Lestrade freed his servant just before the departure of the expedition as a reward for many years of faithful service.[6] The notarial act in this case specifically stated that Sorlier was enrolled as a soldier in the regiment—thus gaining a liberty tax exemption for military service commonly available to slave soldiers or slave family members of soldiers in wartime. Even M. le Baron had better uses for the few thousand *livres* he otherwise would have been assessed for manumitting an adult male slave.

One of the most prominent roles for coloreds—both free and slave—in the French military was that of *tambour*, or drummer. Military music, especially the drum, was a necessity for the linear infantry tactics of the eighteenth century. Soldiers needed the beat of the drum to keep in step and to load and fire their weapons on command. Music could penetrate the noise of the battlefield where the voice of an officer would not—modern human-factors engineers have made this discovery in the design of jet aircraft cockpits, making warning signals play musical tones. Military bandsmen stood by the regimental flag in battle, near the officers, and were required to demonstrate considerable coolness in playing the appropriate calls and rhythms while under fire. The flag, of course, was intentionally noticeable, and bandsmen typically wore more colorful uniforms than the rest of the regiment, in the interests of making them as visible as possible to the rest of their colleagues.

As a corollary, the bandsmen were particularly at risk from enemy fire. The infantry weapons of the eighteenth century were not particularly accurate, nor were they generally used for aimed fire. Tactics of the time stressed massed volley fire by whole companies of infantry at a time. Any snipers or skirmishers that there were in the eighteenth century, though, would tend to concentrate on the color party in the hopes of disrupting the enemy's fire discipline and morale. The Prussian army pioneered the use of the long-ranged and accurate rifle by small groups of snipers during the Seven Years' War. However, the buccaneers of the Caribbean, and to a lesser extent their Spanish opponents, had developed smoothbore sniping to a high art in the late seventeenth century. The famous and deadly accurate "long gun" or "buccaneer musket" is a fixture of tales of the expeditions of Morgan and Levasseur. On the North American continent, the backwoodsmen, both French and English, adopted the rifle for hunting and brought it to war with them. The battle of Saratoga, in the War of American Independence, was marked by the successful sniping of a party of Virginia riflemen who disrupted a crucial British charge by shooting most of the officers and the color party at ranges up to 1,000 yards from their position. The poor *tambours* would have had a short life expectancy indeed.

Because of the danger of this position, it was often relegated to blacks, and most often to slaves seeking their freedom. Without discussing the reasons, British military historian Peter Voelz notes that many drummers in British units were blacks or, alternatively, Irish.[7] In fact, service as a *tambour* for a long period of time or through an active campaign customarily substituted for any specific claims of gallantry in petitions to the government for manumissions "for cause" of slave servicemen throughout the Americas.

Special bravery by any slave soldier could occasionally result in that slave being freed by the state. The *Code Noir* makes specific provision for such manumissions.[8] This procedure was not common, though, since the master of the slave would have to be reimbursed. Only one case of this appeared in the sample, that of Jean Hulla, *tambour* in a militia regiment, freed in 1779.[9] In his case, it is unclear from the act whether Hulla was a slave of the state or of the local militia commander.

Much more common was the waiving of the tax normally assessed on manumissions. In wartime, such waivers were very common and applied to family members as well as the soldier himself. No special bravery on the part of the soldier need be alleged for the waiver to be granted; the fact of military service—for a certain period of time or the duration of the emergency—alone sufficed. Of the 607 acts in the sample that freed slaves, 110 were tax-free manumissions of soldiers or their family members. There was a great rush of manumissions during the War of American Independence, says Moreau de St. Méry, because of this practice.[10]

A soldier who served in the expedition to Savannah or in the militia over a period of at least three or four years could have liberties confirmed tax-free between 1778 and 1783. This was obviously a substantial inducement to recruitment, especially because it allowed those living "as free," with the permission of their masters, to regularize their status. The act creating the (abortive) Chasseurs-Royaux de Saint-Domingue was specific in this regard: persons without proper liberty papers were required to serve in the unit for one year, instead of the three months required of all other free coloreds, but they would receive good manumission papers tax-free at the end of that time.[11]

THE MARÉCHAUSSÉE

The only unit that granted tax-free manumissions to its members in peacetime was the *maréchaussée*, or rural police—for them, active service never stopped. The lowest rank of the *maréchaussée*, the supernumeraries, were mostly slaves earning their freedom. The mulatto Caquoin, who accompanied the Lamotte brothers in their hunt for the missing horse, may have been such a supernumerary.

The *maréchaussée* was the organization in Saint Domingue that most directly addressed the problem of maroon bands and disorder in the slave quarters, which the slave owners saw as the primary security threat to the colony. The colonial government and the Ministry of Marine in Paris were more concerned with British or Spanish attack, as witness the very extensive papers—and corresponding substantial budget—of the Colonial Fortification Service. The *maréchaussée* was, to them, a secondary service, an administrative function, instead of being at the core of the colony's defense. This difference in perception meant that the *maréchaussée* was funded from local sources and often had to adopt extraordinary expedients to fill its ranks and fund its activities. One such expedient was the extensive, and in the end exclusive, use of free coloreds as rank-and-file troopers and midlevel leaders. This expedient was adopted later in the militia and other services, but very early in the *maréchaussée*.

The *maréchaussée* first appears in the laws of the colony as a simple "group" in a regulation of 1705 from the city council of Léogane. The regulation reiterated and strengthened a number of the *Code Noir*'s restrictions on slaves' right of free assembly (for seditious or, only slightly less bad, pagan purposes). It established a group of 36 men in each of the parishes of the *jurisdiction* of Léogane (Léogane, Grand-Goâve, and Petit-Goâve, the most heavily populated part of the West province at the time) to enforce the slave regulations and to chase runaway slaves. These men were to be paid a monthly wage by the council and rewards by the slave owners whose runaway slaves they recaptured. The rewards were also not specified; examples drawn from the 1776–91 period suggest that they ran about 10 percent of the price of the slave. The *maréchaussée* was not explicitly defined in this act as an organization composed of free coloreds. However, the promised pay was small, and that, along with the testimonial of Governor de Fayet dating from this period and quoted at the beginning of this chapter, suggests that the *maréchaussée* was mostly composed of free coloreds.[12]

The *maréchaussée* was extended in a law of 1721 to the North province. One company of 75 men was established to support the rural policing efforts of the royal troops. This company was to be divided into three brigades and was primarily responsible for patrolling the frontier with Spanish Santo Domingo. (The term *brigade* comes from the metropolitan French *maréchaussée*, where it signifies the basic local unit, numbering about seven. These brigades in St. Domingue were fleshed out by unpaid supernumerary officers and so were somewhat larger than seven people, but the similarity in name to a regular army unit of some thousands of soldiers is coincidental, if confusing.) The preamble to the law stated that the Spanish border was a route by which many slaves escaped and accused the Spanish of encouraging slave flight.[13]

A secondary responsibility of the group so created, which later became of overwhelming importance, was to search the slave quarters of any *habitation* in the province, in the presence of the master, for arms or runaway slaves. The *maréchaussée* was also responsible for arresting deserting soldiers, smugglers or other unauthorized frontier crossers, and sinister Spanish agents seeking to cause disturbances among the slaves.[14] One can visualize the dreaded Spanish agent with sneering mustachios and a voluminous cape, the better to hide the poisoned daggers, no doubt—the prose of the ordinance is pretty purple on the threat to French interests from the perfidious Spanish. At this time, France and Spain were wrapping up about two hundred years of intermittent conflict. Spain had invaded the colony several times in the seventeenth century, at one point destroying Cap Français. The famous "family compact" of the eighteenth century was only a few years old when this regulation was penned, and perhaps still somewhat questionable, even though active hostilities had stopped with the Treaty of Ryswick. Thus, the *maréchaussée* was originally seen, at least in the North province, as a primarily military organization addressing a foreign threat.

The 1721 ordinance said that the race of the *maréchaussée* men was to be "white or mulatto, free blacks not being received except for lack of whites." Archers were to be paid 360 *livres* a year, which was a 20 percent raise over what their colleagues in Léogane got in 1705.[15] Again, they were to be paid a bounty on each fugitive slave or soldier they caught. The bounties were to be distributed in shares throughout the company—one share to the archer who made the capture, $^1/_{65}$ of a share to each of the other archers all the way up to five shares for the provost.[16]

In 1733, the *maréchaussée* was again reorganized and extended to cover the West province as well as the North. The explicit mission of the expanded force of one hundred men was subtly different from that of the northern unit established in 1721. The perceived threat from the evil Spaniards seems to have declined after peace was made between France and Spain in Europe. The principal mission of the force was now internal and complementary of the militia, not the regular troops.

Archers in the new act were now to be free mulattos or blacks. Officers were to be *habitants*, slave-owning capitalist farmers, certified by the governor-general for their probity, valor, and capacity, and received equivalent benefits to militia officers. Some free coloreds served as militia officers at this time, but none were identified in the *maréchaussée*. A subsequent reorganization of 1767 expanded the *maréchaussée* to the entire island and enlarged it to some two hundred men in twenty-six brigades, each commanded by a *brigadier*. The *brigadiers* were noncommissioned officers and, like militia noncommissioned officers in general, were prominent local free coloreds. One or more *brigades* were assigned to each parish, under the command of a *prevôt*, or *exempt* white officer, at the parish level, who reported to a *lieutenant* at the subprovincial jurisdiction level, to a *prevôt-général* at the provincial level, and finally to the *grand prevôt* in Port-au-Prince. The ordinance made no other changes in the organization.[17] An act of 1788 dealt with some abuses and regularized pay and discipline, but it did not change the composition of the force.[18]

As police forces go, the proportion of *maréchaussée* "sworn officers" to the population they were supposed to be policing was quite small. In 1767, there were 200 *maréchaussée archer/cavaliers* for some 250,000 slaves.[19] By 1789, there were 450,000 slaves but still only 200 regular officers. The *maréchaussée* responded to this shortfall in numbers the same way the Haitian armed forces did in later years—they appointed unpaid volunteer adjutants, known as *attachés* in the pre–U.S. "intervasion" Forces Armées d'Haiti and as supernumeraries in the *maréchaussée.*

Recruitment for this position worked as follows: Free colored militia units were often called out to support major *maréchaussée* operations. They rarely took leading combat roles but patrolled roads, bridges, and plantation boundaries while the more skilled and higher-motivated *maréchaussée* troopers actually confronted the maroon slaves or other evildoers. This duty, called *piquet* service, was cordially detested by the wealthier free coloreds, as they had to be absent from their farms without pay and rarely had the opportunity to profit as the *maréchaussée* men could from these forays. Julien Raimond makes this complaint in his memoirs to the minister of marine in 1786.[20]

However, militiamen who showed themselves especially diligent in these duties were sometimes asked to join the *maréchaussée* patrols, as in the case of Charles *dit* Balata, freed in 1777 for "services that . . . he has given in the militia and in the hunt for maroon slaves."[21] This act makes clear the linkage between militia service as a *piquet,* the hunt for maroons, and the *maréchaussée.*

Above the supernumeraries were the *archers,* or, as they were called in some notarial records, the *cavaliers.* Although supernumeraries must certainly have dreamed of promotion to "official" status, the sample does not identify anyone who actually made this step. *Maréchaussée cavaliers* were actually almost noncommissioned officers, with authority over a half-dozen supernumeraries, and numbered as few as four in some parishes, exaggerating their local importance by their scarcity. The *archers'* superiors, the *brigadiers,* were among the more powerful and respected free colored noncommissioned officers. These were sought-after positions. Their incumbents were among the most important members of the free colored military leadership group in any parish.

The *maréchaussée* troopers were policemen. Their work consisted of a goodly amount of guard duty, sometimes paid by the state, as when they were called upon to police religious gatherings in 1766 during the white militia mutiny.[22] Sometimes, they would perform guard duty for private citizens for a fee, as when they would be called upon to guard the assets of an estate between the death and the inventory.[23] They also enforced the colony's ordinary laws, as when they raided an illegal gambling establishment in Cap Français in 1790.[24] Mostly, though, they rode on patrol through the wilder or more unruly portions of the colony, visiting *habitations* and small farms, looking for runaway slaves and other malefactors. An example of this sort of mission is the time in 1782 when a party of *maréchaussée* men led by the Chevalier de Puisaye raided an abandoned plantation in Dondon, in the North province, and stumbled into a wasp's nest of local controversy. The *maréchausée* got involved in a struggle between a white and a free colored landholder, exercising, it appears, considerable restraint and delivering something resembling justice.[25] Large groups of maroon slaves, their primary targets in the 1760s and before, had pretty much been cleaned up or had made peace with the colonial government by the 1770s, at least in the areas studied. However, when such groups would gather or their presence was suspected, or when some other suspect gathering of slaves was detected, the *maréchaussée* would take the leading role in police operations against them, which might also include militiamen and even regular troops.

THE MILITIA

In theory, all free men of military age in the colony belonged to the militia, coloreds as well as whites. The militia was an ancient institution in France, descending from the medieval levy. However, in the eighteenth century, the militia in France began to change in fundamental ways. Before this time, the French militia had been a local and quite irregular armed mob, called up in time of danger and led—to use the term loosely—by local notables. However, especially in the border provinces, under the stimulus of the military revolution of the seventeenth and eighteenth centuries and enlightened despotism's reforming urge, it began to change into a professional, albeit part-time, armed force, equipped and paid by the public purse and officered by specialists. This transition was incomplete in France at the time of the Revolution but laid the groundwork for the revolutionary *levée en masse*. The militia in Saint Domingue also owed a great deal to its roots in the early days of settlement, and participants experienced some of the same pain at changes to a more modern system that their colleagues in France suffered through.

The earliest French settlers in Saint Domingue were the famous buccaneers, who set out to be hunters of wild cattle but often ended up as pirates. They were warriors but were far from disciplined members of an organized force. The buccaneer scorned military discipline as next to slavery. Formidable fighters, the buccaneer crew was a jointly owned for-profit organization in which the lowest-ranking member could and often did question tactical decisions by the master. Ship's crews often signed articles of incorporation before a voyage carefully delineating the command rights of the officers and the duty of each crewman. Major decisions were often put to a vote, sometimes even in the face of the enemy.

The buccaneers settled the island of Saint Domingue in the late 1620s and had more or less ceased military activity by the end of the century, as the more successful pirates settled down as planters. The expedition to Cartagena (1697) and the subsequent treaty ratifying official French control of the colony, already conceded by the Spanish de facto since the 1670s, mark their last hurrah. Their descendants did not share their martial skills but nonetheless inherited many of their social attitudes. Contempt for the regular military was a strong social tradition in Saint Domingue even a century later. Rank-and-file regular soldiers were seen as the equivalent of slaves; "slaves of the state," perhaps, but still servile and thus below the free white man.[26] This attitude toward military service opened up opportunities for free coloreds to make themselves useful to the state and fulfill some of the obligations of citizenship while at the same time further devaluing those contributions in the eyes of white society as a whole.

The low status of private soldiers in white society, however, seemingly did not affect that of the officers, who were important members of the local aristocracy.

Of course, many settlers who arrived in the eighteenth century had served in the royal armies in Europe, and frequently some Chevalier de St. Louis living as a planter in Saint Domingue would proudly include his title in a notarial act. As part of the transformation of the militia throughout the empire, colonial governors beginning with Jean-Baptiste Ducasse (1691–1700) and continuing through the Comte d'Estaing (1764–66) encouraged regular military officers to settle as planters and serve as militia commanders.

Parish military commanders often acted as informal judges, even in places where there were official courts. Evidence of this can be seen in the fact that several government regulations and court decisions seem intended to rein in local commanders who had overreached their judicial authority.[27] In 1755, the *intendant*, or civil governor, of the colony sourly observed that the militia commander of the parish of Port-au-Prince judged more cases in two days than the official court of the city (the *sénéchausée*) heard in a week.[28] The Conseils Supérieurs and the other courts of the colony saw themselves as the *parlements* of the colony, upholding a legalistic order of the "robe" at the expense of the "sword" nobility's aristocratic autonomism represented by the militia officers' civil jurisdiction. A 1770 order sharply reducing the frequency of militia musters for whites also removed civil jurisdiction from parish militia commanders but maintained their authority to judge "disturbers of the peace."[29] *Maréchausée* officers often exercised a more informal judgment in the field, as policemen often do, determining who to arrest and who to let go with a warning, and perhaps even which evidence to lose or find.

Through the 1750s, the militia officer corps was not exclusively white. Indeed, each racial community—blacks, mulattos, and whites—had provided the officers for their own companies, and there were African-descended parish and provincial commanders of colored troops. In the 1750s, governors ceased to appoint black officers, and the practice was officially ended with the first d'Estaing militia reorganization edict of 1765.[30] Even after the formal end of their status, though, former free colored militia officers retained enormous status in their communities and were even given considerable marks of respect by whites both officially and unofficially.

Eight free coloreds who served as officers in the militia before 1765 and who were still alive during the period under study appear in the sample: *Capitaine* Vincent Olivier, commander of all free colored troops in the North province, Cap Français; *Capitaine* Barthelemy Ibar *dit* Bertole, Petite-Rivière de l'Artibonite; *Capitaine* Laurent Milloy, Cap Français; *Capitaine* François Jupiter, Cap; *Maréchal de Logis* Jean-Baptiste Baudin (cavalry lieutenant), Fort Dauphin; *Lieutenant* Guillaume Manigat, Fort Dauphin; *Ensigne* Augustin LeMoine, Fort Dauphin; *Capitaine* Etienne Auba, Limonade. Presumably, at least one free colored officer had been named in each parish. Socially and economically, these men and their families were members of the free colored elite who gained a great deal of respect from their neighbors of both racial castes. They are considered along with their social and economic successors, the noncommissioned officers, who filled the same position in colored society after 1765 when free colored opportunities for advancement were reduced.

Special privileges attaching to the role of militia officer did not trickle down to the enlisted ranks among whites, however. White rank-and-file militiamen clearly saw service as an onerous *corvée* and avoided it whenever possible. In the first half of the eighteenth century, militia service was not a particularly time-consuming obligation. Reviews were held monthly, at most, and since officers were frequently absent from their parishes, even those reviews were often canceled.[31] Militiamen came out when there was a threat, like a band of maroons or an actual enemy landing, but they could not be prevailed upon to man checkpoints, batteries, and standing patrols. The government got by more or less with regular troops, and a lot of security functions just did not get done.

The colonial government in the 1760s, especially under d'Estaing and de Rohan, attempted to address this problem by regularizing the militia in line with proposals for changes in the system in the *metropole*. Militiamen were to serve for a few weeks at a time on garrison duty, in rotation. Officers were to be professionals. Equipment would be standardized and issued by the state. In time of war, as in the ongoing Seven Years' War, regular units of paid soldiers were to be recruited from the ranks of the militia. However, white resistance, violent at times, forced the government to abandon this plan.[32]

As an alternative to a predominantly white militia, the government increasingly turned to the people of color to provide the manpower for the active militia that the security situation seemed to demand. People of color were less able to use political pressure to resist recruitment, although some were able to make their opposition known during the white-led unrest.[33] Colored resistance was overborne, however, and the colored militia became the mainstay of colonial defense by the 1770s. Colored and black militia companies numbered 104 out of 156 in the total force in 1789, although blacks and coloreds made up only 42 percent of the total population of free persons in that year.[34]

In addition to being more numerous, the black and colored militiamen were better-prepared troops. White militiamen mustered at their parish church every three months. After the uprisings of the 1760s, the officers were not expected to give their men any training whatsoever during these musters—they were merely to verify that each militiaman had presented himself armed and equipped as required in the manual.[35] Colored troops, on the other hand, were called out regularly to assist the *maréchaussée* in the pursuit of runaway slaves. Colored dragoons especially found themselves regularly on duty, either mounting guard on bridges or road junctions or acting as orderlies for militia commanders.

Wide participation of free coloreds in this sort of duty, although not usually active combat service, nonetheless served to give the colored militia increased unit cohesion. The colored militia company in Port de Paix, for example, refused recruitment en masse to support the *maréchaussée* in 1786.[36] This is only one of many occasions on which the militia company served as a collective avenue for communal self-expression or self-help. In a similar case, involving the Chavanne family of Limonade, militiamen collectively resisted when they felt they had been too frequently assigned to picket duty. Three members of the Brilliant family, for whom this is the only appearance in the records, joined Hyacinthe Chavanne, the brother of revolutionary leader Jean-Baptiste Chavanne, Jean-Baptiste Laporte, an illegitimate child of the wealthy Laporte family, and Jean-Pierre Guerin or Guerineau, their noncommissioned officer, in refusing to continue mounting guard on the Limonade–Sainte-Suzanne bridge. They claimed that they had been on duty there for two weeks and that their crops and plantations would suffer from their absence. Parenthetically, one notes the irony of Julien Raimond's argument along these lines when he said that the free colored proprietors' absence from home on militia service left their "goods at the discretion of their slaves and their discipline to their good-will."[37] Free colored planters worried about the loyalty of their labor force just as did white planters.

The general commanding all troops on the island sentenced the unknown Brilliants to eight days in prison and the better-known people to twenty-four hours in the stocks.[38] It is interesting to note in this case that the more prominent people, including the one person of higher military rank, received what one would think of as the less severe punishment. Seemingly, the leadership felt that the social punishment of a day in the stocks was more severe for the proud members of the free colored planter elite than eight days in the lockup for the ordinary poor *affranchi*. In any case, here again is an example of free coloreds using the militia unit structure to resist what they felt was inequitable treatment by the white hierarchy. This solidarity was expressed even across class and color lines and suggests the powerful role of the military in free colored society.

In addition to being more coherent units, colored troops were also better equipped than their white counterparts. White militiamen were required to bring their own weapons, and thus their equipment varied from the sublime to the ridiculous. Colored militiamen were issued arms by the government, since racist legislation mandated that they not own any otherwise, and thus they were at least uniformly armed. Colored militiamen who were recruited into the *maréchaussée* as supernumeraries were armed by that organization to a quite high standard. Regular officers serving in the militia, with professional standards of uniform and equipment, would equip their dragoon orderlies, always free coloreds by the 1770s, at their own expense—as was traditional even for white orderlies in the regular army at this time.

Colored cavalrymen continued to bring their own horses, however, and remounts were an ongoing problem for all the local cavalry. English cavalry officer Lt. Howard, of the York Hussars, noted the absence of good cavalry horses on the island during the Revolutionary War and the flow of livestock from the Spanish to the French part of the island.[39] Santo Domingo was an important source of livestock of all sorts for the colony from the times of the buccaneers. As a matter of fact, the French colony raised some livestock of its own, especially in the mountain parishes like Mirebalais, but still a common foreign figure encountered in the notarial archives was the Spanish horse and cattle trader. Horsemanship was an important social mark of distinction among people of color.[40] Colored cavalrymen, therefore, were loathe to risk such valuable and high-status assets in unpaid militia work. Furthermore, the qualities important for a prestigious saddle horse are not often very useful to a cavalry horse.

The most important duty of the free colored militia was the internal security function: *piquet* duty at bridges, entrances to cities, mountain passes, and other choke points, and occasionally more active sweeps for runaway slaves in cooperation with the *maréchaussée*. It appears that this duty took a couple of weeks at a time. Participants served in rotation, but whether this was strictly observed or whether there was some aspect of favoritism is open to question, given the case of the Limonade militiamen's complaint. Of secondary importance was garrison duty at fortifications. The colony was full of forts and batteries, mostly pointing out to sea, to protect it, at great expense, against British (most likely) naval attack. These fortifications were manned by a few professional gunners and sometimes companies of the regular regiments in that province, but the bulk of the guard force that would be assigned there in times of international tension would be the local militia. This was another service of which militiamen probably did not think very highly, but after the creation of the overseas expeditionary forces during the War of American Independence, the internal garrison troops probably counted their blessings to be so close to home.

REGULAR MILITARY FORCES AND THE EXPEDITIONARY CORPS

Free coloreds participated in overseas expeditions launched from the colony starting from the very early days of French presence there. As the French military in general, and the colony's militia in particular, got better organized, these overseas expeditionary forces also grew in effectiveness and organization. Service in these units changed in character from participation in a buccaneering expedition to something approximating a tour in the regular army. In addition, some free coloreds were even members of the regular French armed forces, under various rubrics.

The best known of the special expeditionary corps was the Chasseurs-Volontaires de Saint-Domingue. This force, consisting of some 750 free colored soldiers, left Cap in August of 1779. It went with the Comte d'Estaing's expedition to Savannah, Georgia, to attack British troops, which had seized this port during the War of American Independence. The Chasseurs-Volontaires made up about one-third of the ground strength of the expedition. There was a parallel force, the Chasseurs-Grenadiers, who were white, but recruitment for this unit was weak, and they only numbered about 200 soldiers.[41] There were about 800 French regulars in the expedition; about 275 were from the regiments stationed on the island, and about 525 were brought out directly from France.[42]

The Chasseurs-Volontaires, as well as their white colonial colleagues, were expected by the expedition's leadership to be auxiliary troops. They were employed digging fortifications and moving supplies while the regular soldiers did the fighting. Although these duties may not have been as romantic or prestigious as the *volontaires* had anticipated when they were encouraged to enlist, they were crucial to the expedition.

The attack on Savannah followed traditional siege practice of the time: that is, the attacking army built a fortification surrounding the place to be besieged and outside effective weapon range from it. Then, the French and Americans dug zigzag trenches to within cannon range and brought up guns to set up in emplacements to batter a hole in the British works. Finally, when the bombardment had sufficiently beaten down the defenders, the attackers launched an infantry assault to carry the position. Troops with engineering duties played a crucial role in the first steps of this process.

In the case of the siege of Savannah, however, the final stage did not go as planned. The French regulars, instead of sweeping all before them, were thrown back by British reserves waiting at the breach. The French regulars were "broken," that is, their troops fled in all directions and their leaders lost command control. They were out of action as a useful fighting force. In the confusion, the British defenders counterattacked and threatened the French camp. The only troops ready to fight were the Chasseurs-Volontaires. The Chasseurs formed a line at the edge of the French camp and protected the noncombatants and disordered regular troops from the British counterattack. The Chasseurs' performance in this, the only combat of their short existence, proved crucial, as the French forces were able to withdraw safely to their ships. The commander of the expedition recognized a number of individuals as having distinguished themselves by their heroics in this fight.[43]

After the battle, the regiment was split up into smaller units and dispersed around France's empire. Two companies went to Grenada and one to St. Lucia to reinforce colonial garrisons. At least two companies returned directly to Cap Français. Another small group whose size cannot be determined returned to France with the rest of the defeated expeditionary force, where some appeared at court and were commended for their valor.

The official recognition was not enough to placate the men of the Chasseurs-Volontaires sent to Grenada or elsewhere, who considered themselves the victims of sharp practices. In France, the militia had begun to serve as an avenue of recruitment into the regular army, and the Chasseurs-Volontaires suspected that the free colored militia of Saint Domingue, and they as members of it, had been used in the same way. After being recruited for a "special expeditionary corps" as stated in the original enabling act, the Chasseurs-Volontaires had become regular troops, freely distributed where the demands of empire called for them.[44] This dampened colored enthusiasm for overseas service considerably, as is discussed below in the case of the follow-on Chasseurs-Royaux de Saint-Domingue.

Initially, recruitment for the "special expeditionary corps" was heavy, and the troops were enthusiastic. There were considerably more than 1,000 recruits for the Chasseurs-Volontaires, although a number of these had to be left behind for various reasons. In fact, recruiting exceeded expectations by at least 40 percent. The original establishment of the regiment provided for 10 companies of 60 private soldiers, each led by 15 colored noncommissioned officers and 3 white officers. A month after the original table of organization was laid out, the governor-general had to enlarge the companies to 84 *chasseurs* each and add 4 (colored) corporals to each company.[45]

What prompted a young man to abandon civilian life and join the Chasseurs-Volontaires? Colonel Le Noir de Rouvray, commander of the regiment, in his letter protesting the deployment of Chasseurs-*Volontaires* companies to Grenada and St. Lucia, lays stress on the opportunities in civilian life that his soldiers were giving up by joining the Chasseurs-Volontaires. "The *Chasseurs* are almost all landowners who have abandoned their fortunes in order to serve the King," he wrote.[46]

This made a good argument but was not true in all, or even most, cases. In fact, the Chasseurs-Volontaires attracted men from both the haves and the have-nots of colored society. Recruitment was principally from the militia, but almost all colored men participated in the militia at least to some extent, so this did not limit the social scope of the recruitment. In fact, many of the Chasseurs-Volontaires were acting as free but were de jure slaves at the time they entered service. They were taking advantage of the government dispensation from liberty tax offered to persons in military service during the war. Others were free themselves but had family members still in slavery that they wished to free without having to pay the tax. Since liberty taxes were increased in 1775 from 1,000 *livres* to 2,000 *livres* for an adult female slave, and from 500 *livres* to 1,000 *livres* for a male, this exemption created a powerful financial inducement to serve.[47]

Patron-client relationships with whites also led young colored men to sign up for the Chasseurs-Volontaires. Several particularly direct examples of this can be found among the entourage of *Sieur* Antoine Augustin Aubert Defoix *Seigneur* Dupetithouars, *habitant*, minor noble, militia captain, and newly commissioned captain in the Chasseurs-Volontaires. On 10 July 1779, he freed his slave Aman, a *mulâtre*, and enlisted him in his company of the Chasseurs-Volontaires, incidentally benefiting from the tax exemption—even important white planters could find a better use for 1,000 *livres* than to give it to the government.[48] On 4 August, he performed the same service for Pierre Charles *dit* Floissac.[49] After his company returned from the expedition, on 14 April 1780, he freed another of his soldiers, Fabien Genty or Gentil *dit* Tollo. Genty went on to become a substantial landowner and "big man" among the Cap military leader group, and later he was an officer in the revolutionary Army of Saint Domingue.[50]

Dupetithouars, as the captain of the mulatto militia company, was an important person in the lives of free coloreds in his community. Good relations with the militia officer could result in very concrete benefits to the ambitious young free colored man: better security and advantage in small military officeholding, of course, but also access to credit and an entrée into the white business world. Militia officers

and, to some extent, even colored noncommissioned officers were important figures in their communities and good people to know.

The recruiting net for the Savannah expedition was spread wide, however,
sweeping the free colored elite into the ranks alongside the wealthy white man's
slave client. Eleven of the fifty-five elite colored families identified in this book
had at least one member in the Chasseurs-Volontaires.[51] The inducement clearly
cannot have been financial. The pay rate authorized for Chasseurs-Volontaires de
Saint-Domingue was 105 *livres* (*Tournois*) per year plus 22 *sols* 6 *deniers* a day subsistence allowance in lieu of rations (which, one hopes, were furnished while in the
field).[52] This was the same as for *chasseurs* in the French regular army. While some
soldiers may have hoped for loot, more sensible ones must have surmised that siege
warfare intended to recapture a friendly city was unlikely to provide many opportunities for self-enrichment. Neither of these prospects could have been a particular inducement even to a younger son of a free colored planting family.

Building connections with locally influential whites might have been a motivation for a wealthy family's providing a member for service in the Chasseurs-
Volontaires. The local militia commander turned Chasseurs-Volontaires officer
often had a good number of people from his own parish in the ranks of his company, but many, perhaps a majority, of the members of each company would have
come from other parishes where their officer's influence would have been slight.[53]

By process of elimination, it must be assumed that wealthy free coloreds' en-
listments in the Chasseurs-Volontaires were the result of patriotic sentiment and
desire on the part of the free colored community to stake a claim to full citizenship
through military service. John Garrigus has interpreted the rush to enlist in the
Chasseurs-Volontaires as a way to stress masculine attributes of people of color in
the face of racist images that feminized them in the public mind.[54] Certainly there
were few public roles more "masculine" than that of combat soldier.

As can be seen in Rouvray's complaint to the Ministry of War about the posting
of his soldiers to other islands, there was also an attempt by local elites to portray
the Chasseurs-Volontaires as men of property.[55] While this portrayal was exag-
gerated in many cases, nonetheless, it served the purpose of playing up the sacri-
fices of the soldiers and thus further validating their claims to citizenship. This
claim has become part of the popular history of the Chasseurs-Volontaires and has
influenced our view of free coloreds as a class.

Nationalist patriotism was a growing force in the French society of the time.
Many free coloreds, especially younger sons of the wealthier classes, had been educated in France, and many more had read the books and newspapers that their
contemporaries had brought back. Thus, the idea of patriotic sacrifice might very
well have been strong in the motivations of this group. Certainly, patriotism played

an important part in the inducements offered to free coloreds. Expedition commander d'Estaing had served as colonial governor in the 1760s. At that time, he had attempted to encourage free colored participation in the militia through a scheme that would "whiten" *mestif* militiamen and offer them a wide variety of medals from an appreciative nation.[56] Another of his abortive militia reforms would have created a regular army Légion de Saint-Domingue, to be primarily made up of free colored troops under white officers, receiving tax-free manumissions and recognition for their service to their country.[57] He was familiar with the important role played by free coloreds in the colony's defense and was very enthusiastic about the creation of the Chasseurs-Volontaires. He declared that free coloreds, by enrolling in the Chasseurs, would be advancing their own class in the eyes of white society as well as serving the king.[58]

Capitaine Vincent Olivier, former commander of all free colored troops in the North province, was an active recruiter for the Chasseurs-Volontaires. As an extremely influential figure in free colored society, he must have had an important effect on recruitment. He stressed the importance to all free coloreds of participation in the expedition. Moreau de St. Méry notes his "patriotic exhortations" of the free coloreds and points out that two of his family members (grandsons, apparently, instead of sons, as Moreau de St. Méry described them) were participants.[59] In general, the lesson was not lost on his fellow free coloreds.

Vincent Olivier was one of the last survivors of the French expedition to Cartagena on the Spanish Main in 1697. This is the first overseas expeditionary corps from the colony of which any records have survived that included people of color. The expedition included some regular troops but mostly locally recruited freebooters.

This expedition also marked the climax of the transformation of the buccaneer into the planter. Pluchon discusses the reinvestment of the enormous booty of Cartagena in the sugar industry in his history of the French Antilles.[60] Most people in Saint Domingue prior to the 1690s lived off freebooting, hide hunting in the interior, and smuggling to the nearby Spanish colonies. Ever since the time of Governor D'Ogeron in the 1660s, the administrators of the colony had attempted to encourage tobacco planting, but the success of Virginia tobacco in the European market had severely wounded this industry. Various alternate crops had been tried, but few were successful due to the lack of capital or for technical reasons. Plantation slaves were few in Saint Domingue in these early days; there were 2,100 in 1690 according to Pluchon.[61] In the effective absence of the "plantation complex," the line between free and slave and even between black and white can blur. Moreover, the *filibustier* mentality appreciated and rewarded courage on the battlefield and paid relatively little attention to color or status lines. These are the creatures of a settled society. The freebooters were transfrontiersmen to whom the usages of French racism meant very little. Peter Voelz, in his extensive survey of the role of the black soldier in the British Americas, cites many examples of free colored pirates and even officers.[62] Thus in very different times from those covered by the data in this book, it is not surprising to find a talented slave rising high in society thanks to a successful performance in battle.

Vincent was not the only Cartagena survivor living during the last years of the colonial period. In 1781, says Moreau de St. Méry, "Etienne Auba, born in Quartier Morin in 1683[, died]. A slave of M. le Long, who brought him to the siege at Cartagena [at the age of 14], Auba was freed upon his return along with all the other blacks who joined the expedition. His exemplary conduct led M. de Sorel, Governor-General, in 1723 to name him captain of the free blacks of the *circonscription* of Fort-Dauphin. At this time, Auba led his company aboard the frigate *l'Expedition,* under the command of M. de Sirac, to go to the rescue of a French convoy blockaded in Samaná Bay [in what is now the Dominican Republic]."[63]

It is interesting to note the marks of respect accorded to both of these soldiers, not only at the time of their military successes, which seems natural, but also in their declining years, as conditions for free coloreds in general got worse. Moreau de St. Méry himself, by no means a believer in the inherent dignity or equality of the free coloreds, described Olivier as "a happy figure, whose dark skin and white hair command respect," and said he was "admitted everywhere; one sees him at the table of M. le Comte d'Argout, the Governor-General, seated at his side—not puffed up from this mark of distinction but instead from that [conduct] which caused it to be granted to him."[64] He says of Auba that, on 11 August 1779 (just as the fleet was preparing to depart for Savannah), he was granted a "pension of 600 *livres* a year on the *caisse* of liberties, more as a recognition for his services than as a monetary aid [600 *livres* would be a very comfortable annual income, even given the inflation of the war years] . . . he always appeared in public in uniform with his sword. He spoke with good sense and interest of what he had seen . . . he was showered with marks of estimation and benevolence which his white hairs converted into marks of veneration."[65]

The freebooters were gone, and their relaxed attitudes about color and status with them, and the colony had developed a quite substantial plantation complex by the time colored troops served France again, in the Seven Years' War. It seems that their service was again both of some importance to France and rewarding to the soldiers themselves. The colored Chasseurs-Volontaires de l'Amérique regiment, formed for this struggle, was important in the defense of the colony itself. Rather than going overseas, this unit remained in the colony and served as a garrison. France's strategic position in the Seven Years' War was poor. English fleets were dominant at sea. What resources could be spared from the epochal and horrendously expensive ground struggle on the European continent were sent to North America, where France was trying to hold onto its enormous Canadian and Mississippi possessions. Any other French colony had to look to its own resources to protect itself.

In addition, the Caribbean was a very hostile disease environment. French metropolitan troops sent out to Saint Domingue and the other islands were usually decimated by disease. Even the long-service colonial regiments, the Régiment du Cap and the Régiment de Port-au-Prince, suffered enormous losses every season from malaria, yellow fever, diarrheal diseases, and respiratory infections. Beefing up the garrison of Saint Domingue to resist a feared British invasion would have been a terribly expensive proposition in human lives and treasure.

Local whites were unwilling to serve even in a very part-time organization at this time. While perhaps effective enough against stray privateers or freebooters, an untrained militia would have been little use against British professional soldiers in any case. What was needed was a regular or at least semi-regular garrison force that could free up French regulars for service in North America and that would not suffer the great disease casualty rates of the colonial regiments.

It is in this context that the government recruited the Chasseurs-Volontaires de l'Amérique. Consisting of some 550 soldiers, the regiment was based at a camp at Trou du Nord from May 1762 until the end of the war. Moreau de St. Méry was interested in the establishment of rural, preferably high-altitude, camps for the white, regular garrisons of Saint Domingue. In his *Description Topographique, Physique Civile, Politique et Historique de La Partie Française de l'Isle de Saint Domingue,* he goes on at some length about how the white troops who lived alongside the Chasseurs in their rural camp experienced relatively low mortality. Parenthetically, he notes that in the Chasseurs, "among the 550 men of color, there was never more than one sick per twenty, and only three died in two years, a loss rate which was $1/12$ that observed among the soldiers of [the regiment of] Querci" who were their neighbors in the camp.[66] Even in the most salubrious areas, free colored troops were much less subject to disease than whites.

The regiment seems to have spent a quiet couple of years in its cantonment, awaiting an invasion that never came. The English, while committing considerable naval resources to the Caribbean and attacking some smaller island colonies, never attempted to assemble the large amount of resources that would have been needed for an assault on Saint Domingue. Who knows to what extent the Chasseurs-Volontaires de l'Amérique deterred them?

Recruitment for the Chasseurs in 1762 seems to have taken place without the patriotic fanfare that accompanied the enlistment of their namesakes in 1779. There was no talk of overseas expeditions and of opportunity for colored men to strike a blow for their own dignity—perhaps at that somewhat less oppressive time, they did not feel the lack of dignity so strongly. The recruits seem to have joined for reasons that are more traditional: pay, manumission, building of networks within a military caste, and so forth.

In fact, while many men who served in this unit must still have been alive in the time covered by the sample of notarial records, only one veteran of this unit saw fit to identify himself as such in the notarial records. He was Louis la Rondière, of Fort Dauphin, who also served as a sergeant in the free black militia of that city. He was described in one act as having "served in the *nègres volontaires du roy*," which, given his age and his death in 1778, could only mean that he was a veteran of this force.[67]

The experience of the Chasseurs-Volontaires after the retreat from Savannah did not inspire confidence among the free coloreds of Saint Domingue. The 30 to 40 percent disease casualties experienced by the units that went to Grenada must have been particularly chilling—different island, different disease environment, pretty much as challenging to the poor Chasseurs as to white troops from France. To colonial and metropolitan officialdom, though, the Chasseurs-Volontaires were a great success, and a follow-on force was in order to take advantage of the newly available pool of colored manpower. The commander of the Savannah expedition made the point that "sickness and hospital costs of white troops quadruple the value of a local infantryman. White troops from France are too weak to deal with the local climate. Creole troops, especially the free coloreds, hate the rebel slave and are fit to deal with him. A standing corps of Chasseurs-Volontaires would save the lives of French soldiers and the king's budget . . . all persons of color wishing to be freed should be required to serve for eight years."[68] This was the genesis of the Chasseurs-Royaux de Saint-Domingue.

Five companies of Chasseurs-Royaux were to be raised from the free colored militia: three mulatto and two black. Members of this force were to be conscripted. According to the edict establishing the Chasseurs, all free men of color were obliged to serve. Boys were to serve for a year starting at age 15. The newly freed or those whose freedom had not been properly registered also had to serve for a year, following which their liberties would be properly registered at no charge. All other adult males were to serve for three months.[69]

The intent of this edict was clearly to establish a permanent standing force of regular soldiers; this was not an emergency measure for the duration of the war. One assumes that the conscription scheme was never truly intended to be as universal as the phrasing of the edict makes it seem. Either the authorities were making allowances for evasion on a massive scale, or exemptions were to be granted liberally. Establishing five companies of approximately eighty private soldiers each would total four hundred spots in the Chasseurs-Royaux. There were considerably more than four hundred free colored males turning age 15 in the colony each year, to say nothing of the large numbers of persons with irregular manumissions that this measure was clearly designed to attract.

Free coloreds reacted to the possibility of mass conscription in the same way whites had two decades before. The effect of their outraged rejection of this idea on the militia led to mass refusals to appear for musters. Many local militia officers did their best to frustrate recruitment for the Chasseurs, trying to protect their *protegés* in the ranks. Perhaps they were also acting out of motives of regional autonomism such as those that motivated the white militia rebels in earlier years. One example of an officer who resisted conscription of his men into the Chasseurs was Capitaine Jacques Mesnier, who was commander of a mulatto militia company in Cap and also representative of a major mercantile house. He both verbally protested the orders to select members of his company for enlistment into the new formation and refused to pass on those orders to his unit. Arrested on 2 July 1780 while exercising his men on the quarterly militia review day, he was imprisoned in Fort Picolet, north of the town of Cap, for several weeks. On appeal to the governor, he was transferred to house arrest, where he spent an additional couple of weeks. On 6 August, he summoned a notary to complain of his treatment in prison and the decline in his health that resulted from his incarceration. Sieur Casamajor, *aide-major* of the staff, a professional officer, was named to his place as commander of the militia company.[70] A subsequent notarial act describes Mesnier as still a militia captain but "ready to depart for France."[71] Mesnier returned to the colony in 1783, at the end of the War of American Independence, and resumed his mercantile activity and at least the title of militia captain.[72]

Militia officers, and the elite free coloreds they were protecting, seem to have been fairly successful in resisting the Chasseurs-Royaux. The handful of Chasseurs-Royaux who appear in the notarial archives were uniformly poor. One, Pierre Gauthier of Fort Dauphin, was described as "knowing nothing else to do but serve in the military" and hence had volunteered for the regiment.[73] His colleagues listed in the same act included one immigrant from the Spanish side of the island whose liberty was to be confirmed by one year's service, one 15-year-old boy of a poor family, one *bossale* free black conscripted for three months, one person whose claim to have been a veteran of the Chasseurs-Volontaires was disputed, and one deserter from the Chasseurs-Volontaires avoiding punishment for desertion by his service. Only one Chasseur-Royal recruit had any pretensions to gentility at all. This was one Toussaint *dit* Champaign of Limonade whose sister Marie Jeanne, upon her marriage, could muster 3 slaves, 8 *carreaux* of land, 4 horses, and a living allowance of 500 *livres* per year coming to her from the estate of their presumed father.[74] This is not elite wealth, but a comfortable middle-class existence.

Apart from this exception, the only evidence of the remaining Chasseurs-Royaux is reports of their recruitment or their manumissions, performed tax-free because of their military service. This assortment of financial motivations and the feeling that one has little else to do is characteristic of recruits into a long-service professional force, which, of course, is how the government envisioned the Chasseurs-Royaux.

A number of free colored men served in the regular French military, sometimes for long periods. These men filled a number of different roles. Military bandsmen and personal servants of officers served in various regular units. Besides them, regular soldiers served in line regiments in France and throughout its empire. The life of a professional soldier in the eighteenth century was hard, but it was not without its rewards in the form of a certain dignity, stability, and regular pay. None of these men appear to have encountered any special hardship resulting from their color, although none appear to have risen to commissioned rank.

Four of these free coloreds served in the French navy. All countries' navies were notorious at this time for their willingness to accept, indeed to force, the services of anyone and everyone. In fact, three of these men served first in the British Royal Navy, were captured during the War of American Independence, and agreed to serve in the French navy as an alternative to being held as prisoners of war. The only naval veteran native of Saint Domingue appearing in the sample was Bertrand LeMoine. He was a free black, the son of Augustin LeMoine, a free black militia officer and landowner from Quartier Morin. Bertrand was cook on a French Royal Navy vessel in 1777, at the time of his father's death. At the end of the war, he moved over to civilian seafaring work. It is interesting to note that, perhaps in keeping with the ideal of the navy as the scientific branch of service and thus as perhaps more attractive to freethinkers, the two LeMoines, father and son, were among the very few free coloreds in the colony not to profess faith in the "holy Catholic, Roman, and Apostolic faith" in their wills.

Denis Castanet, substantial white merchant and planter, sent his two free colored sons into the military. One, Daniel, served in the Chasseurs-Volontaires, enlisting in the colony, while the other, Etienne, living in France, enlisted in the Régiment de Piémont in the French regular army.[75] Illegitimate children of white men had to be taken care of, and professional military service provided a living and a trade to young Etienne. Daniel did not make any further appearances in the notarial record after his enlistment and manumission, so one suspects that if he survived, he, too, became a professional soldier.

DIFFERING IDEAS OF PATRIOTISM

It has often been suggested that free coloreds served in the military in order to increase their standing as a group in the eyes of whites. Vincent Olivier and the Comte d'Estaing both stressed this theme in their recruiting pitch for the Chasseurs-Volontaires. Julien Raimond used colored military service in his argument, made in the late 1780s before the royal government and later to the revolutionary assembly, that propertied free coloreds ought to be granted equal citizenship with propertied whites.[76] Free coloreds were trying to use a model of patriotism tied to martial virtue to enhance their status in the eyes of the colony's whites.

Unfortunately, during this period martial virtue nearly ceased to be a part of colonial white society's cultural values. Resistance to militia service by whites was rampant during the period—leading to the widespread use of free coloreds in a military role in the first place. Colonial discourse redefined patriotism as "commercial, not martial."[77] At the time of the formation of the Savannah expedition, the colonial newspaper of Cap Français said that the classical ideal of civic virtue demonstrated through military service was too "severe" and "barbaric" for the modern, enlightened age. The paper suggested that instead the loyal white citizens of Saint Domingue should present His Majesty with a warship.[78]

It seems that free colored military service probably had the intended effect more strongly among metropolitan government figures than it did among colonial whites. The Comte d'Estaing felt that the Chasseurs-Volontaires had made the "whites blush for the scorn they have heaped upon [them] and for the injustices and tyrannies they have continually and with impunity inflicted on [free coloreds]. [The free colored] must prove to [whites] that as a soldier [he was] capable of as much honor and courage and more loyalty."[79] The Comte d'Estaing was recruiting for his expedition, but he clearly was impressed at least by the possibility of free colored martial patriotism. Maréchal de Castries, the minister of marine, responsible for the government of the colonies, received Raimond's memoranda between 1786 and 1788 and seemed impressed by their invocation of colored military service. Raimond later claimed that the royal government was preparing significant changes in the legal position of free coloreds as a result of his efforts, although the Revolution of 1789 intervened before anything could happen. Raimond's efforts before the revolutionary assemblies were also more effective with metropolitan than with colonial representatives. Indeed, it was the opposition of the Club Massiac, the planters' lobby in the Assembly, that scuttled the May 1790 law granting political rights to free colored property owners equal to those granted propertied whites under the constitutional monarchy.

Colored martial patriotism was severely battered by the experience of the Savannah expedition, though. The attempt to turn the Chasseurs-Volontaires into regular soldiers caused great resistance to the new Chasseurs-Royaux.[80] The only people to join the new organization voluntarily were those seeking long-term military service, and the attempt to fill the ranks through conscription failed in the face of the resistance of colored property owners and white militia officers.

By 1782, after the twin catastrophes of the long stay abroad of the Chasseurs-Volontaires and the poor recruitment for the Chasseurs-Royaux, the white leadership of the colony was reduced to begging to encourage free colored military service. In April of that year, anticipating that a further draft of his regular troops would be taken out of the colony, the governor-general of the colony wrote to Paul Cairou, the commander of the Limonade militia, to ask him to encourage the local free colored militia to take a more active role in the defense of the region. "I believe it would be useless," he said, "to ask you to appeal to their patriotism; but instead [I urge you] to make known to them the needs of the colony and to insist on their zealous service. I ask you to assure them that I want to find a way to make their service as little onerous as possible . . . when you give the order for assembling the militia, please do not forget to let them know that it is only to serve in the colony, under the orders of their current officers, and that so long as they are on active service, they will receive the same treatment as regular troops . . . troops are to appear in uniform with weapons but dragoons are to serve on foot with the regular infantry companies." Allowing the dragoons to serve on foot meant that their prestigious and valuable horses would not be at risk.[81]

Clearly, colored ideas about martial patriotism had changed significantly during the War of American Independence, becoming more like those of their white neighbors. The colonial government found itself increasingly unable to get significant contributions to the colony's defense from either free coloreds or whites.

CONCLUSION

The military was an important institution in the colony's society. Given that this was a society where 90 percent of the population had to be kept in subjection by the remainder, this should not be surprising. What is surprising is the degree to which this task was entrusted to free persons of color, even, in many cases, those who were still juridically slaves.

Free coloreds served in the *maréchausée,* or rural police, chasing fugitive slaves and enforcing order in the slave quarters. They served in the militia, supporting the *maréchausée* in their public safety role and backing up the regular troops in defense of the colony. Finally, they served in the regular army, both as long-service professionals and as participants in special-purpose expeditionary corps. Service in the most famous of these, the Chasseurs-Volontaires de Saint-Domingue, in 1779–81 earned them the respect of French officialdom while at the same time discouraging free coloreds from further participation.

This heavy free colored participation in the armed forces offered free colored men a route out of slavery and up the economic and social scale. Manumission, for oneself or family members, was an important benefit, but it was only the beginning. Militia and *maréchausée* officers were powerful local figures. When free coloreds served as commissioned officers, they shared in this power. To the extent that free coloreds could become trusted subordinates, they could stand next to power, or maybe behind it. This is the argument pursued in chapter 12 of this book, which considers the free colored military leadership group.

PART TWO

The Free Colored in Society and the Economy

CHAPTER FIVE

Slaveholding Practices

Zabeau Bellanton of Cap Français was one of several free colored women in the sample to qualify for the status of economic elite. Unlike some wealthy free colored women, she seemingly achieved success through her own entrepreneurship and not as a gift or inheritance from anybody. Her background is hazy. She was a *mulâtresse* but did not bear a French name and seemingly had no close white relatives. She had a girl child, a *quarteronne,* who was also surnamed Bellanton and who also did not have a visible white father. Her only white business associate was her *procureur,* or business manager, Maître (a title implying status as an attorney) Justin Viart or Viard. She was always described in the notarial acts as a *confiseuse,* or jam and jelly maker, and also occasionally as a *marchande,* which would be a title of respect when linked with the low trade of food preparation. Official appellations to the contrary notwithstanding, her business was apparently slave dealing, and she reinvested her profits in urban real estate.

The free colored as a slave owner is the subject of this chapter. It is with this remarkable, if not exactly typical, case that consideration of the striking differences between the slaveholding activities of free coloreds and those of their white neighbors begins.

Zabeau Bellanton's name appeared 26 times in the sample of notarial acts. Only eight of those acts were not related to purchase and sale of slaves, and one of the eight was her will. When she made her will in 1782, upon her departure for France, she was quite a wealthy woman. She left real property worth 15,000 *livres* to her godmother in usufruct, with title to the godmother's children. She left 3,000 *livres* to the priest of the parish of Cap Français with instructions that it be distributed to the deserving poor of the parish, white and free colored, thus quite liberally satisfying the requirement of piety that was a part of "respectability" (and with the added fillip of a free colored giving charity to whites). She left her aged mother a quite decent 132 *livres* a month living allowance. Her *procureur* got 2,000 *livres* as well as 10 percent of the total estate, on condition that he manage the remaining property for her daughter until the child reached adulthood and see her well married— another step toward "respectability" that Bellanton herself had not achieved.[1] In an accompanying power of attorney, it is revealed that she owned several houses in Cap and 6 domestic slaves. Two of these slaves were freed upon her departure and were probably quasi-free before.[2]

She operated her business in what seems to have been a heartless and abusive fashion, even by the standards of the time. She bought African-born, or *bossale*, slaves one by one, either rejects from slave ships or from smugglers. Much of her "raw material" was cheap because they were either very young or ill, or both, so she had to face a heightened risk of mortality in the first months in the colony. To share the risk of their "seasoning" while seeking permanent owners, she pawned her slaves out, selling them to temporary employers for a fraction of their value "with right of recovery" in a few months to a year. If a permanent buyer came along, she could repay the pawn and sell the slave, if he or she had survived, at a handsome profit. If the slave died, all she would lose would be the difference between the small payment she had received at the time of the pawn and the small purchase price—the eventual market price of the slave being an opportunity cost, which did not have to be realized very many times for this strategy to pay off handsomely. One imagines the effect on the psychological health, acculturation, and survival of the new immigrant.

Pawning capital goods for ready cash is often an extreme expedient to stave off financial ruin. In the case of Bellanton, though, it seems that pawning slaves was not a strategy of economic desperation, as she seems to have had little need for liquidity or credit. At approximately the same time as she was pawning some slaves and recovering others, she made several purchases, including one of a house in Cap Français for the impressive sum of 18,000 livres, paying with letters of credit on large merchant houses in the city and planters in the countryside.[3] On another occasion, she asked the notary to formalize a debt repayment schedule with Sr. Jean Baptiste Fontaine, a member of the *comédie* of Cap, who had loaned her 13,884 *livres* —he may have been a silent business partner, and the "loan" may have been his share of the profits. Bellanton's business was sleazy, but the enormous profit margins gave the white elite reason to want to have been associated with it, if it could be done without loss of face. In any case, these are quite substantial sums for a humble jam and jelly maker.

Bellanton's slaves came through unusual channels. One of them was described as "speaking only English" (he was a *bossale* of the Soso "nation," so one would presume he also spoke Soso). This suggests that at least some of her slaves may have come to her through the interloper trade from the English colonies and not through the official channels. This sale took place in 1780 during the War of American Independence, suggesting she was trading with the English when good Frenchwomen were doubly prohibited from trading with perfidious Albion.[4] The requirements of patriotism applied doubly to free coloreds, who were striving to be recognized as full citizens, but in this case, at least, the Caribbean tendency to free trade overcame the demands of the national war effort. The general impression that Bellanton's slaves came to her outside normal channels is reinforced when one considers that she was the one holding the paper of the large merchant houses and not the other way around—that is, they were buying more slaves from her on credit than they were selling slaves to her that they imported. Of course, the worst abuses of the transatlantic slave trade are associated with the illegal trade.

Bellanton did not restrict her purchases to smugglers, though. She seems to have had contacts in Martinique, as three of the slaves she sold were from there. All three of these were expensive technical experts; one was the seventh-most valuable single slave out of 4,197 slaves in the sample. Cesarion, a 30-year-old cook and jelly maker (those *confitures* again) worth 6,000 *livres* to the merchant house of M. M. Clément Frères. In this case, the purchaser even had to leave the slave with her until she took ship for France. Maybe she did make some jams and jellies when she could spare the time from slave trading. Or maybe, like many white skilled workers, she was an absentee master whose slaves did the skilled work while she was an entrepreneur.[5] She sold only two adult Saint Domingue–born slaves, suggesting that she was not buying very many slaves in the colony. (Creole, or native-born, slaves made up a third of adult slaves owned by free coloreds and half of those owned by whites.)

However, even Bellanton did not use all of her slaves as money-making commodities. Having four domestic slaves made a quite comfortable, almost opulent, lifestyle, especially for a free colored woman. This opulence was clearly a part of business strategy. She lived on a level comparable with her clientele, the planters and merchants of all colors in Cap Français. Two of her slaves gained their freedom, without any evidence of self-purchase. In her case, as in many others, it is interesting to watch the clash between different views of the slave: as commodity in the market, as kin (pseudo or real), as appurtenance of social respectability, and only sometimes as labor unit in a productive enterprise.

As Zabeau Bellanton's story suggests, slaveholding was very important to free coloreds, and their practices hold a key to understanding their attitudes. The differences between the way different groups of free coloreds used slaves for social and economic advancement, and the differences between those groups and the white population, are very important to any analysis of the society of the colony.

Study of free coloreds' slaveholdings is important to understand the overall situation both of free coloreds and of slaves on the island. Free coloreds owned on the order of 30 percent of the slaves on Saint Domingue. The sample of notarial acts used as the principal source for this book contains about 4 percent of all notarial acts in the archives during the period 1776–91. Those acts record 4,197 identifiable slaves (persons identified by at least three of the following: name, age, place of origin, gender, price, occupational title, and family relationship to another identified slave). Dividing 4,197 by 0.04 gives 104,925, or about 30 percent of the 340,000 slaves reported in the 1786 census, the closest to the midpoint of the time series. This is admittedly a rough estimate. It presumes that all slaves, regardless of the color of their owner, were equally likely to be mentioned in the notarial record. It also presumes that free coloreds (and their slaves) appearing in the sample of notarial acts are broadly representative of free coloreds in general, which has been assumed throughout and which was tested in chapter 1. Given these assumptions and the rather large sample size, it seems clear that free coloreds owned a significant minority of the slaves in the colony—significant enough that an understanding of the condition of slaves in the colony would require investigation of this contingent. This is especially true since their situation was remarkably different from the larger slave population.

To examine the differences, this chapter first looks at the published secondary sources on the slave population of Saint Domingue. Their findings are compared with similar sources on slave populations in other plantation areas in the tropical Americas, and the comparison indicates that the white-owned slave population in the colony was not very different from similar populations elsewhere. Next is a general, and somewhat schematic, look at conditions of work for slaves in the colony.

An examination of the new sources on which this work is based and what they reveal about the free colored–owned slave population follows. This examination shows that free coloreds owned slaves who were different in many respects from those owned by whites, and that free coloreds used their slaves in somewhat different ways than did whites.

The first variable is the ethnic origin and color of slaves from the two populations. This was the variable that was most often noted about a slave in a bill of sale, lease, or inventory (more frequently, in fact, than age, gender, or occupation). Ethnic descriptions used in the archives do not accurately reflect the slaves' ethnic origins in many cases, but, nonetheless, these labels were important to slave owners and merit consideration. The division between native-born (creole) and African-born (*bossale*) slaves was crucial, as was the distinction between persons with some white ancestry and persons with none. Divisions among different African ethnicities were poorly understood, but considerable attention was paid to them anyway.

Next comes the variable of occupational description. Generally, slaves rated an occupational designation in a notarial act only if their occupation was prestigious and valuable—no one was described as a "field hand" or "cane cutter" in the sample. This variable appears to have had an important effect on the value of the slave and the prestige that the slave gave his or her master.

Then, the variables of gender and age are explored. Women were a distinct minority in the Atlantic slave trade and, as a result, in the populations of African-born slaves in the Americas. White masters seem to have had equivocal feelings about female slaves, sometimes seeking more females and sometimes preferring males, who supposedly had greater physical strength. In contrast, free coloreds were much more likely than whites to own female slaves and purchase new ones. Their slave workforces grew naturally as a result, a very unusual condition for slave populations in the Caribbean.

One important thing that free coloreds did with their slaves was to free them. All free coloreds were either freedmen and freedwomen or were descended from them. This chapter explores the procedures of manumission, its frequency among free colored and white masters, and its effect on the economic and non-economic value of slaves.

While reporting on the characteristics of slaves owned by free coloreds, this first part of the chapter gives us an opportunity to look at the non-economic value slaves had for their masters. The prestige that a slave owner got from his or her slaves could be as important to the master as the cash value of those slaves.

This chapter concludes with an in-depth exploration of the way free coloreds got economic value out of their slaves. Saint Domingue was a plantation colony. Slaves did most of the productive labor. Slave owning was almost a sine qua non for economic success of any free person. In addition, a person's social position could be defined in terms of the number of slaves he or she owned. Of large planters it would often be said that "this one has five hundred" or "that one has two hundred and fifty," indicating the number of slaves and thus the relative social position.

Large planters were not the only slave owners in the colony. Many free persons of color, even though of quite modest wealth, owned slaves. Only two of the twenty-seven death inventories in the sample do not contain at least one slave. One of those was the death inventory of a woman named Babet, apparently a dependent of the quite wealthy Pincemaille free colored clan in Limonade; while she may have possessed no slaves at the time of her death, they had plenty as a family.[6] This is significant because of the propensity of free coloreds to execute wills and otherwise to use the notarial system to protect their property.[7] Even quite humble people executed wills and had their property inventoried as part of the probate process, and even those humble people owned slaves.

Slave owning was not only common among free coloreds, even those of modest means, but slaves also made up an important part of their total capital. It was common for the value of the slaves in death inventories to be the single largest component of the total wealth. The average value of all the decedents' property reported in the twenty-seven death inventories in the sample was 26,032 *livres*, while the average value of slaves in those inventories was 16,536 *livres*, or 64 percent. Even those of very modest means invested around two-thirds of their capital in slaves: for estates evaluated at under 10,000 *livres*, the average value was 6,221 *livres*, and the average value of slaves was 4,066 *livres*, or 65 percent.

Slave-worked agriculture gave significant economies of scale. This effect is more marked in some crops (like sugar) than in others (like tobacco or coffee), but in general, in plantation agriculture, one hundred slaves were much more than a hundred times as productive as one slave. Thanks to the very small units of slaves (often amounting to only one or two individuals) that many of these free coloreds of modest means owned, they needed to find alternate ways to employ them profitably. As agricultural workforces, by themselves, they could not compete profitably with the larger slave workforces owned by whites. Owners of small units of slaves found ways to keep them employed productively.

The first step in this exploration is to look at the differing characteristics of slaves owned by free coloreds and by whites. These differences illustrate varying cultural attitudes toward slaves and wealth held by the white plantocracy and by the free coloreds in the colony.

An early but still important secondary source on the slave population of the French West Indies is Gabriel Debien's *Les esclaves aux Antilles françaises, XVIIe–XVIIIe siècles*.[8] Debien worked primarily from plantation records—specifically 108 sets of plantation papers culled from French departmental or national archives during his career. All the proprietors in Debien's sample were white. Almost all were absentee owners of quite large estates. In fact, the papers he studied were, for the most part, copies of correspondence between the proprietor in France and the *économe*, or resident manager, in the colony. His records date from the 1780s for the most part, with some from earlier decades back in the second quarter of the century, and some records of absentee administration under the British occupation in the 1790s. The French archives are quite rich in this sort of material. Debien made a stellar career out of an examination of these records and barely scratched the surface.

More recent research has looked at Saint Domingue's slave population in a somewhat more nuanced fashion, taking into account the differences between sugar and coffee estates. However, much of this newer work also relies on plantation records for its data. Most of the owners of the plantations whose records were used were, like those at the core of Debien's work, whites. Debien himself wrote the chapter on slavery in the standard French-language history of the French Caribbean, *Histoire des Antilles et de la Guyane*, edited by the best-known historian of the colony, Pierre Pluchon.[9] Debien's bibliographic note at the end of the chapter refers the reader principally to published plantation records. David Geggus's groundbreaking study of the colony, composed principally from English sources, cites administrative records of the effects of absentee landlords as its principal French source on conditions of slaves in the colony.[10] Geggus also cites the Debien *oeuvre* extensively in his first chapter, on the pre-revolutionary context. Since *Slavery, War and Revolution*, Geggus has published a study specifically dealing with the slave population of the island, based on records of absentee owners under the English administration. Michel-Rolph Trouillot has also given us a chapter further exploring the coffee revolution, especially its impact on the slaves.[11]

From this new work, it appears that there was a striking difference between slaves working on coffee plantations and those working in sugar cultivation. Slave workforces on sugar plantations were more likely to be creole (47 percent of adults compared to 22 percent for coffee plantations), somewhat less likely to be children (Trouillot found around 300 children per 1000 women as opposed to over 400 per 1000 for coffee plantations, while for Geggus the figures were much closer), but about equally likely to be male (both types of plantations had an oversupply of men, slightly more noticeable in coffee plantations, says Geggus). The explanation for the differences lies in a combination of factors. First, coffee cultivation was a newer development in the colony. Sugar plantations might be several generations old, hence a higher population of creoles is understandable. There were various preconceptions about the ability of different groups of Africans to withstand different types of work or to learn different skills, which made plantation owners seek out members of particular African ethnicities. These differences explain some of the differences between white and free-colored slaveholdings. However, the generalizations about coffee slaves in these newer works do not all apply to slaves on coffee farms owned by free coloreds, nor were all slaves who were owned by free coloreds employed on coffee plantations.

The findings of Debien, Geggus, and Trouillot are comparable to similar values elsewhere in the slave societies of the tropical Americas. Slaveholding units were somewhat smaller in Saint Domingue than in Jamaica, for example, where they averaged at least 250 on sugar plantations.[12] In Brazil, especially in the early sugar boom of the seventeenth century, the work of sugar production was performed, in large measure, by *lavradores*, who contracted with the planter to cultivate small portions of an estate on a sharecropping basis; their slave workforces averaged about twenty.[13] Increasingly replacing this sharecropping system as capital flowed in and the sugar industry took off a second time were very large plantations that equaled and even exceeded those of Saint Domingue in terms of size of labor units. In Cuba, in later years and in areas where the plantation complex had fully taken hold, slaveholding units were exceptionally large, with one planter's workforce surpassing 1,475 slaves in 1857.[14]

Slave workforces in these other plantation areas generally did not grow naturally, with the notable exception of the United States. The British colonies in North America, and the United States from 1776–1808, received about 427,000 slave imports yet had a slave population of about 4.5 million at emancipation in 1863.[15] The demography of other plantation areas in the Americas was much bleaker for the slaves: Cuba received 748,000 slave imports during its long participation in the slave trade yet had a slave population of 436,495 in 1841, the high point of slave population in that colony.[16]

To give a basis of comparison for the data to follow on slaves owned by free coloreds, let us look at the slave workforces on large white-owned plantations as reported by Debien, Geggus, and Trouillot. The plantations that provided Debien with his data had workforces averaging about 100 slaves. The largest was the Bréda sugar plantation at Plaine du Nord in 1784, with 210, while the smallest was the Santo Domingo sugar plantation at Léogane in 1781 with 34. Geggus found a similar range for sugar plantations: the mean ranged over the years of his survey and from province to province from 170 to 200, and the overall range was from 34 to more than 500. His coffee plantations, though, were markedly smaller, with a mean from 34 to 82 and extremes from 7 to over 300.[17]

Debien counted 3,568 slaves from the 1770s to 1790.[18] The single largest "national" origin of these plantation slaves was creole, or native born (2,041, or 57 percent). Among the African-born slaves, the most common "nationality" was Congo (633, or 18 percent). The nationalities of the Slave Coast (modern Togo and Benin; national origin names used: Nago, Arada, Mina, Thiamba, Barba, Foeda, Adia, Cotocoli, Aguia, Mallé) were the next most common (454, or 13 percent). Slaves of mixed race were very uncommon; only 68 were reported, for a total of less than 2 percent. A wide range of African ethnic groups provided the remaining 10 percent, from areas ranging from the mouth of the Senegal River to Mozambique. On the sugar plantations Geggus studied, 47 percent of the adult slaves were creoles, while on coffee plantations, only 22 percent were creole. The African origins of *bossale* slaves that Geggus found were similar to those in Debien's sample, while Geggus notes that Congo slaves were much more common on coffee plantations.[19]

Unfortunately, Debien does not give a precise gender breakdown of the slaves in his reports. Often, gender would not be stated in notarial acts, although it can almost always be assumed from the name given the slave or the gender of the French adjective used to describe him or her; Debien obviously preferred not to assume. However, he reports a significant overall gender imbalance in favor of males.[20] He even refers to attempts toward the end of the colony's existence on the part of plantation managers to encourage better plantation discipline and increase birth rates by purchasing more female slaves.[21] Geggus, on the other hand, reports that gender balances were closer than either censuses or anecdote would suggest. He found sex ratios of 115 men per 100 women on sugar plantations and 120 men per 100 women on the coffee plantations he studied. He feels this relatively low gender imbalance was the result of higher mortality for men than for women, and he deduces that the mortality rates were higher in Saint Domingue than in other colonies.[22]

The literature on the slave trade emphasizes the predominance of males among those transported to the Americas. The overall average appears to have been about 179 males for every 100 females.[23] It is unclear if this imbalance was the result of masters' preference for male slaves to do heavier labor, or of African sellers' preference to keep female slaves for themselves. This gender imbalance persisted among slaves owned by white masters despite the fact that women slaves were somewhat cheaper and despite attempts, reported by Debien, by many white masters to increase the number of women slaves they held in order to increase slave birthrates.[24]

A shortage of women slaves as well as poor treatment and nutrition contributed to very poor fertility rates on white-owned plantations, according to Debien. For example, on two plantations in the southern parish of Aquin, out of an average roster of 149 slaves, there were only 6 births between January 1784 and April 1790, or 6.36 births per 1,000 population per year (assuming 40 percent women, this works out to roughly 15.5 births per 1,000 women, or a fertility rate of 78 children aged 0–4 per 1,000, still quite low).[25] The sugar plantation Galbaud du Fort had a slave population that averaged 120 between 1741 and 1772 and yet never had more than 2 births a year. The workforce increased to 190 slaves over the next twenty years, and yet the number of births never exceeded 3.[26] Geggus found very low fertility levels in the sugar plantations he studied and found no more than 277 children aged 0–4 per 1,000 women in the North province, with a colony-wide mean of 328 over the period 1755–91. Fertility on coffee estates was higher, 356 for the colony as a whole between 1767 and 1792.[27]

Meanwhile, mortality rates were high. The white planters and their managers estimated mortality among slaves at 50 percent during the first eight years after purchasing a slave newly imported from Africa, and equal or higher within the first five years of a native-born slave child's life. Barring an epidemic or other demographic crisis, between 5 and 6 percent of the slave population died each year on these large *habitations*.[28]

Mortality and morbidity were highest among the agricultural laborers, especially those on the sugar plantations. The sugar plantation's workforce was divided into several slave gangs. About one third of a plantation's slaves would belong to the primary gang. Masters hoped to fill the first unit with the younger and healthier slaves. The first unit would do the heavy labor of clearing fields, digging irrigation ditches, cutting timber, and building structures and, most importantly, would cut the mature cane and operate the plantation's sugar mill during the harvest season. Heavy labor in the tropical sun, especially on the generally poor rations offered to slaves on these large plantations, could result in serious health problems, and it is no surprise that laborers did not last long on the first gang. Debien gives the example of the Grandhomme sugar plantation in Croix des Bouquets where the manager bought 8 slaves in 1764, of whom 4 survived the "seasoning" period by 1768, but 2 of the survivors were incapable of work in the first gang and were assigned to lighter tasks. Twelve other new slaves bought that year off a different ship by the same plantation were reduced to 7 by 1767, but of those 7 slaves, 2 were physically unable to do field work.[29]

These ill, injured, older, younger, and female slaves not able to perform the tasks demanded of the first gang were assigned to a second gang with lighter tasks: weeding, overseeing food gardens, cleaning irrigation ditches, and occasional stints of heavy labor when the pace of harvest demanded it. Perhaps a third of the plantation's slaves would belong to this second group. On plantations with significant numbers of children, often some sort of labor assignment would be given to them, more as a form of on-the-job training and socialization than in the hope of getting much economic value out of them.

Coffee cultivation required a wider variety of tasks out of each slave and also permitted the owner to work them more evenly throughout the year. A more even pace of labor was easier on the health of the slaves, especially for the creole slaves. African slaves on coffee plantations, according to Geggus, suffered more serious illnesses than their creole coworkers.

Field work was not the only form of labor demanded of slaves in the colony, though. Numbers of domestic servants were not fully reported in Debien's compilation, as he admits in his discussion of the Foäche sugar plantation of Jean-Rabel, where the plantation list of 1779 named more than 500 slaves and only 4 domestics.[30] Of 1,065 slaves with occupational descriptions in Geggus's sample, only 95 were domestics.[31] Debien points out that many domestic servants belonged to the managers personally, instead of the plantation, and so do not appear in its records. A wide variety of tasks are subsumed under the designation "domestic servant," from scullery maid to cook to coachman to mistress of the house and of the white manager. Hours could be long and tasks onerous and undignified, but slaves who could perform this work had better living conditions than their colleagues in the field.

The leaders among the plantation slaves, though, were the *commandeurs,* or boss slaves, and the technical specialists. These slaves, mostly men, were exceptionally valuable to their masters. The most expensive single slave in the sample was Grand Pierre, *premier commandeur* of the *habitation* of the free colored Daugé heirs in Croix des Bouquets, who was freed by the plantation manager in 1777 in return for a ransom of 8,000 *livres.*[32] *Commandeurs* were community leaders whose authority transcended and eventually outlived that of their masters. Carolyn Fick attributed the success of the great slave insurrection of 1791 to the fact that the organizers were *commandeurs* and technical specialists, not the disgruntled domestics and malcontent field hands who had been at the head of previous disturbances.[33]

Technical specialists performed a wide range of tasks on the plantations. The principal refiner on a sugar plantation might be a high-priced white specialist, but parsimonious owners often sought to replace such craftsmen with slave labor. Skilled labor at a lower level was almost always performed by slaves: every plantation list contained carpenters, masons, coopers, teamsters, midwives, seamstresses, and the like. Persons with these skills were valuable, but their work gave them access to resources that permitted promotion, and even manumission.

Most of the technical specialists on plantations were creole rather than African, according to Geggus. Of twenty-seven occupational categories, *bossales* outnumbered creoles in only four: carter's mate, master boiler, sugar boiler, and fisherman. Among the *bossales,* the masters had preferences for some ethnicities over others in particular jobs, but the clear overall preference was for creoles.[34]

Technical specialists also found work in the cities. Training in technical skills was delivered through the time-honored institution of apprenticeship, with the twist that masters could place their slaves as apprentices without losing ultimate possession of them. One could be both apprentice and slave. Many free skilled craftsmen operated their workshops at least in part with slave workers. For example, Augustine, the wife of Pierre Pasquier, *negresse libre,* placed her slave Pierre in 1785 as apprentice for five years to Antoine Profit, a master carpenter who was also a free black.[35] In 1790, she would have become the proud owner of a journeyman carpenter, whose income would be sufficient to support himself and his mistress.

Urban areas also had a heavy population of domestic slaves. Whereas many absentee planters lived in France, a significant minority were resident in the large cities of Saint-Dominigue. The white population in general looked on visits to the city as times to show off and indulge themselves—this is apparent from the list of amusements and spectacles available in the cities, from taverns and houses of ill repute to the *comédie* and the Philosophical Society. Domestic servants were retained in large numbers predominantly in order to impress, and it was in town where Saint Domingue's wealthy whites sought to impress the most.

Saint Domingue's free coloreds also owned domestic slaves, although in much smaller numbers than their white neighbors. Of the more than 4,000 slaves in the sample, only 79 were identified as domestic servants, of whom 14 were to obtain their liberty in the act in which they appeared in the sample. Although this is only a little lower than the proportions of domestic slaves found in Debien's sample of white plantation populations, the free colored sample includes urban areas whereas Debien's excludes the town houses and the professional managers' slaveholdings, which contained between them the large majority of domestic servants owned by whites. Three reasons explain the paucity of domestic servants in the workforces of free coloreds. First, slaveholding units averaged much smaller among free coloreds, meaning that fewer individuals could be spared for full-time nonproductive labor. In fact, many of the domestic slaves owned by free coloreds were working in a business rather than seeing to the domestic needs of one master. As an example, Alexis La Combe, a free *quarteron*, rented the services of Rosalie, a *blanchisseuse* (washerwoman) for six months at 48 *livres* a month, not, one presumes, in order to wash his sheets but to help in his business of hair care and wigmaking.[36] Secondly, free coloreds were discouraged by law and (white) social convention from "excessive" displays of "style." Hordes of domestic servants were more impressive than useful. Finally, free coloreds were natives of the colony, or at least long-time residents, and thus they did not need domestic servants as cultural intermediaries, which was an important role that higher-level domestics—*menagères* and *valets*—fulfilled for new white immigrants.

Outside the cities and the plantations, smaller agricultural establishments also were homes to slaves. It was very common for a family of free colored (as they were, for the most part) small farmers to own a family of slaves, with the household divided about evenly between servile and free members. It was not unusual for a white father to will or donate to his illegitimate colored offspring a small piece of land and a family of slaves. In an example of this process, *Sieur* Louis Aramy, a modest planter in the mountainous canton of Cotelettes in Limonade, gave 10 *carreaux* of undeveloped land and 4 slaves to his presumed children with a succession of slave mistresses.[37] The children could rent the land and slaves out to other planters for a modest income: undeveloped land in coffee country in Limonade rented for about 200 *livres/carreaux/*year, and healthy adult slaves were worth between 100 and 150 *livres*/year apiece; 400 to 600 *livres* a year could procure a modest but comfortable lifestyle for a family in a rural area. Alternatively, the children could work the land as very small planters, hoping perhaps to advance with the ongoing economic boom. Many free colored planters of the "middling sort" got their start in just this way.

The working conditions of these peasant slaves would be, as one would imagine, very different from those of their brethren on large plantations. A peasant's work demands a great variety of tasks, and thus the slaves' skill levels would be higher. More variety of skills means greater value to the master and thus a less unequal power relationship between master and slave, as in the case of the technical slaves on the plantations. For example, the slave Pierrot, belonging to the widow Poupart, who appears later in this chapter, seems to have been the next thing to a serf. On two occasions, during times of economic hardship for them, in 1779 and again in 1787, the Pouparts leased a piece of land belonging to them in the canton of Fons-Bleux, in the mountainous south of Limonade.[38] On both occasions, Pierrot, described as "guardian and caretaker of the said place," was rented along with the property. At a rental of 100 *livres* a year, neither the land nor the slave must have been very valuable—this was a peasant holding. Obviously, unlike a medieval serf, Pierrot had no legal right to accompany the land, but nonetheless, his attachment to this piece of land was respected. The remainder of the Poupart slave labor force lived and worked on their principal holding, in the area known as the Savane de Limonade, a collection of very small farms, for the most part owned by free coloreds and most of them producing only food crops.

In addition, as they often lived in the same house with their masters, these peasant slaves would have social relations with their owners that were much more intimate than those of the field hands. Their masters retained them for longer periods of time—the Pouparts had owned Pierrot for at least fifty years before they found themselves forced to rent him—and even then, they retained title. This could be good or bad, as in the case of the domestic servants in the white plantation homes. Opportunities for sexual exploitation of female slaves were certainly great in these circumstances. However, since family structure was much stronger among free coloreds than among whites, sexual exploitation was not as pronounced among peasant slave families, and in general, the *griffe* child of a mixed-race master and his slave was a much less common figure than the mulatto child of a white master and his slave.

Having relied on Debien, Geggus, and Trouillot to describe the white slaveholdings of the colony, we turn now to the sample of notarial acts and see what it reveals about the unreported minority. We begin by looking more closely at the ethnic subcategories of slaves owned by free coloreds and examine how they compare with those reported by other scholars. Colonial practice was to refer to these distinctions as "nationalities," and that practice is respected here.

In order to understand important differences in the way European and free colored masters dealt with their slaves, it is important to understand the variables of color, status, and ethnic origin within the slave community. Masters used, or tried to use, these variables in order to improve the productivity and quiescence of their labor force.

Mulâtre, griffe, quarteron, and other terms refer to combinations of African and European heritage. Slaves of mixed heritage were extremely uncommon, as white or mixed-race free fathers were under strong social pressure to see to it that their offspring were freed. Debien's compilation of 3,568 slaves living on white-owned plantations in Saint Domingue between 1760 and 1785 includes 68 mixed-race persons, or 2 percent.[39] Geggus's sample contains about 2.7 percent mixed-race slaves on sugar plantations and 1.6 percent on coffee establishments.[40] Of the compilation of 4,197 slaves either owned by free persons of color or becoming free persons of color themselves who appear in notarial acts, 531 were of mixed race. However, this number includes all those obtaining liberty, whether granted by white or free colored masters. When one omits those receiving freedom in the act in which they appear in the notarial record and slave children under age 12 owned by a relative and presumably destined for freedom, there were only 87, or 2.1 percent.

Much more common were the creole black slaves. They were the most common "nation" in Debien's records: 2,041 of 3,568 slaves were born in the colony, or 57 percent.[41] Geggus found that 56 percent of slaves on sugar plantations between 1760 and 1792 were creoles, while he found that Creoles, at 36 percent, were relatively uncommon on coffee plantations in that period. Creoles were also uncommon as slaves of free coloreds: only 1,314 of the 3,617 in the sample for whom "nation" was recorded fell in this category, or 36 percent.[42] This is partially a result of the fact that many free coloreds were coffee plantation owners. However, the reason given in Geggus's work for the high proportion of *bossales* on coffee plantations in his survey was that those plantations were relatively new, and so the populations had not had time to creolize. The coffee plantations owned by free coloreds were among the first set up in most areas, so one would normally expect them to be among the most creolized of the coffee sector. However, free coloreds owned no more creole slaves than did their latecomer white neighbors.

Bossales were the single largest group of slaves owned by free coloreds in the sample. The different "nations," or origins within Africa, were important to owners because they thought these differences resulted in different outcomes with their slaves: certain "nations" were thought to be more tractable, others stronger or harder working, some better suited to skilled labor, others healthier, and so forth. Certain cultural influences were visible in slaves of different "nations," including some cultural differences and some very marked differences in the market.

The "national" origin of slaves was very important to their owners and served as the principal means of identifying them in notarial acts and plantation registers. The small number of slaves of mixed race were the aristocracy of "national" origin, and after them came the creoles. *Bossales* were the least esteemed, but even among the Africans there was a ranking of value. The Congos and their neighbors from central Africa were the most common "national" designation, and potential purchasers thought of them as somewhat more civilized because of their contact with Catholicism in their home country, according to Moreau de St. Méry.[43] He also says that women in Congo were primarily responsible for agriculture, and so female slaves placed in fieldwork were often Congos. Planters thought of Senegalese slaves as sober, discreet, quiet, hard workers, but they were less healthy than the central Africans since their dietary staple was the less well rounded rice. Bambaras were thought to be indolent and likely to steal, the Mandingues were considered cruel as overseers but good workers, the Sosos were looked upon as good woodsmen and guardians for outlying fields. Most of the slaves from modern Guinea and north were Muslims, and Moreau de St. Méry, at least, considered this a selling point. He uses the most offensive adjectives in his *précis* of slave origins to describe the "idolatrous" slaves of forest west and central Africa. The slaves of modern Liberia and Cote d'Ivoire were mostly brought to the colony by the interloper trade with the English and were thus, said Moreau de St. Méry, the rejects of the English—there's no evidence that Zabeau Bellanton ever had any discipline problems, but then she seems to have been the sort of person who commands respectful obedience. Colonists worried, though, that people from these areas were likely to commit all sorts of crimes, including revolt and desertion. The slaves of the Gold Coast and the Slave Coast were thought to be lazy and pretentious but interested in commerce and marketing. Potential purchasers feared that the Ibos were more susceptible to suicide than other slaves, and this lowered their value to their master, unless there was a large group of fellow countrymen already in the potential master's slave workforce to provide support to the newcomer. Arada women were quarrelsome, said conventional wisdom, so masters would rarely consider them as domestic servants.

Table 3 presents the reported African origins of the slaves in Debien's and Geggus's samples and in the sample of slaves of free persons of color. Both sugar and coffee plantation figures from the Geggus articles are included here for comparative purposes, but it is best to use the coffee plantation figures to compare white to free colored slaveholdings, as these were the type of plantations free coloreds were

TABLE 3

African Origins of Bossale *Slaves on Plantations in Saint Domingue as Compared to Those Owned by Free Coloreds*

AFRICAN ORIGIN	BOSSALE SLAVES ON LARGE WHITE-OWNED PLANTATIONS[a] PERCENT OF ALL BOSSALES	ALL BOSSALE SLAVES, SEPARATED BY TYPE OF PLANTATION[b] PERCENT ON SUGAR PLANTATIONS	PERCENT ON COFFEE PLANTATIONS	FREE COLORED-OWNED BOSSALE SLAVES[c] PERCENT OF ALL WITH KNOWN ORIGINS
Senegal	0.7	1.4	0.7	2.7
Gambie	0	n/a	n/a	0.06
Mandingue	0.4	3.0	2.9	2.7
Fula	0.2	0.7	0.4	0.6
Dia	0.2	n/a	n/a	0
Bambara	5.1	4.0	2.0	2.3
Cap Labon	0	n/a	n/a	0.06
Senegambia region	6.9	6.0	146	8.5
Soso	1.3	1.2	0.3	0.9
Miserable	1.0	n/a	n/a	0.8
Mesurade	0.9	2.5	0.9	0.7
Timbo	0.6	2.5	1.1	1.0
Guinea and Liberia region	3.9	2.3	59	3.4
Capelot	1.7	0	0	0.5
Coromanti	0.2	0	0	0.5
Cote d'Or	1.0	0.9	0.7	0.3
Fonevas	0	n/a	n/a	0.06
Ivory Coast and Gold Coast region	3.0	0.7	24	1.4
Arada	8.4	10.5	8.9	11.3
Nago	11.8	8.9	5.5	7.1
Mina	3.0	3.4	1.0	1.3
Thiamba	2.8	2.5	1.1	2.3
Barba	0	0.8	0.1	0.2
Foeda	1.2	1.9	0	0.6
Adia	1.1	2.0	0.7	1.3
Cotocoli	0.8	0.3	0	1.5
Malle	0.4	n/a	n/a	0
Ataqa	0	n/a	n/a	0.1
Ajouba	0	n/a	n/a	0.06
Slave Coast region	29.6	17.3	443	25.8

African Origins of Bossale *Slaves on Plantations in Saint Domingue as Compared to Those Owned by Free Coloreds* (continued)

AFRICAN ORIGIN	BOSSALE SLAVES ON LARGE WHITE-OWNED PLANTATIONS [a]	ALL BOSSALE SLAVES, SEPARATED BY TYPE OF PLANTATION [b]		FREE COLORED–OWNED BOSSALE SLAVES [c]
	PERCENT OF ALL BOSSALES	PERCENT ON SUGAR PLANTATIONS	PERCENT ON COFFEE PLANTATIONS	PERCENT OF ALL WITH KNOWN ORIGINS
Ibo	3.9	2.5	2.3	8.6
Hausa	0.6	0.7	0.4	0.4
Aguga	0	n/a	n/a	0.2
Bobo/Bibi	0.1	0	0	0.3
Fond	0	1.3	0.4	1.3
Aguia	0.6	n/a	n/a	0
Benin/Calabar region	5.2	3.1	187	10.9
Mondogue	1.8	2.5	4.2	2.2
Ouango	0	0	0	0.2
Congo	44.8	40.8	63.9	47.7
Central Africa region	46.6	43.3	68.1	50.1
Other	4.8	4.1	1.5	0.4

[a] These figures are drawn from Debien, *Les Esclaves,* 64–65. Debien got his counts from reports sent by professional plantation managers to their absentee employers in France, thus these figures represent the population of slaves owned by prosperous white planters, 1760–1791.

[b] These figures are from Geggus, "Sugar and Coffee Cultivation," 81, using figures for the north province for 1775–1791. Geggus drew his counts from a wide range of sources including reports to absentee owners and records kept by smaller producers, bills of sale. These figures represent a more general cross-section of the slave population in the colony.

[c] From a sample of notarial records executed by free coloreds in the colony, 1776–1791.

most likely to own. Before analyzing these figures at length, though, we look at the comparative value of these different nationalities.

Once we put aside the stereotypes of Moreau de St. Méry, it is unclear how useful these sweeping "national" designations used in notarial acts would have been as a tool to help the slave owner understand his slave's culture. A plethora of smaller ethnic groups interpenetrated the large ethnicities that provide most of the "national" designations (Bambara, Ibo, Hausa). One wonders, for example, at the very large reported numbers of Minas, a small coastal ethnic group in Togo, and the absolute absence in both samples of Ewes, a large ethnic group living just inland of the Mina. One wonders if "Mina" just meant "someone sold to Europeans by the Minas or at Mina castle." Some of the "national" designations mean no more than the port from which the slave embarked for the colonies. Aradas, for example, entered the Atlantic slave trade from the coast of modern Togo and Benin but might have come from any one of the more than 70 ethnic groups of the interior of those countries. Occasionally, Africans' ethnic designations got excessively specific. So, for example, the free black Lucrèce, making her will in 1777 in Port-au-Prince, described herself as being of the "nation" Bangouya.[44] A fellow native of the "nation," François Thomas *dit* Salmigoudy, made his will in 1782 in Mirebalais.[45] Now, as it happens, Bangouya is a small town (with a population around 1,500 in the 1990s) about 70 kilometers north of Kindia in the modern Republic of Guinea. Its people are of mixed Peuhl (Fulani) and Soso ethnic origin, the Peuhl having come to the area in the eighteenth century as part of the Fulani occupation of the Fouta Djallon highlands and having reduced the Soso to slavery at that time. The village has a debatable tradition of political independence from the Fulani theocratic kingdom in the mountains. Clearly, these people were asked at some point what "nation" they came from and they gave the name of their village. More common in both the sample and Debien's were the "Timbo" or "Timbouts." Timbo is another village in the modern Republic of Guinea, about 50 kilometers east of Dalaba in the Fouta Djallon. However, Timbo was the capital of the Fouta Djallon Fulani kingdom during the period under study, so it would be somewhat appropriate to describe people from this area as coming from the "nation" of Timbo —although the "nationalities" used in all three samples also include the Peuhl or Fula.[46]

Other non-ethnic titles snuck into the ethnic categorization system. Debien reports the presence of four persons described as being of the Dia "nation" among his sample of plantation slaves. Dia is a common sept name among the Fulani and Soninke.

Keeping these caveats in mind, we clearly see that there were some survivals of African cultural practices and values among the Haitian slave population. Slave masters, by seeking to know the "nation" of their property, were striving to use this fact to their advantage. John Thornton noted the continuity of African military and political traditions from the Kingdom of Congo to the slave rebel armies of Saint Domingue in his article "I Am a Subject of the King of Congo."[47] In fact, much of Thornton's work has served to explore and enlarge our view of African cultural survivals among slaves in the Americas. The second half of his book *Africa and Africans in the Making of the Atlantic World* concentrates on this subject.[48]

The traditional religions of the Slave Coast of west Africa and of the Congo area are closely related to Haitian voodoo. David Geggus discusses the African roots of the Haitian religious tradition as revealed by linguistic links in his article "Haitian Voodoo in the Eighteenth Century."[49] Various fragments of voodoo liturgy have been preserved from the period, including a fragment of a chant in Moreau de St. Méry, and specific and identifiable African traditions were being invoked.[50]

The structure of slave society in Saint Domingue favored African cultural survivals inasmuch as slaves lived in family units in small huts and were encouraged to produce much of their own sustenance on provision-ground farms. In the few examples of slave marriages in the sample, members of one's ethnic group seem to be favored as partners—presumably, the same held true for informal relationships. Conventional wisdom has it that masters practiced conscious ethnic fragmentation, but Moreau de St. Méry's comments on the Ibo's tendency to suicide if not surrounded by fellow ethnics seems to contradict this in at least one specific case. Debien's records show a pattern of ethnic concentration, with most plantations having one group comprising at least a quarter of the total workforce.[51]

It is unclear exactly how successful slave owners were at identifying real cultural traits among different African-born ethnic groups and using them to their advantage to assemble a more productive or less restive labor force. Geggus reports some significant differences among African nationalities who were assigned to different specialized tasks, with Hausa, for example, being especially favored as sugar mill workers and Bambaras as craftsmen.[52] Regardless of how much actual advantage they gained from these maneuvers, slave owners clearly thought that differences in "nation" implied differences in utility. The sample permits us to assess the differences in market value of slaves from the different "nations."

When corrected for age and gender, some "nations" were clearly worth significantly more than others. Contrary to the impression given by Moreau de St. Méry, Congos, with an average value of 2,006 *livres,* seem to have been worth somewhat less than comparably aged and significantly more feminine populations of Mandingues, at 2,110 *livres,* and Ibos, at 2,047 *livres.* The supposedly sought-after Senegalese slaves in the sample, with an average value of 2,016 *livres,* probably owe most of their superior value to their remarkable youth—they averaged 23.5 years of age, almost five years under the average for all *bossales.* Debien notes the changing pattern of slave imports throughout the period, with Slave Coast imports declining and being replaced by shipments from Congo; this would account for the greater average age of the Arada and Nago population in the sample and thus their lesser value.[53] Interestingly, however, the Arada, a "national" descriptor without even the slightest cultural or ethnic validity, at 1,949 *livres,* nonetheless commanded a higher price on the market than the nearly identical, in terms of geographic origin, Nago, at 1,785 *livres.* Like Moreau de St. Méry, white society in general attached a positive image to the description "Arada." Transmitted to free coloreds, this image was worth an average of about 100 to 150 *livres* a head (taking into account the differences in age and gender balance between the two populations) during the period under study.

It is more difficult to judge the difference in the market between creole slaves and *bossales*. Certainly the presumption would have been that creoles were more valuable; this is Moreau de St. Méry's position and is borne out by our knowledge of other slave societies.[54] In addition, an indirect measure of value is the use of an occupational description that would ordinarily be stated only for high-status occupations. The percentage of a group that received an occupational description would also be a rough measure of value.

Adult *bossale* slaves of free coloreds in the sample, with an average value of 1,987 *livres*, were only slightly less valuable than adult creole slaves, with an average value of 2,048 *livres*. On the other hand, a moderately higher proportion of *bossale* slaves rated occupational designations—7.0 percent as opposed to 6.1 percent—and the value of these top-quality slaves was slightly higher among the African-born slaves—2,942 *livres* for the *bossale* high-value slaves as opposed to 2,876 *livres* for the creole slave specialists. Thus, free coloreds valued their creole and *bossale* slaves more or less equally.

This differs sharply from the perception of the comparative value of these two groups of slaves held by the very careful observer Moreau de St. Méry and, indeed, from the received wisdom from most observers of slave societies. Results in this sample notwithstanding, it can safely be assumed that in the colony as a whole, all other things being equal, creole slaves were more valuable than *bossale* slaves. Observations from Moreau de St. Méry at the time to the very detailed statistical survey conducted in 1995 by Laird Bergad and colleagues of the Cuban slave market tell us this.[55] There was clearly something different about the types of slaves that the free coloreds of this colony owned, or the ways they placed values upon them, which would produce this anomalous result.

The explanation for the anomalously high value placed on *bossale* slaves in this sample of free coloreds' slaveholdings is twofold. First, many of the Creole slaves in the sample were quasi-free or bound for manumission. Masters would be likely to keep the reported or assessed valuation of these slaves down in order to reduce the tax assessed on the manumission. Slaves would also have an interest in reducing the reported or assessed value, especially if there was some unspoken or informal agreement for self-purchase between them and their master. In addition, a master might be tempted to make a long-term investment in productive capacity in a slave he expected to keep; although freed slaves were expected to have some skill or resources for their support, it would take an exceptionally generous or well-off master to invest as much in fulfilling this requirement as he would in increasing the productivity of his permanent labor force.

Second, and perhaps more importantly, was free coloreds' cultural attitudes toward their creole slaves. In the African societies from which the free coloreds or their ancestors sprang, slaves were divided into two groups: "domestic" and "trade" slaves.[56] "Domestic" slaves were born in the master's household or village and thus had some rights as junior members of the society; they typically could not be sold without judicial approval and often had rights to work a piece of land assigned to them. They might mutate into a semi-free peasantry over a period of several generations. "Trade" slaves were those purchased from afar. Their rights were much more limited, and they could be put to work directly on the master's land or traded freely in the market. Free coloreds were much more likely to own African-born slaves than were the white plantation owners. The majority of their creole slaves were the children of their *bossales*. The average age of free coloreds' creole slaves was 17.9 years, whereas that of their *bossale* slaves was 28.4 years. Thus, the creoles can be seen as the "domestic" slaves while the bossales were the "trade" slaves, subject to commodification in the market. To the extent that African culture influenced the free coloreds—and in this case it seems that it had a significant influence—the *bossale* slaves fulfilled a different and much more important economic role. They were the more appropriate candidates for specialist training, as their work could be more easily exploited for financial gain within cultural mores. They could be commodified on the market much more easily, and thus their value as stated in a notarial act would tend to be inflated as much as possible (for an act of sale), whereas the creoles' value would be deflated (for an act of manumission).

Among the African-born slaves, the free coloreds seem to have collected workforces composed of the most prized "nations." Free coloreds seem to have owned a higher proportion of the sought-after Muslim slaves than their white coffee-planting counterparts, but they also owned more of the despised English "rejects" (although almost a third of these are Zabeau Bellanton's stock in trade). The Senegambians, favored by Moreau de St. Méry, were more common among free coloreds' holdings than they were in the other two samples (8.2 percent of all slaves owned by free coloreds versus 7.0 percent of plantation slaves in Debien's sample and 6.0 percent of coffee plantation slaves in Geggus's sample). The "idolatrous" Slave Coast slaves, again, were marginally less common in the free coloreds' slave labor forces than on the larger plantations, replicating Geggus's finding that these slaves were less common on coffee plantations than on sugar estates. The possibly suicidal but hard-working Ibos were more commonly found in the hands of free coloreds than white planters.

Debien attributes much of the internal differences in ethnic makeup of the ser-

vile labor forces that he found in his sample to differences in the age of the plantation itself.[57] The coffee plantations, Debien noted, had a much higher proportion
of Congos than did the sugar plantations. He felt this was a result of the relatively
recent development of coffee as a major crop. He cites several plantation records
from the 1750s to show that Congos' share of the slave import market was steadily
increasing throughout the last half of the century. Geggus, on the other hand, gives
some weight to the preferences of the sugar planters, pointing out that those nationalities considered stronger, on average, found more of their men going to sugar
plantations and more women going to the mountains.[58] This may be a result of the
greater buying power of the sugar growers, who could often board the slave ships
when they arrived in harbor and pick out the individuals they wanted in advance
of a general sale.

Since many large free colored landowners frequently got their start in the pre-
1750 period, their labor forces might tend to reflect the distribution of "nations"
common at that time. In fact, referring once again to Debien, Ibos were the most
common "nation" in 1755–57, with the Slave Coast "nations" coming in second
ahead of the Congos, reflecting the pattern found in the free colored slaveholdings
in the sample.[59]

Another factor that would influence both *bossale*-creole ratios and the distribution of African "nations" among the free coloreds' workforces was the relatively
lower mortality and morbidity of slaves experienced by free colored proprietors.
Debien's estimate of 50 to 60 deaths per 1,000 population per year on the large
plantations appears to be much higher than the rate observed among free coloreds'
slaves.[60] Of course, no estimate can be precise, but of the 4,197 slaves appearing in
this sample, 38 are stated to have died during the course of execution of the notarial act. Most of these deaths occurred while the slave in question was leased or part
of an administered inheritance; the lessor or executor was responsible for the price
of the dead slave and thus they were carefully accounted for. There are 153 rental
contracts in the sample averaging approximately seven slaves, for durations of approximately four years. There are 170 disputed inheritances or wardship accountings, containing approximately four slaves each, with durations of approximately
ten years. This admittedly fragmentary data suggests a "background" mortality for
slaves owned by free coloreds of about 35 per 1,000 per year. If fewer slaves died,
bossales would live longer and would thus make up a greater share of the work
force, and the ethnic balance of populations of slaves imported in earlier decades
would persist longer in the free coloreds' workforce than on the white-owned
plantations. For all these reasons, it is not a surprise to find Ibos and the other
older nationalities more numerous among free coloreds' than among whites' slave
populations.

Moreover, free coloreds, as investors with an eye to the long term, could afford to wait for the slaves that they wanted. White planters, seeking quick returns and desperate to increase their workforces as much as possible in as short a time as possible, or at least to stay ahead of their very high mortality, would have to take whatever was offered on the market. It is not surprising, therefore, that white-owned plantations, especially the large number of coffee-growing establishments created in the third quarter of the century, had heavy investments in the supposedly lower-quality "nations."

Slaves were occasionally described in notarial acts by an occupational label. These occupational titles, when they were used, were uniformly complimentary instead of simply descriptive. Thus, no slave would be described as a field hand or laborer in a notarial act. Masters describing their slaves by an occupational title were seeking to enhance the slave's apparent value. Slaves could be given leadership titles, usually *commandeur* (commander, or boss slave). Boss slaves were almost exclusively male in the sample (only one female was described by a leadership title in a notarial act in the sample). These slaves were generally exceptionally valuable. Slaves could also be designated as tradesmen or technical specialists. Most traditional skilled trades were represented among the slaves, such as carpenters, masons, wheelwrights, and coopers. Slaves practicing these trades had often fulfilled apprenticeships with free skilled tradesmen and were qualified journeyman practitioners of their trade, while some, especially craftsmen, were *bossales* who had apparently come from Africa with useful skills. Finally, slaves might be classified as domestic servants of various descriptions. Possession of domestic servants was important for status, but free coloreds owned few, preferring to commit their limited resources to productive workers. Slaves also served in the military, but when this service was mentioned in a notarial act, it was almost always because that slave was being freed. Thus military occupational designators have not been considered at all in this chapter.

Specialist slaves made up about 4 percent of all slaves owned by free coloreds. Of these, about one-half were domestics, one-tenth were supervisors, and the remainder technical specialists. The mean values of the different occupations were 3,520 *livres* for leadership types, 3,162 *livres* for technical specialists, and 2,618 *livres* for domestics. The average for the entire population was 1,751 *livres*. When we take into consideration the fact that the specialists were generally older than the average for the population as a whole, the added value represented by the specialized training becomes even more marked: leadership types were almost two and a half times as valuable as a comparable group of nonspecialists, while technical and domestic slaves were around one and a half times more valuable than a comparable grouping.[61]

The gender ratio was another important difference between slaves owned by free coloreds and the plantation slaves studied by Debien, and, indeed, slaves in the Caribbean in general. About 65 percent of the slaves who crossed the Atlantic were male.[62] The general Saint Domingue slave population was predominantly male—about 55 to 60 percent, depending on the source. Bergad et al. note that females comprised between 40 and 45 percent of the Cuban slave population in their sample, with ratios gradually becoming more balanced during the nineteenth century.[63] Bergad and his collaborators do point out that their records contain disproportionate numbers of sales of female slaves as Cuban masters sought to balance the gender ratios of their work forces in response to a cutoff of imports. This factor exaggerates the apparent number of female slaves by several percentage points when considering only sales contracts, as the authors of *The Cuban Slave Market* do.

It is also true that gender ratios tended to be more equal on smaller *habitations*. Geggus actually found that sugar plantation workforces had gender ratios that were a few percent better balanced than those on coffee estates, but this can be explained by the greater creolization on the sugar plantations.[64] The few sugar plantations owned by free coloreds in the sample employed about 70 percent men.[65] Most free colored slaveholdings were small, and thus one would expect more even gender ratios than on the overwhelmingly male big sugar plantations.

However, even these factors do not explain the marked predominance of female slaves owned by Saint Domingue's free people of color, especially as the sample of notarial acts along with sales contracts contains many death inventories, wills, sales of entire plantations, and other acts in which the reported gender ratio would not be skewed in the fashion Bergad et al. suggest. An imposing 57 percent of *bossale* slaves and an even more surprising 64 percent of adult creoles owned by free coloreds in the sample were female.

Part of the explanation may lie in the relative poverty of free colored masters when compared to white planters. Female slaves were fractionally cheaper and thus perhaps were more appealing to penurious free colored masters. However, the difference in reported price was not marked. Females cost about 94 percent of the price for males in the sample. The price difference may have been greater by a few percentage points in white-owned populations. In Bergad's Cuban populations, prices for males were about 10 percent greater than prices for females between 1790 and 1810 (and were approximately equal after that time).[66] In addition, Debien lays great stress on the shortage of slaves and thus on white slave owners' willingness to purchase almost any slave that was offered.[67]

To fully explain the preference of free colored masters for female slaves, the possibility of African cultural survivals in free colored society must be considered. The preference that African slave owners showed for female slaves has been proposed as one reason for the predominance of men in the Atlantic slave trade.[68] Females increased the slave owner's kin group, goes the theory, serving as wives without inconvenient brothers or fathers, and provided children without divided loyalties in what were often matrilineal societies, while male slaves were potential trouble-makers best exchanged for useful products from labor-hungry Europeans. Thus, female slaves were more valuable than males at the point inland where slaves entered the Atlantic slave trade circuit, so fewer made it to the coast where European records were kept. African values affected slaves' view of the world, as we have seen. To the extent that these values also molded their free cousins' behavior, free coloreds' preference for female slaves is comprehensible.

As demonstrated above, fertility rates of slaves on white-owed plantations were quite low, despite expressions of interest by slave owners in increasing them. In striking contrast, free coloreds' slaves were highly fertile. For 1,072 women aged 15 to 44, there were 316 persons under age 5. Assuming 40 percent infant mortality up to age 5, about the figure for modern Haiti and a reasonable assumption for any eighteenth-century population, this works out to a fertility index of 413 children per 1,000 women, a rather impressive birthrate by Caribbean slave population standards. This compares favorably with Geggus's figure of 356 for coffee plantations 1767–92 and 328 for sugar plantations 1755–91.[69] This figure is even more striking when one considers that a large proportion of the adult population (much larger than on the white-owned plantations) were *bossales*, imported as adults without their children, usually, and subject to disease and psychological stress that would be expected to reduce their fertility. Whereas creole mothers in the sample began childbearing at an average age of 20.3 years, *bossale* women had their first recorded child more than a year later, at age 21.6. Giving up at least one physically possible pregnancy, then, this *bossale*-dominated population nonetheless far outperformed the creole-dominated white-owned plantation slave population in the production of future Haitians.

The steady natural decrease in slave populations as a whole in the Caribbean has led most students of the field to the conclusion that children had little value in the market compared to the cost of maintaining them. Thus, conventional wisdom has it that pro-fertility strategies among slave owners were not economically motivated, at least in the absence of limitations on slave imports. Even in the American South, where slave numbers increased dramatically throughout the first half of the nineteenth century in the absence of legal slave imports, slave breeding for profit was a "myth," according to the foremost economic history of the period.[70]

Applying Fogel and Engerman's logic to the economy of Saint Domingue, it is clear that pro-natalist policies were even less viable economically. An adult creole worker in good health cost between 1,500 and 2,000 *livres* during the period under study. Food for the slaves would be the largest component of their maintenance expense. One act in the sample gives a "market basket" of bulk commodity prices in the colony at a small store owned by a Sieur Guillemet and his free black partner, Marie Josephe, in Fort Dauphin in 1785, a year of peace and (relative) plenty. A sack (of about 20 kilograms) of rice cost 12 *livres*, a sack of beans 8 *livres* 5 *sols*, a pot (about two liters) of cheap cooking lard 1 *livre* 5 *sols*, and a pound of chili peppers 3 *livres*.[71] The weekly ration established in the *Code Noir* for slaves was six pounds of starches and two pounds of salt beef or three of fish.[72] Debien reports that masters usually replaced the meat with beans and oils or lard. Therefore, food for one slave for a year purchased at wholesale by the *grasserie* Guillemet would cost about 175 *livres*. In addition to food, there were secondary expenses such as clothing (the four yards of cloth a year specified by the *Code Noir* sold at the *grasserie* for 5 to 8 *livres* apiece), housing (a new *case à negres* cost about 150 *livres* to build, housed a family of five or six, and might be expected to last a decade before needing major renovation), and medical care. Many masters provided their slaves with provision grounds, expected them to grow a goodly proportion of their sustenance themselves (contrary to the requirements of the *Code Noir*), and used slave labor to produce some of the other goods needed on the plantation, but this calculation at least gives some idea of the cost to maintain a slave, either in cash or in productive capacity lost to the primary crop. Debien has calculated the cost of food from plantation records and came up with a somewhat higher figure, based on better rations given to the first gang workers: he estimated that daily sustenance cost 25 *sols* 6 *deniers* a day, or about 465 *livres* a year.[73] A child's ration would certainly have been less than that of an adult, but how much less is unclear.

Even using the lower figure derived from the sample, raising slave children must not have been financially profitable for Saint Domingue slave owners. A pregnant woman needs to be taken off heavy labor for several months on either side of her delivery and then needs to devote at least a significant minority of her time to caring for her child at least for its first year of life. The child must be fed by the owner from, at the latest, its third year of life until age 9 or 10 before it can begin to make any significant economic contribution to the plantation whatsoever, and the child must reach its midteens before it becomes as valuable as an adult worker. Infant and childhood mortality ran about 50 percent. Twenty or so years of support (taking into account support provided for the children who did not survive to adulthood) at even 150 *livres* a year—about two-thirds of the estimate from the sample for an adult's sustenance or one-third of Debien's estimate—for each new adult worker rapidly becomes unprofitable.

Once again, the non-economic value of slaves to free coloreds must be taken into consideration. Creole slaves, born in the owner's household, in the African paradigm, were junior or second-class members of the household and increased the owner's social position. Thus, a creole slave's value to his free colored master in Saint Domingue cannot be measured in terms of a market price, the more so since it would have been significantly less likely that such a slave would ever enter the market. Indeed, excluding purchases from whites and sales where the objective was the liberty of the slave, only 67 of 249 slave sales contracts performed by free coloreds (26 percent) included creole slaves (and some of these contained a mixed bag of creole and *bossale* slaves), while creoles made up 36 percent of free coloreds' slaveholdings.

This attention to non-economic value of slaves is especially visible when one considers the value ascribed to female slaves by free coloreds. They tended to have more women in their slave labor forces than did white owners. White masters valued women for some jobs on the plantation, but men were overwhelmingly favored for leadership positions. Men also dominated most technical jobs such as sugar refiner, cooper, coachman, carpenter, mason, and other trades that were more or less exclusively male in free society. However, some technical fields were open to women. Indeed, some very valuable technical jobs were exclusively female. The best example is the healing trades—professional medical doctors were all white men by law, but most medical care of slaves was provided by nonlicensed, mostly female, *accoucheuses* (midwives) or traditional medicine practitioners of various descriptions. The term *sage femme,* or professional midwife, was reserved for free birth attendants, but *accoucheuses* who made it out of slavery might aspire to this status. Two appear in the sample: Marie, widow of Pierre, lived in Fort Dauphin in somewhat straightened circumstances, while her wealthier cross-town competitor, Magdeleine Godin, was buying and selling slaves, land, and buildings on several occasions.[74] Thirteen female slaves were described as *accoucheuses*. Their average value was 2,998 *livres*.

Domestic slavery was another way in which women could obtain higher-status jobs, but there were drawbacks to domestic work—loss of privacy by moving from the mostly single-family slave huts to the big house and the possibility of sexual exploitation by their masters. Nonetheless, women served in domestic roles in free colored households in proportion to their numbers in the sample: 48 of 79 domestic slaves in the sample were women. Female domestic slaves averaged 2,427 *livres* in declared value (male domestics averaged 2,925 *livres*).

Among free coloreds, though, it was as mothers that female slaves were especially valuable. Even though it was difficult to get economic value out of slave reproduction, nonetheless free coloreds valued women slaves with children over those without. Adult female slaves averaged 1,922 *livres*. The 539 female slaves who can be identified as mothers were worth an average 2,004 *livres*, despite the fact that their average age was 32 years, past the productive peak, while the average age of all adult female slaves was slightly lower at 30 years. This further reinforces the view that the free colored's slave workforce was assembled for social as well as economic reasons.

MANUMISSION

It is important to study manumission because all free coloreds were either freedmen themselves or the descendants of freedmen. A custom so crucial to the existence of the caste requires our attention.

Family relationship between master and slave was an extremely common reason for manumission, but by no means the only reason. The sample of notarial acts includes acts of manumission for 984 slaves. Of these, 539 were owned by whites and 445 by free coloreds. Half of those freed by whites were persons of mixed race, whereas 73 percent of the slaves freed by free coloreds were black. Creoles outnumbered *bossales* among blacks freed by 267 to 170, with the proportion of creoles being somewhat higher among free colored masters than among whites. Females outnumbered males among the newly free by a ratio of about two to one, with both groups of masters showing the same degree of gender bias. However, whites were freeing mostly women from a slave workforce that was dominated by men, whereas free coloreds freed women in something close to the proportion they comprised of their total slave population. Children accounted for about 40 percent of those freed. About 30 percent of slaves freed by whites were their family members. Among free coloreds, this percentage climbs slightly to 34 percent. In the case of whites, however, all but a few of the family relationships had to be inferred from supporting data, while among free coloreds, almost all of the family relationships were freely admitted.[75]

In the period under study, legal and official manumission was the result of a formal act of donation, performed before a notary. In order to perform such an act, the master of the slave needed to prove title and needed to have special and individual permission from the chief administrators of the colony. Such permissions were routinely granted upon request, but usually masters were required to pay a quite large tax. The standard tax was increased several times during the eighteenth century, reaching 2,000 *livres* for an adult female slave and 1,000 *livres* for an adult male in 1775.[76] The changes in 1775, even though approved by the governors of the colony in that same year, did not actually take effect for some time. Liberty taxes in the sample did not reach the 2,000 *livres* mark until 1781 at the earliest. Liberty taxes in the 1770s averaged around 1,000 *livres* for a female slave and about 500 *livres* for a male, absent some tax exemption or reduction.

These taxes could be waived or reduced for cause. Slaves who had nursed their masters through illnesses, saved them from maroons or rebel plots, or served in the colonial military benefited from tax amnesties. Tax exemption for military service was particularly common in wartime. Influential masters, as one would expect, found it easier to convince the authorities of the merit in their slave's case for a tax reduction. Finally, in cases where the economic value of the slave was very low—for aged or very young slaves and those with crippling illnesses—the tax would often be waived as long as it could be established that the slave had some means of support after manumission.

These taxes appear to have played an important role in colonial finances. Debien attributes the imposition of the 1745 tax in Martinique to "financial exigency."[77] It is unclear what these revenues would represent as a proportion of the total colonial budget. However, if the 1,765 manumissions between 1785 and 1789 cited by Moreau de St. Méry were taxed at an average of 1,500 *livres* each, this would produce an annual average of 529,500 *livres,* which is a healthy 1.2 percent of the 43,236,316 *livres* spent on purchases of slaves in the markets of the major cities of the colony in 1786. It seems from context that this represents only new imports of slaves and not sales between plantations or sales of slaves born on the island. This would also be the wholesale market price and would not include any value added while bringing the slaves to their ultimate consumers. Even so, it is impressive that slave owners would have been willing to spend a noticeable proportion of their budget for new slave purchases on liberating more senior slaves. The figure of 1,765 manumissions from 1785–88 is from Moreau de St. Méry.[78] Julien Raimond claims there were considerably fewer (giving a figure of 204), but because the limited sample used for this book contains 139 for that period and includes about 4 percent of all notarial acts for the period under study, one is tempted to believe Moreau de St. Méry.[79] The average price of a slave in this 1786 report is 1,996 *livres,* while the average price for slaves noted between 1785 and 1789 in the sample was 2,011 *livres*—the tax, at 1,000 to 2,000 *livres* a head, therefore, was at least one-half the price of a new slave, a pretty significant sum for a slave owner, or for a slave in the case of self-purchase.

It appears that manumissions continued reasonably unchecked in spite of these taxes, perhaps because many slave owners successfully evaded the tax. Slaves receiving manumission make up 23 percent of all slaves appearing in the sample for all years, while slaves receiving manumission between 1785 and 1789 make up only 21 percent of all slaves appearing in the sample during those years. This is a minor variation plausibly explained by the fact that slave purchases would be more common, and manumissions thus proportionately less common, even if steady in absolute terms, in peacetime.

Once the tax was paid, the master was free to appear before a notary and perform the actual act of manumission. Often, however, especially in cases of self-purchase, the master would not actually perform the act in person but would grant a power of attorney to a (free) family member or patron of the slave. In fact, the master's last involvement in the case would often be the first step, requesting permission. Particularly after the 1775 "Ordonnance" took effect, raising the taxes and changing the procedures, masters could make their appearance before the notary at the beginning of the process granting irrevocable permission to anyone acting on behalf of the slave to seek his freedom. The permission granted by M. Jean Barthelemy Leclerc, former militia captain and local white elite, to his slave Julienne, *mulâtresse,* and her son Auguste, *quarteron,* to seek their freedom serves as an example of an "irrevocable permission" act.[80] The boy was born in France, so his status was in question. It is unclear if this act was a case of self-purchase or the freeing of an illegitimate son; it cited dutiful service from the mother to the master's wife, including two trips to France. Another "irrevocable permission" case was that of Madelon Guyany, who granted permission to her daughter Therese, aged 50, to seek her freedom; the mother was clearly feeling pangs of mortality (being at least in her late 60s) and wanted to ensure that Therese would not be reenslaved after her death.[81] Same procedure, two very different cases.

The slave would, through a free family member or agent, appeal to the authorities for permission, pay the tax, and officially grant freedom to themselves. This procedure was also common when the master was ill or preparing to leave the colony for France, so use of the "irrevocable permission" form cannot be taken as ipso facto proof that the manumission in question was a case of self-purchase.

However, a significant proportion of the manumissions in the sample were the result of self-purchase or of ransom of a slave by free family members. This occurred despite ongoing efforts by the authorities to suppress the practice, seen as the cause of potential disruptions in the social order. Self-purchase was never outlawed per se, but an appropriate cause aside from mere financial motives had to be asserted in the original request for permission for government approval to be granted, and increased liberty taxes were seen as a disincentive to self-purchase. Once again, the law book serves as a sort of fun-house mirror for society, as the frequency of legislation on a subject reveals the frequency of commission of the offense.

Because of the legislation, cases of self-purchase and ransom were not often labeled as such in notarial acts. Often, even when a slave was freed by an admitted free colored family member who had purchased the slave from a former white master, *bons et agréables services* (faithful service) or some other acceptable motive would still be cited as the reason for the manumission. For example, Barbe *ditte* Léonore freed her godmother, Guittonne, aged 66, in 1780, having obtained her in 1774 from

Mme Dalcourt de Chambellan. She cited "benevolence, friendship, and good services received from the said slave" in the act of manumission, which was granted free of tax in recognition of the advanced age of the subject.[82] Masters and family members were often more frank in the act of purchase of the future freedman. Often, manumission would be made an explicit condition of the sale, to protect the slave against reenslavement if the purchaser's property were to be attached for debt or the purchaser to die before consummating the manumission. For example, militia noncommissioned officer Pierre Amoune sold to his old commanding officer, Jean Baptiste Malic, or Mali, a 9-year-old female creole slave named Marguerite for 1,000 *livres* in 1778.[83] The little girl was described in Malic's marriage contract, though not in the act of sale, as Malic's natural daughter.[84] A condition of the sale was that Malic free the little girl within two years, or the sale would be voided.

Self-purchase remained a significant source of income for slave owners, particularly in bad years. This could reverse to some degree the flow of wealth from whites to free people of color that was a significant part of the economy of the colony during this period. Robert Forster cites the case of the Provenchère sugar plantation in the Plaine du Cul du Sac in which the owner applauds the manager's efforts to sell older slaves to themselves or to their free relatives.[85] In this case, this was one way in which the plantation could get sufficient capital to purchase enough new slaves to overcome losses through high mortality and *marronage*.

Of the 606 notarial acts dealing with manumission, 61 can be clearly identified as being acts of self-purchase or ransom by free family members. Presumably, this significantly understates the prevalence of the practice.

The expense and time-consuming nature of the formal manumission procedure guaranteed that penurious masters would grant their slaves informal freedom, postponing or entirely ignoring the legal niceties. In fact, it is clear from the records that there was usually a long period of time during which almost all freedmen were free de facto while remaining slaves de jure. The example of Barbe *ditte* Léonore, cited above, is only one among many: the godmother, Guittonne, almost certainly did not live the life of a slave during the six years that intervened between her kinswoman's ransom of her from her white mistress and her formal manumission.

Some notarial acts were even more explicit about the granting of temporary quasi-free status. Sieur Arnaud Daignon, master tailor, gave his slave Marie Zabeth Fortin, seamstress, permission to work for her own account in 1784 in order to raise the money for her liberty tax.[86] Demoiselle Rose Vois, widow of Sieur Jean Jude, required her slaves to work for their freedom in her will in 1788.[87] Three of her male slaves were to pay her estate 300 *livres* a year for four years for their liberty, while another male slave, currently an apprentice tailor, was to work for the master tailor overseeing his apprenticeship for two years after the end of the apprenticeship, with his wages going to the estate. A female slave and her two children were to be freed at no charge. All these payments were to be used to say masses for the repose of the Demoiselle's soul, after which the estate was to pay the liberty taxes of the slaves, with the remainder being divided among them.

One of the hazards to the social framework feared by the authorities from the practice of permitting the de jure slave to live as free was the cloak that lent to the runaway slave. The phenomenon of *marronage* is central to the historiography of slave resistance, which rightly sees running away as the most common way slaves resisted or worked to change their status. Colonial society feared the runaway slave, both as a threat to order when operating in bands in the hills and as a threat to the pocketbook of the slave owner.

Of course, the sources used for this book contain very little on this subject. Slaves were not supposed to be making notarial acts. A regulation of 1777, intermittently observed by notaries in the sample, required that proof of free status be presented by all persons of color before they were permitted to execute a notarial act.[88] Many people of color used descriptions of themselves as free in notarial acts to prove their free status in the absence of manumission papers—the marriage contracts of parents were particularly useful in this regard. For example, Jean Maignan used his parents' marriage contract, dated 28/3/61, to prove his free status in a sales contract he executed on Christmas Day, 1782 (Not. 1179n). He must have been alive at the time of the marriage and was merely legitimized by the marriage contract (the age of majority was 25, and there is no suggestion that Maignan was a minor in 1782), hence, the notary in 1782 accepted the word of the notary in 1761 as to his status without any further proof. Many notarial acts, especially in the North province where this regulation was apparently not strictly enforced, do not contain any description of actors' proof of free status. Nonetheless, a person whose titles of liberty were questionable would find it difficult to execute a notarial act, as his reputation would surely be known to someone as highly placed in the community as the notary. On a couple of occasions, notaries did permit persons "living as free" to execute notarial acts, while noting that they had no papers.

Therefore, most of the evidence of the *maron* as well as with the quasi-free in the sample is indirect, through notarial acts performed by owners of runaway slaves.[89] Runaway slaves were mentioned only 33 times in the sample. Most of these were rental contracts or resolutions of inheritances where a slave ran away from someone after a change in possession.

The only significant exception to the rule that runaways did not execute notarial acts that appeared in the sample is very interesting for many reasons. On 14 March 1786, Etienne *dit* La Rivière, a free mulatto butcher, and Pierre *dit* l'Allemand, a free black mattress maker, both from Cap Français, made a deal with Jean-

Baptiste Coutaux *dit* Hervé, a free mulatto planter from the countryside near the small northwestern city of Port de Paix. Hervé's slave, Pierre, had run away some time before, and Hervé had found him living in Cap Français, working as a supernumerary in the *maréchaussée*. Hervé was prepared to take his property back home with him, but the pair who intervened made him an offer he was happy to accept. On behalf of Pierre, who as a slave was legally incapable of making any binding financial commitments on his own initiative, the two paid Hervé 660 *livres* in cash and promised to pay him 396 *livres* more and to give him a newly arrived male slave aged 15 or 16 at the end of the year in return for Pierre's freedom. Hervé agreed to present a request to the government to free Pierre.[90]

This case is an example of the way in which service in the colonial military helped build circles of contacts; it appears here as the exception that proves the rule. Pierre, as a runaway slave, could not execute a notarial act. It was La Rivière and l'Allemand who executed it on his behalf.

The Hervé-Pierre case is also interesting for the light that it casts on the role of the maroon in free society. In this case, the runaway slave was holding down a quite responsible job. The supernumeraries were the bottom rank in the *maréchausée*, but they nonetheless held significant power in the free colored community. There is a certain irony in the fact that Pierre, as a runaway slave, was part of the very organization charged with the pursuit of runaway slaves. Pierre had the ill luck or poor judgment to be somewhere where his old master could find him, doing something noticeable. The case of Maignan shows how flimsy the proofs of free status offered by some persons accepted as free were. It is probable that, for every Pierre who got caught, there were several Jacques who were able to fill roles perhaps less prestigious, but also less noticeable, in free society. With a few notarial acts under their belts, they could become generally accepted as free and could begin working toward a respectable role in free colored society.

THE ECONOMICS OF SLAVE OWNERSHIP BY FREE COLOREDS

The basis of the colony's economy was slave-worked plantations growing tropical staples, principally sugar, with coffee, indigo, cotton, tobacco, and cocoa occupying land not suitable for sugar. These plantations offered economies of scale and rewarded large operators. Most free coloreds owned relatively few slaves. In 27 inventories compiled on the occasion of the death of a free colored person that appeared in the sample, the mean number of slaves owned was 9. Only two persons owned no slaves whatsoever, but the largest reported holding was 40, which would be considered quite small in the world of the white planter that Debien recorded. In one case, the decedent, Nanette Pincemaille of Limonade, actually controlled three quite substantial pieces of land with at least 50 slaves, but they were held in life usufruct with the property rights in the names of her children under the terms of a donation from the white father of her children. She personally owned 16 slaves at the time of her death.[91]

So how was economic value extracted from these (mostly) small slaveholding units? There are several answers. The first was through peasant farming. As an example, there is the household composed of the widow Poupart, Marie Elizabeth, her apparently unmarried sister Marie Thérèse, and their dependents and slaves. The Pouparts had had at least three children, all of whom were minors during the 1770s.[92] They were residents of the peasant village or district known as the Savane de Limonade, which was dominated by free coloreds. The sisters were apparently related to the locally powerful free black militia officer Vincent Olivier. The family seemingly fell on hard times in the 1770s and pawned, leased, or sold a number of slaves, appearing a total of 24 times in the notarial archives between 1778 and 1788. In 1783, Marie Elizabeth died, and the sisters' remaining possessions were carefully inventoried.[93] They owned 7 slaves at the beginning of this process, seemingly the venerable Pierrot, already introduced above, and a family composed of a father and mother, three children, and an unrelated woman or second wife. Nothing in the records suggests that the sisters were anything but peasants, although they always maintained the fiction that their holding was an *habitation*, or plantation. Their home was small and sparsely furnished, according to the inventory. No standing crops or stockpile was noted in the inventory or in any earlier transactions related to the land. It would have been highly unusual to have overlooked any cash crops in an inventory, sale contract, or lease of a plantation. In any case, the family did not have enough land for a profitable plantation: their so-called *habitation* totaled 8 *carreaux*.[94]

The Pouparts were only one example of a commonly overlooked phenomenon in Saint Domingue slavery: the slave-owning peasant household. The small agricultural operator, growing mostly for the subsistence of the family and its slave dependents, was a common figure in the colony's countryside. He or she would perhaps produce a small surplus intended for the retail market, where it would be sold alongside the surpluses from the slave provision grounds from which the farm would hardly be distinguishable. The slaves on such a farm could not truly be considered capital goods, since they came to their owner in most cases through donations and were neither intended for the market themselves nor principally producing for the market. If we work from the example of the modern Haitian *restaveks*, or child servants, the existence of a substantial precapitalist rural slave economy, which may have duplicated African conditions at the time pretty accurately, can be deduced.

Peasants who prospered in the rapidly growing economy of the third quarter of the century could aspire to a large enough presence in the market that they became capitalist farmers. A good example of this process would be the half-brothers Laurent and Charles Durocher. In 1779, the brothers enlisted in the Chasseurs-Volontaires de Saint-Domingue to fight at Savannah in the War of American Independence. They both made their wills before departing, and it was clear from these documents that they lived at a quite modest level, although, like most wills, theirs contained no detailed inventory of property.[95] Laurent's only bequest was to a white neighbor to purchase the freedom of his two children, still slaves of his former master. If his estate did not suffice to buy the slaves and pay their liberty tax, they were to be bought by the patron and permitted to work on their own account to raise the liberty tax. Charles had no slave children, so his will took care of their (or only his?) mother and another brother, both slaves of their former master, with the provision that the mother was to be given priority if the estate did not suffice to obtain liberty for all. From this evidence, presumably, neither brother's net worth exceeded about 6,000 *livres*. By 1785, the brothers were capitalist farmers. In that year, Laurent rented an *habitation* with an unspecified number of slaves and 6 *carreaux* of good land for the princely sum of 1,800 *livres* a year. Part of the payment was in the form of personal property of good quality, including furniture made of high-status *acajou* wood worth 3,300 *livres*.[96]

These rags-to-riches stories were not uncommon in the colony. However, the free colored planter families of the planter elite in many cases had already achieved this level before the time under study. Michel-Rolph Trouillot's "Motion in the System" and John Garrigus's "Blue and Brown" show the way free coloreds came to have an important role in the development of secondary crops in the mountains of the colony around midcentury.[97] These landed elites benefited from many of the economies of scale available to their white counterparts. In addition, they were much more likely to be resident on their plantations and thus avoided administrative overhead, and they also had other competitive advantages over white planters.

Finally, small-scale slave owners could benefit in some degree from the economies of scale available to large plantation owners by renting their slaves to their economic superiors. Slave rental contracts were relatively formalized by this time. The standard contract was for a duration of five years, although there was a wide range. The rent was usually between 10 and 15 percent of the assessed value of the slave per year. All charges—food, clothing, housing, medical, head taxes—were typically the responsibility of the renter. If the slave died, ran away, or lost value in some way during the lease period (excepting a natural decline in value through age, it appears), the renter would bear full responsibility. The generosity of these contracts says much about the shortage of labor in the colony.

Rental contracts were very attractive to small, free colored proprietors, and 159 leases for slaves appear in the sample. As already suggested, it was the large-scale white landowners who were the most desperate for manpower, so it is not surprising that in 73 of these cases free coloreds rented slaves to whites, while in only 14 cases is the white the owner and the free colored the renter of the slaves.

Renting slaves to a wealthier or more entrepreneurial neighbor was a way free coloreds could ensure themselves an income without the necessity of peasant farming or the risks of getting into planting for the market. One often sees the mixed-race child of a white planter renting the slaves given the child by the father right back to him or to one of his neighbors.

Of course, the rental completely commodifies the slave and rejects any non-economic value the slave might have for his or her master. Inventories, wills, and marriage contracts were very careful to list and describe all slaves that were the subjects of rental contracts, specifically because property rights to them were not backed up by public recognition—that is, the "master" of the slave, as far as society was concerned, was the renter, not the owner. It was the renter who got the credit in white society for having the slave, where social position among planters was often determined by the size of the slave workforce. In free colored society, a slave rented out to a relative or neighbor did not increase the household of the owner, nor did he or she bring nearly the social *éclat* of a slave who could be put on display. Thus, those free coloreds most concerned about the non-economic values of their slaves would also be the most likely to work them themselves as opposed to renting them out: only 20 of the 159 rentals of slaves feature a member of the planter elite as the lessor, and in a number of those cases, the lessee is a family member.

The ultimate commodification of the slave was when he or she was traded in the market. Saint Domingue was absorbing tens of thousands of new slaves a year by the 1780s. Curtin estimates the French exports from Africa at 271,500 for the period 1781–90 and calculates that about 75 percent of this traffic was going to Saint Domingue.[98] Assuming a mortality rate of 5 percent, as he does for this period, some 25,800 slaves were entering the colony each year after the end of the War of American Independence. The census for 1786 reported 21,652 arrivals at the four main ports that year. An added unknown number of imports were made by smugglers and would not have been recorded in the census.[99]

Almost all of these new official imports were purchased and resold upon their arrival by one of a number of French mercantile houses, such as the house of Stanislas Foäche described by Debien in his book on their sugar plantation.[100] The only large free colored merchant was Vincent Ogé, and there is no record of his house participating in the wholesale slave market.

Free coloreds would become involved in the slave market at a lower level, either as retail purchasers of the imported slaves or as future owners and traders at some later point in the slave's career. Free coloreds owned a higher percentage of *bossales* than did whites. And although the non-economic value that slaves had for free colored masters was important and would impel them to keep their slaves off the market, it is clear that free coloreds were frequent users of the slave market, both as buyers and as sellers.

The net flow of slaves into the hands of free colored is clear from the table. Free coloreds in the sample bought 139 groups of slaves (of varying sizes) from white sellers for an average value of 7,755 *livres* per group, which works out to 1,077,945 *livres* worth of slaves moving from white to free colored owners. At the same time, free coloreds sold whites 205 groups of slaves, with an average value of 3,267 *livres* per group, which works out to 669,735 *livres* worth of capital moving from colored hands to white. The relatively large average value of free coloreds' purchases from whites was a result of many large transactions both with plantation owners, who were sometimes the buyers' relatives, and with the merchant houses in the major ports. Even leaving aside donations of slaves from whites to free coloreds, which outnumbered the reverse by a substantial majority, the reader can see the steady flow of capital from white ownership to free colored ownership that was one of the defining economic facts of the colony during this period.

Many of these slaves purchased by free coloreds went to work and remained employed on their masters' estates for years. Since free coloreds' slaves had lower mortality rates and the planters were generally more efficient businessmen for reasons explored in later chapters of this book, they generally made above-average profits and often sought to expand their workforce.

Whites needed slaves, and free coloreds were sometimes prepared to sell. Most sales to whites, like sales between free coloreds, were of small lots of slaves—typically, an individual slave or a single slave family. Small sales such as this seem to have been more expensive per individual slave for the purchaser than purchases of large numbers of slaves at a time from the large white-owned mercantile houses. Unfortunately, since many of these sales were barter transactions or included credit terms that varied widely from sale to sale, a precise evaluation of the extra profit free coloreds were able to extract from white purchasers through these small sales is impossible. In any case, the free colored seller had absorbed the expenses of "seasoning" during the first couple of years of a slave's working life in the colony and so deserved a higher price for his slaves than the big merchants for theirs, who were mostly right off the ship.

The 205 acts in the sample of slave sales from free coloreds to whites include 22 pawns. Slaves were very commonly pawned—their high rental value, especially on short-term contracts, meant that the lender could recoup at least 20 percent on his investment, and the risk of loss would be limited to the amount loaned, usually no more than half to two-thirds of the market value of the slave. Some pawns of slaves were accompanied by rental contracts where the pawned slave would be rented back to the borrower; these contracts were always for exorbitant rents. In a typical example of a pawn of a slave, Jacques Coidavy, a free black militia non-commissioned officer, pawned his slave Marie Therèse Celine, 12 years of age and a member of the Fond "nation," to a white retail merchant named Pommeau in 1786. Coidavy received 330 *livres* in forgiveness of outstanding debt and 660 *livres* in cash and had to pay 24 *livres* 15 *sols* a month rent to Pommeau for the four-month life of the pawn in order to have the use of his slave.[101] This comes out to a 30 percent annual return on Pommeau's investment, pretty good even for boom times in Cap Français. A rule of thumb for slaves under 16 was that they were worth about 100 *livres* per year of age; even if one considers Marie to be worth 1,200 *livres,* this rent is still about one and one-half to twice what she would fetch on the open rental market, while the pawn price was at most three-fourths of her market value.

Pawning a slave was not necessarily an act of economic desperation, though. We have seen how Zabeau Bellanton used it to share the risk of "seasoning." Coidavy performed five notarial acts related to pawns in the sample: three pawns of slaves and two recoveries of pawns. Like Bellanton, but on a much smaller scale, he commonly bought inexpensive slaves, often quite young *bossales* like Marie Therèse, off the slave ship, pawned them quickly, and used the capital to purchase more slaves. If a permanent buyer came along for one of his pawned slaves, he would pay off the loan, recover the pawn, and then sell the slave, often at a significant profit. The lender in the pawn deal bore most of the risk of the "seasoning" of the slave, although perhaps children were less at risk than adults from the new disease environment.

CONCLUSION

Free colored masters owned slaves who were different in many ways from those owned by their white neighbors. Their behavior toward their slaves was also different in many ways from that observed among their white neighbors. Why was this? Was it only because of the economic role—as small coffee planters—that free coloreds played in the colony? Or must cultural explanations be considered alongside economic ones?

The reader can discard the notion that racial solidarity led to a generalized benevolence toward their slaves on the part of free colored masters. Many free coloreds owned large numbers of slaves, and almost all benefited, directly or indirectly, from the slave system. Many, like Zabeau Bellanton, were capable of callousness toward slaves that rivals that of the whites. They appear to have been willing enough to profit from the labor of the African-born slaves. It is only toward the creoles that they behaved anomalously—in some cases, at least. Free coloreds were more likely than whites to grow up on their plantations and thus to have formed close personal relations with their slaves from an early age. However, this tendency would seem to be outweighed by the much greater frequency with which white men formed sexual unions with their slaves. Their resulting tendency to free both mistresses and offspring illustrates at least one form of personal relationship between master and slave that free colored masters do not seem to have engaged in to any great extent.

At the time of the French Revolution, free colored political activists appealed to French republican sentiments of equality by laying claim to their "Frenchness."[102] Moreau de St. Méry, while clearly holding the racial prejudice against free coloreds that almost all the whites in the colony shared, nonetheless attributed some bourgeois values to the free coloreds and perhaps saw them as verging on whiteness. The whole ideology of whitening, seen in perhaps its purest form in *hispanidad* in the Dominican Republic or in Brazil in the early years of this century, has as its core idea that "white blood"—or cultural values—would overlay and suppress African and native American ones. The free colored in a slave society, cut off from the majority African culture by familial or clientage ties to whites, by class prejudices and interests, and by status, would seem to be the best candidate for a quasi-total "whitening" of values. However, one possible explanation for the differences between the behavior of free coloreds and whites as slave owners is the persistence of African cultural values among free coloreds.

In general, free coloreds owned more *bossale* slaves, were more willing to sell them than their creole slaves, and also were more ready to give them training in hopes of increasing their value. Similarly, they were more willing to manumit their creole slaves than were white masters. This data is subject to a number of explanations. Free coloreds' slaves lived longer, and so high-valued *bossales* would stay on the plantation's roster longer. In addition, they were more fecund. This would tend to redress creole-*bossale* ratios—both in the skilled trades and in the population as a whole—in fairly short order. Many establishments owned by free coloreds had been in business for many years—longer than those of many whites—and yet they continued to show the preponderance of *bossales* at all levels. This suggests, as the evidence bears out, that free coloreds were liberating their creole slaves at a very high rate.

It would be going too far to suggest that free coloreds were consciously aping

African models of slavery. Clearly they were not—the most cursory study of the literature on African slavery in the eighteenth century demonstrates this.[103] Cultural influences on behavior are much more subtle than that. Free colored masters would simply have had a different set of nearly unconscious assumptions and priorities when deciding which slave to buy, which to sell, which to send off as an apprentice or to promote to a skilled position, and which, if any, to consider for manumission.

In addition, part of the explanation for the observed differences between free coloreds and whites as slave owners lies in the *mentalité* of the free colored planter. The free colored planter—especially the most wealthy who owned the most slaves —emulated, more or less consciously, the French aristocrat of the *ancien régime*. As the real French nobility was hesitantly becoming more bourgeois—seeking to increase profitability of estates through new agricultural techniques, finding socially acceptable ways to invest in manufacturing or trade, even participating in republican revolution like the young Lafayette—the free colored planters of Saint Domingue, with the fervor of the *converso*, were yielding to nobody in their conservatism. Meanwhile, white plantation owners in Saint Domingue were often from bourgeois backgrounds and valued profit above all else. Thus it was that free coloreds were more willing than their neighbors to wait for the most valuable "nations" when purchasing *bossale* slaves. Looking at slaves as long-term assets in a quest for social acceptance instead of labor units producing quick bonanzas might have driven them to provide better living conditions. This would contribute to the observed lower mortality and higher fertility among free coloreds' slaves. A feudal sensibility might also go some way to account for their unusual tenderness toward their creole slaves.

Both of these proposed explanations can be no more than guesses and are offered here in the hopes that others will evaluate and build on them. What is clear from the data, though, is that free coloreds owned a significant minority of the slaves in the colony. They treated those slaves very differently, both on a personal and an economic level, than did their white relatives. The explanation for these differences is elusive but does not lie wholly in differences in the role free colored slave owners and their labor forces played in the colony's economy.

CHAPTER SIX

Landholding Practices

Sieur Thomas Peignanan, a sugar planter originally from Bordeaux, made his will in 1782.[1] He wanted to leave his sugar plantation to his *menagère* (housekeeper) of twenty-five years, Julie Dahey, a free Creole black, and her (presumably their) seven mulatto children. He had a legitimate heir in Bordeaux, however, his sister Catherine. He willed all his personal property, a quite luxurious collection of furniture, household utensils, jewelry, clothing, and so forth, to Dahey directly. Then, he left the plantation and slaves to his sister with the condition that she be required to lease the property in perpetuity to Dahey for 25,000 *livres* a year in peacetime and 15,000 *livres* a year in wartime. This appears to have been a more-or-less reasonable rent for a developed large plantation, although there is no exact inventory in this case.[2] He included the proviso that if the sister attempted to contest the will, she was to be struck from the succession and replaced as universal legatee by two of his white neighbors, who, one presumes, could be counted upon to make sure that his children got their rights. Later in the year, seemingly uncertain about the strategy he had adopted, he recast the will, granting 12,000 *livres* to Dahey and 3 slaves of their choice to each of the children, with life tenancy in the slaves to Dahey.[3] The average value of adult slaves in 1782 in the sample was 2,179 *livres*. Twenty-one slaves times 2,179 *livres* plus the 12,000 *livres* outright cash gift to the mother works out to an estimated value of 57,759 *livres* for this bequest. It is unclear what the value of the original bequest might have been—there are too many variables, from the business climate to Dahey's skill as a plantation manager. Slaves and cash could have been invested safely through rentals or loans or could have set Dahey up in business as a middling capitalist farmer, without, of course, the burden of that 15,000 to 25,000 *livres* a year payment to the sister in Bordeaux. The same provision protecting the colored heirs by threatening the white heir with removal from the succession appeared in the second will.

Foiled in this first attempt to become a sugar planter, Dahey tried again in 1781. She rented at least 75 *carreaux* in the *Plaine* near Croix des Bouquets to four white men in 1781, land that she had gotten as a grant from the government—presumably with the support of her patron, Peignanan, although this is, of course, nowhere stated. The lease was to last for twelve years, longer than the traditional seven, and was for a quite modest 600 *livres* a year (suggesting a value of about 80 *livres* a *carreau*, quite low for flat, undeveloped, irrigable land in Croix des Bouquets). However, the renters were obliged to construct a sugar mill and a number of other structures, build irrigation canals and live fences, and leave 40 *carreaux* in growing sugar and 4 in food crops at the end of the lease. Dahey reserved 25 *carreaux* of the original 100, and 4 "inches" of water, for her own market garden for the duration of the lease.[4] In 1793, at the expiration of the lease, Dahey expected to be a sugar planter, and in the meantime, she could live fairly comfortably on 25 *carreaux* of irrigated land and 600 *livres* a year in cash.

This was not her only income, as she apparently owned a coffee plantation with 30,000 coffee bushes growing on it in the mountain district of Pays Pourri near Croix des Bouquets that rented in 1779 for 3,600 *livres* a year.[5] She also operated a pottery and roofing tile manufacturing facility, which eventually failed during the War of American Independence but generated substantial income in the years before that. The story of this enterprise is told in the 1782 act of dissolution of the partnership between her and Sieur La Bacheliere.[6] Dahey's story is unusual for the scope of her undertakings, but it illustrates many characteristics of the free coloreds' attitudes toward landholding. They were entrepreneurial, to a point, but also longed for the stability of landed wealth. They hoped to gain both wealth and social cachet from their land holdings. There were significant differences between the planter class, to which Dahey belonged, and the military class, on all these levels.

This chapter first looks at agriculture as it was practiced by free coloreds in Saint Domingue. The primary vocation of the colony was agricultural. The production, and basic processing, of tropical luxury crops, particularly sugar and coffee, provided the economic raison d'être of the colony. Participation in these industries, either directly or indirectly, was almost the only way to advance economically.

The second half of the chapter considers the free colored landowner, and in particular how free coloreds obtained land. In addition to considering questions of market value of land, this section looks at how non-economic values of land were extracted. The colony of Saint Domingue, while well developed by the standards of Caribbean island colonies, nonetheless contained large expanses of land that were relatively unexploited by plantation agriculture.[7] Settlement of these remote areas was still underway at the time of the Revolution; land values varied widely from place to place and could change sharply from one year to the next. This variation provided a fertile field for speculators of all colors.

The free colored families who became wealthy coffee planters in the 1770s and 1780s mostly had their roots in relationships between white men and free colored or slave women in the 1750s or before. Julie Dahey and her family got into the game late, but they permit us to observe the process as it must have worked in earlier decades. Many of these families received gifts of land and slaves from their white forebears, with the land often located in remote areas not suitable for sugar but eminently appropriate for coffee when the coffee boom came. Additionally, many of the white inhabitants of the colony in the 1760s, 1770s, and 1780s, the *petit blanc* class who were trying to make their fortunes in the coffee boom, were not natives but instead newcomers who came in a wave of white immigration after the end of the Seven Years' War. The established white sugar-planting families were generally less enthusiastic pursuers of coffee wealth, having already achieved success in another field. The fact that the free coloreds were mostly native to the island and that the planter elite among them were tied in, often through family relationships, to high levels of white society, while the white immigrants were often poor and not well connected, meant that the free coloreds had easier access to good land in coffee-growing regions than did their *petit blanc* competitors. As long-term residents with good knowledge of the territory, free coloreds were well positioned to do well in the land market, and many did.

The French colonization of Saint Domingue, to recap, started in the North province on the island of Tortuga and then spread on the mainland plains along the north coast, driven by colonial governors in the seventeenth century who wanted to provide an alternative industry to freebooting and hunting of wild cattle. Next were the coastal plains around Léogane, Saint Marc, Gonaives, and Archaye, as the sugar boom took hold in the colony in the first half of the eighteenth century. The South province and the area around Port-au-Prince were developed around midcentury as sugar took over almost all the land that was suitable for its cultivation— flat, well watered, close to water transport. It was during this period that free coloreds became a significant proportion of the colony's population, and they were well positioned to participate in the third wave of internal colonization after 1760.[8]

The mountains of the colony had been neglected until midcentury, thanks both to lack of a suitable crop and the presence of aggressive bands of runaway slaves. Once the commercial properties of coffee were demonstrated by daring investors, the maroons were exterminated, driven out, or bullied into treaties that kept them quiet, and the extensive highland regions of the colony were opened to settlement by plantation owners and their slaves.[9] Coffee quickly came to rival sugar as the colony's most important agricultural crop (although never surpassing it). Coffee can grow on land with sharp relief and does not need irrigation or extremely fertile soils. Coffee land was significantly less expensive to develop and use than was sugar land. Coffee bushes are pretty good at competing with or coexisting with weeds of various descriptions, do not require much extra watering, and can grow on (and stabilize the soil on) very sharp relief. Their cultivation does provide economies of scale but not so strongly as does sugar, permitting an investor to start a coffee plantation with much less capital than a sugar planter. Trouillot estimates the startup cost of a sugar plantation as six times that of a coffee establishment.[10]

Free coloreds were important beneficiaries of the coffee boom. Rumors of fabulous wealth brought many whites of modest means to the colony, especially after the end of the Seven Years' War. These young men (as they were, for the most part) hoped to become wealthy coffee planters, but they found, in many cases, that the free coloreds were there before them. Free coloreds who had acquired poor mountain land—by donations or inheritance of the 'back ends' of their white relatives' plantations or by government concession to them as the pioneers who cleared the land—in the 1750s and before had turned this land into coffee plantations in the 1760s. There were 106,570 *carreaux* in coffee in 1780, according to the census of that year.[11] Free coloreds in the sample controlled 3,459.84 *carreaux* in coffee for at least part of this period, and the sample includes about 4 percent of all notarial acts in the colony's registers during the period 1776–1791. Thus, an estimated 80,000 of those 110,000 *carreaux* came into or passed through free colored hands during the period, or about 70 percent, while they made up less than half of the free population. There was still plenty of land and plenty of demand for coffee in France, but the new immigrants were fighting an uphill battle against free colored proprietors who had already acquired an important share of the market. This competition led to considerable friction between free coloreds and poor whites, with political repercussions in the form of discriminatory legislation in the 1760s, 1770s, and 1780s. None of the legislation dislodged the free colored coffee planters from their commanding position atop the hills of the colony, though—they grew wealthier during the 1770s and 1780s.

Aside from expansion into formerly waste land in the mountains, another source of new land available to white and free colored proprietors in the third quarter of the century was valley land brought under irrigation. The expansion of sugar into the Port-au-Prince area and the plains of the South province around Torbeck was made possible by irrigation, as was a considerable expansion of the arable land around Archaye and in the valley of the Artibonite River. This was a method that was less profitable to free coloreds, as they often lacked the substantial capital needed for construction of irrigation canals and dams. There were a few exceptions: the Daugé family of Croix des Bouquets was one. They used water rights coming to them as landowners (albeit of rather poor land) in the Grande Rivière de Cul de Sac watershed in the parish of Croix des Bouquets to irrigate several hundred *carreaux* that they owned and to turn themselves into sugar planters. Much more common, though, were the free colored proprietors who sold or leased land and water rights to white investors who had the capital to develop the land. As an example of this process, in 1779, Marie Magdelaine Guiot *dite* Plaisance sold 12 *carreaux* and 7 *pouces* of water (inches of irrigation pipe or ditch, presumably) to Sieur Victor Antoine Pere Deshormaux, a prominent local planter, for 6,000 *livres*.[12] Five hundred *livres* a *carreau* was a quite respectable price for that parish and time, but far less than what Deshormaux would have had to spend to develop the property.

LAND VALUE

Land was classified under several categories in notarial archives, corresponding to its utility for agriculture and its level of development. Evaluating land by these descriptions is difficult. This is true both because plantations were often sold or rented as a unit but contained parcels of land with different descriptions, and because land values fluctuated sharply on other variables: distance to market, access to water, anticipated fertility, relief, and a host of other factors. Nonetheless, the descriptive categories employed by the notaries and their customers have some analytical value if only because they were so frequently used and seemed to mean a good deal to the participants. Therefore the following is an attempt to attach cash values to the descriptive terms. Let us look at the most common of these categories.

The least valuable category of land was *hallier*, or brush, indicating land that had been cleared for agriculture but had been allowed to regrow. This is in contrast to fallow land, usually referred to as *savane*, which was kept clear even while not cultivated. Land described as *hallier* varied widely in value, depending on its location, access to water, and so on. This description was used 24 times in the sample. Values ranged from 91 *livres* per *carreau* to an anomalous 720, with the mode being around 125.

Some *hallier* might have been useful for grazing, especially for pigs, but mostly pastureland was kept cleared for larger animals and termed *corail* (corral) or *parc à bêtes* (pasture) depending on whether it was fenced or not. Keeping pasture clear, of course, is simple as long as the livestock are kept on it, but the initial clearing would be a laborious task. Unfenced *corail* was often priced much like *hallier*. These descriptive terms were used 26 times in the sample. The lowest-valued single piece of land in the sample was described as *corail*, at Double Montagnes at the head of the Grande Rivière de Cul de Sac. The place was very large at 225 *carreaux* but sold for a mere 2,040 *livres* in 1785.[13] At 9 *livres* a *carreau,* it was practically given away. The same pasture had been bought in 1778 for 4,000 *livres,* and since that time the maroons of the area had made peace with the authorities, so one must suspect either overgrazing or considerable degradation of what infrastructure there was.[14] Most *corail* land was somewhat more valuable than this, though, and the mode is about 80 *livres* a *carreau,* varying between 50 and 100 depending on access to water.

Fencing added considerably to a piece of land's value, as the fence itself was expensive both in labor and, increasingly as wood became scarce, in materials. Live fencing with hedges came to be a favored alternative to wooden fencing as wood became in short supply. Woodland with useful timber on it, or *bois de bout* (the term suggests native or old-growth forest but seems to have been used for mature second growth as well) was valuable in proportion to its local scarcity. Near towns, woodland was sometimes more valuable than cleared agricultural land. Acts of sale and rental of land often contained stipulations regarding the right of one party or another to cut wood, either for sale or for agricultural needs, and stockpiles of cut timber and construction wood feature prominently in many notarial acts. For example, in 1786 in the remote and still forested parish of Mirebalais, Jean Baptiste Alexis Bremond (formerly known as Bourbon) and his wife, free coloreds, sold 50 *carreaux* of mixed cropland and *bois de bout* to Sieur Jacques Penide.[15] An explicit condition of the sale was that the sellers were permitted to cut fence posts, shingles, and planks on the land. The term appeared 101 times in the sample. *Bois de bout* varied widely in value depending on its location and the conditions imposed on its sale or rental, but it seems to have averaged about 350 *livres* per *carreau* colonywide, with extremes of 100 *livres* per *carreau* in another sale in Mirebalais and 1,029 in Grande Rivière in the highly developed North province.[16]

Generally, the term *savane* was used for agricultural land developed but not currently under cultivation. In some cases, *savane* seems to have been a somewhat less-pejorative term for *halliers.* More generally, agricultural land was referred to as *jardin* or *place.* The *jardin* of a plantation might take up only a quarter or less of its total area but was by far its most valuable land. The value lay in the growing crop, of course, and varied widely by what that crop was. On the 225-*carreaux* piece of pastureland at Double Montagnes in Croix des Bouquets, the 1785 purchaser found some *jardins.* However, they were described as "old," and no standing crop was reported—suggesting that the 1778–85 owner tried to live as a peasant on the land, probably letting most of it return to *halliers,* although it retained its description as a pasture in the act of sale—descriptions were often copied verbatim from previous notarial acts.[17] The 1785 purchaser sold half of the land to a neighboring white *habitant,* including the *jardin,* in return for the price of a survey of the land, which had not been done since before 1778. The public surveyor might charge up to 1,000 *livres* for his services on a large piece of land. However, it is clear that in this case, the value of the land described as *jardin* was only marginally greater, if at all, than the wasteland that surrounded it.

On the other hand, well-maintained land in cash crops could be exceptionally valuable. A plantation in Limbé, composed of 32 *carreaux*, half in coffee and half in *bois de bout*, with 3 slaves, rented for 3,500 *livres* a year in 1788.[18] While the officially approved rate of interest on overdue loans was 5 percent, based on metropolitan French conditions, notaries in the colony generally calculated reasonable return on investment in land rentals at 10 percent, so this plantation was worth 35,000 *livres*. Deducting 6,000 *livres* as the declared value of the 3 slaves and 8,000 *livres* as the assumed, and liberal, value of 16 *carreaux* of *bois de bout* leaves 21,000 *livres* for 16 *carreaux* of growing coffee, or 1,312 *livres* a *carreaux*.

Sugar fields were even more valuable. The Baugé heirs rented their land to their brothers to be turned into a sugar plantation.[19] The brothers got the land rent-free for seven years, during which one assumes they were to be setting up the sugar plantation they were obliged to establish by the terms of the lease. By the end of that time, they were to have established six fields of 4 *carreaux* each in sugar cane, for which, for the remainder of the lease period (two more years with an option to extend), they were to pay 3,600 *livres* a year. That works out to an assumed value of 1,500 *livres* a *carreau*, among family members. Anne Françoise Roy brought a sugar plantation to her marriage with René Nicolas in Croix des Bouquets in 1779.[20] Her plantation of 163 *carreaux* and 40 slaves rented for 15,000 *livres* a year plus the requirement on the renter to make some improvements. While the precise size and value of the *jardin* in this act cannot be ascertained, the average value of the 163 *carreaux*—wasteland and pasture as well as sugar *jardin*, was 492 *livres* per *carreau*. The term appears 50 times in the records.

Land was also traded in urban areas. Often, the land traded would have a building of some sort on it, and the value of the building would typically far exceed the value of the lot, so it is sometimes difficult to determine the value of undeveloped land. A number of acts were for undeveloped plots, though. From these, we find that the average value of urban land ranged from 0.07 *livres* per square foot in Mirebalais to 0.76 *livres* per square foot in Cap Français. Average lot sizes varied from 4,037 square feet in Mirebalais to 14,389 square feet in Croix des Bouquets.

The anomalously high price of land in Croix des Bouquets, at 0.46 *livres* per square foot, and the low value for the much larger and faster-growing metropolis of Port-au-Prince, at 0.28 *livres* per square foot, require explanation. Clearly, the government's willingness to permit expansion of the urban area must have had an impact on land values in that area. Croix des Bouquets was not supposed to be an urban area at all. Government policy was to concentrate urban services in the region in Port-au-Prince, with the exception of a parish church. The government did not award small urban lot-type concessions in the area around the church; instead, local landholders resold portions of their agricultural land for urban development. Without free government donations to encourage urban development, the cost of land there was artificially inflated. On the other hand, the government was encouraging the expansion of Port-au-Prince during this period and had just created (in 1770, after a major earthquake) the "New Town," granting hundreds of new lots throughout the 1770s. The low value for Mirebalais was also an anomaly: defined as a town because of its status as a capital of a *quartier* and given free government land, it was nonetheless a very small urban area, and several of the ten undeveloped "lots" in this parish that appeared in the sample seem to have been gardens rather than being reserved for development as urban building lots. The expansion of Cap Français was hindered not by official reluctance but by geography; the city is located on a narrow strip between the bay and a steep hillside leading up to the 2,500-foot Cape Mountain. The city could expand only to the south and only with difficulty as there was considerable swamp land that first needed to be filled in during the eighteenth century.[21]

An important secondary use (after agriculture) to which landowners put their land was to be the site of structures. These structures were useful—providing shelter against the elements, offering defense against potential enemies, and housing important equipment necessary for agricultural entrepreneurship. Of course, buildings also have non-economic value. Houses luxurious and otherwise were important markers of status in Saint Domingue society as well as being capital goods.

Buildings defy easy categorization. Construction standards varied widely. In the countryside, most buildings were wattle and daub with thatched roofs. Better-quality houses might be made of whole logs, palm or hardwood, and in exceptional cases, there might be plank walls and a ceiling covering the thatch on the inside. "Bricks" were occasionally used, although whether this term referred to fired bricks or adobe is unclear. *Briques de Provènce* were clearly fired bricks imported from France, while ordinary bricks could be anything. Haitians and west Africans today use adobe, so it is not unreasonable to suppose that their ancestors knew the technique also. Bricks were often used for flooring in better-quality buildings. Buildings with pretensions might have roofs made out of shingles or even tiles from France. In the towns, wooden construction was more common, and only the lowest class of house used mud construction. Concrete made an appearance in the city, often mortared over bricks. Stone construction was the height of luxury but was uncommon outside of Cap Français, where fire regulations required it for new construction throughout the period under study.

Buildings used as primary residences could be humble: the *case*, or hut, owned by the widow Poupart and her sister in 1783 was 30 feet by 15, wattle and daub, and was appraised at 150 *livres*.[22] They could also be spectacular: Vincent Ogé brokered a deal for a house on the corner of the rue d'Anjou and the rue du Cimetière in Cap Français in 1785. The building was built out of masonry, had three main rooms, a *cabinet* (smaller room), a kitchen with oven and chimney, and a separate apartment upstairs (servants' quarters, apparently) with two more rooms, a paved courtyard, and another kitchen and some other outbuildings at the end of the courtyard.[23] He leased the place from its white owners for 13,500 *livres* a year and sublet it for a profit of 1,320 *livres*. In European context, the Duc de Saulx-Tavanes, a wealthy and powerful member of the sword nobility, paid 7,320 *livres* (Tournois, or 10,980 *livres* colonial) rent on his Paris townhouse in 1787.[24]

ACQUISITION AND TRADING OF LAND

Land, and its acquisition, were crucial parts of the economic strategy of everyone who lived on the island, from the slave in his provision-ground garden to the greatest planter in her sugar plantation. As the last chapter showed in the case of slaves, land was also moving quickly from white to free colored hands throughout the period under study.

Donation of land was a common method by which land moved into the hands of free coloreds. Fathers of illegitimate persons of mixed race discharged their obligation to provide for their children's support through giving them land. Gifts of land, often in combination with slaves, were one of the more common categories of notarial acts in the sample. It is hard to ascertain the precise value of these donations. Estimated land values throughout this book were calculated based on values of land revealed through acts of sale or rental for the most part. Occasionally a precise value could be ascertained for land involved in an act of donation, most often when the recipient sold or rented the plot. These values were included in the overall calculations of estimated land values found elsewhere in this chapter.

Grants, of course, ran the gamut from tiny to immense, but most were of sufficient size to support a family and employ a couple of slaves. A half-dozen *carreaux* or even less would suffice if the land were suitable for fields producing food crops. The census of 1780 found 67,319 *carreaux* in food crops, supplying a total population of 282,000, or an average of slightly less than one-quarter *carreau* per capita.[25] If grazing was to be the primary activity, 25 to 50 *carreaux* of *corail* might be needed for a subsistence herd: the 1780 census found 118,167 *carreaux* of pastureland for 253,239 sheep, pigs, cattle, and horses, or about one-half of a *carreau* per head.[26] Someone trying to make a living from livestock would have to have at least 50 head of animals. The average size of all rural land donations was 31 *carreaux*.

Donations had an important social meaning in the context of a father's responsibility to his illegitimate offspring. It turns out that 62 out of 146 donations of land in the sample of notarial acts were from parent to child. Most of the remaining donations were within the kin group, often between unmarried partners, although there were a couple of cases of non-kin donations that were probably part of an exchange or sale that was not explicit in the notarial act. Whites were the donor in 54 cases and the recipients in 12 others, while in the remaining 80 cases, the donation was from one free colored to another.

The law discouraged donations by whites to free coloreds, as this was seen as a route through which capital was flowing out of white hands and into colored hands. The Louisiana *Code Noir* of 1724 forbade free people of color to receive *any* gift or legacy from a white person.[27] This law code was never formally accepted by the courts of Saint Domingue, but Moreau de St. Méry included it in his *Loix et Constitutions* because many of its provisions became customary law in Saint Domingue as well as other French colonies. As is clear from numerous struggles during the eighteenth century in metropolitan France between *parlements* and royal authority, the fact that the law court failed to enroll a royal decree did not necessarily mean that that act did not become part of the law. In any case, this legal provision demonstrates the state of feeling of the metropolitan government and, one presumes, its representatives in the colony, on the subject of donations to free coloreds.

However, donations from whites to free coloreds were rarely overturned in colonial courts. Donors were, almost by definition, people with resources to spare. Wealth mostly translated, in this society dominated by capitalist agriculture and commerce, into influence over government. Donors were also, by definition, alive at the time the donation took effect (otherwise we would call it an inheritance). Therefore, they could defend their actions personally, should the gift be called into question by the authorities or family members.

Bequests to free coloreds, on the other hand, were occasionally challenged in colonial courts by white heirs, but even then with only indifferent success. On 5 October 1775, for example, the Conseil Supérieur du Cap Français found in favor of the illegitimate mulatto sons of Charles Hérivaux, deceased in 1770, who had been willed two coffee plantations in the North province, totaling 348 *carreaux*, 240 slaves, 30 head of livestock, 80,000 coffee trees, and "certain other buildings and utensils."[28] These items came into the mulatto sons' possession only after a drawn-out lawsuit. Although unique in the sample for its scale, their success as heirs was repeated many times in the courts of Saint Domingue. Colored heirs were not guaranteed to receive what had been willed them, but in the struggle between racism and the unrestricted property right of the testator, property rights generally had the upper hand. A few examples will serve to demonstrate the trend.

In 1778, the (presumed) illegitimate sons of Sieur Gilbert Viau, real estate developer in Cap Français, named Jean and Jean Baptiste, came to a settlement with their white step-mother and half-sister, also resident in Cap.[29] The deceased had willed the two young men a *pension viagère,* or living allowance, of 1,800 *livres* a year shared between them—a quite substantial sum. This would have been a good salary for a plantation manager or other professional employee. Viau's legitimate family, living in Cap Français, had appealed to the lower court that the will was inequitable since it left them insufficient means to support themselves. The court reduced the colored children's allowance to 1,200 *livres* a year. The legitimate Viau heirs, who seemed to accept that some provision would have to be made for the two boys, offered them 3,000 *livres* in cash and a seven-room masonry house on 5,120 square feet of land on the rue du Lion, in a mixed neighborhood in Cap Français. The free colored heirs accepted, stipulating that all legal costs were to be borne by the legitimate family. It was quite common for *pension viagère* bequests to be fulfilled by the executors with a grant of some capital good worth something like ten years' worth of living expenses, or 18,000 *livres* in this case. This house was worth an estimated 15,000 to 25,000 *livres,* as similarly sized houses in Cap were going for at least that much at this time.[30] In this case, the free colored heirs seem to have gotten something close to, or even a somewhat better deal than, what their father had intended for them, and in the form of a concrete asset that would give them status and permit entrepreneurship instead of a simple cash dole.

White heirs who were not present in the colony had even less power than the Viau women to argue with free colored heirs who were in Saint Domingue. The Conseil Supérieur de Port-au-Prince ruled twice on similar cases where white heirs in France contested legacies by deceased whites to free coloreds, in 1782 and 1784.[31] Both were for moderate sums, 6,300 *livres* in 1782 and 24,000 *livres* in 1784. In both cases, lower courts ruled that the legacies were appropriate, and the higher court rejected the white heirs' appeals.

Nonetheless, on occasion the heirs in France would prevail. In 1781, M. le Vicomte Maille obtained an order in a metropolitan court to compel one Roger Auguste, a free colored, to turn over property illegally willed to him by his presumed father, M. le Roux, which should have gone to the Vicomte as the husband of le Roux's daughter.[32] One presumes that the nobility had an easier time of it in *ancien régime* courts, especially in the metropole.

In order to avoid any chicanery by metropolitan heirs, white testators would often make an alternate bequest to a (white) neighbor or friend that would take effect if a particular bequest to a free colored heir was challenged. Such a provision appears in the will of Thomas Peignanan, introduced at the beginning of this chapter.

Another inventive tactic adopted by white testators was to disguise the bequest as repayment of a debt. Debts of an estate had to be paid by the executors before bequests could be satisfied, so the rights of the colored heirs would thereby be even more securely guaranteed. Quite frequently a white testator would declare that his *menagère* was owed many thousands of *livres* as back wages for many years of service. In addition, testators in this situation were often careful to state in the will that some important pieces of property were actually owned by the children or *menagère*. As an example of both of these processes, there is the will of Sieur Léonard Simiat, *habitant* of Croix des Bouquets. He stated in 1781 that he owed his employee Louise, a free black, back wages of 600 *livres* a year for three years and, in addition, that she had loaned him a further 1,800 *livres* on various occasions. He also said that she owned 2 horses that were housed in his stables.[33] It appears that he had a falling-out with her the next year, because at that time he made a codicil to his will denying the debts that he had formerly acknowledged and alleging that she was required to serve him for the remainder of his time in the colony—thereby revealing the true character of the former bequest.[34]

It appears that inheritance of land followed the same pattern as donations; that is, grants ranged in size from sufficient for a peasant family and a couple of slaves at a minimum up to enormous plantations and hundreds of slaves. Specific description of the land transferred often awaited the death inventory, frequently absent from the notarial record. The wills generally referred to pieces of land transferred to free coloreds as *places,* or *habitations;* both terms suggest complete agricultural operations, small or large, and not subdivisions thereof, which would be described as *morceaux de terre, jardins, emplacements, champs,* or similar terms. Land was not an indispensable component of provision made for one's illegitimate children in a will, but, as in the case of the Viaus, even when the testator originally specified cash, the heirs would often get real estate—indeed, one gets the impression that they generally *preferred* real estate, for social reasons and because they trusted in their own ability to extract value from capital assets.

Another way free coloreds got land was by buying it. Free coloreds were active participants in the land market. Land acquisition could be part of a long-term strategy of capital acquisition. Free coloreds also bought land for short-term speculative gain, especially during the great economic boom of the 1780s.

It should not surprise us that total value and unit value of land transactions were higher in the major cities, as these were the places the wealthy and powerful of all colors came to buy and sell capital. Thus, Cap Français had a total of 104 land sales including free coloreds, with an average value of 12,651 *livres.* Rural land sales in Cap Français (a parish with only a few square miles of rural land) had an average size of 205 *carreaux* and an average value per *carreau* of 845 *livres.* The average value for the whole sample was 5,793 *livres,* while the average size for all rural land sales was 84 *carreaux,* with an average price per *carreau* of 279 *livres.* Many of the largest of these transactions obviously refer to high-valued property located in other parishes. Mirebalais was a very isolated area and thus had a higher proportion of the high-valued transactions carried out before the local notary than did those areas that were closer to the large cities. Almost 40 percent of the rural land sales in the sample were registered in Mirebalais. Croix des Bouquets is an interesting anomaly, with the highest average size of rural land transactions of any parish in the sample at 222 *carreaux,* perhaps because sugar growing was very strong there during the period under study. The enormous value of the sugar plantations traded would tend to push up the average value and size of land sales there, even if the very biggest transactions were still reserved for the notary in the big city.

The proportion of urban plots traded that were undeveloped suggests the balance between "improving" and "speculative" uses of the urban landscape. An "improving" urban landlord would obtain a piece of land, either through purchase or government grant, develop it, and rent or sell it, while a speculator would be more likely to obtain undeveloped land on the outskirts of town cheaply and sell it, still empty, when the wave of development reached it. Cap Français, an older town, had a lower rate of this sort of speculation than did Port-au-Prince, with 61 percent of Cap's urban land sales being of developed properties, as opposed to 38 percent in the case of the capital. In rural areas, it was harder to determine how significant any improvements made on the land really were.

Characteristics of sales of land differed markedly between racial categories. Sales by whites to free coloreds were just about as common as the reverse (25 and 26 percent of the sample, an insignificant difference), but the average value of sales by whites was much greater (10,640 to 5,473 *livres*). Once again, as with slave-related transactions, the reader can see the pattern of crucial capital goods flowing from white hands into free colored ones through the market to supplement the important flows through inheritance and donation. This was a very important social trend that might provide an explanation for the nervousness of the colonial government about the growing power of the free colored population.

The proportions of land sales made by white sellers, made by colored sellers, and between two free coloreds were not notably covariant with the racial balance of the free population but instead remained remarkably stable throughout the period studied. This suggests that the economic interdependence of whites and free coloreds in the colony was affected not by the growing size of the free colored population but perhaps by other factors. The two parishes where the proportion of sales from free coloreds to whites was largest, Fort Dauphin and Croix des Bouquets, were parishes where the pace of transformation of plains into sugar plantations was highest during the period under study. The places where sales between racial categories were least common, on the other hand, Limonade and Port-au-Prince, were places where coffee was strong, and the few sugar plantations there were old and well established (in Limonade in the northern plains and in Port-au-Prince along the south shore of the Cul de Sac River). Whites were the most likely to sell to free coloreds in Mirebalais, a place on the outskirts of both agricultural transformations, and one where the white population was stagnant, while the free colored population was growing rapidly.

The number of years a piece of landed property was held before it was sold suggests whether the seller used that piece of land in a speculative or improving way. Free coloreds in general held their land for much longer than whites, suggesting that they were increasing its value before commodifying it as well as seeking non-economic value in being landholders in preference to transient monetary profits from being land speculators. Whites, on the other hand, often speculated in land —getting government concessions to develop unoccupied land and then selling it very quickly, often to free coloreds, or snatching a quick profit from a piece of developed land and then selling out, with the eternal dream of returning to France with full pockets.

The label of *habitant* (implying a gentleman farmer, above peasant scale) meant a lot to free coloreds of all economic and social levels. The widow Poupart and her sister, relatives of black militia captain Vincent Olivier, were, in the economic sphere, typical of peasant farmers with a couple of slaves. Nonetheless, the surviving sister, Marie Therèse, was careful to have her farm defined as an *habitation* in the death inventory of her sister, Elizabeth.[35] André Poupart, Elizabeth's husband, did sell 4 *carreaux* to a neighbor in 1779.[36] Obviously, this sale was the result of economic distress and was followed by further economic collapse. However, from the time of André's death in that year until Elizabeth died in 1783, while the sisters sold a half-dozen slaves and rented out portions of their land, they never sold another inch of land. It seems to have been the least dispensable part of their capital. This is despite the fact that Limonade was experiencing considerable economic growth during the period, and they probably could have gotten good money for their plot. Land in Limonade had the highest average value per *carreau* of any of the rural parishes. Instead, the sisters preferred to keep living on the portion of their land they had not rented to neighbors, making a subsistence crop with their remaining slaves and clinging to the title of *habitantes*.

It is clear that landholding had important non-economic value to free coloreds of all economic levels. Non-economic values of capital goods, especially of land, had an enormous value for the planter elite. But next door to the Laportes, Raimonds, and Chavannes, their peasant neighbors loved their land just as much.

Many free colored peasants in Saint Domingue who managed to acquire title to their land hung on to it for generations. The longest-held pieces of land in the sample were invariably those pieces conceded back in the first half of the century to a free colored proprietor who grew a small amount of food and maybe a few coffee bushes. The government even recognized this non-economic value when the intendant de Liancour proposed in 1781 that no liberty should be approved by the government unless it could be demonstrated that the newly freed person would own at least a small amount of land to support himself.[37] The proposal was not adopted by the minister of marine, but this suggests the way the high officials of the colony, the people responsible for approving petitions for manumission, saw landholding among free coloreds—not only as a hedge against indigency but also as a way to create a landed small farming class who might then find their interests connected to those of the gentlemen farmers through economics *and* status.

Renting a slave to another sacrificed the non-economic value of that slave: renters had to be careful in wills and death inventories to list all slaves rented out lest title to them be lost. Similar logic did not apply to renters of land. The lessor of a piece of land did not necessarily sacrifice all the non-economic value associated with land ownership. Renting land to small peasant occupiers was a traditional part of land ownership in rural France. "Respectable" landowners were supposed to let their land out—operating it oneself, in the metropolitan context, was a step down, and scientific farming was the next worst thing to engaging in "trade." Even if the power relationship was more equal, or tilted in favor of the renter, the owner was still an *habitant,* while the renter was a speculator of somewhat suspicious gentility. This was one of the curses of rural development in early modern France, as entrepreneurial tenants were not rewarded either socially or financially. It can even be argued that the act of leasing one's land to another converted the peasant into the more respectable landlord, or at least solidified the right to the title. For instance, the Poupart sisters had rented out their paltry 8 *carreaux* in 1779 and still rated the honorific title.[38] To the extent that free coloreds, at any social level, had adopted the *mentalité* of the French rural landholder, the *mentalité* that they would have learned from white ancestors and from education in France, the route to "respectability" for them lay specifically in renting their land out, even to white planters. Rental of one's land to another was a socially appropriate as well as potentially financially rewarding choice.

Let us look, then, at some general characteristics of rental contracts in the notarial archives. Value of a lease contract has been set, for the purposes of this analysis, at ten times the annual rent unless the value of the property was otherwise stated in the act. This conforms to practice at the time in estimation of the value of land in cadastral surveys and death inventories. This appears to slightly undervalue the land when compared with what it would have fetched on the market, but the evidence for this conclusion is not sufficiently strong to overturn the notarial practice of the time in estimation of property values.

Overall, the West province, and especially Croix des Bouquets and Mirebalais, had the most valuable rental contracts. These two parishes averaged over 24,000 *livres* per contract, while the colony-wide average was around 20,000. Rural land was the subject of about two-thirds of all rental contracts. The average size of rural land rental contracts was 34 *carreaux*, with a range from 6 in Limonade to 70 in Croix des Bouquets.

A significant number of rental contracts imposed improvement conditions on the renter that clearly added value to the lease without allowing estimation of this value for statistical purposes. For example, in 1777, M. and Mme de Chambrun, acting through their agents in the colony, rented 40 *carreaux* of mountainous land from their *habitation* in Mirebalais to Louis Blanchard *fils*, a *quarteron* son of their neighbor Sieur Louis Blanchard, for seven years.[39] The land appears to have been undeveloped at the time of the rental. Blanchard *fils* was to pay his landlords 1,200 *livres* a year in rent and, in addition, was to construct on the land a three-room principal residence, four slave huts, and an indigo refining facility with all its hardware. In addition, he was required to leave the land with 6 *carreaux* planted in indigo, 3 in yams, and 1,500 hands of bananas standing, and to hedge all the fields. This represents a substantial improvement, probably increasing the value of the land by much more than the 8,400 *livres* in cash rent that Blanchard had obliged himself to pay during the life of the lease.

Such practices were common in cases where free coloreds rented their land to white lessors. Julie Dahey's second attempt to become a sugar planter in 1781, related at the beginning of this chapter, is an outstanding example. This sort of contract can be seen as a commitment by the owner to the long-term value of the land, since immediate return on investment was sacrificed in favor of long-term improvements. Free coloreds were more likely to impose such conditions on white renters, in fact, than whites upon colored renters; 24 percent of rentals of land by whites to coloreds included such charges, while 34 percent of rentals by free coloreds to whites were in this form. These sorts of contracts cannot be evaluated and must simply be counted at their stated cash value, even though this leads to an undervaluation of the real cost of renting land.

Undeveloped urban land was almost never rented, and so there are no reliable figures on value per square foot in the rental market. Urban rentals, at least among free coloreds, were generally for developed land. There were usually sections of towns, at least the large towns, where free coloreds congregated for residential purposes, although there is only fragmentary evidence of official residential segregation. Free coloreds owned quantities of land outside these areas, but they were generally investment properties.

Many rentals of urban property were not the subject of notarized acts. Short-term rentals were common, as can be seen from secondary evidence. For example, in 1788, former Chasseur Volontaire Jean-Louis Robineau had to apply to his brother Jean-Baptiste for assistance with his living expenses. Jean-Baptiste promised to pay Jean-Louis's landlady, Rosalie *dite* Duperrier, 241 *livres* 5 *sols* 3 *deniers* for six months' back rent.[40] There's no sign of a notarized rental contract in the sample, and the original act does not refer to one. Several of the entries in the cadastral survey refer to "various renters" or describe the property as "lodgings."[41] However, only 3 of the 129 rental contracts for urban real estate were for periods of less than a year.

From the fragmentary evidence that does exist, it is apparent that short-term rentals were a potentially very profitable way of using urban real estate. At the top end of the scale, Vincent Ogé, acting for an absentee white proprietor, rented out three apartments in very fashionable sections of town.[42] These apartments were rather small, typically one large room and a hall or antechamber. They were well located and perhaps intended to serve as business premises instead of, or in addition to, residences. The rents ranged from 198 to 375 *livres* a month. These are quite important sums. Houses in the wealthier section of town would contain four or more large rooms, hence each of these rentals was at most a quarter of a house. The most valuable house in this neighborhood in the sample sold for 64,000 *livres* in 1784; anyone who could count on receiving 1,000 *livres* a month in rents for such a house would be realizing a rate of return on investment of at least 20 percent.[43]

But it was not only people at the level of the Ogés who made high profits on short-term rentals of urban land. Sieur Pierre Arnaud, a merchant with a shop on the Place de l'Intendance in Port-au-Prince, rented two *cabinets* (small rooms) in wood in the courtyard in back of his shop to one Marie Thérèse, free black, in 1785, for 36 *livres* a month.[44] The value of the land is not easily determined, but constructing small wooden buildings was relatively inexpensive. These were a mere seven feet square each and could not have cost over 500 *livres* to produce. Sieur Arnaud, to the extent that he could keep his rental property full, would have realized a truly princely 85 percent annual return on the cost of building these shacks.

Short-term leases, of course, had the drawback of lacking stability—36 *livres* a month for those outbuildings would be nice, if one could get it every month. Of course, there is no way to estimate what occupancy rates were, except inasmuch as the sale and rental price of urban property is suggestive of demand—high in Cap and Croix des Bouquets, deflated in Port-au-Prince.

There were other drawbacks to short-term rentals. In 1785, former Chasseur-

Volontaire Fabien Gentil, who appears again in chapter 11, leased a rather large house to a white man, a *Sieur* Edouard Niort or Niord, described as an *aubergiste* (innkeeper). The house must have been fairly well located if it was to serve as an *auberge;* in any case, Sieur Niort was willing to pay 2,000 *livres* per year for a term of three years.[45] However, the house came with an unexpected tenant—a Sieur Anbossy, almost certainly a single white man, who was residing in one of the rooms of the house and who refused to vacate. The lease included no mention of his rights, and Gentil declared that Anbossy's tenancy had run out some time before and he had been asked to leave. He had refused on several occasions to move out, though. Niort tried to nail Anbossy's door shut, but Anbossy caught him at it. He threatened to beat Niort; then he went into Niort's home and "mistreated" his wife, who had to protect herself with a stick. Niort and Gentil brought the whole matter before the local courts by making out a declaration before a notary of the facts of the case, which they presented to the *sénéchausée* of Cap Français on 9 February 1786.[46] As is common in such cases, there is no record of the outcome. However, it gives an idea of the kind of trouble that tenants could make for landlords in short-term rental situations. One presumes that the presence of the irascible Sieur Anbossy was one motivation to Gentil to put his building on a long-term lease to a white man who might have a better chance in the courts.

If we compare the average value per *carreau* of rural plots rented with similar data on plots sold, we can see that, like urban plots, rural land was more likely to be developed when rented. The average value of rural land in rental contracts was 634 *livres* per *carreau,* while for sales contracts the average was 279 *livres.* Some rental contracts specified further improvements as a condition of the lease, but on the whole, the lessor was most likely to seek steady income from land he had already put into production. The improving tenant was a rarity throughout the French world, and the world of Saint Domingue's free colored landowners was no exception.

In the West province, especially Croix des Bouquets, the coffee and sugar booms were putting more and more land into production during the period under study. For this reason, in these parishes free coloreds were the most likely to be renting their land to whites—both the number of such acts and their average value was much higher than in the other parishes. The average value for white lessors in Croix des Bouquets was 65,636 *livres,* more than twice the colony-wide average of 23,970 *livres.* The average value for all leases in the sample, regardless of race of participants, was 18,638 *livres.*

In the big urban market of Cap Français, whites seem to have been the lessors more frequently than in other parishes. This is no doubt an artifact of the increased proportion of white lessors in urban leases as a whole: whites executed 26 percent of urban rental contracts in the sample as opposed to 20 percent of all leases. The rental market in Cap was dominated by urban real estate business to a much greater extent than that of Port-au-Prince, reflecting the much more extensive rural hinterland included within the borders of the latter parish.

Notarized leases were for land within the parish for the most part. This is in sharp contrast to land sales, where large trades were quite often executed before a notary in a nearby large city. Land rental contracts, as more evanescent documents, were perhaps not seen as so crucial to either party's social standing or requiring the special skills of an urban notary. Of the 134 rental contracts executed in Cap, only 5 were for land outside the borders of the parish, and of the 52 contracts in Port-au-Prince, only 4 were from outside the parish limits.

Aside from donation, purchase, or rental, another way free coloreds often gained legal rights to the soil was through government concession. The colony's government claimed all land within its borders that was not already settled by Frenchmen at the time of the formal establishment of the colony at the end of the seventeenth century. In return for a minimal fee, this land was given to any person who promised to develop it. Grants could be of any size but were typically blocks of considerable size: units of 100 *carreaux* in the countryside of Port-au-Prince, Fort Dauphin, Limonade, and Croix des Bouquets and as much as 225 *carreaux* in the upper Artibonite around Mirebalais. Recipients of concessions were required to survey the land and place boundary stones. The surveyor's fee could be substantial and perhaps even greater than the undeveloped value of a piece of land. Wimpffen has described the process in his *Voyage:* "with enough fortune (for effectively, there is no plantation without capital), he [the newcomer] can start his plantation. The first expense, which I estimate at three to four thousand *livres,* would cover the concession fee and the surveying. His first step should be to reconnoiter in person, accompanied by his surveyor, the land conceded, to ensure that it had not been previously ceded to another, which sometimes happens. . . . he must then set border stones, to avoid all discussion with his neighbors."[47]

He then goes on to explain the process of developing the land for agriculture, clearing it, planting food crops to feed the slaves, acquiring a work force, planting the cash crop, obtaining water, and other necessary duties. This was clearly a time- and capital-consuming process, which many small operators could not afford. For this reason, many concessions of land that appeared in the sample did not result in the creation of plantations but instead in the development of a small subsistence farm, to satisfy the government regulation that the land be worked, surrounded by a vast expanse of scrub land used, perhaps, as marginal pasture. Some conceded plots remained in this state for many years. For example, Jean François *dit* Dramanne sold 13 *carreaux* to his neighbor, the white *habitant* Sieur Charles Dangoise, in 1787, for 858 *livres*.[48] This works out to 66 *livres* a *carreau*, which is quite low-valued land—less than half the average value per *carreau* even for remote Mirebalais. No improvements were mentioned in the act of sale. The land had been conceded by the government to Jean François in 1752.

Conceded land was often resold rapidly and without any significant effort to develop it, however, despite government regulations that the concessionaire must develop the land himself. In 1781, Marie Louise Descaline of Limonade, free black, sold an urban lot in the village of Embarquadaire de Limonade to Sr. Jean Baptiste Vasques.[49] She had been conceded the plot in the spring of 1780 and had built what is described as a "ruinous" *case*, or hut, on the land to satisfy the letter of the regulations, but it is clear from the price (600 *livres* for 720 square feet) that the buyer's interest in the lot was in its potential as a construction site and not the presence of any small outbuilding. The price was somewhat higher than average, so perhaps he gave her some credit for the wood in the hut as building materials.

Free coloreds occasionally went ahead with agriculture and construction without having legal title to the land. This took place in that shadowy world inhabited by the quasi-free slave or the maroon, and indeed it was these persons who were frequently the squatters. Almost by definition, squatting cases rarely appear in the notarial record. However, Wimpffen's advice to the new proprietor to check his conceded land carefully to see if any piece of it had already been conceded to someone else suggests land title was never too clear.

Often, surveys of pieces of land would reduce or increase their supposed size by enormous quantities. Battles over property lines are a feature of Haitian rural life to this day and were no less troubling in colonial days, so the definition of squatting was often very dependent on the situation and with whom one was talking.

An example of marginalization and questionable land titles is offered by the story of Pierre Perodin and Sieur Navarre.[50] Perodin, a free colored, was a coffee planter in the hills of Dondon until 1780, when he seems to have run onto hard times and perhaps also have provoked the hostility of a powerful white neighbor, Navarre. Their story first appeared in the sample in a 1781 act, a report from the *maréchausée* when they paid Perodin's farm a visit during a sweep for runaway slaves. They were armed with a complaint by Navarre that accused Perodin of harboring "bad sorts" and of having sold his slaves and having ceased to work his plantation. Failing to work the land conceded to him would have threatened his land title. In any case, Navarre claimed that the horses kept by one of Perodin's "bad sorts" were wandering on his, Navarre's, land. Perodin had taken one of Navarre's slaves, he claimed, without good title. Several of the people living there, according to Navarre's claim, had dubious titles of freedom. The Chevalier de la Puisaye, *maréchausée* officer for the parish, and his detachment of *cavaliers* came and took several of these people away, although they did not arrest Perodin. Letters from other neighbors supported Perodin and his dependents, leading to a suspicion that Navarre's complaint was an attempt to divest Perodin of his land. The slave that Perodin supposedly stole, said the neighbors, was actually originally Perodin's or perhaps belonged to one of his dependents on the farm and had been taken by Navarre without good reason. The Chevalier concluded his report with a recommendation that Perodin and two of his dependents be dismissed with warnings and another "bad element" living with Perodin should be expelled from the *quartier*.

This story shows us the social importance of being able to refer to oneself as a planter. Although the dispute with Navarre obviously had a long history, Perodin, as an *habitant* with slaves and cash crops, had never been troubled by the *maréchausée*. It was only when he ceased production and sold most of his slaves that he entered the shadowy netherworld of the squatter and the quasi-free, and his title to his remaining slaves and land came into question.

CONCLUSION

Free coloreds were important players in the land market in the colony. They both bought and sold land, and they were often recipients of inheritances and donations of land from white relatives or patrons. Since their sales of land were generally small and their purchases large, in combination with the gifts received, their share of the colony's landholdings increased sharply over the time under study. When one takes into consideration the growing share of the colony's slaves that they possessed, it is clear that they were a very significant and growing presence in its economy.

Nonetheless, typical landholdings were small. The free colored was, in general, a more careful and knowledgeable planter than his white neighbor. However, there were economies of scale in plantation agriculture, even in the coffee business, and in this sense, anyway, free coloreds suffered under a handicap *vis à vis* their white competitors.

CHAPTER SEVEN

Entrepreneurship

The la Bastide family of Croix des Bouquets, military leaders who reappear in chapter 12 of this work, launched its family fortune with a gift from a white man, possibly the father, although this is hazier even than such things usually are, to two young mulatto men named Pierre and Joseph la Bastide in 1755, just after their liberties became final. They received a piece of land in the hills between Mirebalais and Croix des Bouquets.[1] From these humble beginnings, the la Bastide brothers built a substantial collection of real estate, both urban and rural, located in three parishes. In a notarized agreement in 1778, Pierre, the older brother, formed a partnership with a white man to operate the original piece of land as an indigo plantation. In a reversal of the usual pattern, this plantation was to be operated by the white man, who invested "sweat equity" to make up for la Bastide's greater contribution of land and slaves.[2] The brothers also grew coffee and indigo in Mirebalais, and they ran cattle and owned urban properties in Port-au-Prince and Mirebalais.[3] The brothers were not as well supplied in land or slaves as the greatest free colored planting families, owning about 400 *carreaux* of rural land of varying quality, no more than a dozen urban lots, at least four of which were undeveloped, and no more than 50 or 60 slaves. Nonetheless, these men were living quite comfortably and could have great confidence in the long-term safety and growth prospects of their investments. They were producing two different important cash crops, coffee and indigo, and, in addition, were producing food to satisfy the great appetites of the growing sugar plantations of the Plaine de la Cul de Sac, which lay between their different pieces of land. Moreover, with investments in urban real estate, they were well positioned to supply the housing needs of a free population growing at some 5 to 6 percent per year. Absent a colony-wide catastrophe, the la Bastide family fortune was assured.

The last chapter covered the acquisition and trading of land. This chapter turns to the entrepreneurial use of land, defined as the aggressiveness with which owners sought to extract economic value from their land and their willingness to sacrifice its non-economic values for economic ones. Free coloreds varied widely in their entrepreneurial use of the land. Many remained very small agricultural operators, adopting the attitudes of peasants toward their land. That is, they preferred to hold land for long periods of time, as they held their slaves. They produced primarily for their own consumption and only secondarily for the market; they were connected to the capitalist market in tropical cash crops in only a very tenuous way. Some free coloreds who rose in economic status above the peasantry began to use the land and their slaves very aggressively, trading rapidly on the market, leasing capital goods that they needed, seeking to maximize the economic return on their property. It was at this economic level that free coloreds often left the countryside and began to operate in the cities, saving money for the day when they might once again return to the countryside, this time as *habitants* instead of as mere peasants. In contrast, the planter elite tended to use their assets more conservatively even during the early stages of their careers.

This chapter also considers the urban entrepreneur and the link between urban and rural free colored populations. The tendency to maximize economic value of assets at the expense of non-economic value—part of entrepreneurship—is most marked among urban free coloreds in the colony. At the same time, urban free colored populations were significantly younger, more likely to be childless, and less likely to be married. It does not seem too much of a stretch to suggest that these variables were connected. Young, single free coloreds moved to the city to seek their fortunes. As middle age and parenthood set in, those who had achieved some reasonable facsimile of a fortune moved back to the countryside and, having something to conserve, became conservative.

Thus, although free coloreds were perhaps pursuing non-economic goals, both in slave and land ownership, it was important for them to make money and to be seen making money. Luckily, as a group, free coloreds were pretty good at making money. They were not the largest capitalists on the island, but they were among its most successful.

RURAL ENTREPRENEURSHIP

Colonial observers laid great stress on the fragile nature of the fortunes obtainable though tropical agriculture. Wimpffen devotes two chapters to revealing the "fragility of colonial fortunes" and exploding the "myth of the Dominguan millionaire." "Believe me, Monsieur, when I tell you," he says, "there is no country where individual fortunes are less solid [than Saint Domingue], and . . . nowhere where wealth and happiness are less synonymous than they are here." [4] Similarly, Brueys d'Aigalliers reported that the (white) colonists of the French Antilles, seemingly as wealthy as Croesus, were actually bowed under a weight of debt and disaster and were no more than "ill-at-ease" at best. [5]

The merchants of La Rochelle, reports Robert Forster, routinely had to write off loans to impecunious planters in the colonies who could not repay their debts. Abandoning the colonial trade for landowning in rural France not only was to the social advantage of the merchant family he studied, but it was also a wiser use of their capital than continuing to do business with the sugar barons of Saint Domingue. [6] Paul Butel described the wealth of the colonial planter as "fragile . . . in the face of climatic catastrophe, and even worse, market fluctuations which left him without any real possibility of reaction. . . . the social history of the Antilles from the Seven Years' War to the Revolution is perhaps more strongly marked by the confrontation between merchants and planters than by that between masters and slaves." [7]

Free colored agricultural entrepreneurs occasionally failed, also. Families as different as the Chavannes and the Pouparts of Limonade (the former the family of free colored rebel Jean-Baptiste Chavanne and the latter family the relatives of black militia captain Vincent Olivier) suffered major economic setbacks during the period under study. Certainly Pierre Perodin, victim of *maréchaussée* raids and the harassment of his neighbor, was not going up the economic escalator in the late 1770s and early 1780s. However, these stories attract the chronicler's eye because they were exceptions. The general rule, at least for the middling to wealthy free coloreds who appeared in the notarial record, was of steady success.

The Laporte family, whom we met at the beginning of chapter 1 and whom we encounter again in chapter 8, were among the upper ranks of the planter elite in the 1780s. The family launched its fortune sometime in the 1750s when the first Louis arrived in the colony as an immigrant from France and settled down to farm coffee according to the model put forward by Wimpffen. A few years later, after a first marriage to a white woman of modest property ended with her death, leaving him with one son, this Louis Laporte married a free colored woman who owned undeveloped land in the area where coffee growing was starting up. A couple of other pieces of property held by the family in the 1780s had been conceded to the ancestor by the government during the 1750s and had been handed down. [8] Other pieces of land came to the family through purchase or more recent concession, as they capitalized on their favored position as one of the first to get into coffee production to become an important force in the regional market by the 1780s. By the mid-1770s, they had no close white relatives (the original Louis Laporte having died sometime before 1776) and received no donations of land during the period under study. Notarial records do not contain much information on day-to-day matters like coffee sales, but with a galaxy of *habitations* in the hands of various members of the family totaling at least 800 *carreaux*, employing at least 300 slaves, they were among the leading producers in the parish. Having gone in one generation from new white immigrant and free colored peasant farmer to the owners of a collection of very large coffee-growing establishments suggests that they were efficient producers.

Compare the happy situation of the la Bastide brothers or the Laportes to the white entrepreneur described by Brueys d'Aigalliers, owing enormous amounts to his business agent in the large city, at the mercy of price fluctuations in the single primary product he produced, always worried about the hazards of war, flood, epidemic in the slave quarters, and dishonesty or mismanagement on the part of his *économe*, or manager.

The general point is clear without the need to further multiply examples. Free coloreds, as resident proprietors, were closer to the ground and could respond more quickly to major changes in the marketplace, such as the coffee boom, or to minor fluctuations that were more common, if less earth shattering. Also, as resident proprietors, they could dispense with a great deal of professional management talent and also decrease corruption on their plantations. If managers were needed, the large free colored family could generally provide a candidate without having to search among the ranks of the *petits blancs*. Free colored proprietors also could, and did, diversify their capital, as in the example of the la Bastides, making them more resistant to the vagaries of the marketplace.

Scale was another difference between white and free colored landholding. There were white peasants—one was living among the "bad sorts" with Pierre Perodin on his defunct coffee habitation in Dondon, a certain Joseph Thibault, said by the *maréchaussée* officer to be a malingerer who was giving himself to laziness.[9] Most poor whites, though, seem to have stuck to the socially acceptable roles of manager or technical worker on a large plantation or tradesman in the cities. Whites who could buy farms, following the advice of Wimpffen, were much more likely to sink themselves deeply into debt in order to become large planters rather than start with something within the reach of their capital and work toward long-term growth. White purchasers in the sample of notarial acts bought on explicit credit terms 17 percent of the time, while only 11 percent of sales between free coloreds were on credit terms.[10] This greater willingness of the beginning white *habitant* to buy land on credit suggests that he was stretching his resources farther to get a bigger place. The goal of the white immigrant was to establish himself, make a fortune, and return to the *metropole* to live the good life. Finally, those white *habitants* who had succeeded in their quest for fortunes had enormous operations, even when compared to the upper levels of the free colored planting elite. The plantation that Pierre Pluchon chose as typical for his chapter on colonial society in his standard general history of the colony, the Cottineau sugar plantation, consisted of 520 *carreaux* and 171 slaves.[11] This is much larger than any but the very biggest *habitation* owned by a free colored.

Size produced economies in agricultural production, especially in sugar. One needed a certain level of production to use a sugar mill economically, and no sugar plantation in Saint Domingue could make money without its own mill. The institution of small sugar farmers supplying a central mill, found in the nineteenth century in Brazilian sugar country, did not catch on in Haiti until the late nineteenth century with the introduction of narrow-gauge rail lines to carry the cane to the central mill. Even in coffee or indigo, one gained a certain advantage from buying one's slaves in large lots, wholesale, and a large market share would give the planter a better negotiating position with buyers.

However, there were also reverse economies of scale. The intimacy that grew up between master and slave when both lived together in a small unit on a remote plantation could be expected to have had a positive impact on the slave's morale and thus productivity. Keeping watch on the slaves would also have been easier with fewer of them per free overseer, and thus runaway rates would have been lower. Seeing to their health must also have been easier, perhaps explaining in part the demonstrated lower mortality of slaves owned by free coloreds.[12] A smaller production unit meant more variety of tasks, which would also help keep slave morale up as well as build the slave's value to his master. In addition, if slaves were more likely to have more than one specialty, as would more commonly be the case on smaller plantations, death, illness, or flight of slaves with specialized knowledge would be less of a disaster to the organization's efficiency.

Smaller units meant less total income, even if margins were higher, and so the free colored master would have less wherewithal to travel to the cities. Having the master on hand on the plantation would seem inherently more efficient than having him resident in Cap or Port-au-Prince or Paris. Certainly, in the aggregate, free coloreds were much more likely to be resident on their plantations than were white proprietors.

Whites were absent so frequently from their plantations that the colonial military found it difficult to provide officers for the rural parishes' militia units who could be reliably counted on to be present for duty. M. de Carnage de Mailhert, the colony's military commander, complained about this problem to his superiors in France in 1739, but there is no evidence that the situation got any better in the ensuing fifty years.[13]

Absenteeism among whites usually meant that the plantation would be administered by an *économe*, or manager. This was a profession greatly in demand, with 1,636 appearing in the 1780 census out of a total white population of 20,543.[14] Some of these men were quite professional. For example, the former master of Toussaint Bréda, later Louverture, Bayon de Libertat, managed several plantations in the North province. Owners clearly felt he was worth his considerable fee. Many *économes* were rank amateurs, however, recruited from the class of poor whites, with little or no experience in the colony, with the crops, or with the slaves. Wimpffen's letter from the *habitation* Désert, in the mountains north of Jacmel, laid great stress on the "stupidity" and "laziness" of the *économe*.[15] In many cases, not only their professionalism but also their honesty was in doubt. Sieur Pierre Abadie, *économe* of the *habitation* Borgello and Fontelaye in Croix des Bouquets, lying ill in 1777, was so conscience-stricken about his disservices to a former employer that he willed him 600 *livres* to repay the costs of his "negligence."[16]

When free colored owners were absent, management of their lands was often carried out by a family member. In 1788, Jean-Baptiste L'Eveille *dit* Riché, fully involved in land deals in Cap Français, sent his son Jean-François Edouard L'Eveille to manage his *habitation* in Boucan Quimby, in the parish of Grand Rivière du Nord.[17] The land had been leased to a white man, and the son's responsibility was to reclaim it at the end of the lease, repair any damages, and get the land back in production. The strength and size of the free colored family meant that there were usually family members around to carry out these tasks so that expensive and unreliable outside help did not need to be employed.

White planters were much more likely to be on their own in the colony. Although there were creole white families, some of which owned extensive plantations, most whites on the island were recent immigrants who came without families. Those who were able to marry on the island might have relatives to help them with management tasks, as would the creoles. Even these families, though, suffered from the strong desire of whites to "return" to France, whether they were born there or not. Young creoles, male and female, often traveled to the *metropole* for their education, and many remained there, leaving their places on the family farm to a hireling.

Frequently, a colored family would form a partnership in which the junior member—child, younger brother—provided management services and some resources, and the senior family members provided most of the capital. For example, we have the long-standing and apparently quite successful partnership between Dame Marie Madelaine Duchemin, widow of Sieur Turgeau, apparently a free colored although her racial status was never specified in any of the acts, and *le nommé* Pierre Turgeau, her son. Pierre was apparently the oldest of a substantial brood of Turgeaus (others of whom are frankly described in the notarial record as *mulâtres/*

mulâtresses) and was the one chosen to take responsibility for the family farm. In 1773, the widow Turgeau declared before a notary that her "great age" prevented her from seeing to her own affairs, so she formed a partnership with Pierre to last five years. Her age could not have been too great nor her handicaps especially life-threatening as the partnership was renewed three times in the notarial registers.[18] The younger Turgeau was to manage capital provided entirely by his mother, pay one-third of the operating expenses out of his own pocket, and get for his pains half of the gross income. Greatly formal, the two visited the notary every year in early November for an accounting. Nine of these accountings have survived, from 1777 to 1786, omitting 1781. They cleared about 6,500 *livres* a year during the War of American Independence and up to 9,500 *livres* a year in peacetime. The mother never actually paid him more than 800 *livres* cash in any one of those years, and the son usually took substantially less. A professional manager for such an estate would have demanded at least 800 *livres* a year salary and would have insisted that it be paid out of the proceeds of each harvest. The rest of his "management fee" was added to a running total in each of the annual accountings, which was to be paid "later"—from her estate, one presumes. This case is a neat example of a pain-less way of transferring one's assets to one's heir of choice while protecting them (as debts) from attachment by other claimants to the estate, circumventing the re-quirement under French law that assets be divided equally among all heirs. For our purposes here, let us note that the plantation got a manager dedicated to its long-term success who did not need to be paid large sums of cash in salary.

Free coloreds occasionally formed partnerships like the Turgeaus' with whites, either family members or patrons. This also often proved a handy way to transfer assets without it appearing to be either a bequest or a donation—both of which were officially frowned upon between whites and free coloreds, as was discussed in chapter 6. As an example of this process, we have the partnership established by Jean Pierre Pavie, *quarteron*, and the widow Cochet, a white woman, presumably his step-mother.[19] She provided a piece of land and 3 slaves, and he provided 3 slaves. She was to build a house on the land and reside in it, and she had the right to personal service from her 3 slaves. She also had the right to take one of the slaves with her if she traveled. He was to manage the farm and had a right to 50 per-cent of the profits. This sounds like a young man getting control over property and managing it, while taking care of an aged relative.

Credit is an important component of entrepreneurship. A business transaction that is performed on credit can be said to be almost automatically entrepreneurial, as a certain level of economic return on investment is required or the capital good will be lost. Agricultural credit was available to free coloreds. *Négociants* were will-ing to put as much as two-thirds of the price of slaves sold to planters on credit against the harvest.[20] Mercantile houses in France extended vast amounts of credit to planters as well. Sometimes they found themselves saddled with uncollectible bad debts as a result, like the Depont family of La Rochelle merchants. The Deponts were owed more than 50,000 *livres* by various creditors in Saint Domingue. Some of these debts were decades old.[21] Free coloreds could also touch unofficial support networks composed of patrons and family members, as we have seen, probably with greater ease than could immigrant whites operating far from their families.

Actual cash payment was unusual for the expensive capital goods that were typically the subject of notarial acts. Real French cash money was rare in the colony, and a host of substitutes from Spanish currency to pounds of sugar circulated in its place. Of 1,408 sales contracts for all commodities in my sample, sales made at least in part for cash totaled 487, or 35 percent. On occasion, acts that stated that a sale was performed for cash payment were actually credit sales, as explained in chapter 2; occasionally the subterfuge would be revealed in subsequent acts when the purchaser failed to live up to the unwritten payment agreement. Only 299 sales, or 21 percent, were on some explicit credit terms. In the majority of acts, no terms were explicitly stated, and often the sale would be said to have been made *comptant,* or on account.

The most common form of credit was variously termed a *billet, obligation, mandat,* or *lettre de crédit,* but in all cases it was a personal promise to pay at some time in the future that was negotiable in the issuer's economic universe and in proportion to his creditworthiness. That is, Stanislas Foäche's billet was negotiable in France or anywhere in the colony, while a planter could count on having his billet accepted in the port city where he traded and in the immediate vicinity of his *habitation* to the extent that he paid his bills. Billets could change hands several times between issuance and recovery, and frequently we find sales being paid for in the seller's paper, in the hands of another person than the one to whom it was originally issued.

Commercial paper had a lifespan, though. In some cases, this might be only a couple of days, between the negotiation of the contract in the notary's office and the recovery of cash from a strongbox on a distant plantation. In other cases, obligations would be good for years, with elaborate payment plans carefully laid out.

Credit cost, of course, but religious objections prevented the cost from being specifically stated in these notarial acts. Obviously, the price was inflated if the payment was to be delayed. Interest of 5 percent was often assessed in court orders for payment of past-due debts, as permitted by law, but creditors often went to great lengths to negotiate with overdue debtors instead of taking them to court. One presumes that creditors saw 5 percent as insufficient recompense (with legal fees eating up too much of that). The profusion of different types of payment terms make it impossible to determine the precise actual rate of interest, but given the relatively standard 10 percent annual return on investment used to estimate rental value in cadastral surveys and notarial acts, we must assume that money cost at least that much.

Free coloreds, though, do not appear to have been the aggressive consumers of credit that white proprietors were. As smaller-scale operators, on the average, their paper did not have the same broad geographical range as that of large white planters. Racial prejudice may have led merchants to be less willing to accept their paper. Finally, their natural conservatism, particularly among the planter elite, made them less willing to plunge as deeply into debt as their white competitors.

For example, Wimpffen stated that the white planter needed to pay only one-third of the value of his slaves in up-front costs and would get the remaining two-thirds on credit.[22] On average, only about 20 percent of the purchase price of slaves bought by free coloreds from whites in my sample was credit. This marked preference for cash sales was not forced upon free coloreds by white sellers, for in sales between free coloreds, an average of only 23 percent of the purchase price was loaned.[23]

So what, then, motivated the free colored landowner and entrepreneur? Obviously, avoiding financial losses was important. Breaking even financially, at least over the long term, meant staying in business.

The essential motivation of the white proprietor was to get rich and go "home" to France. Even whites born in the colony thought of France as home; a "Mecca" to which they aspired like "Mohametans," said observer Cornelius de Pauw, to journey at least once in their lives—so they could see and be seen and flaunt their wealth.[24]

This motive meant much less to the free colored, although they did travel to France and did consume conspicuously while there. The Police des Noirs regulations of France were concerned with the overweening display of wealth by visiting free coloreds.[25] Many white men would send their colored sons (and sometimes daughters as well) to France to learn a trade or make valuable contacts. Individuals as diverse as Vincent Ogé and Zabeau Bellanton, the slave dealer we met in chapter 5, made long commercial stays in the *metropole*. Free coloreds' public spokesmen, however, alleged that they saw the colonies as their home.[26]

Certainly their behavior supports this assertion that the free coloreds viewed their plantations as home and were more likely to manage their land for the long term. We can see from the statistical description in chapter 6 that the pattern of land ownership by free coloreds indicates that they held onto pieces of land, on the average, for much longer periods of time than did whites. If they had to sell land to whites, it was in smaller units and lower value, both total and per unit, than what whites sold to them, suggesting that they were sacrificing small or undeveloped portions of their establishment while whites were selling whole plantations to them.

As landlords, or junior partners in the agricultural partnerships described above, free coloreds were "improvers," seeking a structure that would reward them for developing the productive capacity of their capital goods. Occasionally, they were content to be *rentiers,* especially in urban real estate, but as rural landlords they were more likely than white proprietors to rent to tenants who would improve the land, not asking for high cash rents in order to have the right to installations built and fields planted.

As businessmen, rural free coloreds avoided the trap of easy credit, even in a cash-poor society, and stayed within their means. They built for the ages, economically speaking, in the expectation that their children and grandchildren would enjoy what they had worked for.

URBAN FREE COLORED ENTREPRENEURS

The conservative free colored planter elite contrasts with the rather aggressive behavior of the free colored in an urban area. As we have seen in the demographic investigation contained in chapter 3, the free colored populations in urban areas tended to be younger than their relatives in the countryside and were also less likely to be married or to have children. Young, single people are notoriously willing to take risks. Urban free coloreds went into business, retail or wholesale, on a shoestring, bought and sold land aggressively, and developed land with the expectation of fat profits. To some extent, they shared the "boom times" mentality of their white neighbors, profiting off the great river of wealth that flowed between the sugar and coffee plantations and France in the 1780s. To a considerable extent, though, they were laying the bases of what they hoped would be longer-lasting fortunes, in much the same way, if on a smaller scale, as French merchants like the Deponts, who took their gains from their La Rochelle mercantile house and bought nobility and royal office.

Whatever else they did in the cities, free coloreds were very likely to be involved in the urban real estate market. The colony was growing so rapidly during the third quarter of the century that it was difficult *not* to make a profit in urban real estate. The cities were growing rapidly, along with the countryside; Cap Français, for example, grew from a free population of 1,751 in 1775 to 4,123 in 1788.[27]

As we have seen, free coloreds in the countryside tended to hold onto their property for the long term and frequently saw it as a family patrimony that would build social status as well as produce financial gain. In the cities, they focused much more tightly on financial gain and were willing to buy and sell land quickly. Free colored sellers in the sample held urban land for an average of 5.5 years before selling it, significantly less than their average tenure in rural land, which was 8.25 years. Free coloreds were also more willing to deal in undeveloped land in urban areas. Of 130 sales of land in urban areas by free coloreds, 74 were of undeveloped plots. This suggests that, whereas free colored landowners in rural areas preferred to buy land, turn it into a farm of whatever level of sophistication they could afford, and then work it, free colored landowners in urban areas were often content to buy a piece of land, await the city's expansion, and then sell the piece at a profit to someone who would improve it—constituting speculation, an extreme form of entrepreneurship.

Furthermore, as landlords, urban free coloreds were more likely than their rural cousins, and, indeed, even more likely than their white neighbors, to take the income of their lands rather than build for the long term by seeking improving tenants. In only 6 of 129 urban rental contracts in the sample where free coloreds were the owners, was the renter required to make significant improvements on the property. All but one of these simply required repairs or minor renovations instead of the often major developments that were a significant part of many rural lease contracts. On the other hand, of 31 rental contracts where whites were the owners, in 7 cases the renter was obliged by the terms of the lease to do some work, and in 2 cases this was important construction adding significantly to the value of the place.

Alongside land trading, urban free coloreds engaged in other businesses. Many were involved in commerce, from the most humble to the highest levels in the colony. At the very top was the future revolutionary leader Vincent Ogé. Ogé's father was a prominent white *négociant* (a term implying the highest level of wholesale merchant); upon his death, Vincent, as his legitimate son, took over his business. The Ogé house shipped sugar and coffee to France as its primary business. Vincent Ogé also owned inter-island boats, one of which traded with North America. On one occasion, he criticized the captain of one of his vessels who was said to be planning to take his schooner *La Normande* to New England without his permission—Ogé may have been trying to cover himself in case he was accused of violating the *exclusif*.[28] Ogé was also involved in urban real estate, apparently in his own name, in that of his mother, and as an agent for absentee owners in France.

In an example of free colored urban entrepreneurship that is closer to the bottom of the economic scale, Marie Josephe, free *negresse,* formed a partnership with a *Sieur* Guillemet in 1785 to manage a small retail business in Fort Dauphin. Their total capital was 2,362 *livres* 10 *sols. Sieur* Guillemet was to manage the store, which would operate in rented premises.[29] The source of their money is unknown, but it is perhaps significant that a white *habitant,* Formel des Rivières, acted for Marie Josephe before the notary. This may have been how he set up a dependent, perhaps a former lover or mother of his children, to take care of herself. In any case, in the Spartan furnishings of the store, the tight conditions imposed on the white manager to refrain from granting credit to his friends, and the very small amount of cash reserves (only 462 *livres*), we can get a good idea of a desperate attempt to break out of poverty and be one's own master on the part of both the free colored and the white investor in this scheme. The *boutique* Guillemet/Marie Josephe was established originally for one year but seems to have survived at least three, as no act of dissolution or final accounting appeared in the notarial record.

Not all such attempts succeeded, however. In fact, like small business startups in developed and developing countries today, one gets the impression that a sizable minority, if not a majority, failed. Let us consider in this light the 1782 act of dissolution of a partnership between Sieur La Bacheliere and the *menagère* Julie Dahey to operate a pottery manufactory in Croix des Bouquets.[30] La Bacheliere did not do badly in the deal, as he had a 4,000 *livre* annual salary for operation of the facility. Julie was to get the buildings and equipment of the company, with the slaves to be split equally between the partners. The largest share of the 74,651 *livres* that the partnership accumulated in expenses was for the salaries of several skilled employees: 12,000 *livres* for La Bacheliere, 9,000 *livres* for a *Sieur* Richie, 3,300 *livres* for a *Sieur* Croziat who made bricks, 600 *livres* for a *Sieur* Redas, and 3,000 *livres* for a *nommé* Thelemaque (for whom rental charges as a slave were also paid, suggesting that he gained his freedom during the life of the company). The partnership also rented widely varying numbers of slaves, as many as 22 at one point, for a total of 18,500 *livres* with the usual conditions that the renter pay the cost of missing or deceased slaves—costing them an additional 5,500 *livres* for dead slaves and several expenses of 8 *livres* 5 *sols* for slave catchers to bring back their runaway slaves (the *maréchaussée* would have charged them much more, according to official price schedules). The business seems to have made 36,214 *livres* in income, which is not detailed in the final accounting.

This was a fairly substantial business. Again, the free colored partner was a woman, possibly supported by a white man in the background—in the case of Julie Dahey, such support might have come from Thomas Peignanan, whom we also already met in chapter 6.[31] It is interesting to note in the case of Dahey's pottery plant that she kept the land and buildings as her share of the partnership's assets. This is entirely consonant with her class identity as a member of the planter elite. Land meant much more to her than it would to an urban free colored. While Vincent Ogé was managing an established business, both of the other two businesses discussed here were considerably riskier than the agricultural partnerships to exploit this or that plantation that appeared so frequently in the sample. Free people of color seem to have been willing to take great risks when engaged in business in the cities—although the experience of the pottery manufactory seems to have cured Julie Dahey of risky business ventures. Her subsequent appearances in the record reflect a more conservative approach, as indicated in chapter 6.

The urban areas were the place where most skilled workmen plied their trades. With the exception of the technical skills required for crop transformation—sugar and indigo mill workers—tradesmen concentrated in the urban areas. Many free coloreds identified themselves in the notarial record as practitioners of a skilled trade, even if they did not gain much or any of their income from that trade. It was socially respectable to teach one's free colored illegitimate son a trade, and free coloreds could be members of the trade associations. One Joseph *dit* Aubry, a free black, for example, identified himself as a *compagnon orfèvre* (journeyman goldsmith) in an act of sale in 1787.[32] He thereby laid claim, not only to technical skill, but to membership in a social and political fraternity of French journeymen tradesmen which has variously been identified as an early step in the creation of a labor movement or as part of the death throes of the medieval guild system.[33] Aubry probably joined the *compagnonnage,* if indeed he was entitled to claim membership, while studying his trade in France. There was a white Aubry family living in Cap, perhaps former masters, who may have helped Aubry travel to France to study. He was a reasonably prosperous man, as one would expect for a journeyman goldsmith in a boom town like Cap Français. He owned at least 2 slaves, including one talented and expensive woman termed a *marchande* in the act of sale.[34] Perhaps she was his shop clerk, and perhaps she was destined for freedom, as this was a term most often applied to free colored women who had succeeded in business.

More common was the tradesman who had learned his trade in the colony. The few white master tradesmen who could be convinced to come to the colony and set up shop had no difficulty finding labor. Along with slaves, who were frequently sent by their masters to learn technical skills through the apprenticeship process, many young free coloreds' families were looking for opportunities to get them training. Apprentices typically worked for their masters for a number of years, with payment from the apprentice's family reducing the number of years required. The guilds were not strong enough, seemingly, to significantly limit the number of practitioners or keep free coloreds out. Only white craftsmen were described in the notarial record by the term "master" carpenter or tailor or what have you. However, by the time under study, free coloreds, even without the title, were doing the same thing their white teachers had done before them. The white masters do not seem to have gotten much more money out of the deal, either: the average fee for apprenticeship with a white master was 1,262 *livres* while the overall average fee, including apprenticeships supervised by free colored journeymen, was 1,166 *livres*.

Not all people identified in the notarial record as practitioners of a particular trade got much, or any, income from that skill. One of the most successful military veterans of the Chasseurs-Volontaires de Saint-Domingue was Pierre Augustin, who was first mentioned in the introduction in this book. A landowner in Cap turned *habitant* in the countryside, he was described in the notarial record throughout his early career as a wig maker. At one point, his notary formally noted that he was "once a wig maker in Cap, and now an *habitant* in la Souffrière, Limbé."[35] Clearly, at some point in his past, Augustin, a *bossale* from somewhere in west Africa, had been trained as a wig maker, and the description stuck even after it would have been more accurate to have termed him a "real estate investor and developer."

Persons who were active in their trades seem to have been able to make good money, although once again, like the retail merchant, the skilled workman was a sole proprietor with a heavy investment in tools and slave workmen and nothing to protect him against fluctuations of the market.

All of these urban businesspeople, thus, were aggressive and entrepreneurial users of capital, in contrast to most of their cousins in rural areas. Their *mentalité* may have been the result of their youth, childlessness, or perhaps a product of the difference in attitudes between the planter elite and the military leadership group, which are described in chapters 10 and 11 of this book. Of course, the conditions of the businesses described above are further indications of the risky nature of free colored economic behavior in the cities. The free colored plantation seems to have been a quite safe investment, as indicated in the previous subsection. Not so for the free colored commercial enterprise: even the mighty merchant house of Vincent Ogé was always close to the precipice, at risk of war (and France's disadvantageous position in the naval struggle with England), bad debts or bad faith by their customers, the planters, changing government regulation, or changing conditions of their market in France. The small *commerçante*, like Julie Dahey or Marie Josephe, was much more at risk. Certainly in my sample, almost half of all nonagricultural partnerships were dissolved.[36] High risk, high gain, seems to have been the consensus strategy for free coloreds in the cities.

URBAN-RURAL LINKS AND ENTREPRENEURSHIP

So far, we have considered urban and rural entrepreneurship as two distinct phenomena. However, individuals and families seem to have moved back and forth between city and farm with great ease and to have split their resources in a complicated response to changing circumstances. This mobility of capital and people reinforced the unity of regional communities of coloreds. This places Saint Domingue's free coloreds in sharp contrast to other Caribbean populations of free coloreds, such as Jamaica's, for example, where the free coloreds in the towns were sharply distinct from the—often maroon—free people of color living as peasants in remote rural areas.

As an example of the regionwide range of free coloreds, the family of Toussaint Louverture was moving from slavery to the status of small planters during this period. Toussaint's son-in-law owned a farm and two dozen slaves in rural Grand Riviere, and Toussaint himself operated that farm from 1779 on.[37] At the same time, Toussaint himself was an urban landlord. He owned a small amount of land at Haut du Cap, an outlying area of the city of Cap Français, part of which he sold in 1781 as urban expansion reached him.[38] His wife was to receive a house in Cap as a rental property in the will of Pierre Guillaume Mirebalezia and subsequent codicils (although it is unclear whether Mirebalezia actually predeceased her).[39] The same family could be both urban and rural.

Another example of the same process was the miscalled wig maker Pierre Augustin. Augustin moved from tradesman to urban land speculator to proud rural *habitant* in the space of about two decades. Even as an *habitant*, he did not abandon urban land speculation.

Even the planter elite Laporte clan of Limonade was not immune from the lure of the city. They seem to have done business with a Cap notary who was not among those sampled. However, on one occasion, their in-law Guillaume Castaing (*fils*) appears in the records as renter of a town house on the rue Royale.[40] On another occasion, Catherine Françoise Ardisson, the daughter of Marie Anne Laporte, resided in Cap for some time before being placed in a convent by her mother.[41]

The question remains, then: if urban and rural free coloreds were the same people, why was their behavior so different? To recap: free coloreds in rural areas were generally more conservative than whites both as landholders and as slave owners. They held land longer than whites and often sought to improve it rather than extract maximum cash rent or sale value from it. They were less likely to use credit than their white neighbors. They did not trade speculatively in land or slaves, to any great extent, and they built their land value for the long term. The rural planter elite seemingly saw themselves as a group of *seigneurs* for the New World. Military leaders resident in rural areas, while not nearly as conservative as the planter group, were typically more conservative than their urban counterparts. The rural free colored poor, for their part, were a peasantry (foreshadowing the return of the newly free to peasantry after the Haitian Revolution). In the cities, on the other hand, free coloreds were active land speculators. They bought and sold land rapidly, often without improving it at all. They were much less likely than rural landlords to require renters to make improvements. They used credit more commonly than their country relatives. They got involved in non-agricultural businesses that were much more risky than the diversified and well-managed plantation, albeit potentially much more rewarding. Why?

Part of the explanation lies in the generational difference between urban and rural free coloreds. We can see from the demographic data that the city was full of young, single free coloreds. This is where individuals went to start their fortunes. Mixed-race children of whites would often be trained in a trade and would be most likely to practice it in town. Younger children of rural free colored families, like Guillaume Castaing or Catherine Ardisson, would make their way to the cities to see and be seen and to wheel and deal.

Some of the difference might also lie in distance from slavery. Freed slaves also often had trades that they had learned and through which they accumulated the capital necessary to move out of slavery. They, too, would most likely set up in business in the city. The newly freed from rural areas who were young and energetic and who wanted more than a peasant farm next to the provision grounds on the old plantation would head for Cap Français or Port-au-Prince. If any of these people were successful, they would reinvest some of their profits in the safe, conservative environment of the countryside, as a hedge against misjudgment or business downturn and to provide a comfortable environment for middle age.

Marriage was postponed among free coloreds as it often was among metropolitan whites of similar social class. Marriage was much more likely to take place in the countryside than in the cities, as is explored at greater length in chapters 10 and 11. In fact, marriage often spelled departure from the urban environment as the newly respectable *habitant*, husband, and father settled into his country lands and began striving for social promotion—for the benefit of his children as much as for himself—along with financial advancement.

The differences in aggressiveness and entrepreneurship between the military leadership group and the planter elite provide the remainder of the explanation. Military leaders were commonly, though not exclusively, freedmen and began their careers as urban tradesmen or workers. Even after retiring to the countryside, many had important urban holdings still in their portfolios. As is demonstrated in chapters 10 and 11, the differences between these two groups combine with the generational divide between rural and urban populations to produce the apparent differences between the free coloreds in rural and urban settings.

Making money, though, was not the only thing one needed to do to get ahead in this tradition-bound pre-revolutionary society. Money had to be mediated through variables of status to truly affect the social position of the individual. Success as an entrepreneur, urban or rural, merely put one in a position to acquire social status, as is explored in the next chapter.

CHAPTER EIGHT

Non-Economic Components
of Social Status

The Raimond family of Aquin are among the most famous of the free coloreds of Saint Domingue. Their most illustrious member, Julien Raimond, was sent to France as an unofficial envoy of the free colored planter elite to help gain legal protections from the royal government just before the Revolution. He was still in France in 1789 and played an important role in the debates of the revolutionary assemblies over slavery and civil rights for people of color. His writings constitute an important source for students of the politics of race in the French Revolution.[1] The Raimond family offers an object lesson in the way free coloreds manipulated non-economic markers of social status to assume a higher place in society than that assigned to them by racial prejudice. For example, rarely in the notarial record are the Raimonds referred to as *le nommé* or *la nommée* although this formula was supposed to be used for all free coloreds. Instead, they are often referred to as *Sieur* or *Dame* Raimond, although these terms were generally reserved for whites. When the *nommé* formulation is found, it is often interlined as if the notary put it in the second copy in his files but, presumably, not on the original given to the client.

Writing in the 1780s at the beginning of his civil rights campaign, Raimond suggested that *quarterons* be considered legally white and benefit from full citizenship.[2] Raimond himself was a *quarteron*, but he reflects the attitude of the lighter-skinned *gens de couleur* who might have been thought to be approaching white. Raimond, in any case, was not alone in making this suggestion: the influential Chambre de l'Agriculture de Cap Français had made a similar recommendation in 1776.[3] Other proposals would have limited this official "whitening" to "legitimate" *quarterons* or to those who had performed military service, but the principle remained that free people of color could somehow whiten themselves through some combination of racial titles, proper behavior, patriotic values, and wealth.

"Whitening" remained an unattainable holy grail in colonial times, but manipulation of an extremely complex galaxy of different indicators of status could grant social status. Status was a goal unto itself, as well as a way to secure economic gains.

It should be no surprise to the reader that race and color were socially defined concepts in colonial Saint Domingue. It is hardly unusual in modern scholarship to refer to race as a malleable idea, although observers at the time and since have tried to treat it as a scientific and invariable classification. Free coloreds in Saint Domingue manipulated the variable of color in their quest for social advancement.

The incomparable Moreau de St. Méry, in his *Description* of the colony, spent many pages discussing the thirteen racial types he identified, both by their physical appearance and moral character, in an attempt to create an invariable scheme of scientific genotypes.[4] Even he was aware that these categories were by no means stable. He noted that the "*sang-mêlée* [one-sixteenth African ancestry] approaches the white" in appearance and, he did not add, became identical in official characterizations after a while.[5] From long before the time of Moreau de St. Méry, as soon as the *Code Noir* and other legal disabilities began to draw a line between mixed race and white, those who were mostly white began to try to slip into the dominant group. Hilliard d'Auberteuil used the phrase *tache ineffaçable* (indelible stain) to refer to the principle that even one part in a thousand of African and slave ancestry made a person a member of a lower social order, but in practice, there was a point at which mixed race became indistinguishable from white.[6]

Many light-skinned people of partial African descent climbed up a racial category by passing as partially Amerindian. A March 1642 regulation of the Compagnie des Indes declared the Indians of the French Caribbean islands the equals of whites in all respects. Moreau de St. Méry took the case of a purported *sang-mêlée* woman who was able to prove to the satisfaction of the court that her only nonwhite ancestor was a Carib Indian.[7]

At the time of his visit to the colony in 1721, Father Jean-Baptiste Labat said of the early settlers of the Plaine des Cayes in the South province that there was hardly one who was pure white, all being suspected of some sort of racial mixing.[8] Yvan Debbasch, modern French student of racial stereotyping in the colony, cites a Chevalier de la Rochelard who complained from Cayes in 1734 of the "lack of white people of pure blood; they are almost all mulattos."[9] Moreau de St. Méry confirmed the partial African ancestry of many families reputed to be white. "After three or four generations," he said, "although public opinion would have it otherwise, black physical traits tend to weaken, and even in some 'white' families, these indiscreet appearances of African characteristics occur from time to time and are always remarked upon, but the family remains officially 'white.'"[10] He also described a case in which a purportedly white man, who had served as an officer in a French regular regiment and who had even obtained a metropolitan French court decree confirming his whiteness, was refused a commission as an officer in the militia because his ancestry was in doubt. A decision in his favor by the colonial authorities was insufficient to impose the man on the militia company, and in the end he had to appeal to the Conseil d'Etat in France before he could establish his right to be a militia officer.[11]

More recent observers have also occasionally succumbed to the temptation to treat racial categories as absolutes when they should have known better. C. L. R. James, for example, made of the free coloreds a *petit bourgeois* class as unitary in its economic determinism as Moreau de St. Méry's were in their racial determinism.[12] Interestingly, in so doing he resorted to racial categorization, using the term *mulatto* repeatedly to describe all free people of color. In fact, the term *mulatto* had and still has a colloquial implication of wealth, as in the Haitian proverb *neg wiche sé mulat, mulat pov sé neg* (a rich black is a mulatto while a poor mulatto is a black). In any case, free blacks were almost as numerous as free persons of mixed race in the colony. Sorting out variables of caste, class, and personal alliance becomes more difficult when the observer, in the 1780s or the 1940s, relies excessively upon unitary categories.

The color of marriage and other partners was an important part of the family strategies of free coloreds. A good example is given by the Laportes of Limonade, whose family tree is found in appendix 3. They seem to have chosen marriage partners so as to whiten their offspring as much as possible, becoming by the fourth generation an almost uniformly *quarteron* family.

Color descriptions in the archives were flexible and responded to changing economic and social circumstances of the people described. Officially, the categories used by Moreau de St. Méry were to be used in all cases of referring to a person of color in official documents. In the "scientific" paradigm of racial categorization, a person's racial category clearly could not change over time. It could be precisely determined from the racial category of his or her ancestors. It could not respond to appearance, style, wealth, or social respectability; color was not supposed to be an acquired characteristic.

The terminology actually used in the notarial and parish records was simpler than Moreau de St. Méry's complicated categorization system. As described in chapter 2, most notaries restrained themselves to *blanc, nègre, mulâtre, quarteron, griffe*, and occasionally *mestif*, and their feminine forms. Very rarely, someone would be described as *tierceron*, which seems to have been the equivalent of a *mes-*

tif. Mamelucs, sacatras, sang-mêlés, and the like existed only in the pages of Moreau de St. Méry's apprentice *Encyclopédie.*

In reality, we find that people changed their racial categories with relative ease. It was quite common for wealthy people of mixed ancestry—even those somewhat less wealthy than the Raimonds—to appear in the notarial record without any racial identifier appended to their name. The Laporte family tree illustrates how this process worked among the planter elite. The "official" categorization of members of this group ranged from black to white, with mulattos and *quarterons* predominating. Frequently, however, no racial identification was made in the act referring to them. Often, racial identifiers would be used when referring to another person not present, but when that person appeared to perform a notarial act, the notary would defer to them and omit the descriptive. Often, all descriptives would be omitted, especially in crucial acts that marked important turning points in the life of the family as a whole, such as marriage contracts, wills, and death inventories. The marriage contract of Charles Laporte and Catherine Françoise Ardisson is notable in this regard in that twelve Laportes or their relatives assisted in the tying of the knot, all but one of whom (the father of the groom, child of the white immigrant Louis Laporte's first marriage to a white woman) were identified elsewhere as people of color, and yet no racial descriptions were used anywhere in the text of the act.[13]

This notary, Michel of Limonade, was particularly egregious in his omission of racial identifiers for notable free coloreds, In general these omissions were more common in the North province than in the West, but all notaries did this to some extent. The widow Turgeau of Port-au-Prince, whom we met in the last chapter, was never identified by a racial title, and yet, as the mother of a number of frankly identified *mulâtres* and *mulâtresses,* she could not have been anything but a woman of color herself.[14] It is strange that her invulnerability to racial categorization did not extend to her children, but she *was* the one who controlled the resources and hired the notary.

Vincent Ogé, prominent merchant of Cap Français and future revolutionary leader, never was identified by color in any notarial act. It is only through knowledge of his revolutionary activities that the reader of the notarial archives would be aware that he was a person of color. There is no hint of his color in the archives, although his mother was occasionally referred to as *la nommée* in acts in which she appeared, and this was usually indicative of a person of color.

The intermittent social redefinitions permitted the elite of free colored society were paralleled by a species of "passing," or more permanent redefinition, that took place lower down in that culture. Pierre Augustin, who came from somewhere in West Africa, no longer identified himself as an African after he became a respectable freedman land developer. The Durocher brothers, veterans of the Chasseurs-Volontaires de Saint-Domingue, were described as free blacks in the original act in which they appear in the notarial record and were enrolled in a company of free blacks.[15] At the time, they were socially marginal figures with close relatives still in slavery and with insufficient means to purchase and free these relatives. As they achieved economic success and social advancement, coming to be known as *habitants*, and pretty comfortable ones at that, their racial categorization mutated to mulatto.[16] In 1789, in an act that identified their older brother Laurent as a mulatto, the brothers' father was described as a *griffe* while their mother was a *nègresse*, a combination that does not produce *mulâtres* as offspring according to the "calculus" in Moreau de St. Méry.

The redefinition of children was even more common than the redefinition of an individual during his or her lifespan. Two parents with dark classifications often had offspring with lighter classifications. For example, François Le Roy *dit* Gautier was described in his marriage contract as a *mulâtre libre* although, as the child of a *nègre* and a *mulâtre*, he should have been considered a *griffe*.[17] However, his father Jacques Le Roy, was a returned veteran of the Savannah expedition and an important member of the Cap military leadership group. François himself was a legitimate child. Moreover, by marrying his long-time lover and freeing her and their children from slavery, François himself attained further respectability. Hence, he got a racial promotion, one can only presume, to reflect his and his father's increased status.

Occasionally, racial demotion would take place from generation to generation. Alexis Duchemin of Mirebalais was almost always identified in notarial acts as a *mulâtre*. His wife, Gertrude Chaulet, was almost always identified as a *quarteronne* and generally rated the title *Demoiselle*. Their children were invariably described in the notarial records as *mulâtres* and *mulâtresses*.[18] Moreau de St. Méry's *Description . . . de la partie française* is clear in indicating that the racial calculus was not gender-biased—*mûlatre* or *mûlatresse* plus *quarteron* or *quarteronne* produces *quarteron* or *quarteronne* every time. However, the observer cannot help suspecting that the racial demotion of these children was a product of the fact that their mother was apparently lighter-skinned than their father.

As we can see, most of these color-based promotions and demotions paralleled and seem to have been part of social and economic promotions and demotions. As Pierre Augustin went from slave to businessman, he also went from *bossale* to simple *nègre*, without ethnic label. As Demoiselle Chaulet "lowered" herself by marrying a man with more African grandparents than she, her children were similarly reduced a level on the ethnic stepladder.

Demoiselle Chaulet used a title that was supposedly restricted to white women.

In France, the titles *Sieur, Dame,* and *Demoiselle* were indicators of gentry status. Any common person would be referred to as *le nommé* or *la nommée* (so-called) in an official act. In Saint Domingue, we know that whites were divided internally between wealthy landowners and merchants on the one hand and the poor whites, the *petit blancs,* on the other. However, there were few whites with actual noble status on the island. As a matter of practice, and of policy, to encourage racial solidarity among whites and to make a mark of distinction from the free coloreds, all white people received these honorific titles as if they were members of the gentry. As a poem of the time had it:

> *En France, l'on tire avantage de l'éclat du rang*
> *du courage, du savoir, des biens ou du sang:*
> *mais pour se croire un personnage,*
> *laissant là tout cet étalage,*
> *il suffit ici d'être blanc*

> In France, [social] advantage comes from rank,
> courage, wisdom, wealth, or blood:
> but to [be able to] consider yourself important,
> leave all that pomp over there,
> here, it is sufficient to be white.[19]

Thus any white person was *Sieur, Dame,* or *Demoiselle. Monsieur, Madame,* and the like were terms still reserved for members of the aristocracy. Free people of color and the very occasional white malefactor were the only people in Saint Domingue who rated *le nommé* or *la nommée* before their names.

The "normal" white titles, though, were occasionally hijacked by free coloreds seeking to raise their apparent status in notarial acts—like the Raimonds. Usually, when the notary omitted the color designation, he also referred to the person as *Sieur* or *Dame.* Persons who received this accolade were typically free coloreds of high status, and typically they received this deference only in their home area. So, for example, Marthe Castaing, mother of revolutionary Jean-Baptiste Chavanne, and her numerous brothers and sisters were always referred to as *Dame* or *Sieur* in Limonade.[20] When they went into Cap, they became, for example, *le nommé* Guillaume Castaing, *mulâtre libre.*[21]

Occasionally, however, the color designation would be omitted but the notary would preserve the formula of *le nommé* or *la nommée,* perhaps as a compromise or intermediate designation. Cap notary Bordier *jeune* stopped referring to the Desrouleaux heirs, Louis and his sister Madeleine, by color after Louis returned from the Savannah expedition, while restraining himself from going the extra step and calling them *Sieur* and *Demoiselle*.[22] This would have been about the time that Louis, at any rate, reached his majority at age 25. His increased social status as a responsible adult and returned serviceman, the financial success of his property under the management of Pierre Attila of the Malic *dit* Mali clan, and his connection through Attila to the powerful military leadership group of Cap free coloreds might have combined to raise Louis Desrouleaux's social standing enough for the notary to notice and give him some mark of distinction.

Finally, on occasion, but rarely, an individual would be described as *Sieur and* the racial designator would be applied. This last case seems to have been reserved for people of color with truly high status, perhaps when the inspector from the central court might be expected to enforce the regulation requiring the use of racial descriptives. Color descriptives in such cases are often interlineal, suggesting that they might have been added before the second minute of the act was sent to the regional court for safekeeping and perhaps did not appear on the first minute, retained by the participants in the act, although there is obviously no way to check on this.

Another way free coloreds could obtain socially significant titles was by holding public office. Most offices had been closed to free coloreds during the progressive tightening of racist legislation during the second and third quarters of the eighteenth century. The largest example of office holding still open to free coloreds throughout this period was military service.

Outside the military, however, there were still a few places free coloreds could go to gain social position through service. One was the church. *Margouilleurs,* or ushers, could be free coloreds, as could *syndics,* or vestrymen. Vincent Bleakley was *syndic* of the subparish chapel at Sainte-Suzanne in 1785.[23] Bleakley, a *quarteron*, was almost never referred to in the notarial records by his racial category. He was a large coffee planter in Limonade, and his daughters were marriage material for the Laportes and the Castaings.

The professions were forbidden to free coloreds during this period. Health care professions were progressively closed to them throughout the 1750s and 1760s and were finally closed completely in a regulation of 1764.[24] Laws that forbade whites married to free coloreds to hold seats on the various courts of the colony, or to act as lawyers before them, presupposed that no free colored could ever hold such a position.

However, free coloreds practiced many less prestigious professions and occasionally rated occupational labels of some social weight. Vincent Ogé was one of a select few *négociants* who were people of color. The term was generally reserved for merchants who did substantial business outside the colony. Few free coloreds were so well capitalized. The lower-level title of *marchand* was quite commonly applied to free coloreds, either alone or in combination with some trade-related title. *Marchand* implies retail trade and certainly disqualified the bearer for noble rank or high government position, but free coloreds were disbarred from those roles anyhow. The title was, however, more impressive than the simple craft title and suggested respectable wealth in a society that valued money.

Trade or craft titles were also permitted to free coloreds, up to a point. The *compagnon orfèvre* (journeyman goldsmith), Joseph Aubry, seen in chapter 7, is the most dramatic example of a craft title held by a free colored, since there do not appear to have been any nonwhite officially designated craft masters. The power to create masters was the privilege of the metropolitan guilds, and perhaps jealously kept at home by them, while few free coloreds would have remained in the *metropole* long enough to achieve this status even if racial attitudes there permitted it. However, as we have seen, free coloreds mentioned the journeyman status in official documents even when it was clear that they no longer worked actively in their trade, so the title must have meant a good deal to them.

More important even than title was the name used to identify oneself to the world. The surname was the privilege of the free, for the most part, and the French, or French-sounding, surname to some extent was the privilege, or at least mark, of the mixed race. Treading in the territory of other groups in self-identification was a good way to pretend to membership in those groups or to advance oneself socially.

Masters chose names for their slaves. Sometimes, very rarely, those names would be African or what the master fondly thought was African: one Cadiagnon appears in the records (probably a variant of Kadija, the first wife of the Prophet Muhammed and a popular women's name among West African Muslims) along with a couple of Muhammeds, an Attila, a Mali, several Dahomeys, and a few Scipions. The last suggests both Africa and Classicism, which was a much stronger influence on masters' choices of names for their slaves. Many plantations could boast a Caesar and more than one a Platon (but no Spartacus).

By far the most common personal names given to slaves, though, were ordinary French names. Plantation lists abound in Jean-Philippes, Gérards, Marie Claires, and Jeannes. Creole slaves seem to have been named after members of their families, so perhaps the parents had some role in the choice of their names.

All families tend to reuse the same personal names, often those of illustrious ancestors, and free coloreds in the colony were no different. The first son was often was given his father's personal name. This can make identification of individuals difficult, as witness the six members of the Laporte family bearing the name "Louis." There were two in each of the second and third generations, all four of whom were actively producing notarial acts during the time under study. In the absence of surnames, however, or in case of illegitimate birth where the father's role is not officially admitted, the personal name often helps keep relationships straight. When a black woman slave named Constance and her son, a *mulâtre* named Louis Lamotte, were freed by down-at-the-heel white *habitant* Louis Lamotte, even the absence of any verbiage in the act of liberty about support for the child does not invalidate a presumption of the family relationship.[25]

French names were preferred by free coloreds, for the most part. This was not unusual in slave societies as a whole; free coloreds frequently sought to be assimilated as much as possible into the dominant culture. In some cases, freedmen would take a new personal name upon changing status, and this was more typically the assumption of a French-sounding name by a classically or African-named person than the reverse. Some freedmen kept their African-sounding names, especially free blacks, obviously without real French relatives after whom to name themselves. Whether this was done out of familiarity and convenience or in an attempt to proudly claim African roots is unclear from the official record. The free military leaders exhibited this characteristic disproportionately, a tendency that is further explored in chapter 11.

A 1773 ordinance of the administrators of the colony forbade free persons of color to name themselves after former masters or white relatives. The law, designed to prevent what it said was a custom likely to "destroy the insurmountable barrier that public opinion has placed between whites and *gens de couleur,* and that government has wisely preserved," required all unmarried free women of color who baptized their children to select a surname for the child "drawn from the African idiom or their profession or color."[26] Newly freed persons were required to follow the same rules in choosing a surname for themselves. "Usurpations" that had taken place prior to the publication of the regulation were to be corrected after a certain delay. Public officials were not to accept declarations, notarials, or other official documents bearing surnames chosen in contravention of this regulation.

Obviously, this was a law more honored in the breach than the observance. The Laportes and other legitimate colored families continued to use the name of their white forebears with little or no hint of diffidence. In the case of recognized bastardy, metropolitan French practice permitted the child to use the name of the father. In some cases, this recognition overrode the aforementioned colonial regulation and in others not. For a negative example, "Marc Corbeille, formerly known as Daniaud, *mulâtre libre*" the recognized illegitimate child of Augustin Daniaud, was married in Mirebalais in 1786 under a name that was not his father's.[27] On the other hand, less than a month later, "Jean-François Thoreau, *tierceron libre,*" recognized illegitimate son of Etienne Thoreau, white, was married in the same church under his father's name.[28] Perhaps the difference lay in the lighter skin of the second groom, (*tierceron* in this notary's usage being what this work, and most notaries, term *mestif*), perhaps in the marginally greater wealth of the second couple (the first couple owned 4 cows and about 7,000 *livres* in personal articles between them while the second couple had 3 slaves and 8 cows as well as several thousand *livres* in personal articles).

The situation became even more difficult for unrecognized illegitimate offspring. In most cases, these people were officially referred to with the qualifier *ci-devant connu sous le nom de* (formerly known as) or *dit* (called) or even *vulgairement dit* (popularly called) preceding the name of their white ancestors. Often, another surname would also be used, as in the case of Marc "Corbeille." This obviously must have been humiliating for the free person, by diluting their right to claim kinship with whites, as was the intent of the law. However, the claim was not altogether eradicated, and one can presume that most people in daily life referred to Marc as "Daniaud" and not as "Corbeille" (as, indeed, the qualifier *dit* implies).

Often the alternate names simply changed the spelling of the white progenitor's name without changing the pronunciation. Spelling had been formalized in official, printed French by the eighteenth century, well in advance of English. However, it was still subject to numerous and comical variations in the informal written language; frequently both whites and free coloreds seemed uncertain in the official record as to how their names ought to be spelled. Even signatures were occasionally spelled differently from one act to another (while clearly being in the same handwriting), and going to a different notary might produce an almost unrecognizable change of spelling in the body of the article. A small variation would be practically unnoticeable to the ordinary person while satisfying the letter of the regulation. This is what John Garrigus said the Raimonds did, changing the spelling from their white forebear's "Raymond."[29]

Newly freed persons were supposed to assume a personal name drawn from the African or from their profession under the 1773 regulation. Again, this restriction was observed for the most part officially but only intermittently in ordinary daily practice. The act of manumission almost invariably stated that the newly freed person was to be henceforth known as something African. When that person appeared later before the notary, either they would be identified by the "African" name and described as *dit* a French name, or, more commonly, the "African" name would simply disappear. An example of a similar change in surname was that of Louis, presumed son of Louis Lamotte, referred to above. In the act of manumission, young Louis was given the surname of "Dahomet."[30] This was a favorite "African" name among notaries of Cap, being given to several dozen unrelated newly freed people in the sample over a period of several years. In fact, one gets the impression that the notaries did not really think much about the names they were giving to the freedmen because they knew that such names would probably never be used. In any case, young Louis used Lamotte for several years, joining the *maréchausée* and learning the trade of mason. He then seems to have gotten into some trouble— the reasons are unclear, but seemingly his father apparently was no longer in the colony to protect him—and made a notarial declaration, in connection with another act, saying that he was now going to use the name Dubois since he lived in a wooded area.[31] From that point on, he was known to the official record as Dubois, with no hint of Lamotte. Unable to use the French name of his father, he chose, not a name "*tiré de l'idiom Africaine*" but another French-sounding one. Cultural assimilation was an important part of social promotion.

Some free coloreds, of course, kept the African names or simply abandoned surnames altogether. These were often the poorest of the class, but sometimes quite wealthy and powerful individuals, such as the famous Malic or Mali, kept their non-French names. This tendency is found both among the *bossales*, who might have been expected to try to keep their African names, and among creoles, like Malic.

Among those born in the colony, both colored and white, having been to France was also very important. French Police des Noirs regulations in France attempted to restrain the flow of status-seeking free coloreds to the *metropole*, without marked success. For one thing, the Parlement of Paris never registered the key edicts, and thus they had dubious legal weight.[32] Free coloreds regularly made notarial acts that announced their intention to travel to France or their recent return from there in a manner calculated to parade this evidence of status achieved before all readers. So, for example, Louise Lucrèce, known as Dufon, a *mulatresse libre*, on the occasion of her departure for France, gave a procuration to a white businessman to manage her affairs and sell one of her slaves. In the notarial act, she is quite clear about her plans, and the reader can see the pride she took in having achieved this step.[33]

Just as in modern society, physical possessions were important markers of status, and display of material wealth was important to social advancement. The progress of sumptuary regulations marks the acquisition of wealth by free coloreds. These laws were designed to limit the ability of free coloreds to usurp the privileges of wealthy whites in the area of material culture. The whole island was affected by a regulation of 1779, in which, in the name of modesty and the color bar, free coloreds were forbidden to "affect" the dress, hairstyles, style, or bearing of whites.[34] Other, local ordinances forbade free coloreds to ride in coaches, have certain types of household furnishings, keep indoor privies (in the tropics, without running water, who would want to?), and so forth.[35] The growth of these sorts of regulations in the period after 1770 suggested the growth in wealth and ostentation of high-status free coloreds. A law forbidding possession of coaches suggests that at least some of the affected group had enough money to afford a coach.

None of these regulations, of course, did much to prevent free coloreds who could afford it from acquiring the forbidden articles and, indeed, may have encouraged them by allowing all to identify the specific items that would grant the most status.

A collection of 27 death inventories found in the archives gives a better idea of what sort of status possessions free coloreds acquired and how they used them. Although all parishes but Mirebalais are represented in this sample, Fort Dauphin and Limonade are the most common locations. Apparently, in these two parishes, the notaries copied the actual inventory into the second minute of the act as a matter of routine, while in the other parishes this laborious task was only performed if the family requested it for some reason. One very likely reason was to preserve for the ages evidence that the family owned some particular items, so those inventories coming from other parishes where this practice was not routine are doubly valuable as guides to status items.

Some, but not all, marriage contracts also included extensive inventories of the property of the couple. These inventories were seemingly not as detailed or complete as the death inventories, as they were based on reports of the parties and not a physical survey by the notary. The items reported can be presumed to be the most valuable; when the cash value is low, we can further presume that the social value must be high. Thus, the 190 marriage contracts in the sample are also useful to understand the different meanings of the possessions of free coloreds.

Generally both types of inventories carefully enumerated the slaves owned by the party or parties, especially in cases where they were rented out to some neighbor. Land was generally only peripherally mentioned in these inventories, since the titles to the land described them precisely and were much more likely to have been conserved than the notarial acts of sale of the slaves. Most important in the death inventory, however, was a description and evaluation of the deceased's personal possessions. Not all possessions were enumerated, however. There were obvious omissions in all of these inventories, death as well as marriage. Consumables were almost never mentioned, unless they constituted the stock in trade of the deceased or were cash crops from his or her farm. Kitchen and eating utensils were also rarely mentioned unless they had some extraordinary value—fancy silverware, for example. Clothing for everyday use was also not often featured, unless it was worthy of special note. Furniture, jewelry, silverware, weapons, and livestock were the most important items and were sure to be mentioned in the inventories.

These inventories, like other kinds of notarial acts performed by free coloreds, concerned people from all levels of society. The inventories in the sample range from that of one Babet, a dependent of the wealthy Pincemaille family (and perhaps their former slave) who died in 1786 owning a bed, in *acajou* wood, with mattress; curtains in Indian cotton, in poor condition; a *buffet*, lockable; two tables, in *sap* wood, in poor condition; a small water container "of Provence"; six chairs with straw seats; a dresser, in *sap* wood; another *buffet*, also in *sap*; and two donkeys, one pregnant.[36] Even in the enumeration of the effects of this quite poor woman, care was taken by someone, probably her executor, the locally prominent free colored and her patron Michel François Pincemaille, to make sure her status goods, such as they were, were not overlooked. Hence, the bed was noted as being built of hard and durable *acajou* and as having its hangings made out of cotton cloth from India. Among the kitchen equipment, the water storage jar imported from France was the only one enumerated.

Things that came from France were the most status-enhancing and thus most likely to be mentioned in the inventories. Clothing imported from Asia or from the mother country was sure to rate a line, as, for example, in the case of the deceased carpenter Pierre of Limonade. A humble man, with only 4,179 *livres* in his estate, Pierre nonetheless boasted a number of outfits in *jinga*, or gingham.[37] Some status clothing verged on the comical: a beaver coat was among the possessions of militia officer Augustin LeMoine when they were inventoried in Fort Dauphin in 1777.[38] The climate of Fort Dauphin, now Fort Liberté, makes it unlikely that the coat was ever needed; perhaps the fact of owning one implied that the owner had traveled to more temperate climates where such things were useful.[39]

Women's clothing included large numbers of scarves to be tied around the head and shoulders. Moreau de St. Méry remarked on the frequency with which women of color bought and wore enormous numbers of scarves in high-quality imported fabrics at the same time. Luxurious clothing, he says, was their principal method of showing their status.[40] We find evidence of this in the inventories: Nanette, the matriarch of the Pincemaille clan, owned 31 old and 12 new scarves, along with 17 blouses, 20 dresses, and 28 corsets at the time of her death in 1784.[41] Nanette's clothing was worth only a few hundred *livres* altogether, but Marie Jeanne, *griffe libre*, was a much snappier dresser: her 12 dresses were in Indian cotton and alone cost 200 *livres*, and her 12 best head scarves cost another 72 *livres*.[42]

We have already seen the Provençal water jug in the estate of Babet; imported daily use items figured prominently in death inventories. The elegantly dressed Marie Jeanne also owned a coffee set and teapot in French pottery. Anne *dite* Fraicheur, another independent urban free colored woman, had pottery plates and cups from France, all lovingly detailed in her inventory in 1788.[43]

Furniture was very expensive to bring out from the *metropole*, and so almost all of it was manufactured in the colony, of tropical hardwoods. It varied widely in quality but always rated lengthy mention in the inventory. When it included important works of craftsmanship, it could make up a significant part of the economic value of a small estate, but even when it was a minor part of the cash value, clearly its social value was high. An *armoire* with locking glass doors and copper hardware, standing seven feet tall and made out of *acajou,* worth 250 *livres,* had a prominent place in the inventory of the effects of the estate of young Gaspard Ardisson (III) in 1783 and absorbed considerable verbiage in its description, even though his total net worth was almost 65,000 *livres.*[44]

Moreau de St. Méry did not speak to the importance of jewelry to public display by free coloreds. However, it is unmistakable in the notarial record. Both men and women owned and wore as much silver and gold as they could afford. This is common in west African culture as well as in other cultures in the modern African Americas, so this should not come as a surprise to the observer. Aubry, the *compagnon orfèvre* mentioned in chapter 7, had plenty of potential customers among free coloreds as well as whites. Two prominent free colored men of Cap Français, Jean-Baptiste Petigny and Jean-François Leveille *dit* Riché, made the sale of a watch, produced by Baltazar of Paris, a more prestigious name than Aubry's, the unique subject of a notarial act.[45] Garrigus indicates the propensity of free coloreds to protect valuable property by getting notarial acts to attest to their ownership of it; we can see from this act that this piece of masculine jewelry was as important to these men as, say, a piece of land or a slave, the usual subjects of notarial acts. Nicholas and Charlotte Le Roy brought their daughter to be married to Jean Charles Dorien in 1778, and the only personal item she owned worthy of specific mention in the marriage contract was a gold watch, worth a whopping 700 *livres.*[46] Besides his freedom, Sieur Pierre Guillon left his presumed mulatto son Alexis his gold watch and 1,200 *livres* meant to pay for him to learn a trade.[47] While perhaps of secondary importance when compared to wealth or slaves or white ancestors, these examples show that the watch was a component or symbol of gentility.

Feminine jewelry was an equally crucial part of the female identity. Part of the standard marriage contract was the provisions for division of property between principals and heirs should the community of property be dissolved by death or separation. In almost all contracts, parties were permitted to claim some portion of the community property as theirs before the official division took place; this was called a *precipit.* The *precipit* usually included clothing and sometimes cash or a stated value in other personal articles as well. The most common specific provision in the *precipit* was to give the wife the right to her jewelry. Of 138 marriage contracts in the survey with *precipits,* 90 included this provision.

Other pieces of male jewelry sometimes took pride of place alongside the watch. The shoe buckle in some precious metal was a marker of masculine gentility, especially because its possession and shininess implied that the owner had no need to get his feet dirty. The most notable and significant piece of jewelry to the free colored man, though, was the decorated sword or brace of pistols. Suggesting pretensions, not just to middle-class respectability, but to nobility, and stressing the free coloreds' military role, arms were the most gendered, and controversial, possession a free colored man could have.

Arms bearing by free coloreds was a frequent subject for official pronouncements. The *Code Noir* and other early legislation spoke only of limiting the right of slaves to bear arms. However, a 1721 edict required that whites without domiciles, and all mulattos and free blacks, register all purchases of firearms with the administration.[48] In the same law, however, all *habitants,* of any race, were required to have weapons and rations at their homes for all free persons in case of insurrection or invasion.[49] Once again, the law code found it difficult to deal with the contradiction between the desire to maintain a color bar and the desire to have all free citizens ready to defend the system against whatever threats might arise. A 1761 regulation of the Conseil Supérieur of Cap forbade free blacks and mulattos to bear arms in the city limits, citing the risk to public order and the great number of armed fights between individuals.[50] A 1762 law forbade all free mulattos and blacks who were not militia officers to bear arms except on active militia or *maréchaussée* service. In this case, the prohibition was extended from the cities only to all areas of the colony. The intent of the legislation as expressed in its preamble also shifted from the preservation of public order to the maintenance of social and color barriers.

Nonetheless, plenty of free coloreds in the 1770s and 1780s owned weapons, many of which were clearly designed for display and must have been displayed on any possible occasion. Colored militia officers Captain Vincent Olivier and Lieutenant Etienne Auba were never seen in public without their swords, said Moreau de St. Méry.[51] They were taking advantage of the special permission accorded them as commissioned officers, but they were not alone in having weapons on display. The owner of the beaver coat, Augustin LeMoine, a militia noncommissioned officer in Fort Dauphin, also owned a brace of pistols with silver chasing and two swords, one with a copper hilt (for show, one presumes) and one described as Spanish (Toledo steel was notorious for its ability to hold an edge), which was most likely intended for use as a weapon.[52]

Free coloreds were often described by whites as somehow "effeminate." Feminine characteristics were attached to them by popular prejudice and observers at the time.[53] Racial and gender stereotypes fused to some extent, as a growing group of free coloreds appeared who passed most whites on economic grounds. Owning weapons, as a powerfully masculine activity, was one way that free coloreds could combat this gendered attack.

Most *habitants* kept some sort of weapons around the house. These might range from simple spears or machetes to hunting firearms to frankly military weapons such as muskets with bayonets. The widow of Joseph de Bury had *twelve* muskets at her home when she died in 1783.[54] Free colored *habitants* were required to keep arms on the premises by security legislation of the colony. Colonial censuses routinely kept track of the number of firearms and swords in private hands in each area. However, the very presence of these weapons gave the free colored *habitant* legitimacy as a defender of the social system against its enemies. Nonetheless, the only people who owned weapons designed for display—with gilded or jeweled hilts, scabbards, or barrels—seem to have been members of the colonial military.

Along with the firearm, the other status possession beloved by people of color was the horse, but the horse was not as firmly attached to the masculine gender as the gun or sword. However, horsemanship and possession of fine horses, like bearing arms, was a way for free coloreds to escape from "slave-like" as well as "effeminate" roles and act as full-fledged members of Saint Domingue's white-dominated society.

Moreau de St. Méry noticed the free coloreds' love of the horse: "dancing, riding, and making love are [the mulatto's] three passions. . . . As far as his love of the horse is concerned, only one fact need be cited to prove it: in all the colonies, the deadliest insult for a mulatto is to call him *volor choual,* or horse-thief."[55]

This passion is clear from the notarial records. After slaves, the horse was the most popular item of movable property to be the subject of notarial acts. Like the watch sale cited above, horse trades could be the subject of notarized sales contracts even when the value was relatively minor. In 1781, for example, Pierre Roux sold Baptiste Clement, the postman who carried the mail from Gonaives to Cap, an English horse, described in considerably greater detail than most slaves.[56] The sale price was 786 *livres,* much smaller than the average for land or slave sales. Notarial fees at the time averaged about 30 *livres,* almost five percent of the cost of this sale. One cannot escape the conclusion that the expense of the notary made registering this sort of sale an uneconomical proposition, and yet they did it. In this case, Clement had a professional need for a fine horse, but what about Catherine *dite* Cavailly, who bought a roan horse for an impressive 1,450 *livres* in 1778?[57] This was no draft horse, but a fancy riding mount. She did not regularly perform notarial acts, owned no land, and was apparently a humble urban retail trader. Like a modern teenage American with his car, her horse was probably her most valuable possession, and certainly her proudest. Nineteen notarized sales including only horses appeared in the sample, and 14 other sales included horses along with other objects traded, while 14 donations included one or more horses. Twenty-six wills made specific bequests for horses, while 87 marriage contracts mentioned horseflesh owned by one or both parties.

Among the wealthy, the horse and its companion, the carriage, assumed great importance as well. The coach was another object, like the sword, that the colonial government would have liked to have kept an attribute of white gentility. Like the sword, free coloreds found ways to appropriate this symbol for themselves, and indeed, the very restrictions on the use of coaches gave them even greater *cachet*. In addition to the fine horses and expensive decorated tack of Marie Anne Laporte (II), her estate included a carriage.[58] What strikes the reader of this act is the matter-of-fact way in which this item was listed, given that it was at least officially forbidden her as a free colored. Anne Françoise Roy was somewhat more effusive about her carriage in her marriage contract in 1779 — it came with a slave coachman and was worth 1,500 *livres* (while the slave was worth more than 3,500).[59]

Along with slaves, real property was the central capital good of the colony, however, far outweighing the high-status, movable possessions in economic value. Land was also a central component of social status. Being an *habitant*, as discussed in chapter 7, was almost the sine qua non of admission to the upper class of the colony. Planters were what the colony was all about. Being a planter meant that one shared in the wealth and power of Saint Domingue, even if only in small measure. Thus, for example, we have the widow Poupart and her sister, *habitantes* with 8 *carreaux* and no standing cash crops. Land, however, was not often carefully described in the death inventories, as notarized deeds and surveyors' reports usually existed and their transfer to the heirs was simply mentioned. However, it was normal to note the existence of buildings and describe them with short phrases that were loaded with meaning. These phrases appear throughout the notarial record, not just in the inventories, and can be analyzed for a clue to attitudes toward real estate ownership.

Case, or hut, was a widely used descriptive term for buildings of all sorts. It was not unusual to find *cases* in the country and in the city, used as outbuildings, as residences of slaves and other dependants (*case à negres* was a very common phrase), or for storage. When the term was applied to a principal residence, though, a value judgment was being made. That the judgment was not made of the size or construction standards is evident from a few examples of quite luxurious *cases:* the home of Marie Françoise *dite* Merthille at number 200, rue St. Thomas d'Aquin in Croix des Bouquets, was described as a *case* despite its 3,000 *livres* a year rent, cement construction, tiled floor, shingle roof, and quite respectable dimensions of 48 × 24 feet.[60] Similarly, the family home of the socially descending Chavanne family was described as a *case*, albeit *grande*, although it measured 84 × 34 feet, in wooden construction.[61]

In addition to these large and impressive *cases*, one finds occasional small and unimpressive *maisons*, the more highly valued term used for the residences of the socially prominent. For example, Sieur Jean Dabadie, an *habitant* from Fort Dauphin, took a lease on a *maison* in Cap Français that was a mere 33 × 16 feet, in plank construction, with earthen floors, and rented for a mediocre, for Cap, 600 *livres* a year.[62] Despite the presence of the important accessories of an oven and a well, one presumes that had the owner, a free mulatto named Dubertet *cadet*, rented this structure to another free colored, it would have been termed a *case*, or at best a *magasin*.

The term *magasin*, meaning warehouse or shop in modern French, was used indiscriminately in the notarial acts to mean either an urban structure of any sort or a rural storage facility. In fact, the terms *maison* or *case* were also used for retail premises—the *case* of Marie Françoise in Croix des Bouquets was her shop as well as her home. *Magasin*, then, was an intermediate step, and the term was frequently used for the homes of free coloreds of the middling sort. So, for example, when Sieur François Nicolas Tribon, himself a white *habitant*, apparently of the middling sort, sought to provide for his children with Marie Jeanne Laroche, free *quarteronne* of Mirebalais, he gave them a *magasin* at the corner of the rue de la Crête and the rue St. Louis in Mirebalais.[63] The *magasin* was clearly combined retail and residential space. Along the street there was a gallery, and in back were two rooms and another hallway, with a detached kitchen in the courtyard.

Thus, the progression from *case* to *magasin* to *maison* was a social progression rather than necessarily one from smaller to larger living quarters. Of course, the quarters could and usually did improve. However, the acquisition of a *maison* was an important step in the "arrival" of a person in the ranks of the elite of free colored society. We can tell, for example, that Zabeau Bellanton had arrived, when, in 1781, she bought a *maison* from the notary Maître Grimperel, Bordier *jeune*'s junior partner, at the corner of the rue St. Pierre and the rue du Gouverneur in Cap for 45,000 *livres*.[64] The house was enormous for downtown Cap, 60 feet square, and had five rooms, two separate kitchens, and a paved courtyard, all in masonry construction. Proving her economic credentials, Bellanton paid two-thirds of the price in cash and assumed a mortgage that Grimperel had taken on the house for the remainder. To own this house, described in these terms, was the mark of a wealthy and socially important person.

Another nonmaterial means of laying claim to full membership in the dominant culture was to adopt, publicly and enthusiastically, the religion of that culture. The official religion of Saint Domingue was Roman Catholicism, confirmed in the *Code Noir*.[65] However, many of Saint Domingue's whites were Protestants, royal prohibitions to the contrary notwithstanding. Prominent *négociant* Stanislas Foäche was regularly mulcted by members of the Roman Catholic parish council of Cap Français when they elected him to minor church offices he could not accept because of his Calvinist faith and then required him to pay a fine to escape the duty.[66]

Many more prominent whites had adopted the fashionable deism of the Enlightenment and were unenthusiastic Catholics, at best. Anti-clericalism was strong in the comments of observers of the colony's society, such as the Baron Wimpffen, who described the clergy of the colony thus: "tranquil in their rectories, most of the *curés* await peacefully a considerable income that allows them to live at their ease. Divine services are performed, more or less well, in churches where nobody goes, and, rather than preaching to nobody, they don't preach at all."[67] Free coloreds occasionally complained of the services they received from the local clergy, too. The children of the widow Antoine Drouillard could not get the *curé* of Mirebalais to bury their mother in a timely manner, so they had to do the burying themselves and make a notarial declaration to take the place of an entry in the parish register.[68]

Nonetheless, free coloreds tended to be strongly pious in the period under study. In an interesting parallel to their attitude toward military service, which free coloreds took up as a route to acceptance in white society just as whites were ceasing to regard it as a virtue, free coloreds took up Roman Catholic piety just as whites were drifting away from it.

Notarized wills and marriage contracts typically included religious boilerplate. Each notary had his preferred formula, from the freethinker Bordier *jeune* of Cap, who eschewed the practice altogether, to the pious Leprestre of Fort Dauphin, who usually had persons making wills before him begin their declaration by stating, "As a good Christian, Catholic, Apostolic and Roman, [the testator] has recommended his/her soul to God, supplicating his divine majesty very humbly to take pity on him/her, pardon his/her sins, and receive him/her in his holy paradise among the blessed by the merits of the Passion of our Lord Jesus Christ and the intercession of the Very Holy Virgin, and all the saints of Paradise."[69]

The presence of the formula means little as regards the piety of the individual making the act, but its absence or modification means much. When the reference to "Apostolic" and "Roman" was usually present, but dropped in one instance, it can be assumed that the testator was a Protestant. Only three free colored persons made such deletions; two were father and son, Bertrand LeMoine, of the French Navy and merchant marine, and his father, Augustin LeMoine, militia noncommissioned officer and beaver coat owner.[70] Especially notable was that both the LeMoines preserved the remainder of the formula, about paradise and even the Virgin Mary; they were pious men, just not Roman Catholics.

Occasionally, freethinkers would omit the formula. If we leave aside the records from Cap Français, where formulas were uncommon, 11 out of the 242 acts where a religious formula would be expected that were performed by free coloreds (4.5 percent) omit the formula altogether. Persons not wishing to be identified in their wills or marriage contracts as religious ran the gamut of social class and color. With such small numbers, it is difficult to make any generalizations except to say that this form of public religiosity was significantly more common among free coloreds than among whites—of the 63 wills performed by whites in the sample, again excluding those from Cap Français, 6 (almost 10 percent) omitted the formula.

Much more common among free coloreds was a strengthened religious formulation. Often, this would be combined with some other evidence of piety: a bequest to the church for charitable purposes, a wish to be buried in some particular place or manner, or an invocation of a particular saint. Twenty-five of the 242 acts contain some such strengthening of the religious content. In addition, 5 acts from Cap Français have some religious provision where any mention of God at all was unusual.

Finally, notations of burials in the parish registers stated whether the deceased had received extreme unction before death. Parishes, and priests, were few and far between in rural Saint Domingue, and this sacrament was rare in the colony. Whites especially do not seem to have made much use of priests to ease their final passage. Free coloreds were more likely to have the services of a priest at their deathbeds, even though, given the greater likelihood that their *habitation* or peasant steading was located in a remote area, it would likely be harder for the priest to get to them in an emergency. Of 108 burials of free coloreds in the sample, in 40 cases the deceased had received the church's services before death.

Another mark of prestige and social achievement was the ability to sign one's own name. All notarial acts were signed, by or for all actors. The notary read the act to persons who declared themselves incapable of signing and signed for them. As previously pointed out, the declared ability to sign notarial acts had little to do with actual literacy. The most prominent example of this phenomenon was Toussaint Breda, later Louverture. The traditional hagiography has it that he learned to read and write from a kindly priest who lived nearby. He may also have been taught by his former master and patron, Bayon de Libertat. Louverture's first role within the revolutionary leadership was as secretary to early leader Jean-François. Later, as leader of quasi-independent Saint Domingue, he regularly read and wrote extensive reports. As Napoleon's prisoner in the Jura, he wrote his memoirs and a number of appeals to the emperor. There seems no doubt that he was functionally literate throughout his adult life. However, as a middling *habitant* in this period, he always claimed not to be able to sign notarial acts that he executed.[71]

The opposite effect occurred in the case of Jeannette Reine of Cap Français. As her social status declined, she "forgot" how to sign her name. In 1785, described as a *marchande* but apparently in financial difficulties, she sold a *maison* that seemingly served as her residence and business quarters.[72] In this act, she declared that she had signed notarial acts before but had forgotten how, and so the notary signed for her. In a follow-up act a year later, Reine, no longer described as a *marchande*, succeeded in getting the remainder of the sale price of her business, and once again declared that she had forgotten how to sign.[73]

In the case of Jean-Baptiste Leveille *dit* Riché, prominent Cap Français free black and future general in Toussaint's army, we have an even clearer demonstration of how free coloreds chose to sign or not to sign notarial acts. He made his first appearance in the notarial record in February 1779 in an unusual manumission case where a white man, apparently the former master of Leveille's slave son, objected to the manumission.[74] The objections were overruled by the court, and Leveille proudly signed the act with a flourish. He appeared two months later, however, as a properly humble illiterate, when he was described as *nation* Foeda i.e., a *bossale*), further reducing his apparent status. He requested permission from the government at this time to free another family member, seemingly with the permission of her master.[75] Still later in 1779, he rented land and slaves in Limbé from a white *habitant* and again declared his inability to sign the act.[76] In 1781, by then a respected man and noncommissioned officer in the militia, he acted as the official mourner at a burial. The other witness was a white man; both signed the act.[77] Leveille signed again as the proud father of the groom at the wedding of his son, Jean-François Edouard *dit* Leveille, or Riché's wedding in 1782.[78]

Signing one's name to a notarial act was a claim to social status. Such a claim had to be made when the two participants could be assumed to be of different social statuses. Thus, of 728 sales contracts between free coloreds and whites, in 330 cases at least one participant signed the act. Not surprisingly, in 66 percent of the acts that were signed, the only one to sign was the white participant, in 26 percent, both participants signed, and in only 8 percent was the sole signer the free colored. On the other hand, of 613 sales where all participants were free coloreds, only 160 had at least one signature.

CONCLUSION

In conclusion, Saint Domingue's free coloreds adopted many markers of status from their white neighbors, albeit in somewhat modified forms. Their attitude toward color was principally driven by the desire to manipulate it in order to advance themselves or their offspring in a color hierarchy as much as physically and socially possible. As discussed in chapter 10, they indulged in class prejudices, especially among the planter elite, but do not seem to have cared about color except in an instrumental fashion, as part of a strategy of social advancement.

Free coloreds used titles, personal and official, to increase their status. They manipulated names, often over the objections of white officialdom, in order to stress their links to white relatives and to distance themselves from their slave antecedents in the public eye. Free coloreds owned and displayed status goods, from clothing and furniture to weapons and horses, in a further attempt to show both their wealth and their willingness to defend the system that produced it. For free colored men especially, the display of weapons and fine riding mounts helped combat gendered stereotypes of their caste.

Along with the public patriotism of military service, public displays of piety were another route many free coloreds used to show how firmly they were attached to the mores of the dominant culture, even though, ironically, the dominant culture was moving away from traditional Catholicism. Public displays of literacy served as another claim to social status. It is clear, and unsurprising, that literacy admitted officially in notarial documents had little to do with actual, functional literacy and much more to do with social position.

There is really no way to say what these findings mean, in the larger sense. It is almost banal to say that money does not translate directly into social position but must be mediated through a set of markers of social position. Some of these markers can be acquired by the smart, lucky, or well-connected without spending a great deal of money. Other individuals—especially free coloreds in this case—labor under a handicap caused by their birth and must be smarter, luckier, or better-connected to succeed. In this sense, the only contribution of this chapter is to show how the details of this process were different in Saint Domingue than in other societies in other times and places.

However, although it is unremarkable that free people of color should have done the same things as whites to get ahead in society, it is unfortunately not yet banal to say so. Students of slave societies, even relatively sophisticated ones, tend to think of free coloreds' skin color as the only thing about their lives that mattered. Ignoring the complex web of relationships that tied them to each other, to slaves, and to whites, ignoring the ways they presented themselves to the world as free people and citizens, the unreflective racialist theorist simply treats them as a caste caught between a color line and a status line. Lumping them into an undifferentiated intermediate class on the basis of color, as the colonial authorities tended to do, or because of the limited economic success of free coloreds is a simplistic and fundamentally wrong way to approach this group.

CHAPTER NINE

Family Relationships and Social Advancement

In 1777, in Mirebalais, Jean Pierret *fils,* a *quarteron,* 27 at the time and seriously ill, called the notary to witness his will. After a fairly flowery affirmation of his Catholic faith, Jean's only bequest, to his brother, was funds to pay the liberty tax of his slave housekeeper Charlotte, *negresse,* and her two children Jean Charles and Marie Jeanne, *mulâtre et mulâtresse.* Once the liberties were confirmed, the two children were to receive 2,000 *livres* each "to take the place of a living allowance." Any remaining property was to be retained by the brother, the only legitimate heir. One gets the impression that Jean did not expect that there would be much left over, although, as is common with wills, there was no inventory.[1] From the "living allowance" phraseology, we can presume that Jean Charles and Marie Jeanne were Jean's children and Charlotte his long-term lover.

The case of the Pierret household illustrates two common themes in Saint Domingue's society that often come as a surprise to the unreflective observer. The first is the surprising autonomy and even power wielded by free colored women, linked in informal relationships to whites but legally independent, since they were unmarried and thus free to dispose of substantial property without male supervision. The second surprise is the fact that the free colored family was bound together with strong ties, ties that transcend color and even status bars. Married or unmarried, black, white, or in-between, free or slave, Saint-Dominguans generally looked out for their kin. Free fathers did not impregnate their slaves and then ignore them; they established strong relationships with slave mistresses that lasted as long as marriages—maybe longer. The children of these relationships were cared for and preferred, insofar as the father's resources permitted. Slavery did not weaken the Dominguan family; indeed, it may have strengthened it by taking away other sources of support. The family, then, in all its forms, was an enormously important part of free colored Dominguans' lives. This book is about social advancement, and the preceding chapters have explored how economic success and noneconomic markers of social status could produce social advancement. However, in the consideration of social advancement, the unit of analysis is not the individual but the family. If a son became free, most likely soon the mother and siblings would also be free. If a mother was given a plantation, her children joined the planter class. If a man became a military officer or noncommissioned officer, his patriotic gesture would rub off on his kin, helping them all to advance.

The first subject to be considered under the general heading of the family in Afro-Dominguan society is formal and informal family relations between masters and slaves and among slaves. Marriage between master and slave was fairly common among free coloreds and was seen occasionally even with whites. Informal relations were much more common and were often quite stable and enduring. These relationships were the most important, although not the only, avenue to freedom for slaves and thus were crucial to the growth of the free coloreds as a group. In addition, they were important to the gendered view of the free colored class both at the time and in more recent scholarship.

The next topic is gender and relationships within the family and in the larger society, a crucial issue in both the internal structure and functioning of free colored society and in the perceptions of it held by white society. Free colored women occupied a position vastly higher vis-à-vis free colored men than did white women in their society. More numerous in proportion to the total numbers of their caste, free colored women were also much more likely to be independent economic actors and seemed to hold greater authority within the family. Their social role and, because social and economic position were so intimately linked, their economic role form an important part of this chapter.

The chapter next explores the role of the family in free colored society by looking at the institution of marriage in that society. Observers have often noted the prevalence of a "bourgeois morality" among free people of color. Matrimony was central to the free coloreds' social advancement and a state to which many free coloreds aspired. Yet commentators at the time described the free people of color as "licentious" and the product of "illicit unions." For example, Moreau de St. Méry said that "pleasure was the only master of the mulatto," while the "entire being of the *mulâtresse* is given to voluptuousness." Julien Raimond stressed the attachment of the free colored landholding elite to traditional French family structures in his *Réponse.*[2] Marriage was, in fact, a state to which many aspired but fewer achieved.

Marrying put the seal on a claim to traditional bourgeois morality that was important for those free coloreds aspiring to community leadership. The pseudo-*seigneurs*, the wealthy planting families, valued marriage and legitimacy to such an extent that one rarely finds illegitimate children in their ranks beyond the first generation. The military leaders were frequently freedmen, thus almost by definition illegitimate (as there were very few marriages between slaves), but many married, and all seem to have valued marriage and sought the status, though not to the exclusive degree of the planters.

The exploration of marriage and family concludes with a look at the relationships between parents and children in free colored society. It seems that close supervision of free colored children by their parents, especially their mothers, both reinforced their families, by comparison with those of the colony's whites, and perhaps affected their society in surprising ways.

FAMILY RELATIONSHIPS AMONG SLAVES AND WITH MASTERS

Many free colored families originated in relationships between slaves and their masters. However, most slave relationships were with each other. Let us begin with the slave family, important because of its impact on slave fertility and child survival. Formal marriage between slaves was uncommon. The *Code Noir* forbade priests to marry slave couples without the permission of masters.[3] This permission, it appears, was rarely given. The religious establishment did not reach out to slaves in any important way, with the limited exception of the Jesuit priests present in the North province until 1763. Evidence can be found of only four marriages between slaves. Three had been conducted in the North province before 1763, and the fourth in Martinique sometime before 1750.[4]

Nonetheless, family structures were strong among slaves belonging to free coloreds, when compared to those owned by whites. Housing for slaves, composed mostly of single-family *cases*, or huts, helped strengthen family ties. Occasionally, a large slaveholder would have an older person designated as guardian for the plantation's children—this was very common in large white-owned plantations—but in general, women would oversee the upbringing of their own children. Children were usually listed with their mothers on plantation records, and social tradition required that mothers and children not be sold separately until the child was at least 12 years old. Of 620 sales contracts for slaves in the records, only 12 involved slave children under 12 years of age being sold separately from their parents. (Many more records exist of mixed-race children being sold to their presumptive white fathers and away from their slave mothers—and a common although not universal provision in these cases was that the young mulatto, while remaining the property of his or her father, would live in the establishment of his former owner, with the mother, until reaching maturity.)

Much more common than formal marriage between slaves was marriage between master and slave. Free colored males and occasionally white males or free colored females would marry their slaves, thus achieving a tax-free manumission and often legitimating as well as manumitting a host of children. The *Code Noir* encouraged marriage between masters and slave women who had borne their children, and it stipulated that the act of marriage would make the slave spouse free.[5] Informal sexual unions between master and slave often were very stable, and formalizing them was the first step toward respectability, an important goal of free coloreds.

The sample contains 38 occasions where a free person married a slave. Only one of these marriages was between a white man and his slave.[6] In 26 cases, the free spouse was a free black, while in the remaining 11 instances, a free person of mixed race was the free spouse. The slave spouse was black in 30 cases and of mixed race in the other 8. Paralleling the predominance of women among those receiving manumission in general, only 8 of the slave spouses were male, compared to 30 slave brides. Thirteen of these marriages had already been blessed by children, as many as six in one example. Children were also freed and legitimized, tax-free, by the marriage.[7]

This provision of the law, used relatively commonly among free coloreds, seems to have served the purpose clearly intended for it in the original *Code Noir:* to reinforce free colored families and bring illicit unions out of the "closet" and into respectability.

Very many more much less "respectable" unions existed, however. There is, of course, absolutely no direct documentary evidence on this subject. Indirect or negative evidence is rife, however. The law fulminated against the practice of masters having sexual relations with their slaves, in the *Code Noir* and in a follow-up measure in 1713 that further penalized masters for violations of this article of the *Code Noir.*[8] Masters having contracted "alliances" with women of "mixed blood" (either slave or free) were further penalized by being made ineligible for noble titles in 1774.[9] The very repetition suggests how frequent the offense was.

Of 539 slave women identified as mothers in the sample of notarial acts, 155 had children of another racial category than themselves (in all but 2 of these cases, the child or children were of a lighter category than the mother). In the majority of cases, these were black women with mulatto children; in most cases the fathers of these children would have been white, although *quarteron* fathers and black mothers also produced *mulâtre* offspring according to the racial calculus of the day.

Racist propaganda of the day, and even of later days, suggested that colored women offered themselves indiscriminately to whites in an attempt to gain financially or advance their position in society.[10] Modern apologists for the people of mixed race suggest that the black slave woman was little more than a rape victim of her white master, who might sexually exploit any or all of his female slaves.[11] Both of these stereotypes are contradicted by the evidence that large numbers of these illegitimate relationships between master and slave seem to have been of significant duration and required at least some consideration from master to mother. Of the 155 mothers of mixed-race children, 69 had more than one child of the same racial category, which was different from their own, suggesting, although certainly not proving, that those children had the same fathers. Of the 155 mothers of different-colored offspring, 79 received their freedom during the period under study.

More commonly even than the slave mothers, though, one finds that the mixed-race offspring of these unions gained their freedom. According to contemporary observer Hilliard d'Auberteuil, colonial society considered it the moral responsibility of the white father of slave children to see his children freed. He said that this moral obligation led to the establishment of "mulatto factories" in which newly arrived whites would be seduced into relationships with black slaves and then be sold their children at exorbitant prices.[12] The average value of mixed-race child slaves gaining their freedom found in the records was 1,058 *livres,* whereas the average value of all slaves under age 16 was 1,103 *livres.* Thus, d'Auberteuil's anecdote does not seem to be borne out by the facts, but the very existence of this "urban legend" suggests the strength of the societal code requiring that mixed-race offspring be freed.[13]

In almost all cases, fathers provided in some way for their slave offspring, once freed. Acts of manumission did not generally contain specific clauses describing the level of support provided for the newly freed slave, so statistical precision is not possible in this case. However, traditional French legal practice required that fathers of illegitimate children provide for the sustenance of their offspring, either through a living allowance (*pension viagère*), dowry, training in a trade, or by providing them with the means to make a living in some other way. This obligation was widely respected in the case of fathers of illegitimate mixed-race children in Saint Domingue. The general practice was to make a sizeable donation of capital goods to the mother of the children, either while the father was still living or in his will.

There are hundreds of wills and inheritance cases in the sample in which a white testator provided some sort of assistance to a freed slave where there is at least a strong suspicion that the slave was the child of the white. A few examples will suffice to give an idea of the scope of this practice. In 1780, Sieur Jean Morin, aged

60 at the time and unmarried, working as a manager on the sugar plantation in Limonade owned by the Minieu family, made a will in which he left his goods and land in France to a nephew in Rennes and all his goods in the colony to a friend and fellow *économe*. The friend, Sieur Morand de la Sauvagère, was to seek the freedom of a mulatto boy named Joseph, aged 4, belonging to the Minieu plantation, and to "ensure his living."[14] The phrase is a dead giveaway of the family relationship between the two.

As a counterexample to the general faithfulness or at least stability common in master-slave relationships that in some measure proves the larger rule, in 1788, Sieur Jean Baptiste Martin Souffrière, an *habitant* with lands in the North province, lay ill in Cap Français. In his will, he gave liberty to 12 slaves, 9 mulatto children and their 3 mothers (2 *negresses* and a *griffonne*), giving a third of his property in the colony to each of the mothers and their children after a number of bequests to family in France were satisfied.[15] Even though he was apparently somewhat of a rake, he submitted to the general rule that slave offspring were to be freed and cared for.

At the high end of the economic spectrum, there is the example of the illegitimate mulatto sons of Charles Hérivaux, deceased in 1770, who had been willed two coffee plantations in the North province totaling 348 *carreaux*, 240 slaves, 30 head of livestock, 80,000 coffee bushes, and "certain other buildings and utensils."[16] Hérivaux *père* obviously had liberal notions about what constituted an appropriate level of support for his illegitimate children, but the local *parlement* agreed with his right to do so when the will was challenged by legitimate heirs in France.

One interesting feature of the Souffrière and Hérivaux wills that was found in many other such grants was the donation of the land, slaves, and so on in life usufruct to the mothers, if free, and in property to the children. Given the unusual longevity of free coloreds, this system meant that large amounts of property remained under the control of free colored women even after their sons reached adulthood (legally defined as age 25 at the time). This fact further reinforced the position of free colored women in society.

The situation for children of free colored masters was similar to that of the children of white masters. A few examples will suffice to demonstrate the trend. In one case related at the beginning of the chapter, Jean Pierret sought to secure the liberty of his children with a slave mistress. In another case, in Fort Dauphin in 1788, Marie Favardière's will apparently took care of her son's illegitimate slave children, granting liberty to Pierre Louis, *griffe*, and an anonymous *griffe* younger brother, and their mother, Marie Catherine, *negresse*, along with 11 *carreaux*. Favardière's son, living at the time in a faraway parish, got 21 *carreaux* adjacent to Marie Catherine's place—perhaps to encourage him to move back home and legitimize the relationship.[17] I am sure that any grandparent can understand the relationships in play here.

The Favardière case illustrates another commonality among these sorts of acts: that the duty to assist mixed-race illegitimate children extended to the fathers' kin, real or pseudo, when the fathers were unable or unwilling to perform it. Marie was a mother seeing to her grandchildren on behalf of her son, and there are plenty of cases of brothers, cousins, godparents, friends, or neighbors of a runaway or destitute father helping out his children.

FREE COLORED FAMILY STRUCTURES

The previous chapter discussed non-economic markers of status that free coloreds could manipulate to achieve or cement social gains. The structure of the family offered free coloreds many opportunities for social advancement. It was with their relatively stable family structure that free coloreds were best able to challenge the colonial stereotypes of them as "lascivious." Respectability and a further advance toward full citizenship were the rewards of marriage, legitimacy, and gender relations that matched those of the dominant culture. At the same time, in many cases it was by flouting gendered conventions that women of color, in particular, were able to acquire the economic resources that fueled their children's quest for respectability. This fundamental incongruity within free colored society deserves more attention than can be given it in this book, but some discussion of the issue is essential for the reader to understand the position of women in this society and thus understand the role of gender stereotypes in the actions of both the free colored soldiers and the planter elite families.

WOMEN IN DOMINGUAN SOCIETY

Women were the matriarchs of many wealthy rural free colored families, in part because of the provisions of the wills and donations that provided the seed capital for that wealth. Often, the mother would be granted life tenancy on a piece of land and would have control over a group of slaves given to her children by their father, who was usually white and usually not married to the mother. While free colored plantation managers were typically quite successful, and families could often afford to give substantial property to children during the lifetime of their mother, the hold of the mothers on the central agricultural operations of the family gave them considerable power over the younger generation.

In addition, free colored women were important in commerce. In contrast to the dominant position of males among white businesspeople, free colored women had an important role in the colony, rivaling, while not eclipsing, that of men of their own caste. This powerful role of women in free colored society had an important effect on both the internal structure of that society and on white attitudes toward free coloreds as a whole.

An exploration of the role of women in free colored society must take in the role of the *ménagère,* a woman who combined the roles of professional manager and personal companion to white men in the colony. While by no means the only framework under which relationships between free colored woman and white men took place, the institution of the *ménagère* rewards investigation. The relationships were often marked by stability over the long term and by a set of mutual obligations that were often the subject of a formal contract. The institution of *ménagère* represents a route to financial and social success open to free colored women that can be compared in some ways to the institution of free colored military service considered in chapter 11. Successful *ménagères* could become quite wealthy, as wealthy as successful military leaders at least. Interestingly, these women and their children, despite springing from the free colored lower classes or, indeed, from the slave underclass, formed an important source of new recruits for the planter elite group during the period under study.

Women outnumbered men in all groups in the free population of color throughout the colonial period. Female manumissions somewhat outnumbered male ones, even at the end of the colonial period. The population was female-dominated in more than numbers, however. Women played an important role both as economic actors and within the free colored family.

Many free colored households were headed by women. Illegitimacy was high, and even in those households where white fathers lived with their lovers and illegitimate children, social convention and law prevented the formation of a community of property, traditionally to be led by the male partner, as would be found in a marriage. Women in these situations were often important economic actors, as demonstrated by the examples of Julie Dahey, *ménagère* and presumed lover of Sieur Peignanan, pottery entrepreneur, and prospective, if temporary, heir to his plantation, and Nanette, matriarch of the Pincemaille clan.

In free colored households where there was an adult male—especially a husband but to a lesser extent an adult son—French law and cultural tradition would have ascribed him primary responsibility for the family's economic activities. However, cultural values that are still a part of both west African and Haitian society gave women a great deal of independent authority. In the example of the widow Turgeau and her son Pierre, it was Pierre who managed the plantation, but he was very much under the supervision of his mother. She called him formally to account every year, and he justified every expense with great precision. In a telling point illustrating the power relationships between them, no notarial act ever called her *negresse libre*, but instead she was always *Dame* Turgeau, occasionally with *la nommée* thrown in, in case higher authorities checked up, while the son was occasionally identified as *mulâtre libre*.

Women of color made substantial use of their unusual freedom to take part in the economic life of the colony. As managers of their own, or their children's, property, they seemed to move in the patriarchal economic sphere with greater freedom than white women.

They were generally pretty successful in that sphere. For every Dame Chavanne, who lost the family homestead after her husband's death, there were several Marie Anne Laportes, the aging second wife of Louis Laporte (I), who was still protecting the economic position of the family in 1780. In that year, she bought back from a white *habitant* neighbor a piece of land that her son or grandson had sold him and reunited it with the family patrimony.[18] Free women of color were statistically much more important rural landholders than were white women. They were at least four times more likely to participate in sales of land than were white women.[19]

Urban real estate development was a favorite place for people of color to invest gains. Women took a leading role in this activity. Almost half of colored landowners in Cap in 1776 were women.[20] Like men, women used urban landholdings as the basis of family fortunes and social advancement. A good example of this process is the story of one Anne *dite* Rossignol, a free *mulâtresse* and matriarch of a quite successful free colored family. Apparently a citizen of the French colony of St. Louis in Sénégal (and thus that rarity in the eighteenth-century Americas, a voluntary African immigrant), Anne first appeared in the sample as the renter of house in a quite tony, and almost exclusively white, neighborhood in Cap Français in the cadastral survey of 1776.[21] She most likely did not reside there, given the unofficial residential segregation in the city, but probably sublet the house out as apartments. She owned another large house in the Petit Carenage, a neighborhood in which she might have been expected to live, and in 1786 she sold this house and six of her domestic servants to her daughter, Marie Adelaide, for 66,000 *livres* (not cash, but probably assessed against Marie Adelaide's share of the inheritance).[22] The house was quite impressive both for size and for quality of construction, in masonry with a tile roof and a well in the courtyard. It also appears to have been divided into apartments, although no leaseholders were mentioned in the act. Perhaps they, too, were short-term renters or boarders without official leases. In any case, Anne was economically successful through her urban landholding. The transfer of the house and servants to the daughter permitted Anne to convert her economic success into social advancement when, ten days after the sale, Marie Adelaide signed a marriage contract with a white man.[23] Sieur Guillaume Dumont, a surgeon, brought 29,000 *livres* to the relationship, including landholdings in France. The bride brought 79,000 *livres* to the marriage, including that 50,000 *livre* house. The dowry was a quite substantial 10,000 *livres*.

At a lower economic level than the Rossignol clan, the public markets in the colony were dominated by free colored women retailers, and most free women of color at all economic levels seem to have had some money-making activity outside the home. The articles of incorporation of the *société* Marie Josephe–Guillemet in Fort Dauphin is the most detailed look at small commerce by free colored women in the sample (see appendix 3). Marie Josephe and her white junior partner had a stock of very plebian commodities for sale—cheap cooking oil, a little fabric, and suchlike—and some very spartan furniture for the store. Marie Josephe was very strict about not allowing Guillemet to offer credit to his friends, and the cash on hand would not suffice to pay more than a few months' living expenses for the two of them, to say nothing of replacing stock.

Most of these retail operations seem to have been quite small-scale, similar to those found in west African and Haitian markets to this day. As such, they did not leave many traces in the notarial records; the very price of performing a notarial act would make notarial formalization uneconomical for any but the largest transactions these women carried out. When one of these small-time tradeswomen moved up from street market stall to fixed retail quarters, though, she would occasionally rent a shop and require the services of a notary. One such case is that of Victoire Arelise, a free black woman who sublet a room with a gallery facing on the rue St. François Xavier in Cap, plus a storeroom or living quarters in the courtyard of a house leased by prominent free colored landlady Elisabeth Bonne Femme *dite* Jolicoeur in 1784.[24] The rent was 1,650 *livres* a year, appropriate in view of the location of this shop near the docks and in an active retail neighborhood but suggestive by its size of the large sales volume that Arelise would have to make to turn a profit here. Women of color who achieved success in small commerce would be accorded the occupational title *marchande*, or merchant. Whereas for men this term was one with mixed connotations (suggesting that they were not sufficiently important to qualify as *négociants*), for women this was quite a tribute to their success in business. There were 16 colored women who qualified for the description *marchande;* their names are found in appendix 2. The average value of the 45 acts they performed was 10,958 *livres*, 142 percent of the average value for all acts in the sample.

These *marchandes* were women who had, for the most part, not been the beneficiaries of much largesse from whites. Many of them were widows, but none had been married to a white. Some had children of a lighter racial category than themselves, but none seem to have had white lovers in evidence. They did business with whites—for example, Genevieve Dupré of Port-au-Prince acted as the *procureur,* or representative, of Mathurin Mahé, a white who had returned to France, in a lawsuit decided in his favor in 1787.[25] We have already seen *marchande* and slave trader Zabeau Bellanton and her pretty much unaided rise from unknown to leading businesswoman in chapter 5.

Free colored women, thus, were significant economic actors. They owned large amounts of property, they dominated some facets of commerce, and even when they did not own, they frequently controlled important capital through the terms of donations from their white patrons.

GENDER IN PUBLIC ATTITUDES TOWARD FREE COLOREDS

The notarial record does not permit many generalizations about relations inside the free colored family. Just as in the case of discriminatory legislation forbidding this or that activity or possession to free coloreds, their real behavior did not correspond to that desired of them by the laws' framers, so relations inside the family may not have corresponded exactly to the pattern suggested by the notarial acts. What one says in official and public statements is often different from what takes place in private. However, the public impression had an impact on whites' attitudes toward free coloreds.

White society's views of women's roles at the time may have prevented white businessmen from taking colored female counterparts seriously. Also, the existence of so many colored women heads of household reinforced white stereotypes about the "licentiousness" and "effeminacy" of colored society and the "shiftlessness" of men of color. As a result of these gendered stereotypes, free colored males may have sought masculine activities, such as military service, that could increase whites' confidence in the entire group's "gender correctness."

Of course, the mixed-race population sprang in the first place from sexual unions between African women and white men, generally their masters or employers— either directly or some generations back. This meant that free men of mixed race faced a complicated task in convincing the descendants of those white men that the unequal power relationship that once existed could now be equalized. On the one hand, such unequal sexual relationships continued throughout the colonial period, reinforcing the image of the free colored group in the minds of whites as sexual objects and thus reinforcing the "gendering" of the free colored as "feminine." On the other hand, the men of mixed race were the sons or half-brothers of the white men, and this was a family relationship that white society took seriously.

Women's roles in this complicated dance of gendering and gender roles were complex and varied. One role for free women of color that was universally noted at the time was as *ménagère*, housekeeper and live-in lover, for white men. The role of *ménagère* was the best-known role for women of color in Saint Domingue at the time. To read the early white commentators on the society, it would seem to have been the only role open to them. The traditional view, shared by most observers at the time and many since, was that the free colored community was defined by "licentiousness" and immorality. Moreau de St. Méry, while also attributing this conduct to the warmth of the climate and the limited supply of white women, adopts this explanation in his *Description . . . de la partie française:*

> it is thus that the majority of *mulâtresses* are condemned to the estate of cour-
> tesan, where they are associated [in the public mind] with slave women. This
> illegitimate commerce, an offence to morals and religious laws, is nonetheless
> regarded as a necessary evil in the Colonies, where there are few white women.
> This is especially true in Saint Domingue, where this disproportion is larger
> [than in the other French Caribbean colonies]. It seems to prevent even worse
> vices: the weaknesses of masters for their slaves causes the lightening of the
> burden of slavery. One can even say that it is the warmth of the climate which
> irritates the desire, and the facility with which these desires can be satisfied,
> that will make legislative prohibitions against these practices useless. The law
> is quiet when nature speaks imperiously.
>
> It is also possible that the morals of the slave women have an influence on
> the free women. Black women coming from Africa, where polygamy is ac-
> cepted, know that by their illegitimate commerce with white men they can
> ameliorate their condition and that of their children. This is enough to make
> them complaisant. Thus, the influence of the climate, the love of luxury, and
> a distrust of men of their own class, who are the most suspicious and despotic
> of husbands, all lead women of color to flee marriage and to give themselves
> to a lucrative concubinage. This state satisfies their voluptuous inclinations
> and also is the activity to which they owe their liberty.[26]

C. L. R. James, an observer closer to our times who might have been expected to have known better, placed the worst possible complexion on the situation when he said that "in 1789, of 7,000 Mulatto women in San Domingo (sic), 5,000 were either prostitutes or the kept mistresses of white men."[27] The truth turns out to have been substantially more complex than that.

First, not all employers of *ménagères* were white men: Jean-François Edouard *dit* Leveille employed a free black woman named Hélène as his houskeeper on his *habitation* in Limbé for 400 *livres* a year.[28] Vincent Ogé also employed a *ménagère*, Marie Magdelaine Garette—befitting his greater wealth and higher social position as a *quarteron* and a *négociant,* her salary was 600 *livres* a year.[29] Of the remaining 21 women identified as *ménagères* in the sample, 20 were employed by whites. The names of all 23 appear in appendix 2 of this book.

Many employers of *ménagères* demonstrated a surprising and sometimes touching fidelity and tenderness for their lovers. Many men remained with the same woman for decades, fathering large families. At the men's death or departure from the colony, the women were, by social tradition, well rewarded.

We have already seen the colossal payoff that Sieur Thomas Peignanan tried to arrange for his *ménagère,* Julie Dahey. She and her children would have become sugar planters of considerable importance in Croix des Bouquets had his scheme come off as planned. Even under the revised will, he left her with more than 20 slaves and enough cash to buy good land for them to work. If not a sugar planter, she would at least have had the opportunity to become a coffee planter, and moreover, one without a large debt to the metropolitan kin. While the most generous settlement, Peignanan's was not the only deal along these lines.

White planters sometimes used a subterfuge to make bequests to their *ménagères* by claiming they were debts. Similar to the example of the revoked bequest of Sieur Léonard Simiat to his employee Louise, in which he claimed in one will that he owed her a substantial sum of money, only to revise his will and eliminate the "debt," there is the case of Marie Grasse *dite* Balanquin of Limonade. She was *ménagère* for a white man of considerably less wealth than Sieur Simiat, a Sieur François Androuin, seemingly an employee of the sugar plantation Lescarmortier in Limonade who fell ill and died in 1780. His death inventory revealed that he owned 2 slaves and 4 horses, as well as a few personal articles and a guarantee from his doctor promising reimbursement of 3,300 *livres* in fees if Androuin died. He had willed 3,000 *livres* and one of the horses to Grasse "to recompense her for her good and agreeable services, especially during his last illness."[30] The bequest to Grasse, as specific recompense for specific services and as the first mentioned in the will, took precedence over the other bequest, to the young man's parents in France, of 4,000 *livres.* Grasse accepted her payment and then returned 3 more horses and a carriage, which she said belonged to the estate—and which, since they were unmentioned in the will or official inventory, she could easily have kept. So, far from being the grasping and mercenary "prostitute" or "kept mistress," Grasse was careful not to leave herself destitute, but she showed concern for the probably not-too-well-off parents of her lover, whom she most likely had never met, and who most likely would have had little concern for her, given racial attitudes of the day.

Departure from the colony could also leave a *ménagère* bereft. In 1788, Moise Lange, of the house of Lange *frères,* was leaving the colony for France on an extended business trip. He left behind him one Rose Merza, his *ménagère*. In his procuration to the house of Petit *frères*, his business managers, he ordered that 2 of his slaves be placed at Rose's disposition and furthermore that she be paid 33 *livres* a week (1,716 *livres* a year) until his return. This represents a reasonable professional salary, approximately what a junior or less-experienced white male plantation manager might be paid.

Ménagères typically signed employment contracts with their patrons, stating their pay and specific managerial duties they would be required to perform. For example, Marie Louise à Traitte, upon being engaged by Paul Bonneau, *quarteron libre,* promised to "go and live on the said Bonneau's *habitation* in the quality of *gouvernante,* and thereby to take care of his household [*ménage*] and house [*maison*], and of his domestic servants, to see to the conservation of his goods just as a good *gouvernante* and manager [*économe*] must do, and this for as long as the parties judge it appropriate." For these services, she was to be given one slave of a value not to exceed 2,000 *livres* each year, or the equivalent in cash.[31]

The legal relationship between the two was that of employee and employer, and the verbiage was quite similar to contracts signed between absentee white landlords and their professional *économes.* However, Bonneau was not an absentee planter resident in Cap, but a single man resident on his plantation. The relationship between them was both personal and professional, and seemingly much more companionate than even the traditional relationship between spouses in French society. The contract between them, then, served to grant Marie Louise limited rights to use the Bonneau capital as if she really were Bonneau's *économe.* Within the domestic sphere, anyway, armed with this piece of notarized paper, she could buy and sell on his behalf, exercise authority over his slaves, and, indeed, behave both as his junior business partner and as a member of his family. This was presumably the purpose of the act—to give economic rights to a person who was being made into pseudo-kin as the planter's acknowledged and long-term lover.

For the white resident of Saint Domingue, the step beyond acquiring a pseudo-wife and illegitimate children through having a *ménagère* was to marry a free colored woman. Miscegenation was never forbidden, although legislation and social convention sent mixed messages about it. On the one hand, the *Code Noir* encouraged masters to marry the slave mothers of their children. On the other hand, the law forbade men who had contracted *mésalliances* (marriage to someone of far inferior status) to hold public office, ranging from militia rank to noble titles.

Increasing racist ideology, and racially based discrimination against the free coloreds, had led to a significant decline in the rates of such unions from the first half of the century, when they were responsible for the creation of such powerful free colored houses as the Laportes of Limonade and the Raimonds of Aquin. However, for those white men who could find it in themselves to defy social convention, there were significant advantages to be gained from marriage into a free colored family.

Free coloreds were good stewards of capital, as we have seen, and many free colored families were quite well-off. Marriage to a white, combining "whitening" with "respectability," represented quite a significant social promotion and thus was to be sought after and paid for. Of 10 such marriage contracts in the sample, in 8 the bride brought substantially more economic value to the relationship than did the groom. In one of the remaining cases, a long-established relationship producing eight living children was finally ratified by the church, while in the other no estimation of relative economic value can be made. Even in the 8 cases, though, colored in-laws were careful that their family's property was not expended unnecessarily.

The companionate nature of these marriages, based perhaps on a realization that the free colored partner was likely to be a better steward of the family's capital, was frequently stressed in the provisions of the marriage contract. For example, Sieur Pierre Huget, a native of Haute-Guienne, married Françoise Elizabeth *dite* Girardeau in 1788. She brought a lot of very valuable status possessions—clothing and furniture—and a slave to the relationship, for a total value of about 9,400 *livres*. He brought only his personal property, not described, and, of course, his white skin. However, a condition of the marriage contract was that the husband was not to be permitted to "sell any slaves or real property which may belong or come to belong to the family without the written consent" of the wife.[32] Certainly this restriction was likely to be galling to a man raised in French society of the times. A similar case was the wedding of Sieur Louis Charles Cautellier, a professional *économe,* to Marie Louise Turgeau, relative of the Dame Turgeau previously introduced. His economic contribution was not stated in the contract but can be assumed to have consisted for the most part of his earning power as a technically skilled employee. Half of her family's more substantial contribution of land and slaves, though, was withheld from the community of property and remained her personal property.[33] Thus, her independent economic status was not completely obviated by marriage and acquisition of "respectability" as the bride of a white man. In addition, if his skills as a manager were questionable, and because he was an immigrant to the colony and seemingly rather young to boot, her abilities and the advice of her mother might serve to keep the family solvent. Wealthier white women, often widows with substantial means, marrying newly arrived white immigrants might, and often did, adopt the same strategy, but it is interesting to see it used here by a young free colored woman whose entire economic contribution to the relationship came from dowry gifts from her parents. It was as if both parties took as a given that a free colored woman might be a better manager of property in the colony than a white man for whom plantation management was his profession.

BOURGEOIS MORALITY AND RESPECTABILITY

Julien Raimond argued that family structures were stronger among free coloreds than among whites in Saint Domingue, and thus that free coloreds were a more moral people than the colony's whites.[34] This argument flew in the face of the collective opinion of white observers up to that point and through the two centuries since, as we have seen. It also flew in the face of substantial statistical data showing that illegitimacy was much more common among free coloreds than among whites in the colony and that marriage was less frequent for colored women than for white women. However, it gets at a deeper truth about free colored society, which is that it was much more concerned about the stability of the family, whether female headed or otherwise, and that free coloreds aspired to bourgeois "family values" in the colony to a much greater extent than did whites. Of course, whites, especially the many young white men in the colony, often aspired to being considered bourgeois in France upon their triumphant return from their luxurious and decadent, but very profitable, colonial exile. Raimond was right in his larger conclusion, that free coloreds were the indigenous stable middle class of the colony. As Raimond would have had it, the stability of the free coloreds offered France the rock on which to build a society that would remain true to French values and loyal to French sovereignty, if only racial attitudes and revolutionary politics had permitted it.

Illegitimacy rates can be a good indicator of the strength of family structures in a population. Parish registers, wills, and other documents often mention the legitimacy or bastardy of the actors. Of 1,112 free colored persons whose legitimacy was mentioned in the notarial sample, 629 (57 percent) were described as illegitimate and only 483 (43 percent) as legitimate. Almost by definition, all freedmen were illegitimate, although some were legitimized after manumission—marriages of free persons to slaves almost always included significant numbers of offspring to be legitimized—and there were very few marriages between slaves. Of those born free, the sample of notarial acts and parish registers suggest that about half were legitimate. Some families, especially those at the top of the socioeconomic scale, were almost exclusively composed of legitimately born persons—as witness the Laportes, whose family tree is found in appendix 1. In the first generation, at least three of eight ancestors were bastards. In the second, two. In the third, one, and in the fourth, all members identified were legitimate. One would expect that illegitimate offspring of powerful free coloreds would be as quick to claim kinship as similar relatives of white people, so few illegitimate members of this family must have escaped notice. Clearly, family members were solidly committed to marriage as a means of building their family—much more so than comparable white planter families in the colony, who had a substantial population of free colored bastards at each generation.

However, the planter elite were not alone in insisting on the importance of marriage to their family strategies. Members of the Olivier family, the offspring of the famous Capitaine Vincent, hero of Cartegena and black militia officer, seem to have been careful to ensure that as many offspring as possible were legitimate. While he himself was a freedman and illegitimate, he married upon his return to the colony and had a considerable number of legitimate offspring. His daughter had an illegitimate mulatto son, Pierre Olivier, who was nonetheless welcomed into the clan and became quite influential in his own right. Even the widow Poupart, a poverty-stricken member of the family, married and bore legitimate children. Legitimacy was valued as a component of social standing at all economic levels.

Even in those families that were not united by formal marriage, commitment to family stability was high. Men remained with their *ménagères* for decades. There were occasional examples of women of color with illegitimate children by different fathers (either admitted or obvious from their different racial categories), but this was rare. When irregular unions were formalized by marriage, often a half-dozen or more children would be legitimized, as in the case of the 1782 marriage of Sieur Gaspard Bos, from Italy, and Marie Petit *dite* Quercy, *negresse libre*, which bestowed the respectability of legitimate birth on eight young people.[35]

Women who were unmarried mothers often oversaw a promotion to respectable family life on the part of their children. Françoise La Racointe of Mirebalais was a perfect example of this process. Free black mother of six surviving illegitimate mulatto children, whose father left them owners of considerable resources in land and slaves, she oversaw a fairly successful campaign to marry off her children. Her daughter Marie married Jean-Baptiste Nivard, a mulatto *habitant* in Mirebalais. Marie and Jean-Baptiste, by 1777, had built an *habitation* worth 110,000 *livres*.[36] Françoise's son Charles died before 1776 but left legitimate heirs behind him. His legitimate daughter was herself married by 1777.[37] Françoise's son Jean married Charlotte Dumoyer in the 1750s; their family included eight surviving legitimate offspring. Their daughter Cécile was married by 1788 to a mulatto named Joseph Labattu, who was also an *habitant*, although there is no record of his resources.[38] Another daughter of Jean and Charlotte was Marie Charlotte, who married in 1778 to one Jean Baptiste Filatre, himself a legitimate *quarteron*.[39] Thus were *libertinage* and *concubinage* converted into solid bourgeois morality as the family advanced in economic and social terms.

Marriage was, of course, a vital part of family strategies in *ancien regime* France, both for the acquisition and retention of wealth and for social advancement. Free colored families used marriage for all the same reasons that whites used it, and in very much the same ways, especially at the top of the social scale. In addition, toward the bottom of the social scale, marriage was an inexpensive and highly thought of way to free one's slave lover and children.

MARRIAGE CONTRACTS AND RELATIONSHIPS BETWEEN SPOUSES

As suggested by the economic role of free colored women and by the nature of relationships between free colored women and white men, marriage between free coloreds was a more companionate institution than among whites. Marriage contracts typically detail the resources brought by each partner to the relationship. While traditional practice had it that marriage was a patriarchal relationship, and the combined resources of the couple would be managed by the husband, wives who made larger contributions can reasonably be expected to have had some voice inside the family in the management of those resources. A large dowry would have represented an advantage in the internal family power balance. Free colored women brought large dowries to their marriages, not only to those with whites, but also within their caste. Of 122 marriage contracts in which the comparative value of the two parties' contributions could be ascertained, the wife's contribution was substantially greater in 40 (33 percent), the husband's in 28 (23 percent), and the two were substantially equal in 54 (44 percent).[40]

Interestingly, the average value of the couples' declared resources in those marriages in which the wife was the wealthier was significantly higher (53,935 *livres*) than those marriages where the husband was the wealthier partner (21,750 *livres*). Those where the two couples were of substantially equal wealth had the lowest value of all at 16,238 *livres*. These data suggest that well-off families tended to marry their daughters to men of lesser wealth, perhaps in order to preserve control over family resources. If the power relationship within the marriage was tilted in favor of the partner who brought the larger contribution, then the wealthy fathers- and mothers-in-law would in reality be "gaining a son rather than losing a daughter."

As we have seen, marriage contracts also often stipulated specific restrictions on the husband's right to manage the wife's goods. The traditional arrangement was that marriage created a community of property, supposedly managed by the husband. Occasionally, a marriage contract would depart from this traditional arrangement, stating that no community of property was to be created, and that the wife was authorized in advance by the husband to manage her own affairs. This sort of arrangement was rather common among white widows making second marriages but less common among free coloreds. One gets the impression that it was seen as somehow less than completely respectable. By having such a relationship officially described in the notarial act, the wife was publicly announcing her violation of the traditional gender roles. As many of the things free coloreds did pushed the envelope of racial roles, perhaps they did not feel confident in challenging gender roles quite so explicitly. Only 5 of the 190 marriage contracts in the sample followed this model.

Instead, free coloreds more often settled for other restrictions on the absolute right of the husband to manage the communal property that were inserted in their marriage contracts. Exemption of part of one party's total worth from the community was a common expedient. Either a proportion—a quarter, half, or more— usually of the bride's property, would be set aside for her own use, or a specific amount would be reserved for the bride as disposable in bequests in her will while managed by the husband during her life. Either way, families preserved property given to their daughters. Seventeen of 190 marriage contracts contain some such provision, and they were from generally quite well-off families, as one would expect. The average value of these contracts was 65,930 *livres.*

Another provision along these lines that was sometimes used, as in the marriage contract of Sieur Cautellier and Demoiselle Turgeau, was to give the wife a veto over alienation of capital goods—slaves and land—from the community. This was less common in marriages among free coloreds; only three such cases appeared in the sample. Perhaps this provision bent the gender lines too far for respectability, too.

Finally, members of one side of the family, usually the bride's, were sometimes specifically listed as heirs of the couple as part of their contract. Thus, for example, when Mathieu Cockburn married Marguerite Fauquet in Cap in 1785, their marriage contract, otherwise traditional, obligated the husband to provide a 1,200 *livre* per year pension to his mother-in-law if his wife predeceased her.[41]

Free colored couples who married had frequently been together for years before legitimating their relationship. Often, of course, if one member of the couple had been a slave, this was a cheap and socially respectable way to manumit one's partner and children. However, even when both partners had been free for some time, it was not uncommon for hosts of illegitimate children to be legitimated by the marriage of two free coloreds. In general, these couples were of strained economic circumstances, so one presumes that the expense of a marriage was beyond their means for some years after starting a family. In addition, these marriages often took place when one of the children was seeking increased respectability. It is common to find that the oldest child, often a daughter, was approaching marriageable age in these cases, which leads to the supposition that it was her value on the marriage market that was being enhanced by the parents' belated acquisition of the church's blessing on their relationship. It was rare to find a child born before the marriage in the more wealthy and powerful free colored families—they would have been no more willing to permit their daughters to form illegitimate unions than would the metropolitan rural aristocrats they emulated so assiduously.

RELATIONS BETWEEN PARENTS AND CHILDREN

The marriage contract, of course, illustrates the relationship between husband and wife. It also, however, illustrates the relationships between parents and children, as it serves as part of the family strategy to keep the property of the family intact from one generation to the next, advance the family socially, and provide for the happiness of the children. Wills are another way to look at the relationship between parents and children, as are the many other notarial documents in which members of two generations were participants.

Through all these sources we see a society with an unusual view of generational relationships. In contrast to the relative freedom accorded women, children, even after reaching adulthood, were firmly under the control of their elders in a way that would have been pleasing to traditionalists in France. These attitudes were not at all characteristic of white society in the colony.

Many whites living in the colony were immigrants. They had left behind them a society in the *metropole* that traditionally delayed the acquisition of property by children until after the parents' deaths and that accorded parents, especially fathers, a great deal of power over their children's lives. Living in the faraway colony, without their older relatives about (even the older relatives of native-born whites tended to retire to the *metropole*), the young white Dominguans were their own masters. This may account for a good deal of the effervescence of white creole life that often merited the unfavorable comments of observers at the time. However, members of all generations of free colored families were resident in the colony, and traditional ideas about children's duties and parents' rights were quite strong.

A great deal of land and slaves was held in life tenancy by mothers of mixed-race children as a condition of donations made to them by their white fathers. The widow Turgeau and her son spring to mind as an example of a free colored family in which the mother was clearly the dominant force.

An equally large group of legitimate free colored children whose fathers, of either racial caste, were dead were in a similar position. This was thanks to a provision of many (although not all) marriage contracts that transferred title to property to the children once one of their parents died but reserved life tenancy in all, or a significant part, of the estate to the surviving spouse. These sorts of provisions were intended to ensure that the widow would not be beggared by the death of her husband, but the actual practice proved to be an overreaction.

Counterbalancing these trends were the donations of important collections of capital goods "in advance of inheritance" to children on the occasion of important turning points in their lives, often marriage. This was one of the important spurs that encouraged young free coloreds to marry. Of the 190 marriage contracts in the sample, 37 contain some such provision spelled out in detail. Most other marriage contracts contained gifts from parents, but the acts do not explicitly describe them as advances on the future spouse's inheritance. On the other hand, 15 marriage contracts specifically stated that some portion of one or the other partner's goods came from their own savings or income from their trade and thus were not to be counted against their share of the parental estate, suggesting that the alternative was understood even if not explicitly stated.

Often, the donation from parents to children at the time of their marriage was the right of the newly married couple to live on the family homestead and plant crops. Sometimes, children were offered the right to live under the paternal roof and eat at the family table, which would certainly indicate a subordinate position. This suggests a different relationship between adult children and their parents than with what we are familiar in our culture. More often, parents would set aside a piece of land for the children to use. As usufructaries, the children at least had control over the land, often irrevocable control, but this was a far cry from the ownership and control exercised by young white neighbors. Sometimes, lucky children would receive actual property rights to a piece of land.

In general, though, wills and death inventories show us that parents retained significant portions of their property until their deaths. As in the case of the Pincemaille family, children who actually had title to land might have difficulty laying claim to control of it on the death of the usufructiary parent. Nanette, the free black *materfamilias,* died in 1784, and her children, Michel François and Marie Françoise, had to make quite a stern protest to the notary before their property rights to the family's land and slaves could be accepted.[42]

CONCLUSION

Free colored women had a surprisingly strong public role, both as economic actors and as dominant presences in the lives of their often fatherless children. This feminine, and very un-French, power paradoxically reinforced gendered stereotypes of their caste. At the same time, though, the mobilization of women's labor and management talent may have helped free coloreds be more successful entrepreneurs. Certainly, many were successful in business. Free colored women household managers and companions to white men were successful in advancing their families economically, but at the same time their violation of sexual mores reinforced stereotypes held at the time, and more recently, about free coloreds.

Free colored families were, in fact, quite strong by colonial standards, with families at all levels placing great importance on the institution of marriage. Even those families that were formed without formal sanction from the church were nonetheless quite stable, and this family stability, unnoticed though it was by the stereotypes, was nonetheless important in the economic success of the group. Strong families, though, meant strong controls over children, and free colored children enjoyed much less liberty than their white counterparts on the island.

PART THREE

Group Strategies for Economic and Social Advancement

CHAPTER TEN

Planter Elites

The reader has already met the Laportes, the best-documented members of the planter elite in the sample of notarial acts. They were by no means the only family of free coloreds who achieved power and social position during this period. For another example, there are the Baugés of Galets, Croix des Bouquets, mulatto relatives of the powerful white planting family of the same name. They were small planters who seized the day as the economy boomed after the end of the War of American Independence and became big planters by the end of the 1780s. In 1777, they established a partnership in which the husbands of the four Baugé sisters, including members of the Desmarres and Graine clans, rented four-sevenths of the ancestral plot to the three brothers, along with all the water coming to them from the irrigation system in the Cul de Sac River.[1] One presumes that in this patrilocal society, the sisters were living with their husbands on the husbands' *habitations* and could not exert direct supervision over their land. As usual in free colored families, there were relatives to whom the land could be entrusted rather than seeking out the services of a professional manager.

At the time, the farm was producing small amounts of food for the market, as the notarial act refers to *places à vivres* owned by the four brothers-in-law on the place. Clearly, these were small farms of the "middling sort": above the peasantry and tied to the market, but by no means a plantation. The term *habitant* is used, but it seems more a title of courtesy than a real description. Over nine years, though, the three brothers turned it into a proper *habitation*. By the time this piece of land last appeared in the notarial record, in 1781, it was worth 11,400 *livres* a year in rent, or well over 100,000 *livres* in total value. On that date, four white men, probably professional estate managers seeking to move up and two of them relatives of one of the brothers-in-law, rented the *habitation* from the Baugés for 5.5 years, along with all water rights. They rented 24 slaves and 6 head of mules as well. They also were to complete and maintain two seemingly quite solid sugar mill buildings, with an animal-driven milling machine. The renters were to leave standing six cane fields of 4 carreaux each at the end of the lease period, with the alleys planted in sweet potatoes, protect the fields with live hedges or fences, and leave the whole place in "defensible condition."[2]

This did not represent the entirety of the Baugé patrimony. The brothers had turned their earlier profits into new, large estates worth an additional 80,000 *livres*. One was a coffee plantation within the borders of the parish of Port-au-Prince, above Bellevue, and the other was another sugar establishment still under construction at Fond Parisien in Croix des Bouquets.[3]

In this chapter we turn to group formation among free people of color. The preceding chapters, which treated free people of color as a more or less undifferentiated whole, have served to give a basis for comparison for the two leadership groups that this study has identified. This chapter explores the subgroup to which the Laportes and the Baugés belonged, the planter elite, beginning with an extensive definition of what is meant by the term *planter elite*. While the members of this subgroup were in general wealthy, rural, of mixed African and European antecedents, and at least two or three generations removed from slavery in the time period under study, not all these characteristics apply to every member of the group. Instead, the distinguishing characteristic is the level, intimacy, and frequency of contacts with whites, both personal or familial and financial. These close links with whites mean relatively weak links with other free coloreds not of their group. It is for this reason that this group is referred to as an *elite,* while the people discussed in the next chapter are referred to as the military *leadership group.* The latter were much more the leaders of the mass of free coloreds, even though in many cases they did not possess the wealth of the planter elites.

From this initial definition of terms, the chapter turns to an analysis of the economic role of the planter elite. The first question is the source of this wealth. Bequests and gifts from whites formed the core of the capital of these families. Their generally greater efficiency as agricultural entrepreneurs led to a steady increase in this capital over the generations. By the time under study, members of this group were among the most important planters, especially in the coffee sector, on the island.

An investigation of the *mentalité* of the planter elite forms the final portion of this chapter. The planter elites had an attitude toward their capital that paralleled the attitude common among the landed aristocracy of French society in France. Being a landlord in the *metropole* meant status and an accepted role in society. Part of that accepted role was a feudal attitude toward land and the people who worked it. Speculation in land or labor markets, for the French rural aristocrat, would have been, if not anathema, at least something to be concealed. While many Frenchmen rose from business circles to become landowners, the business practices adopted as urban merchants were generally abandoned when they became rural *seigneurs*. Saint Domingue lacked a noble class, and free coloreds could not aspire to noble status in any case. Nonetheless, these wealthy free colored planter elites imitated, to a great extent, the thought patterns and economic behavior of the metropolitan aristocrat.

GROUP CHARACTERISTICS

The first distinguishing characteristic of the planter elite group was its wealth, surpassing that of any other in free colored society. Members of this group performed 527 notarial acts in the sample. The average value of those acts was 23,145 *livres*, three times the average value for the entire sample.

Some owned great amounts of capital goods, both land and slaves. Inventories reveal members of this group who owned hundreds of *carreaux* and hundreds of slaves, like the two mixed-race sons of Charles Hérivaux, who inherited over 350 *carreaux* of good land as well as many slaves from their white father.[4] The Baugés owned numerous slaves and at least several hundred *carreaux* of fertile and irrigated bottomland in a burgeoning sugar-growing area, as well as subsidiary establishments in the surrounding mountains.[5]

Families generally controlled significant amounts of land and slaves, but some individuals, younger sons or other dependents, might not be so wealthy in their own right. An example can be found in the family of revolutionary Jean-Baptiste Chavanne. Jean-Baptiste's younger brother Achile's marriage contract details his and his wife's effects. She was the illegitimate daughter of a white planter in the Plaine du Nord who dowered her with 9 *carreaux* and 6 slaves of her choice off his *habitation*. Achile's parents turned over to him 9 *carreaux* and 2,000 *livres* in cash as part of the marriage contract.[6] Eighteen *carreaux* of land in two parcels in different parishes and 6 slaves would not have made a very impressive *habitation*. It would permit a comfortable existence, but without any great degree of luxury. As a younger son, Achile had perhaps gotten as good a deal as he could have expected. Nonetheless, we can see that not all persons born to this group were outstandingly wealthy.

Neither were they all rural. The generational connection between rural and urban free colored populations in the colony has already been explored. Younger children of the rural plantocracy, like Achile Chavanne, would have had an economic motivation to move to the cities and seek their fortunes. In addition, imitating the behavior of young rural white members of the upper class, some may have been attracted to the cities as a place to show off wealth and gain status. Several examples of younger children of planters moving to town appear in the notarial record. One was Guillaume Castaing of Limonade, relative of the Laporte clan, who rented a quite luxurious house on the corner of the rue D'Anjou and St. Simon in Cap.[7] This was a mixed neighborhood, where well-off free coloreds might live, and it seems that young Guillaume intended to occupy the house himself. A provision of the lease forbade him to sublet any part of the property without permission from the owner, prominent Cap military leader Manuel Louis Roussame.

But there were also persons who, by attitude and wealth, were members of the planter group, and yet they owned little rural land. A prominent example was revolutionary leader Vincent Ogé, who was the son, apparently legitimate, of a white Cap *négociant*, also named Vincent. Like other *négociants*, Ogé bought colonial produce from farmers and shipped it to France, and he imported goods for the farmers, including possibly slaves, although there is no evidence of his being involved in the slave trade. His principal source of income was as the business agent of absentee landlords in France. In this connection, he had rural activities, supervising the management of estates, but he based himself in the city. He also owned a number of ships that traded within the Caribbean and, on at least one occasion, with North America. Many of his fellow *négociants* also owned plantations in their own names. The best-documented member of the trade, Stanislas Foäche, seemingly made as much off his quite large plantation in Jean Rabel as he did off his equally important mercantile house in Cap.[8] It does not appear, though, that Ogé actually owned any plantations in his own name.

Despite his lack of a plantation, in his attitudes, Ogé was a member of the planter group. That is, he was conservative with his capital. Ogé's investments appear solid as the proverbial rock of Gibraltar. Urban real estate was an important part of his portfolio. He and his mother were listed as owners of 127,000 *livres* of urban property in the 1776 cadastral survey of Cap Français.[9] The Ogés held onto their land, renting out small apartments for the most part. Urban land values and rents were going up unceasingly, and so it was hard to lose money at this game. The most important role that Vincent Ogé played in the urban real estate market, though, was the even safer one of an agent for absentee owners. In this capacity, for example, he rented a large house in a fashionable neighborhood of Cap Français owned by a white widow to a white planter from Plaisance in 1785.[10] The rent was 13,500 *livres* a year, and Ogé took a commission of 1,300 *livres*. He had several properties that he managed in this way. This is the most certain way to make money in real estate, if one has the capital and the reputation for reliability to permit it. Manage others' property, and you risk none of your own capital and stand to lose only possible future business opportunities.

Aside from his involvement in the urban real estate business, Ogé was a merchant, trading with other ports in the Caribbean, North America, and France. The risk of storm or English attack bedeviled all maritime traders in the colony. However, Ogé had several inter-island boats and stood to lose something less than everything he owned in case of disaster. Economies of scale worked for him at the top of the economic pyramid as they did for whites in his position.

Like Ogé, most of the planter group were of mixed African and European ancestry. This was not true of all members, however. In the first generation of almost all planter families was a woman, like *la Dame veuve Ogé*, Nanette Pincemaille, Julie Dahey, or Anne Laporte (I), who was the companion or wife of a white man. Many of these women were of wholly African descent, like Pincemaille and Laporte. Far from being the seduced, or raped, victims of white sexual aggression, or the "lascivious" aggressors seeking economic gain on their backs, many of these women were matriarchs of stable and prosperous families. The short life expectancy of whites on the island, thanks to the unfamiliar disease environment, meant that many of these women significantly outlived their white companions or husbands. Often, these women exercised considerable control over the lives of their mixed-race offspring for decades after those children reached adulthood.

Many of these families had been members of the planter elite for two or three generations by the period under study. It would be tempting to ascribe their observed conservatism to their status as a group of "old freedmen." Alternatively, one could refer to differing attitudes toward race in the happier decades when these families were first gaining prominence. However, as we have seen, the group was growing throughout the period under study. Julie Dahey, *menagère* to Sieur Peignanan, was only one example of this process. She had worked as his domestic manager for twenty-five years, was the mother of his seven children, and was the beneficiary of numerous donations from him. She was a substantial planter in her own right by the 1780s, having gone into partnership with one of her neighbors to develop a sugar plantation in Croix des Bouquets on land Peignanan apparently gave her.[11] He tried to give her his own sugar plantation in his will but settled for 21 slaves and a substantial amount in cash in fear of opposition from his legitimate heirs in France.[12] In the 1770s, he had attempted to set her up in business in a pottery factory, but the business had failed.[13] Her unsuccessful attempt at a more speculative business would certainly have made her more conservative in any case, but all her businesses after that show the hallmarks of the planter elite. Her 1781 partnership to develop the sugar plantation was a deal in which she sacrificed cash income for improvements on the property—in this case, a sugar refinery and irrigation system. This shows the planter group's concern for long-term productivity. One presumes that she had some hand in framing the will in which Peignanan attempted to leave her his sugar plantation, even at the cost of a substantial annual payment to the heirs in France, in preference to giving her a large cash settlement and two dozen slaves. The production of Peignanan's *habitation* is unknown since the plantation was never inventoried. However, given the continuing strength of their relationship, it seems reasonable to presume that the second deal was at least equal to the first in raw economic terms. Her preference for having the land shows a willingness to sacrifice immediate economic gain for potential future gain and, even more importantly, shows that she preferred the status of having a plantation to having liquid assets. Again, placing non-economic values above economic ones was the hallmark of the planter elite group.

Therefore we can see that members of this group were mostly, but not exclusively, rural, of mixed race, and from privileged backgrounds by the time under study. The constant factor, though, was the frequency and intimacy of their contact with whites. These contacts were both economic and personal, and on this variable the group members differ sharply from the military leadership group. Members of the military leadership group were about 10 percent less likely than planter elites to trade in slaves and land with whites. The planters were twice as likely to include whites in their "family acts" (baptisms, funerals, wills, resolutions of disputed inheritances, transactions related to wardship of orphaned minor children, marriages and marriage contracts).

It is clear that, in all categories, the planter group members were significantly more likely to do business with whites. This was true not only of people like Julie Dahey and her children, whose white father was present throughout the period under study, but also for families like the Laportes, whose white progenitor had died before 1776. The extended Laporte family, composed of dozens of adults, contained one living white member in 1776–1791, and yet 45 percent of their notarial acts were with whites during this period.

This is not to say that the planter elite group was dependent on whites or receiving handouts from family members. In fact, while donation and inheritance from whites were usually the source of the initial capital of these families, their economic relationships with whites after this startup period can only be interpreted as equal and not preferential. Julie Dahey's first appearance in the notarial record was as a partner in the pottery factory of Croix des Bouquets, which subsequently failed. Her companion, Peignanan, guaranteed her initial stake in the factory, but her partner was an unrelated white man who seems to have been a technical specialist. The outcome of the deal was unfavorable to her, but the two of them salvaged what they could from the wreck and seem to have shared equitably. Significantly, she took the assets to which status was attached, the slaves and buildings, whereas he got cash and some equipment.[14] Later, she appeared once again in a major business deal with white men, in which she arranged for some of her land to be developed into a sugar plantation.[15] Once again, her role was not as a suppliant or beneficiary of charity but instead as an equal participant in a contract from which both hoped to draw advantage.

Contacts that the planter group had with whites extended beyond the economic sphere into the personal, however. The widest divergence between the two leadership groups was in the area of family acts. Planter group members performed 44 percent of their family acts with at least one white, whereas for the military leadership group the figure is 18 percent.

Planter elite families sprang, on the whole, from relationships between Africans and Europeans. Interracial marriage, while never disappearing, was becoming less and less common in the colony during the latter half of the eighteenth century. It still happened, though, and when it did it was most likely the free colored planter group who managed to marry off their daughters to white men. Of 41 white men alive in the 1770s and 1780s who appear in the sample and who were married to free colored women, 25, or 61 percent, were married to members of the planter group, which was a minuscule percentage of the free colored population as a whole.

However, in the majority of cases, the white progenitors were already some generations in the past. Few families were recruiting new white members, especially as the longer-established families felt strongly that offspring should only come in "respectable" marriage and as whites were less willing to marry free coloreds. Nonetheless, the planter families frequently found a place in the most intimate activities of their families for whites who were in many cases only distantly related, if at all.

For example, the wedding party of Marie Marguerite Jacinthe Bleakley, who was a free *quarteronne* and scion of one of the most prominent free colored planting families of Limonade and who married Jean Jacques May, another free colored planter group member of considerable wealth, included one Sieur Le Roux, the bride's godfather.[16] Godfatherhood of illegitimate children was often a cover for unacknowledged fatherhood, but in this case the bride was unquestionably the legitimate daughter of two prominent free coloreds. They had plenty of relatives within their own caste who could have stood as godfather to their daughter, yet they chose a white man. Interestingly, Le Roux, who owned a small coffee *habitation* in the parish, was probably not as well-off as Bleakley. Certainly his wedding gift of 2 horses worth 350 *livres* does not inspire awe in comparison to the bride's portion of 5,000 *livres* in land and 3,000 *livres* in slaves promised by her father. Were it not for the color issue, one might suspect that Bleakley was Le Roux's patron. In any event, this was clearly a case where the relationship between the two was that of neighbor and perhaps friend instead of patron and client.

Anne Françoise Roy of Archaye, member of a very well known free colored clan, was given away at her wedding to a member of a prominent Jacmel free colored planter family by her white guardian.[17] Although still a minor (under 25 years of age), she was the widow of someone named Molet, about whom the records studied are silent. There must have been some reason why neither one of Molet's other heirs or family or a member of the Roy family in Archaye was named her guardian. Certainly the game was worth the candle, as she brought to the marriage a plantation and slaves that rented for 15,000 *livres* a year. It is suggestive of the attitude of the planter group that the consensus choice to oversee this sizable fortune was a white neighbor.

The closeness of the free colored planter group to whites parallels a relative distancing from other free coloreds of lower social class than themselves. Where the military leadership was very concerned with building networks of people tied to them through patronage, one rarely finds the members of the planter group in this position. Mostly, these large families provided their leaders with enough real kin that the collection of pseudo-kin was unnecessary.

In addition, one can speculate that class-based and perhaps race-based attitudes made association with their "inferiors" distasteful to these individuals in proportion to their desire to associate themselves with whites. Certainly in the military sphere, white observers found this to be the case: in 1783, the commanding general of French troops on the island tried to combine the understrength black and mulatto dragoon companies of Limbé into one formation. The parish militia commander reported on the result of this order:

> On the ninth of this month, I incorporated the company of free black [dragoons] into the mulatto Dragoons according to the orders of the General. I brought the non-commissioned officers of the two companies in to give them their new posts. The farrier sergeant of the blacks will be in charge of the *marechaux des logis* while the sergeant of the blacks becomes a *marechal des logis,* commanding the mulatto brigadiers. . . . I noticed an extreme repugnance of the mulattos to obey the orders of a black. This could have very pernicious results because of the reciprocal animosity between the two species. . . . Prejudice which maintains the mulatto at a higher level than the black must be maintained to ensure discipline in the service.[18]

The dragoons were mounted troops, and since cavalry provided their own horses, these men were among the wealthiest of the area. That this prejudice was based as much on class as race becomes clear when one considers that the *maréchaussée* contained both mixed-race and black members almost from its inception without any sign of racial problems. The infantry companies of the Chasseurs-Volontaires were designated for one racial group or the other. However, the Robineau brothers, socially defined at the time as black, although later redefined as mulattos, served in the mulatto company of Capitaine Dupetithouars. François Vigreux, identified as a mulatto on every occasion he appeared in the records, nonetheless served in the company of Capitaine De Baury, officially designated as a black unit. There do not seem to have been any racial repercussions in either case. It was only the upper-class people of mixed race—in other words, the planter group—who resisted serving alongside other free coloreds not of their group.

Even outside of official service or the economic sphere, most of these planter elites did not have strong contact with other free coloreds. Of the 232 "family" acts (baptisms, marriages and marriage contracts, wardships, resolutions of disputed inheritances, and wills) executed by this group, unrelated free coloreds played a major role in only 66. Of those, 27 were performed by the Limonade-based trio of Jean-Baptiste Chavanne, Michel François Pincemaille, and Vincent Bleakley. Bleakley was *syndic* of the chapel of Sainte-Suzanne and, as such, was regularly a witness at baptisms and funerals at that chapel. Chavanne might have already had political ambitions in the 1780s; in any case, he appeared several times as witness in family acts of nonplanter group free coloreds of the region.[19] Pincemaille clearly adopted a strategy of building a pseudo-kin network, reaching out to lower-class free coloreds through serving as godfather to their children, witnessing and giving gifts at their marriages, and mourning at their funerals. Such a strategy was atypical for members of his group. In fact, he was the only member of the planter group in the sample to do this sort of thing with any frequency.[20] Others avoided contact with free coloreds outside of their own group and extended family, preferring to include whites in family acts if a nonfamily member was required.

A common form of contact between higher- and lower-class free coloreds was manumission. Release from slavery could mark the creation of a patron-client relationship, especially if it was the culmination of a ransoming or self-purchase arrangement in which the manumittor had helped the new freedman get out of the clutches of a white master. Of 984 persons gaining their freedom in the sample, 445 were manumitted by free colored masters. Of those acts of manumission, only 21 were performed by members of the planter group.[21] This remarkably low rate of manumissions by planter group members reinforces the impression that they were not seeking close relations with lower-class free coloreds.

Aside from their low rate of manumissions, we have other indications that the planter group's relationships with their slaves were not as close as those of other free coloreds. Chapter 5 suggested that African cultural patterns and attitudes toward slaves may have affected free coloreds' behavior. These attitudes encouraged free coloreds to keep their slaves off the market, especially their creole slaves, and to seek non-economic benefits from enlarging their pseudo-kin group with these subordinate members. This reluctance to sell their creole slaves was the least marked among members of the planter group.

Among all economic elites, 34 percent of all slave transactions contained at least some creole slaves. Among the planter elite, this figure increased to 48 percent, despite the fact that the creolization of the slave workforces of the two groups was nearly identical. Why this discrepancy?

As a general rule, it could be argued that smaller slaveholding units would encourage more intimate, if not friendlier or more positive, relations between slaves and their masters. The planter group were the largest slave owners in the free colored community, and thus perhaps they simply had less personal contact with their slaves.

White masters often freed their slave relatives—children and mistresses for the most part. In any case, the widespread phenomenon of sexual relations between white master and slave at least meant that many whites had personal relationships with at least a few of their slaves. Likewise, members of the free colored peasantry often had sexual relationships with their slaves, occasionally marrying them and legitimizing large numbers of children. This weakening of the rigors of the slave system, intermittent and morally questionable though it may have been, was mostly absent in the case of the planter group. The records contain very few of the telltale *griffes* and *griffonnes,* the product of mulatto and black. Elite free colored families contained very few illegitimate slave or newly freed children; fewer even than white planter elite families. The Laportes, for example, had two identifiable bastards in four generations. Illegitimate children of wealthy and powerful free coloreds must have been as successful at making their relationship known as did the bastards of white planters, who were quick to claim their fathers' names and financial support. The requirements of "respectability" and the strength of the planter elite family presumably meant that any unsanctioned unions that did occur between planter group men and their slaves remained casual and unacknowledged. This was another factor contributing to a great social distance between the free colored planter group and the general population of African-born Dominguans, free and slave.

SOURCES OF GROUP WEALTH

The planter group were mostly large rural land and slave owners who produced crops for the export market. Some were sugar growers, but most were in the coffee market. While there were some recent arrivals in the ranks of the planter group, as witness Julie Dahey, most of these families had been large-scale agriculturists for at least a generation prior to consideration of them here. What is the source of their wealth? At the root of almost all of these family fortunes was a gift or bequest from a white progenitor.

The Pincemaille family was an example of this process. Nanette Pincemaille was a free black woman from Limonade who caught the attention of Sieur Michel François Pincemaille so thoroughly that she bore him at least five children. Despite her adoption of his family name, there is no evidence that they were married, and from this we can assume they were not, for certainly her children would have publicly claimed legitimate birth. Pincemaille gave or willed his children two pieces of land and several dozen slaves sometime before 1776.[22] This was a common means of taking care of one's illegitimate offspring, and often the size of these bequests or donations could be significant. The majority of the white forebear's property, however, had to go to any legitimate heirs in France. Parents, siblings, and even nephews and cousins were preferred to illegitimate offspring as legal heirs. Provision for illegitimate children in a will would come under the heading of special bequests, which could not be so large as to leave the legal heirs destitute. In any case, if the white father died intestate, the free colored mistress and illegitimate children might be left with nothing, or at the mercy of the legal heirs, who might be ill-disposed toward them on personal or racial grounds.

Legitimate free colored offspring, in cases where the couple was married, suffered from no such handicaps. In such a case, other white heirs in France did not need to be satisfied, and the customary law of France and the colony was on the side of the children of a legitimate marriage regardless of their color. Therefore, the most significant route for capital transfers from white to the free colored planter group members was inheritance within legitimate families.

However, all these transfers from white forebears to free coloreds in the first generation of these planter elite families only provided them with startup capital. Planter group families were very efficient stewards of the capital they had been given.

The original donations to the Pincemaille children totaled a few dozen *carreaux* and a few dozen slaves. This was enough for the mother to rent out and so support herself and her children in comfort, or, alternatively, it was enough to make her a planter of the middling sort. Nanette chose the second alternative. As indicated in chapter 7, planters of the middling sort perhaps missed out on the productivity advantages of scale received by owners of the enormous plantations that Debien studied. However, members of the planter elites invested for the long term. They also personally managed their holdings, on the whole. When forced to turn over management of a farm to another, the free colored member of the planter group would usually have a family member available to whom to entrust his property. Thus, the free colored planters avoided both the risk of loss and the expense that white planters incurred by hiring professional managers. In addition, free colored members of the planter group generally spent less on ostentatious personal property than upper-class whites. Not having to maintain prestigious residences in the major towns, since they were usually resident on their plantations, made a big difference in this regard. Finally, free coloreds were often the first into the coffee-growing areas and thus had the pick of the land. As a result of all these factors, the plantations of these small free colored owners were productive, and some planter group members, like the Pincemailles, moved up in society from small to large planter.

The large plantations owned by free coloreds benefited from the same economies of scale as the large white-owned establishments. In addition, many of the productivity advantages accruing to small free colored planters also applied to their wealthier brethren. Even at the higher economic levels, free colored proprietors were more likely than their white counterparts to manage their own plantations, thus holding down overhead. The deficiency laws, requiring a fixed ratio of white overseers to slaves, while widely ignored or compounded by moderate fines by white slave owners, were not enforced in any meaningful way against free colored masters. This could result in a significant savings, as white *économes* could receive thousands of *livres* a year in wages. Although wealthy free coloreds indulged themselves in certain luxuries—fine horses and trips to France being especially favored—their overhead was never anything to compare with that of absentee sugar barons in Paris, thus leaving more funds remaining for reinvestment in productivity.

A few free colored families achieved economic success comparable to that of the large white planters. John Garrigus tells the story of the Raimond family in his dissertation.[23] Julien Raimond's father was a white man who came to the colony before 1726, at which time he married Marie Begasse, legitimate *mulâtresse* daughter of a powerful white planter. He brought 6,000 *livres* to the marriage, whereas her dowry was 15,000 *livres*. They turned this quite substantial fortune, for the times, into a galaxy of slave-worked landholdings in the South province of the colony by the 1780s, which were distributed among his numerous offspring. His children and grandchildren were educated in France. His son Julien Raimond was a deputy in the French Assembly and one of the commissioners sent by the French government to rule Saint Domingue after the Revolution.

The Raimonds did employ a white *économe*, in the service of Marie Begasse, with whom her children feuded bitterly (even going so far on one occasion, he alleged, as to strike him in front of her slaves, surely subversive of discipline). His presence was unusual for their group and may have been a result of the well-educated Raimond sons' unwillingness to allow themselves to be bossed around by their mother in the manner common in other free colored families. The Raimond boys lived away from the paternal homestead, on land that they had amassed since reaching adulthood. Aside from its dysfunctionality, by the standards of the time, the Raimond family was an unexceptional member of the planter group. Born of a church-sanctioned union between white and free colored, grown through a successful conservative and long-term campaign of land acquisition, growing a safe balanced mixture of cash and food crops, and imbued with the sense that justice demanded full participation by the free colored planter group in a creole plantocracy, the Raimonds were exceptionally well chosen by Garrigus as exemplars of their group.

MENTALITÉ:
ATTITUDES TOWARD LANDOWNERSHIP,
ENTREPRENEURSHIP, AND FAMILY

The combination of substantial gifts and bequests of land and slaves to planter group families and the superior plantation management skills of free coloreds, planter group members and otherwise, meant that there was a steady flow of capital into free colored hands. Once those in the planter group were in control of property, they tended to hang onto it for longer periods of time than did whites. From these trends, it is clear that there was a different attitude toward landholding on the part of free coloreds from that common among whites.

Whites saw landholding in France as a means to approach noble status.[24] Rural land in the *metropole* was valued, not so much for its ability to produce economic gains—rates of return were often considerably less than those available through trade, and improved methods of farming to enhance income were not common—but for its role as a route, along with officeholding, to achieve and confirm noble status.

Whites in Saint Domingue had a very different attitude toward land. They held their land for short periods of time and seemed to be treating it as a commodity and not as the indispensable concomitant of increased status that it would be in France. They were willing to use land in a speculative manner. They often lived in the cities or in France and not on their plantations, but unlike metropolitan landlords, they usually operated their plantations directly through managers, instead of renting them to small operators, as a metropolitan landlord would be more likely to do. They held land in search of fabulous, and often elusive, profits in tropical staple production, instead of a steady 5 percent from a stable rent roll. Instead of the social *éclat* that came to the metropolitan noble from the number of peasants on his rent rolls, the Saint Domingue planter counted his slaves and, even more importantly, the hogsheads of sugar and profits that they produced. These were capitalists pure and simple—there was very little hint of feudalism in their mentality. The Saint Domingue white planter who wished to extract non-economic values from land reinvested his profits in rural land in France.

Free coloreds, on the other hand, did not have the opportunity to climb socially through landholding in the *metropole* (at least officially, they were forbidden to travel there and do not seem to have owned land there to any significant extent, being barred from noble status by their color). Instead, they seem to have been trying, to some extent at least, to duplicate the world view of the French metropolitan *seignieur* in the mountains of Saint Domingue. They still functioned economically as planters—that is, they did not rent their land in significant quantities to poorer persons who produced subsistence crops on small plots, instead producing tropical staples themselves on their land with slave labor.

However, in terms of their use of the land, the free coloreds were less than aggressively entrepreneurial. They frequently sought to maximize the non-economic value of their land, often at the expense of possible economic gains. Like the metropolitan French nobility, the status gain from being a landholder was more important than the financial gain from being a successful capitalist. If entrepreneurial advantage should clash with social advancement, status would win out. Their attitude toward the land they owned can be measured by two variables: the length of time they held land before selling it and the degree to which they required improvements on the land as a condition of leases. In addition, the degree to which they leveraged land purchases is an indication of how willing they were to take risks with their land in the interests of increasing their total business volume.

Length of tenure in land ownership is a very useful indicator of how important the non-economic values of that land were to its owner. Although there are all sorts of reasons why someone might hold onto land for speculative reasons, waiting for the price to reach a profitable level, at some point an owner would be presented with an opportunity to make a profitable sale. This is especially true in a rapidly expanding economy such as Saint Domingue's in the 1780s. Whether the owner took that opportunity says a lot about how important being a landholder was to him or her.

Sellers in the towns had held their land for shorter periods, on the average, than sellers in the countryside. This reinforces our impression of free colored city dwellers as more likely to be entrepreneurial users of their land than those in the country. Whites on the whole tended to be more speculative in the use of the land than were their free colored neighbors, especially in rural areas. For example, whites held onto the average piece of land in Limonade only 2.5 years before reselling it, whereas free coloreds selling land among themselves would have been in possession for an average of 7.6 years. In Cap Français, home to the most speculative group of free coloreds, the average tenancy of a white seller to a free colored was a mere 1.1 years, whereas the average free colored selling to another free colored had held onto the land 6.4 years. Part of this is a result of the larger size of the average rural white's holding and the greater proportion of peasant users of the soil among free coloreds in the countryside (who could be expected to hang onto a piece of land for as long as possible).

However, the planter group hung onto their land for even longer than free coloreds as a whole. The overall figure for the free colored population was 7.7 years, whereas members of the planter group had an average tenure of 10.2 years on pieces of land they transferred.[25] This figure does not show any significant variance with the race of buyer and seller; that is, when both parties were free colored, the average tenancy was 9.8 years; when the buyer was white, the land had been held for an average of 10.7 years. When free colored planter group members disposed of land, moreover, they transferred smaller and less valuable pieces of land than they were receiving from whites, suggesting that they were selling less-desirable portions of their land in order to meet some urgent cash need, whereas whites were transferring entire plantations to them. When planter group members transferred land among themselves, the transactions involved an average of 55 *carreaux* and had an average value of 6,130 *livres*. When planter group members sold to whites, these figures went down to 8.5 *carreaux* and 4,889 *livres*. When planter elites were the buyers, the average transaction was for 65 *carreaux* at an average value of 44,480 *livres*. Thus, even the infrequent land sales by planter group members were less important than their acquisitions.

The planter group members were improving landlords, on the whole, although the urge to improve came in second place to the desire to hold land. The institution of the improving landlord can be seen as capitalist in the European context, in contrast with the pre-capitalist landlord content to collect his rents from his peasants. The improving landlord in Britain was the engine of agricultural transformation that fed the cities of the industrial revolution. We must consider the Saint Domingue free colored planter group in the context of that island, however. The white land speculator was a common figure there. He obtained land grants from the government only in order to resell them as fast as possible to owners who would actually put the land into production. White landowners who intended to develop their land as plantations were only somewhat less speculative. As revealed by Baron de Wimpffen and Brueys d'Aigalliers, extensive debt and extreme measures to increase production as much as possible at the expense of long-term stability were the way to make a profit for the white planter.[26]

The tactics of the free colored planter group were much more conservative. The Baugé family's development of a sugar plantation near Croix des Bouquets, discussed earlier, serves as an example. First, the seven siblings chose three among them to be their agents and then rented the land and water rights to them, forgiving the rent for the first six years of the arrangement.[27] In this way, they concentrated their capital for the purposes of increasing productive capacity without giving up ownership of it nor turning over control to someone outside their family. Next, the three brothers brought in a partner, an older free colored woman who may have been an aunt or cousin.[28] She contributed 16 badly needed slaves to the operation. Finally, four years later, with the preparatory work seemingly more or less done, the brothers sublet the land to three white men, two of whom were white relatives of one of their brothers-in-law, for a big payoff and the obligation to further improve the sugar refinery.[29] While allowing control of the land to slip out of the hands of free coloreds, this rental still kept things in the extended family by dealing with white relatives. In any case, renting land preserved the non-economic values, as we have seen. The value of this piece of land was already established, having gone from 3,600 *livres* a year for the last two years in the first lease to 11,400 *livres* a year in the last. The brothers appear to have taken on some debt in the process of expansion, directing some 29,000 *livres* of the final act's payments to reimbursing creditors. However, the proportion of the total added value of the plantation that was represented by this debt was small: less than 30 percent by the standard calculation of the time that land was worth about ten times its annual rent. The model planter described by Wimpffen in the passage cited above would have bought the majority of his assets on credit and would never escape debt.

This unwillingness of the planter group to use credit is clear from the sample of notarial acts. The average notarized purchase by a free colored was made on only 13 percent credit. The more expensive the purchase, of course, the less likely that it would be made for cash, but only 16 percent of the price of sales evaluated at over 5,000 *livres* was credit. Overall, the planter group's transactions were on a mere 8 percent margin, while credit made up 15 percent of the purchase price of their more valuable purchases. These figures do not change markedly between racial categories of buyers and sellers. Sales from whites to free colored planter group members were on an average margin of 15.7 percent, with credit making up 6.4 percent of the price of transactions where the planter group member was the seller. It is clear that the low level of credit in planter group members' purchases was the result of innate conservatism and not unwillingness of whites to extend credit to free colored purchasers.

Thus we can see that the planter group members were very conservative with their assets. Unlike their white neighbors, they were not willing to risk their capital nearly as much in the search for enormous profits. Why might this be? The most reasonable explanation was that they had some reason to own capital goods, particularly land and slaves, other than simply to generate revenue. For one thing, the social consequences of failure were greater for them than for white landowners. A white who failed as a planter was still a white member of the somatically defined upper class of the colony. He might even be able to reestablish his fortunes through easy credit in a growing economy. For the free colored who failed as a planter, the fall was much greater. The stronger free colored family structure would ensure that no former planter would end up starving. However, from the social point of view, failure as a planter meant that one was cast out of respectability and back into the mass of free coloreds from which one's ancestors had escaped. The reader has seen in the experience of the militia captain the antipathy that existed between these two groups. The difference between being an *habitant,* even a small one, and not being one was much more important than the difference between large and small *habitants.*

As an example of the free colored family that suffered a reverse probably more damaging to its social position than its economic standing, we have the Chavannes. In 1786, the mother of future revolutionary leader Jean-Baptiste Chavanne returned her *habitation* to M. Paul Cairou, the militia commandant of the Limonade region and a fellow *habitant.*[30] She had owned the plantation for only eight years, her husband having bought it from Cairou and having failed subsequently to make the agreed-upon payment of 15,000 *livres* a year. She had given 8 *carreaux* to her daughter Marie-Marthe on the occasion of the daughter's wedding. Marie-Marthe had given permission to return that land to Cairou if needed, but as it turned out, the mother was able to buy the 8 *carreaux* from Cairou and at least not involve her son-in-law in her economic catastrophe. Another child, younger son Achile Chavanne, bought his land back from Cairou separately and was also not involved in the mother's financial collapse.[31] Although the land was clearly used to plant coffee, a business venture, we can detect the presence of a larger and more important non-economic goal that landholding was serving for the Chavanne family. From the use of this land as marriage portions for the children, it is clear that the *habitation,* to Madame Chavanne, was not merely an investment but a lifestyle. It was a part of a family strategy to build holdings of planter property in the North province, which apparently fell apart. One can clearly see, in the mind's eye, the important white patron and possible family member, having put up with seven years' worth of arrears amounting to over 100,000 *livres,* a considerable fortune at the time, finally forcing the family to give up their hopes of landed wealth, standing by sternly as the notary enumerated the buildings and crops, and the servants packed the family's movable property in the background. Perhaps this family tragedy, with its racial overtones, helped drive young Jean-Baptiste to his suicidal rebellion in 1790. The Chavannes, related to some of the wealthiest free colored families in the North and moving in their circle until 1786, suffered an enormous loss of "respectability" by losing the family homestead, whereas a white entrepreneur, far from the homeland where respectability had a permanent value, could just start over again.

FAMILY STRATEGIES

Another indicator of the aristocratic *mentalité* of the planter group is the way they used family strategies to preserve wealth and, more importantly, to advance in status. Marriages and transfers of property between generations were the most important ways this took place.

Marriage provided respectability ipso facto, but marriage to a person of the proper hue could increase the social standing of the next generation. A perfect example of this process among the planter group was the Laporte family of Limonade. Their family tree is found in appendix 1. The first generation of the family was composed of three white men who came to the colony in the 1720s or before, Louis Laporte, Antoine LeMaire, and Gaspard Ardisson, and their free colored companions. Laporte and LeMaire married free black women. Ardisson had a relationship with a free black woman without the benefit of marriage, but, conforming to the prevailing cultural mores, he provided quite handsomely for his son—André Ardisson's widow was able to endow their daughter with 14 *carreaux* and 6 slaves on the occasion of her marriage in 1777, despite the fact that there were at least three other children to be taken care of.[32] Laporte was first married to a white woman, Jeanne Couvert, daughter of a planter, and had a white son, also named Louis. Following Couvert's death, he married Anne, a free black woman, and had at least four other children. Antoine LeMaire's daughter Elizabeth, described as a free *mulâtresse* and legitimate, was the only one of his children to appear in the sample. In the first generation, clearly, marriage was already a state to be pursued.

The white or mulatto children of these couplings tended to marry people such that their offspring were mostly *quarterons*, aided by the helpful provision in the racial calculus that usually made the child of a *mulâtre/mulâtresse* and a *quarteron/quarteronne* a *quarteron/quarteronne*. Thus, the *mulâtresse* daughter of Antoine LeMaire married Louis Laporte *ainé*, the white one, while the *mulâtre* Louis Laporte *cadet* married Marthe Françoise Bleakley, *quarteronne* illegitimate daughter of a white Sieur Bleakley whose personal name has unfortunately not survived. The *mulâtre* Ardisson children, Gaspard (II) and Marie Louise (II), married younger *mulâtre* children of Louis Laporte, so their offspring were still *mulâtres*. The marriage partners were selected for more than their color, of course. One important trait was legitimacy. Of the four marriages in the second generation of the Laporte family tree, both spouses were legitimate in three of them. Finally, of course, wealth was important, and the ability to endow children with as many white ancestors as possible, legitimate birth, and economically useful properties all went into the choice of a spouse.

By the third generation, the grandchildren found spouses such that the legitimate great-grandchildren of the founding patriarchs would all be *quarterons*. For example, Catherine Françoise Ardisson, *mulâtresse* daughter of Gaspard Ardisson (II), married a white man, and Anne Laporte (II) married her cousin Charles Laporte, *quarteron* son of the white Louis Laporte (*ainé*) and Elizabeth LeMaire. There was no further recruitment of whites into this family after what was the elder generation during the 1770s and 1780s, the second generation. Nonetheless, almost all the members of the family in the third and fourth generations would have qualified for Julien Raimond's or the Chambre de l'Agriculture's proposed redefinition of whiteness—no more than one-quarter African ancestry and legitimate birth.[33] Two of three marriages in the third generation also featured spouses who were both legitimate.

Overall, 96 of 253 marriages (38 percent) in the sample of notarial acts would have produced offspring who were racially "whiter" than one of their parents; for the planter group, this figure was 35 out of 87 (40 percent). Among the planter group, legitimacy seems to have been a more important criterion in selection of marriage partners: 57 of 87 marriages (66 percent) contained at least one legitimate spouse, while for the population as a whole, this figure was 139 of 253 (55 percent).

In addition to marriage, transfers of property to the next generation were the other crucial element of family strategies. Families in Saint Domingue labored under the same handicap that most metropolitan French aristocratic families did in this regard: inheritances, by the "customs of Paris" governing the colony, were partible, that is, estates were to be divided equally among all eligible heirs. This was an obstacle to the concentration of capital and thus to the overall advancement of the family, while at the same time it ensured that all members would be treated fairly. This arrangement was obviously of greatest concern to those who had large amounts of capital to pass on from one generation to the next, and so it is no surprise to find the planter elite spending a good deal of energy to circumvent these requirements and concentrate the family patrimony in the hands of one child.

The widow Turgeau, Marie Madeleine, and her son Pierre, of Port-au-Prince, provide an interesting example of how this worked. Sieur Turgeau, probably white, had died before the beginning of notarial recordkeeping in the West province. He had fathered at least four children with his wife, probably free black although she was always referred to by the notary as Dame Turgeau without racial identifier. They were wealthy people, owning at least a large house in Port-au-Prince worth 17,000 *livres* in 1782, 100 *carreaux* of undeveloped land in the mountains overlooking Croix des Bouquets, and 96 *carreaux* of at least partly developed land in the hinterland of Port-au-Prince.[34] These pieces of property were distributed to the children more or less equally before 1776 as marriage portions and the like. However, the centerpiece of the family patrimony was an *habitation* that the provisions of the father's will left in the control of the mother. This plantation produced net profits of around 6,500 *livres* a year during the War of American Independence and up to 9,500 *livres* a year in peacetime. In 1773, citing her "great age" that prevented her from seeing to her own affairs, she formed a partnership with her oldest son Pierre to exploit this *habitation* on terms very favorable to him—he was entitled to half of the income but only had to support one-third of the expenses and provided no capital. This "management contract" was, of course, a thinly disguised way to transfer the *habitation* to him. Over the twenty-five years of their association, his profit on the deal, averaging some 2,000 *livres* a year, was mostly applied against the succession, although he drew at various times up to 800 *livres* a year for personal expenses.[35] This means that, upon her death, the estate would have owed him perhaps as much as 50,000 *livres* before dividing the mother's property among the children. It probably still would have been no small matter for him to buy out the others, but certainly arrangements of this sort made it easier for the older generation to concentrate property in the desired hands.

Ironically, the much lower rate of illegitimacy among the planter group made this sort of chicanery essential and thus much more common. In families formed by nonsanctioned unions, as long as the principal member had no legitimate heirs, he or she could make bequests to anyone they pleased.

CONCLUSION

The reader can see, then, the many parallels between the free colored planter group and the rural landholding classes in France as regards their attitudes and practices toward their capital. While practicing capitalist agriculture, the Saint Domingue planter group nonetheless represented the strongest traditionalist element in the society of the colony. A strong concern for the status that came from landholding was typical of them. They traded with and shared social space with wealthy whites. Whenever possible, they avoided contact between themselves and free coloreds not of their own group, with the exception of several anomalous individuals. Not only did they manage their landed estates with an eye to achieving and retaining status as well as financial advancement, but they also used family acts to enhance their status. Mating patterns show concern for improving the status of their offspring, both in terms of color and, more importantly, through the "respectability" derived from legitimacy. They arranged inheritances so as to concentrate wealth in the hands of one person in each generation, instead of letting the legally required but nontraditional equal division take place. In this way, again, they paralleled the behavior of the rural aristocrats in the *metropole* whom they so resemble in many other ways. When one reads the political tracts of a Julien Raimond and hears him speak of the free coloreds as the stable middle class of the colony, lauding their attachment to traditional family values, he was referring not to the racial caste as a whole but to his own group, the planter group. He was making the same point before the National Assembly that Vincent Ogé and Jean-Baptiste Chavanne made with their muskets in their abortive uprising on the Plaine du Nord: free colored landholders and slave owners ought to be permitted equal status with white landholders and slave owners in a socially stratified, slaveholding society.

CHAPTER ELEVEN

The Military Leadership Group

At the beginning of this book, the reader was introduced to Pierre Augustin, the archetype of the military leadership group. He represents the 1770s generation of military leaders. However, the group was not new to the colony in that decade, and Augustin had many illustrious predecessors. Prominent among them was Capitaine Vincent Olivier, first introduced in chapter 4.

Olivier provides the best example of great economic success among the military leadership. He is mentioned in Moreau de St. Méry:

In the parish of Grande-Rivière (or more properly Sainte-Rose), a free black named *Captaine* Vincent Olivier died in 1780, aged about 120. Vincent, who was born a slave, followed M. Olivier, his master, in 1697 to the siege of Cartagena. As they were returning from the battle on a transport ship, they were made prisoners and brought to Europe. There, the Dutch ransomed him along with sixteen of his comrades who were brought to France. Vincent, who was striking because of his large stature, was presented to Louis XIV. Having developed a passion for the military life from his adventures, Vincent fought in the German wars under Villars, and upon his return to Saint Domingue in 1716, *M. le . . . Gouverneur* named him captain-general of all the colored militias of the jurisdiction of Cap. . . . The conduct of Vincent and his virtues were so striking that they rendered prejudice mute. He was awarded a sword by the King, with which he always appeared, as well as a plume for his hat. Vincent was welcome everywhere; one saw him at the table of the governor-general. . . . He gave to all men of his class a precious example, and his age and extremely faithful memory made him always interesting . . . recounting his former prowess to young men of color who were being enrolled for the Savannah expedition, and showing through his own family, who were among the first to volunteer, that he had transmitted his bravery. . . . He was content with his humble fortune, and possessed an *habitation* in the canton of Bois-Blancs as well as a pension of 600 *livres* a year awarded him by [the colonial government] in 1776.[1]

Members of his family appeared regularly in the notarial archives for Cap. His "humble fortune" put them among the economic elite of free colored society, with three acts over 10,000 *livres* in value. In addition, they owned a seemingly large and profitable *habitation* in Grande Rivière with at least a dozen slaves, about which there is little in the sample since the parish of Grande Rivière was not one of those studied in depth. However, some of the slaves were rented to family members in 1778, an act that seems to have been intended to sort out in advance some questions of Olivier's estate and may mark his retirement from active management of his land.[2] It was at this time that he began to be described in the records as a resident of Cap rather than of Grande Rivière. From at least 1776, he owned a quite respectable house in a predominantly colored section of town, with an estimated rental value of 1,000 *livres* a year in that year.[3] In 1779, in the parish register of the parish of Notre Dame de l'Assomption in Cap, Olivier signed as godfather to the young mulatto Vincent Adrien.[4] In this act he was described for the first time as residing "in his home in the Petit Marécage," seemingly in this 10,000 *livre* house.

Having the patriarch occupy the town house instead of renting it does not seem to have left the family without income, though. Olivier owned a coffee *habitation* in Limonade, of unspecified value, but it was located next up the river from some very valuable land owned by the Chevalier de Rivehaute.[5] The captain's will, in addition to freeing some of his slaves and taking care of a number of godchildren and other extended family members, seems to have left his two legitimate children and their numerous offspring very well taken care of indeed.[6]

The Olivier family fortune probably got its start with the Cartegena expedition. Survivors shared an immense store of loot, which sufficed to set up many of the leaders as planters and has been identified as an important early force behind the success of the sugar revolution in the colony.[7] As a slave, though, Olivier's share was probably rather small. His participation in some campaigns in Europe built his reputation in the colony—how many white militiamen at that time could claim similar experience? The professionalization of the militia under the governors of this period would have made the government especially anxious to obtain the services of Olivier. However, his service in Europe probably did not do much directly for his pocketbook, at a soldier's pay. It was on his return to the colony that he became a wealthy man. His pension from the government, a very healthy 600 *livres* annually, added to land that he was able to obtain and protect thanks to his military connections, allowed him to become an active agricultural businessman without becoming a planter group member. He retained his contacts with other free coloreds, especially other soldiers, and did not build patronage relations with whites other than parading his status by dining with the governor from time to time (when recruitment of free coloreds to the armed forces was a crucial issue, one presumes). By the time the period covered by the sample begins, Capitaine Vincent himself was already semi-retired (and at least in his 90s), but his children seem to have been entrepreneurial and active traders of land and slaves in much the same way as other free colored military leaders. In addition, as mentioned by Moreau de St. Méry, his sons, or more likely grandsons, followed him into the armed forces, participating in the Chasseurs-Volontaires and, apparently, the milita of Grand-Rivière. Here, then, is an example of a family that achieved financial success at the same time as the planter group families, some thirty to fifty years before the period under study, and yet had retained patterns of relationships and attitudes toward capital typical of the military leadership group, rather than adopting those typical of the planter group.

These differing attitudes can be summed up by saying that the military leadership was more aggressively entrepreneurial than its rivals. The military leaders were more willing to speculate, to buy and sell capital goods, to shift from one field of endeavor to another in search of profit.

The group of people that are called the military leadership group were wealthier than most free coloreds, although most fell short of the rarefied heights occupied by the wealthiest representatives of the planter elite. They had many of the characteristics of a rising middle class, compared to the planter elites' aristocracy. However, unlike many successful members of the middle class in France at this time, members of this group who achieved the greatest financial success did not adopt the economic habits and social prejudices of the aristocracy. Instead, even the most successful members of this class tended to retain their arms-length economic relationship with whites and their aggressive attitude toward capital.

The distance from slavery in length of time or number of generations does not seem to have affected the *mentalité* of members of this group either. Many of the military leadership group were freedmen, but others were two or three generations distant from slavery and yet retained the identifying marks of the class. On the other hand, of course, many of the planter elite group, such as the *menagères* and their children, were born in slavery.

The social success of people in the military group was based in large measure on their connection to other free coloreds through ties of kinship, fictive or actual.

Fictive kinship was especially important for freedmen with few blood relatives. These kinship ties were made, recorded, and strengthened through "family" notarial and parish register acts: marriages and marriage contracts, wills, wardship of orphaned children, godparenthood, serving as official mourner at funerals, and the like. One very important element of this process was manumission. Members of this group were very active manumittors, both of their true relatives and of pseudo-kin. This tendency is especially striking given their slaveholdings, which were smaller on average in proportion to their total capital (and in absolute terms) than was the case for the planter elites. This network of relations with other free coloreds, both members of their own group and persons of lower-class status, made them leaders of free colored society in a way that the planter elites were not.

Fifty-two families or individuals appear in the data who merit inclusion in the military leadership group on these criteria.[8] That is, they had little contact with whites, either personal or financial, instead building networks of other free coloreds through family acts, and they demonstrated an aggressive attitude toward capital. Of these, 33 were not economic elites under the definition used throughout this work: having three acts in the sample of notarial acts evaluated at over 10,000 *livres*. Obviously, this group was not as wealthy as the planter elite. Their relative lack of wealth did not mean that they were poverty-stricken, though. All these persons participated in the market on a regular basis, and, indeed, their modern, entrepreneurial attitude toward the market is one of the identifying characteristics of this group. Their demonstrated leadership of free colored society despite their relative lack of wealth makes them, if anything, even more noteworthy.

In the cases of seven of these individuals, no record of military service appeared in the data. Two of these people were women. All seven, though, had close economic and often personal or family ties to military leaders, as well as demonstrating all the other characteristics of their group. The military seems to have been a unifying factor in the lives of most individuals in this group.

With this chapter, the analysis of group formation among free coloreds in the colony continues with an investigation of the military leadership group. The chapter begins, as did chapter 10, with a look at the defining characteristics of the group in question. Next, we look at some of the rewards of military service at this level and the value of this alternative route to economic success. Then, the chapter turns to look at the relationships of the military leaders with other groups in society. Especially important in their case is their relationship with poorer free coloreds through "family acts" such as marriage, funerals, godparenthood, and other methods of creating pseudo-kin ties. Also, they did build networks of whites, not through family relationships but through military service. This chapter looks at how patron-client relations between the free colored military and their white officers worked. Finally, as was done in the preceding chapter, there is an attempt to define a *mentalité* of the free colored military leader by looking at his economic activity.

The first important characteristic of the military leadership group is that, in financial terms, members had sufficient resources to raise them above the mass of free coloreds. Some were exceptionally wealthy, but all had enough to put them above the peasantry or the urban workers. As a body, their notarized sales were worth an average of 5,095 *livres*, as compared to 3,574 *livres* for non-elite free coloreds. However, they were significantly poorer than the planter group, whose average transaction was 23,795 *livres*, although some members such as Capitaine Vincent certainly were on a par with the planter group.

Using the value of sales contracts as a measure of total wealth is somewhat flawed, since military leaders were more active buyers and sellers of capital goods than the planter group and thus would tend to sell smaller amounts more frequently. However, no reliable measure of actual property exists for more than a few individuals —detailed death inventories were not preserved in many cases, and this is the only occasion on which the notaries were called upon to record all property of any individual. Although the use of sales data somewhat understates the relative wealth of the military group, it gives us some impression of where the military leadership and planter elite groups stood vis-à-vis the non-elite population. Sales by both groups were of higher than average value, obviously, and equally obviously the generally wealthier planter elite outpaced the military leadership group in the highest-valued sales. This disproportion was smaller than the difference in the two groups' wealth, however, and the military leadership group matched the planter elite in the very largest sales of land and slaves. This suggests the greater entrepreneurial character of the military leadership group. With fewer resources than their planter elite competitors, they were equally ready to contract for the purchase or sale of large plantations.

This relative wealth of the military group came without the attachments to whites that were so noticeable among the planter group. The military leadership was significantly less likely than either planter group members or non-elite free coloreds to perform business or family acts with whites: about 10 percent less so in the case of sales of land and slaves, and about half as frequently in the case of family acts.

This relative separation from the white world paralleled an integration into the free colored world that the planter group lacked. Recognition within free colored society went to military leaders despite, or perhaps because of, their lack of connection with whites. One method that they used to substitute for their lack of powerful white kin was the creation of a network of free colored pseudo-kin through participation in unrelated persons' family acts. Acting as godfathers at baptisms and witnesses at marriage ceremonies and burials, as well as the more concrete manumissions, served to build a network among these men and to connect them to numerous families, both fellow military leaders and clients of lower social status than themselves. It was this network of pseudo-kin upon which they drew when they needed anything, from financial assistance with their newest project to a buyer for a piece of property to judgment of a dispute. Economic elites, those with more than three acts evaluated at over 10,000 *livres* in the sample of notarial acts, generally used "family" acts quite regularly to cement their real kin groups together: they were 25 percent more likely than the free colored population as a whole to execute such acts. As freedmen, military leaders had fewer kin through blood or marriage, so it is not surprising that they should have been less active in this category than the economic elites, who were mostly freeborn. However, the military leaders were 15 percent more likely than free coloreds in general to use these acts, and their "family" acts were much more likely to be performed with unrelated persons. Of their 149 "family" acts, in 70, or 47 percent, the military leader participating was not a member of the immediate family of the principal actors. This compares with only 66 of 232 acts, or 28 percent, for the free colored planter group.[9] Even families in the military leadership group that had been free for many decades and contained large numbers of legitimate kin—like the Oliviers—used this strategy with gusto.

Sergent of the militia Jean-Baptiste Magny *dit* Malic, or Mali, was one of the most energetic users of the family act in this way. Out of 48 appearances in the notarial record, he was godfather of an unrelated child at least 3 times, a witness at a burial of an unrelated person once, and a member of the marriage party of unrelated couples 4 times.[10] Three of the principal participants in these acts—that is, fathers of grooms or brides, the deceased or bereaved, or parents—were fellow military leaders: Joseph *dit* Cezar, bandmaster of the Cap militia; Louis la Rondière, *sergent* in the Cap militia; and Pierre Augustin, whom we have already met. Three more who were prominent free coloreds of Cap Français and whose military service cannot be ascertained are Pierre Attila, Jacques Magnon, and Alexandre Scipion, each of whom had family members who served in the military. Malic's appearance at Pierre Augustin's brother's funeral returned a social obligation: Augustin had served as a witness at Malic's marriage. At Malic's own funeral, in 1781, Cap's free colored military leaders and their associates turned out in force: military leaders Jean-Baptiste Belly, future delegate from Saint Domingue to the French revolutionary assemblies; Jean-François Edouard *dit* L'Eveille, a future president of independent Haiti and a Chasseur-Volontaire veteran; and Pierre Augustin, along with a number of other prominent Cap military leaders, signed the parish register. These nine people participated in 26 other notarial acts along with Malic, out of a total of 48 that he executed. The social circle revealed by the execution of "family" acts also defined, in great measure, the economic circle.

Another member of Malic's circle was Pierre Simon Zogo, of the Cap militia. He was quite energetic in family acts, and in addition he brought a respectable number of slaves to freedom. Manumission, for the freedmen among the military leadership group, served as another way to acquire pseudo-kin or clients.

It was stated in the act that one of the slaves Zogo freed was his natural daughter, Reine.[11] He appeared with a wife named Elisabet as a witness to a marriage contract in 1781; unfortunately, these two acts tell us all we can discover about his real family.[12] However, manumission, as well as godparenting and participation in other "family" acts, built a network of pseudo-kin in colored society. One is reminded of African family strategies in precolonial times that based personal social standing on the size of the kin group, both blood and fictive pseudo-kin, and encouraged strategies, like slave keeping, that increased the size of the kin group. The Dominguan serial godfather is the child of the African "big man" as well as the father of the Haitian *chef de section*. Zogo rewards investigation as a particularly outstanding practitioner of this strategy of social climbing.

For example, Zogo obtained the liberty of his godson, Pierre Ulisse, a young *bossale* from the Slave Coast, in 1788. This marked one of the few times that he had anything resembling a personal interaction with a white, as Ulisse's master gave him a specific power of attorney to seek the liberty of the young man. (This act was not one of the simple irrevocable permission forms of manumission for the "bearer" but instead specifically named Zogo.)[13] Ulisse got married in the same year with Zogo standing in as the "friends and family of the groom."[14] As his godfather, and in the absence of the father of the groom, this was clearly Zogo's duty. However, it was also a privilege as he saw his kin group increased by one Marie-Rose Baucy and her kin from Borgne, including the Borgne militia noncommissioned officer Xavier Janvier. So Zogo, as the saying goes, did not lose a (god)son but gained a daughter, as well as important contacts in a neighboring parish.

Zogo was also a regular fixture in the wills of women of color. The prominent free black slave trader Geneviève Zangoué Sarazin, when ill in 1780, prepared a will in which Zogo was named executor and tutor of her minor children.[15] She survived that illness, and her next will in 1784 named Pierre Balthazard, another prominent Cap free black and militia leader, in Zogo's place. For four years, however, Zogo was considered worthy to be entrusted with the very considerable resources of this enterprising woman. Zogo may have been ill or absent at that time, as he seems to have dropped a number of obligations in 1783–84 and executed no notarial acts at all in 1785, before returning to activity in 1786–89.[16]

Balthazard's own will gave freedom to 5 of his slaves and named Zogo and another militiaman, Pierre Amoune, as his executors and his alternate universal legatees after his wife.[17] Once again, we see evidence of a tight-knit community of mutual self-help among the free colored military leadership of Cap.

In the wedding in which Zogo's wife made her only appearance with him, in the character of "relatives and friends of the bride," Malic's family was strongly involved. The groom was Jean Baptiste Hypolite from Limbé, a neighbor of Marie Coeflin, Malic's wife, who was part of the bride's wedding party. The bride was the former slave and possibly the half-sister of the wealthy Desrouleaux heirs, the wards of Malic and his partners. It seems that by participating in the wedding party of the groom, Zogo and his wife were both building social connections to fellow militiamen and important figures in the Cap free black world and also laying claim to their right to be considered "respectable" in the bourgeois moral code: Zogo attended with his wife, who was carefully described in the act as his *épouse* (spouse) and not by the more inclusive term *femme* (woman). As a married man, he could legitimately assist others in achieving that state and could also strengthen his claim to be a "big man"—although his economic status was unspectacular.

Military leaders mainly made up for their lack of white relations through stressing the status that came from their jobs. However, their social status was both reinforced and validated by their assistance to nonblood kin free coloreds in "family" acts—baptisms, marriages, burials, wills. Military service held them together and gave them an alternative to the white world for social and economic advancement.

It is not surprising to see military leaders being half again as likely as the population as a whole to be participants in marriages and marriage contracts. They performed 9.1 percent of all acts in the sample but were involved in 12.7 percent of all marriages and marriage contracts. Military leaders' wedding parties were much less likely to include whites than those of other elites, however: 29 percent of military leaders' marriage parties contained whites, as opposed to 50 percent for elites as a whole. The figure for the sample as a whole is 37 percent. Military leaders were also more likely than the population as a whole to use the notarial system for other "family" events—regularizing inheritance-related transactions and governing the effects of minor heirs. They were participants in 11.4 percent of such acts while performing only 9.1 percent of all acts in the sample.

In an interesting sidelight that is indicative of the relationship of this group with their slaves, the unique free colored attitudes toward slaves were especially marked among the military leadership group. They were very likely to treat their own slaves differently depending on whether they were purchased or born into service, a tendency tentatively attributed to African cultural survivals in chapter 5.

Members of the military leadership group, then, were markedly more likely to own *bossale* slaves than were other free coloreds, 59 percent to 50 percent, and those *bossale* slaves were more likely to be trained in an occupational speciality. Ten percent of all *bossale* slaves owned by military leaders rated an occupational specialty designation, whereas for free coloreds as a whole this figure declines to 7 percent. Creole slaves owned by military leaders tended to be younger and less valuable than their *bossales*. This difference may very well be due to a view of slaves that saw "trade" slaves as being fit subjects for commodification and extraction of value whereas slaves born in the household were thought of as junior members.[18] This view is buttressed by the fact that 27 percent of creole slaves noted as belonging to members of the military leadership group were designated as being destined for manumission in the notarial act in which they appear.

The military leadership group was dominated, naturally, by persons holding noncommissioned rank in the colonial armed forces. Of the members of the military leadership group identified from the sample, at least 31 served in the colonial militia as noncommissioned officers. Many of these, and some with no identifiable militia service, were leaders in the Chasseurs-Volontaires de Saint-Domingue in 1779. Since the leaders of the Chasseurs-Volontaires companies who were giving out the stripes were militia officers, it seems reasonable to assume that the sergeants and corporals in the Chasseurs were the same subordinate leaders with whom these men had worked in their own parish militia companies. We can safely assume that all 14 Chasseurs-Volontaires noncommissioned officers identified in the notarial records were also militia NCOs, perhaps in parishes not covered by the sample. The military leadership group contained four *maréchaussée brigadiers*. These were some of the most powerful noncommissioned officers in the colonial military because of their power over the daily lives of all free coloreds. The *maréchaussée cavaliers*, or *archers*, are not considered as noncommissioned officers because, despite the fact that they led supernumeraries in the field, the government did not grant them any sort of independent disciplinary authority and in fact tried to ensure that they not be assigned to independent operations without their officers being present.

MILITARY SERVICE AS INCOME GENERATION

Military service defined this group, and at least a portion of their income came directly or indirectly from that source. Given the nature of the data that form the foundation of this book, these are the easiest sources of income to analyze.

Military service was rewarded in several different ways. Pay is the most obvious but was not necessarily the most valuable. The state also offered rewards to their servicemen, especially those hunting runaway slaves. In addition, the state provided equipment to free colored soldiers. There were informal rewards and unofficial, but legal, opportunities to earn extra income from persons needing special services from the military and police. Finally, the Saint Domingue policemen, like police everywhere, were tempted by corruption, and the soldiers, like soldiers everywhere, hoped for the opportunity to loot, preferably the enemy.

Militia duty was generally unpaid, except in special circumstances, but other free colored military men were paid wages. These wages were generally small but during the time covered by this book equaled those offered to white servicemen in the regular French military.

Some evidence exists of plans to pay buccaneers serving France, but for the most part the men of both colors who went from Saint Domingue to Cartagena in 1697 were expected to seek out their own reward in loot. In this they succeeded beyond their wildest dreams. As the buccaneers faded from the scene and the military professionalized, though, it came to be expected that soldiers would be paid by the state that employed them.

No record was found of how much members of the Chasseurs-Volontaires de l'Amérique were paid during the Seven Years' War. However, records of another, abortive force proposed at the same time gives us an idea of what might have been the reward for these servicemen.

The Premiere Légion de Saint-Domingue, a creature of the abortive militia reforms of the Comte d'Estaing in 1765, would have created a regular force out of the militia. The colored rank and file troops of this unit were to be paid considerably less than their white colleagues of the same rank: 180 *livres* per year for a *fusilier* of color versus 270 *livres* for a white and 270 *livres* per year for a colored dragoon versus 450 *livres* for a white. The noncommissioned officers and bandsmen were, however, paid the same amount regardless of their color.[19] Whites opposed turning militiamen into regular soldiers regardless of the pay, and so the idea was dropped, but it was indicative of feelings at the time about the free colored soldier.

By the next war, though, free coloreds had achieved nominal equality in pay. The pay scales for the Chasseurs-Volontaires and Grenadiers-Volontaires de Saint Domingue contained no overt racial distinctions—soldiers in these regiments received the pay of their titular equivalents in the French regular army. However, *Grenadiers* were the elite of the regular army and received higher pay than *Chasseurs* (or skirmishers) and regular line *fusiliers*. All *Chasseurs* in the units raised in Saint Domingue were free coloreds, receiving 105 *livres* a year, while all *Grenadiers* were white, at 126 *livres* a year. Moreover, noncommissioned officers were paid differently depending on what unit they were in, and the free colored leader types received about ten percent less than their white counterparts.[20]

Members of the Chasseurs-Royaux de Saint-Domingue, the abortive force created after the "success" of the Chasseurs-Volontaires, were also paid on the same basis as other white *Chasseurs* in the regular Army.[21] Militia troops were activated briefly in 1782 and were paid on the same basis as regular *fusiliers*.[22]

One hundred *livres* a year was not very much money, even though the regulations are unclear as to whether this was French or inflated colonial money. However, the soldier received food and housing while serving, and there was little on which he could spend his money. Taking these factors into account, military pay seems to have been competitive with civilian incomes for working-class occupations. Professional salaries in the colony were high: *économes* made from 1,500 to 4,000 *livres* a year, while *ménagères* got from 300 to 2,000 *livres*. The courier who carried the mail between Port-au-Prince and Léogane got 3,750 *livres* annually, although his contract was unclear as to whether he was to carry the mail himself or act as a contractor.[23] Craftsmen made somewhat less: five years of Pierre Aubien's service as a journeyman *charron* (wheelwright) were equated with a 1,200 *livre* debt in an act of 1780 in Fort Dauphin, a rate of pay of 240 *livres* a year.[24] A journeyman carpenter in Cap in 1782 made one *gourde* (8 *livres*) a week, or 416 *livres* a year.[25] Room and board in 92 civilian employment and apprenticeship contracts in the sample averages about 20 *livres* a month, so we can see that the Chasseur's pay of 100 *livres* a year, plus 240 *livres* a year for the value of room and board he received in barracks—the maintenance cost his family did not have to bear—fell toward the middle of the skilled crafts pay scale.

In addition, military pay was not disbursed regularly but usually was distributed at the end of the campaign in a lump sum. Therefore, Chasseurs-Volontaires returning after a few years' service—and forced savings—could afford a small piece of land or craft training and an urban job that could support them modestly.

The *maréchaussée* trooper was not housed or fed in barracks and so received considerably higher base pay. The 1721 act creating the organization fixed the pay of *archers* at 30 *livres* a month. In 1753, the state tried to pay the *maréchaussée* rank-and-file troopers with slave head tax exemptions, presuming thereby that they were slave owners. The term *habitant* was even used in the regulation of 1753 to describe the sort of man needed for the job.[26] By 1767, though, they were receiving regular pay once again, 500 *livres* a year for the *archer* and 750 *livres* for his noncommissioned superior, the *brigadier*.[27] The pay kept up with inflation, reaching a base of 800 *livres* a year in 1788.[28]

This is a modest but adequate professional salary, as befits an important servant of the slave society who had to work independently on many occasions and who had supervisory responsibility (over the supernumeraries, in any case). A *maréchaussée* man could afford to buy slaves and land and probably could live the life of a small *habitant* after a few years' service even if he was not a member of that class before.

The salary of an *archer* was the least of the possible financial advantages accruing to a *maréchaussée* man. Captured slaves, lawbreakers, or deserting regular soldiers escorted to the local jail were worth a varying reward, divided among the capturing troops according to a number of official formulae issued at different times (and unofficial kickback systems, no doubt). Slaves whose masters could not afford to pay the reward plus other fines and jail costs were often sold at auction. Notarial acts often contained the former ownership history of slaves, and so the sample contains several cases of slaves who passed through this system. In one case, for example, Nanon Dada, an elderly free black woman living on the *habitation* Arteau in Limonade, abandoned her usufructiary rights to the slave Guillaume to the heirs of her former master, Sieur Verbod. Dada had been given life usufruct of Guillaume by Verbod, with property rights reverting to Verbod's heirs upon her death, but the slave had run away and then had been recaptured in Cap. Dada was unable to pay the fines, expenses, and rewards, totaling in this case 1,515 *livres*. As a result, Guillaume was sold at this price to Sieur Barbe, living in Haut du Cap. The heirs of Verbod, holding the property rights to the slave, would recoup him from Barbe. Thus, the rewards were paid out of the sale price, and the *maréchaussée* men did not lose out, but poor Dada lost a valuable possession.[29]

The rewards for *marron* slaves specified in the 1788 law were as follows: 100 *livres* for each slave captured on the Spanish frontier, 60 *livres* for all those taken or killed in the mountains (the *maréchaussée* man claiming the reward for a killed maroon slave was to bring back the portion of skin with the slave's brand on it), 30 *livres* for any slaves arrested outside of their own parish, and 12 *livres* for those slaves captured inside their parishes. Arrests in the last case could be made only at night, unless the suspected slave was on horseback, to reduce shakedowns by rogue *maréchaussée* men. Effects possessed by recaptured slaves were to belong to the *maréchaussée*, except if it could be proven that the items had been stolen, in which case one-third of their value went to the *maréchaussée*. Slaves and horses were to be returned to their masters. Recaptured horses carried a reward of one *piastre* (or 20 *livres*). The *maréchaussée* received from the masters a one *ecu* reward for the return of any slave who was caught with a horse or a weapon that could not be proven to be the property of a free person, and the horse or weapon would belong to the *maréchaussée* man who arrested the slave.[30]

Parenthetically, we can see again from this act the importance of horsemanship and owning horses for the free colored identity. The slave on horseback threatened the free colored's separate status of being above slavery and so was a particular target. Additionally, the *maréchaussée*, springing from the militia *dragon piquet*, was a mounted formation. The alternative designation for the rank-and-file officer, *cavalier*, shows this. The acquisition of more horses would, of course, be a professional, as well as social and economic, gain for any *maréchaussée* man.

The official scheme for division of these cash rewards in the 1788 act was four shares for the *grand-prévôt,* or colonial commander, three for the *lieutenant,* or regional commander, two for the *exempt,* also referred to as the *prévôt,* or parish commander, one and one-half for the first *archer* on the scene, and one for each of the other *archers* involved in the case.[31] Some of the special rewards, such as the weapons and horses of captured *marrons,* were exclusively for the *maréchaussée* officer who made the arrest.

One can see from these figures that a *maréchaussée* man would not have to make very many arrests in a year before his reward money would surpass his regular pay as a source of income. Even if, conservatively, the average *maréchaussée* trooper doubled his pay with official rewards, he would have the income of a professional, such as the ubiquitous *économes,* and would be able to afford to set himself up in business as a rural capitalist farmer with little difficulty. The government's conceit that *maréchaussée archers* were to be *habitants* is thus seen to have been well-founded.

Unofficial rewards were common as well. In chapter 4, the reader was introduced to the peculiar case of Sieur Theron and his missing horse. The reward given to the *maréchausée* men who recaptured the horse in this case, divided three ways, comes to 46 *livres,* 13 *sols,* 8 *deniers* apiece, or more than a month's pay for a *maréchaussée cavalier.* They laid their hands on this money perfectly legally and in the line of ordinary business.

Another way *maréchaussée* members could pad their income was through private security work. If individual proprietors felt that they wanted more attention from the *maréchaussée,* this was available, for a price. An *arrêt* of the Conseil Supérieur de Cap Française regularized procedures for the posting of *maréchaussée* members at an individual's house on his request. The *maréchaussée* was available to protect a house especially at risk from attacks by runaway slaves or to oversee the seals placed on the deceased's property before an official inventory. In either case, the homeowner or estate was to pay 6 *livres* per day. *Prévôts* were forbidden by the *arrêt* to charge more than that, which implies that they had been doing so. There is no mention in this case of how much of the 6 *livres* made it into the hands of the individual guard, but the logic of the other laws relating to *maréchaussée* rewards suggests that he would not have been left completely out of the deal. Given that official pay was around 1.5 *livres* per day, this private security work was an important supplement to the income of the lucky *archer* or *cavalier* assigned to the duty.[32]

Both *maréchaussée* men and their counterparts in the free colored militia and special units were issued weapons and uniforms. The uniforms were suits of clothing with high social value, as discussed in chapter 7, but not much value in monetary terms. Augustin LeMoine's officer's dress uniform, white with copper buttons and green taffeta lining, sold for 10 *livres* at his estate sale in 1777.[33]

The weapons were a more significant item. Aside from their high social value, they were also technologically advanced and thus quite valuable in their own right. Gaspard Ardisson's sword, with gold hilt, was evaluated at 50 *livres* when his wife, Marie Anne Laporte, died in 1783.[34] A pair of horse pistols belonging to one Pierre, of the Limonade militia, were worth 37 *livres* in his estate sale in 1785.[35]

All this is modest enough when one looks at it from the perspective of a planter or successful urban entrepreneur. Still, a full outfit for an infantryman would have been worth nearly a year's pay, and a cavalryman's kit even more, because the cavalryman had to outfit his horse as well. For a young man starting out in life with few advantages, this would have been something significant.

However, official pay and rewards were often unpaid, as evidenced by the case of M. de Carnage de Mailhert, general of Royal Troops in St. Domingue, in 1739. In a formal complaint to the metropolitan government in that year, he described the background of the *maréchaussée* to that time. He pointed out that the budget for salaries of *maréchaussée* was too small; it was never sufficient to pay all the troops required by the various edicts. Colonial governments, he said, had responded by engaging all the people they were permitted to raise and then skimping on the pay. Since they were not paid, he said, the *archers* always complained, and occasionally they became "abusive." It is not clear from context if he means they were abusive of their superiors when their pay was short or if they were abusive of the population in order to shake them down for money to replace the unpaid salaries. Both are possible. M. de Carnage found the *maréchaussée* of the colony in a poor state. Morale was poor and recruitment was becoming difficult. To pay enough *archers*, he said, to provide the coverage needed would be very expensive. He cited the poor quality of the white *maréchaussée* leadership, especially the new *grand prévôt*, or colonial commander of the *maréchaussée*. This man, a retired sergeant of infantry, was a "very bad sort," said de Carnage.[36]

In response to de Carnage's complaint, the government in Paris approved the imposition of a tax of 30 *sols* per slave to pay for the *maréchaussée*. If fully collected, this would have provided the princely sum of 150,000 *livres* a year (in 1739; it would have amounted to much more by the 1780s) for the whole colony, enough to pay 360 *livres* per year (as it was in 1739) to 416 troopers. However, the official strength of the force, 193 at the time of de Carenage's complaint, never increased beyond 200, despite the quadrupling of the slave population in the following fifty years.

The 30 *sols* a year per slave tax seems to have become a general revenue source for the colonial government pretty quickly after the departure of General de Carenage from office. Certainly, one of the reasons cited in a later request for permission to raise the assessment on slaves in urban areas was the general financial condition of the colonial government.[37] Earlier taxes had quickly disappeared into the general fund: an edict of 1721 makes this point while establishing yet another special allocation to support police work.[38] All this suggests that official pay probably remained short throughout the period and that the official and unofficial rewards were probably the most important inducement to the *maréchaussée cavaliers*—and, of course, to their supernumerary subordinates who received no official pay at all.

Occasionally pay and rewards that were appropriated failed to make it to their intended recipients due to corruption among the white officers. When the white *maréchaussée* leaders were corrupt, though, free coloreds were quick to protest. Moreau de St. Méry took note of a case that took place in Port de Paix in 1786. The local *maréchaussée* commander had apparently been holding back the archers' pay and reward money and was either pocketing it or handing it out to his favorites. The supernumeraries stopped showing up for work, and the *maréchaussée* commander prevailed upon his superior, the *commandant du quartier*, or parish militia commander, to order a muster of the local free colored militia. At the muster, he ordered each of the companies to provide nine supernumeraries. The white captain of one of the companies, M. Audige, was accused of having incited all his noncommissioned officers to refuse to name anyone. The colored *sousofficiers* were put in prison by order of the parish commander, who complained to the commander of the militia of the North province in Cap Français about Captain Audige. The rank-and-file soldiers gathered in a "noisy troop" and insisted that they be put in prison as well, since they all refused to serve as supernumeraries.[39] At the same time, the official *maréchaussée* men were refusing to perform their duties, and at one muster, the only person present was one of the *brigadiers*. There were only five places in the jail, said the local militia commander, so what was he to do?

It appears that these complaints were common, as an edict of 1790 refers specifically to the problem of officers misappropriating *maréchaussée* pay and reward funds, citing the case of *Prévôt* Picard, of Fort Dauphin, who stole two years' worth of payroll and rewards. The 1790 act required that *maréchaussée* pay be given quarterly in the presence of a notary and required that senior officers carry out regular inspections of financial records.[40]

The Port-de-Paix case illustrates a number of important points about free colored military service. The militia company was a body through which free coloreds could carry out collective resistance to exactions by the colonial government. The noncommissioned officers were the ringleaders of the rank and file. The support of the white officer was very important. The local free colored planter elites were not conspicuous participants.

Maréchaussée troopers in particular sometimes managed to lay their hands on things of value outside of the legal avenues. A court decision cited by Moreau de

St. Méry in 1790 illustrates a solution to a common police dilemma that occurred to the *maréchaussée* of Cap Français, as it has certainly occurred to many other police officers in other times and places. Dame Naugaret, a café keeper in Cap, was condemned by the Conseil Supérieur to pay a fine of 10,000 *livres* for holding illegal gambling games in her café. One-third of the fine was to go to the royal treasury, one-third to charitable institutions in the town of Cap, and one-third to the *maréchaussée*, from which was to be deducted 660 *livres* for the militia detachment that assisted in the arrest. However, the *maréchaussée* were chided for not keeping track of the names of the players of these illegal gambling games.[41] A reward of 3,300 *livres*, less 660 *livres* for the militia, divided according to the official formula among 15 official *maréchaussée* cavaliers, 4 noncommissioned officers, and 2 white officers comes to 117 *livres* 17 *sols* per line trooper, or almost a quarter year's pay. Even deducting something for the supernumeraries still leaves this a healthy recompense for a night's work.

The *maréchaussée* men found other ways to make ends meet, some less ethical and legal than others. The free black Zazon, about whom further information is unfortunately lacking, was dismissed from the *maréchaussée* by order of the general commanding all troops in Saint Domingue on 29 July 1782, in response to his "insolence and exactions from blacks in their *habitations*."[42] This punishment by no means stopped the problem, however. In the act reorganizing the *maréchaussée* in 1788, the leadership was encouraged to pay "particular attention to the conduct of their *Archers*, in order to stop the inconveniences which the avarice of some of them can cause. They must be careful that the *Archers* allow blacks [slaves] to pass freely when the slaves have correct passes from their masters, and not to tear up the passes in order to gain, by this illicit means, the reward fixed in this act. If such a case is revealed, we (the Governor and Intendant of the colony) reserve to ourselves the right to impose such exemplary punishment as the case seems to require."[43]

The *maréchaussée cavalier* Boussens was sentenced to the ultimate exemplary punishment in 1785, although it is unclear if he was attempting to extort money or if he simply used excessive force. On 26 February of that year, he was condemned to death *in absentia* by the Conseil Supérieur de Cap Français for the crime of having shot to death a certain François.[44] The deceased was *commandeur*, or boss slave, on the plantation of Sieur de Buor in Trou du Nord. François refused to stop when called upon to do so by the accused. Details on the case are sketchy; the fact that the judgment was rendered *in absentia* suggests that Boussens had some doubt about the legitimacy of his use of force. The *maréchaussée* man and the *commandeur* might very well have had a clash of authority—one can see how the subordination of the lower slaves to their boss might have been undermined by the free colored slave catcher, and the temptation for the *maréchaussée* man to misuse his authority was great. The state refused to pay Sieur de Buor 1,200 *livres* for his dead slave (a modest price in any case for a *commandeur*), which at least suggests that in the minds of the authorities the responsibility for this tragedy was, to some extent at least, shared between the actors.

A "police brutality" case appears in Moreau de St. Méry's *Description . . . de la partie française,* dating from 1780, that illustrates the level of misconduct in which *maréchaussée* men felt they could indulge and the lengths to which the colonial government was willing to go to protect them. Four *archers* and a *brigadier* beat a white prisoner and cut him with their sabers while the prisoner was said to be offering no resistance. The prisoner died of gangrene resulting from his wounds. The appeals court ordered prison terms of a year or less for the participants in the attack and annulled the fine and expulsion from the *maréchaussée* ordered by a lower judge for the subordinate members of the *maréchaussée* party. The high court also fined the heirs of the dead prisoner 150 livres (five months' salary for a *maréchaussée archer*) for insults to the *maréchaussée*.[45] This result appears to have been at least a partial vindication for the colored policemen. Contrary to what observers such as Hilliard d'Auberteuil have reported, in this case free coloreds struck a white—fatally—and had their knuckles rapped instead of their hands cut off.[46] Colonial administrators seem to have made a decision against the supposedly unbreakable color line and in favor of their need for a loyal, efficient police force.

The participants in the overseas expeditions obviously hoped for loot as a supplement to their pay. The Cartegena expedition in 1697 acquired remarkable quantities of loot, sufficient to change the entire economy of the colony. Subsequent expeditions did not fare so well. Short-range trips might have given an opportunity for "prize money," or the value of a captured ship that was shared among all participants. The *Chasseurs* of the 1760s stayed in the colony, while their successors in the 1770s went to recapture a friendly city. Neither one got much of a chance for extraordinary wealth.

Militiamen also seem to have been largely left out of the opportunities for licit and illicit enrichment open to their *maréchaussée* colleagues. One of the things that must have made *piquet* duty so annoying to free coloreds was that it offered relatively little opportunity for rewards. A runaway slave might be caught at the roadblock, but it was much more likely that the *maréchaussée* patrol would pick up the slave in the hills trying to get around without daring the roadblock. Personnel at an immobile roadblock might be able to shake down passersby, but it also would be easier for authorities to pin the crime on them once the victims complained than on a mobile patrol of *maréchaussée* men.

SOCIAL ADVANCEMENT THROUGH MILITARY SERVICE

Luckily for the militiamen and Chasseurs, though, their service offered opportunities for social advancement perhaps as important as those economic possibilities open to the *maréchaussée*. In general, in fact, the possibility of social advancement was as powerful an inducement to military service for free colored men as was the hope of financial gain. It was possible for people at all levels of free colored society to advance socially through military service.

The supernumeraries in the *maréchaussée* were unpaid auxiliaries who served under the officially appointed *archers*. These supernumeraries were serving mostly in hopes of social advancement through manumission, which was granted free of tax after some years of service. Of course, these men may also have been able to earn reward money as shown above. However, it seems clear that manumission was the principal stimulus for recruitment to this position. It would have taken quite a bit of reward money to equal the manumission tax they were avoiding, to say nothing of the opportunity to bridge the enormous social gap between the quasi-free and the fully free.

Although plebeian supernumeraries must certainly have dreamed of promotion to lofty "official" status, no one in the sample actually made this step. A more typical *maréchaussée cavalier* was young André Leprestre of Croix des Bouquets and Port-au-Prince. A *mulâtre*, André was the natural son of the free *negresse* Ursule and, one presumes, Sieur André Leprestre, *prévôt* of the *maréchaussée* of Croix des Bouquets. In any case, Sieur Leprestre's will, executed on 19 September 1780, leaves his namesake his uniform and weapons to encourage the young man to follow his profession.[47] Sieur Leprestre also left his *brigadier*, Joseph la Bastide, a slave, a bequest that la Bastide passed on to Ursule after he extracted it from Leprestre's white heirs in a lawsuit. Occasionally bequests to the free colored lover and illegitimate children were passed through unrelated friends in order to foil opposition from legitimate heirs—and it appears in this case that Sieur Leprestre expected objections from his French relatives. Brigadier la Bastide got Ursule's slave only after two years of legal wrangling with the heirs.[48] André and his mother and brothers appeared several more times in the notarial archives of Port-au-Prince, and on each occasion he is listed as a *cavalier* in the *maréchaussée*.

A similar case to André Leprestre is that of Pierre Pellerin, a mulatto *cavalier* in the *maréchaussée* of Croix des Bouquets. His relationship to Sieur Pellerin des Prez, militia captain in Port-au-Prince and wealthy planter in the hills overlooking the plain of the Cul de Sac, is even more unclear than these things usually are. The name is not uncommon, and there were no notarial acts in which the two appeared together. Pellerin appears, however, to have gotten on pretty well in life without direct patronage from his possible relative or former master or both. He was a regular member of the wedding parties of other *maréchaussée* men and prominent civilian free coloreds and stood as godfather to the neighbors' children, both a mark of the respect in which he was held. On 7 April 1780, he and another man (possibly a member of the Croix des Bouquets *maréchaussée,* although this is unclear) bought a tannery and pasture in the hills that form the southern limit of the Cul de Sac plain from a white planter for 4,700 *livres* cash.[49] This represents some fifteen years of "official" *maréchaussée* salary, even had it been paid regularly. When Pellerin's partner died in 1782, they seem to have had a herd of about 120 assorted animals.[50] Cattle, the most important component of their herd, were worth at the time about 250 *livres* each, with smaller animals in proportion, so this represents at least another 20,000 *livres* in capital. Pellerin and his partner were *habitants* who had advanced in society at least in part thanks to the respect that they had among other free coloreds springing from their military role.

The *cavaliers* or *archers* of the *maréchaussée,* then, seem to have been financially secure citizens of their communities with considerable social respect. They frequently rated the description of *habitant,* like Pellerin, or François Lamotte, brother of the Limonade *maréchaussée* men Michel and Louis Lamotte. As we have seen, the state expected them to be *habitants,* in the wording of the 1753 reorganization act.[51] The state also presumed that they would be slave owners, granting them an exemption from the tax on slaves instead of a regular salary; it is perhaps significant that this provision was dropped in the 1767 reorganization of the *maréchaussée.* As we will see, military members, especially the leadership group, were considerably less likely to trade slaves than were nonmilitary persons of equivalent social level and financial means, although they may have owned enough for an exemption from the slave tax to be attractive.

The Chasseurs-Volontaires de Saint-Domingue attracted all sorts of free coloreds, from young men escaping slavery to blue-blooded aristocratic younger sons motivated by patriotic appeals. The case of one such Chasseur-Volontaire might give a better understanding of the social benefits accruing to them from service in the expedition.

The career of Fabien Gentil is illustrative of the advantages that service in the Chasseurs-Volontaires could have over the long term for an ambitious young free man of color. Freed by his master, Captain Dupetithouars, shortly after his return from service with the Chasseurs-Volontaires, and most likely quasi-free for some time before that, Gentil seems to have quickly blossomed into a prominent man in colored society. In his success, we can see the hand of his former master, but in a subtle way that illustrates the difference between the intimate relationship between a young landed aristocrat like the children of Julie Dahey and their white father Sieur Peignanan and the patronage relationship typical of the military noncommissioned officers we meet in this chapter.

Both Gentil and Dupetithouars moved off the farm and to town about the same time. Before his departure for the Savannah expedition, Dupetithouars signed a contract with Antoine François Bayon de Libertat, former master of Toussaint Breda Louverture and manager of the Breda plantations in the North province.[52] Bayon de Libertat was to manage the Dupetithouars *habitation* in Limbé during the master's absence. Dupetithouars must have liked Bayon de Libertat's work, as future references to Dupetithouars in the notarial archives describe him as an *habitant* of Limbé, but resident in Cap, rue St. Louis.

Gentil also left Limbé after his return from Georgia and the Lesser Antilles, but he did not install himself in his former master's household in town, as would have been expected of a planter group natural child like the Peignanan offspring. Instead, he went to a neighboring parish and set up in business for himself. Following a common pattern for free colored entrepreneurs, he seems to have split his time and resources between an urban area and the countryside. Less than a month after his own manumission became final, on 10 May 1780, and representing himself as a resident of Cap, he freed a young mulatto slave named Jean, age 18.[53] Presumably, there was a family relationship between them, but its exact nature is unclear. In any case, he began by this step a process of creating his kin group that was common among other free colored military leaders.

Later in the year, though, Gentil moved from Cap Français to open a business in Embarquadaire de Limonade, a seaside village about 20 miles from the city. On 30 November 1780, he promised a slave to little Marie Josephe Sanitte, *mulâtresse libre*, the 2-year-old natural daughter of Jeanne, also a *mulâtresse*, who was working as *menagère* to M. le Vicomte de Labissenaye, a prominent planter of Limonade.[54] The child may have been Gentil's, or perhaps Jeanne was a relative, since the act avoids the giveaway reference to living expenses. The slave was to be delivered in two years; Gentil said he was expecting an inheritance. The act declared that Gentil was planning marriage but not, apparently, to Marie Sanitte's mother, since he appeared in a 1785 act as the husband of a certain Elizabeth Petrouille or Petronille.[55] The live-in partners of white planters may have had outside interests but rarely married, within the planter group or anyone else.

In any case, Gentil was moving up economically and socially fairly rapidly—perhaps too rapidly, as his next appearance in the notarial archives attests. In December 1784, Gentil and a white man, Sieur Pierre Crivel, dissolved a partnership that they had created for the purpose of operating a store in Limonade.[56] Their accounts no longer accompany the agreement to dissolve the partnership, but it is clear that the dissolution was involuntary. They were said to have had more than 5,000 *livres* in outstanding debts, including 2,862 *livres* 5 *sols* to Sieurs Tessier and Martin, prominent *négociants* of Cap Français. The partners were to be individually responsible for the debts of the society, with the first partner to be responsible for collecting from the other. In this act, Gentil was described as "Sieur Fabien Gentil, *marchand*." He had obviously joined the upper ranks of colored society.

On 9 March 1785, having been free for somewhat less than five years, Gentil pawned his personal effects, including a teak bed with Indian cotton bedcurtains and covers, a good deal of furniture of various qualities, six sets of silverware, and a horse to one of the white creditors of his partnership, Sieur Lasalle, in return for forgiveness of 1,930 *livres* of his debt and a piece of undeveloped land in Fort Dauphin.[57] He was obviously looking ahead to future speculations, as well as dealing with the consequences of the last one. In addition, he was diversifying his holdings between urban and rural, a pattern common among free coloreds and especially the military leadership. The quality of his personal furnishings suggest that he had a comfortable middle-class lifestyle, at the least.

Gentil seems to have overcome his reverses and remained near the top, although he never again rated a *Sieur* before his name in any notarial act. He invested in urban as well as rural real estate, including another developed lot in l'Embarquadaire de Limonade, and got involved in the case of the tenant who would not vacate, presented in chapter 6 of this book.

Gentil appeared several more times in the notarial archives, but always without any sign of his former master Captain Dupetithouars. But we need not deduce from this that Dupetithouars had no personal interest in his former slave. The manumission of Gentil should not be seen as a purely economic transaction between him and Dupetithouars, nor did the master cast off his former slave once they left active military service and moved away from Limbé. First, one wonders about the source of all Gentil's assets. Juridically freed in 1780, he was already the owner of a slave of his own whose services he could afford to dispense with through manumission. His act of donation of a slave in the same year to little Marie Sanitte declared that he was expecting an inheritance in two years. It is unclear from where he was expecting this inheritance to come, and it may in fact simply refer generically to substantial income that Gentil anticipated. In any case, he had resources available to him. He obviously must have been quasi-free and active in the market for some time before his formal manumission, but his is not the case of the stereotypical self-purchasing freedman, skimping and saving for decades to afford the price of manumission. Gentil seems to have found the road to financial success smoothed for him to at least some degree. The freedman Gentil moved fairly rapidly into at least middle-class respectability, as a *marchand* and a *sieur*.

From where could these resources have come if not from, or through the assistance of, his former master? Gentil's bride, from the little we know of her, does not appear to have been wealthy, and there do not seem to have been other free colored family members with substantial resources. Slaves clearly had access to money before manumission, through the retail market and the practice of letting them work on their own account. He may have been semi-free to operate on his own economically for some time, but this was a precarious existence. Gentil was never described as practicing a skilled trade, but he could have been involved in small retail before his manumission. However, it seems unrealistic to assume that he accumulated substantial resources on his own before receiving his liberty—a few hundred *livres* perhaps, but not the thousands that he demonstrated that he had in the first few years after his manumission. Presumably, along with his freedom, Gentil received at least a couple of slaves and perhaps a piece of land from his master. Then, when he was in financial difficulties, he discovered that prominent white Cap Français merchants would extend him and his partner credits worth thousands more *livres*—a concession that would certainly have been easier to obtain with some judicious intervention by a respected militia officer and planter. This intervention would have been especially efficacious coming from a white man with a number of honorific titles like Capitaine Dupetithouars, Chevalier de l'Ordre Militaire et Royale de St. Louis. In Gentil, then, we see another way of patronage relations with prominent whites, where the young free colored man receives assistance in meaningful ways from his patron without being a family member or close dependent, as was true of the planter group. For those without influential kin, a relationship with a white officer might serve a similar purpose.

In addition to the Chasseurs-Volontaires and the other special expeditionary corps and the *maréchaussée* was the much more pervasive institution of the militia. Every free colored male was required to serve in the militia. However, only those to whom this service was important socially or economically identified themselves as such in the notarial acts. In essence, this means that the only persons identified from the sample as members of the militia were the quasi-free who achieved tax-free manumission through their militia service in wartime and the leaders of the militia. The latter formed an important part of the group of military leaders. Most expeditionary corps noncommissioned leaders were drawn from the militia companies by their officers when those officers took up regular commissions. In addition, self-identification as a militia leader in a notarial act gives a clue to those members of the milita leadership who placed a high value on their military participation; it was precisely these men who formed the military leadership group.

MILITARY LEADERS AND THE TRADITIONAL MARKERS OF STATUS

Social advancement for these military leaders was a result not only of patronage, either received or given, or of their explicit military role. The more usual status markers also affected society's view of military leaders. Generally, they did not possess these characteristics of high social status in the same measure as the planter elites, although they did surpass non-elites in most cases. Officeholding was obviously at the core of these military leaders' social success. Their courtesy designations in the notarial archives, though, were different from those accorded other free colored elites. Even Capitaine Vincent, who was received at the governor's table, according to Moreau de St. Méry, was never referred to as *Sieur* Vincent by any of the three notaries with whom he did business. His fellow officer Etienne Auba rated a *Sieur* from Limonade notary Jean-Louis Michel, who was notoriously free with this accolade for wealthy or influential free coloreds, but not from any of the other notaries with whom he dealt. None of the other military leaders qualified for a *Sieur*. Military leaders did use civilian occupational titles occasionally, in addition to their military rank, especially in time of peace, but these were generally tradesmen's titles that were marks of distinction for non-elites but generally below the planter elites.

Military leaders generally adopted French or French-sounding surnames, like all other free coloreds. However, they were more likely than non-elites, and especially than the planter group, to keep the names "drawn from the African idiom" that they were assigned upon manumission. Pierre Zogo, Jean-Baptiste Malic, and Pierre Marion Yari are noteworthy examples. All free blacks, all militia noncommissioned officers, they made no attempt to adopt French surnames and gloried in this public identification of themselves as freedmen.

In the realm of status goods, military leaders, as might be expected, concentrated on professionally related items such as weapons, uniforms, and horses. All of them, obviously, owned these items, and typically when we have an inventory of their personal property, the uniform turns out to be their most valuable item of clothing, and the swords and firearms are among their most valuable other personal possessions.[58] In general, these men did not seem to have had very high standards of personal luxury. Their furniture appears to have been more useful than decorative, with a marked absence of copper hardware on armoires, carvings and imported cloth hangings on beds, and the like. Such a Spartan lifestyle was common among the free colored middle class and nouveau riche, as we have seen, with the real status goods appearing in generations following the one that built the family fortune.

The ability to sign one's name was more directly related to one's social status than to actual educational achievement, and thus it is not surprising to find that military leaders were somewhat more likely than free coloreds as a whole to sign their notarial acts (41 percent of their acts were signed, as opposed to only 35 percent for the sample as a whole).

PATRONAGE THROUGH MILITARY SERVICE

Probably the most important social benefit of military service for free coloreds, though, was the opportunity to establish networks of military comrades, especially those of higher ranks and even including prominent whites serving as militia officers. These networks could supplement or indeed substitute for the kin networks that were so important to the advancement of elite free coloreds.

For example, on 14 March 1786, Etienne *dit* La Rivière, a free mulatto butcher and probable noncommissioned officer in the Cap militia, and Pierre *dit* l'Allemand, a free black mattress maker, both from Cap Français, made a deal with Jean-Baptiste Coutaux *dit* Hervé, a free colored planter from the countryside near the small northern city of Port de Paix. Hervé's slave, named Pierre, had run away some time before, and Hervé had found him living in Cap Français, working as a supernumerary in the *maréchaussée*. Hervé was prepared to take his property back home with him, but the pair who intervened made him an offer he was happy to accept. On behalf of Pierre, who as a slave was legally incapable of making any binding financial commitments on his own initiative, the two paid Hervé 660 *livres* in cash and promised to pay him 396 *livres* more and to give him a newly arrived male slave aged 15 or 16 at the end of the year in return for Pierre's freedom. Hervé agreed to present a request to the government to free Pierre.[59]

The intervention of the two not only saved Pierre from an unenviable fate but also served to illustrate the way in which free colored military men could build useful networks of contacts. Both of the men who intervened were prominent free colored businessmen in Cap Français. La Rivière had served in the expedition to Savannah as a sergeant, as well as in the militia. L'Allemand was a colored businessman of some stature who owned several slaves and who was frequently asked to serve as godfather to unrelated children—a sign of social status in the free colored community. There is no record of his military service, but he was part of the social circle that included other military leaders. That these pillars of the community were willing to at least lend their names, if not their financial resources, to the *maréchaussée* man's quest to remain free speaks a good deal to Pierre's importance within the community. Even if he was using his own money to make the payments and only using the pair's names for the transaction, rather than getting a loan from his protectors, they were at least technically extending him credit by making a legally binding promise to pay on his behalf.

LEADERSHIP ROLES

The social advantage that free coloreds gained from military service became more important as the servicemen increased in rank. Free coloreds served as military officers up until the 1760s, and many retired officers were still alive in the 1770s and 1780s. Even after the formal end of their active service, these free colored militia officers had enormous status in their communities, and even whites showed them considerable marks of respect both officially and unofficially.

Augustin LeMoine

We have already met the most prominent member of this group, Capitaine Vincent Olivier. He was not alone, though. A more typical example of the group would be Augustin LeMoine, owner of the beaver coat. He was a free black militia officer in Fort Dauphin with a farm in Quartier Morin. He had served in the militia in the 1760s and died in November 1777. An inventory of the effects found at his household, one of the few death inventories in the sample, was conducted in his son Bertrand's absence—Bertrand having chosen to serve in the French Royal Navy—by his neighbor and the executor of the will, Georges Thomany:

> Inventory of the house in the town of Fort Dauphin, rue de l'Eglise, in which the deceased died 28/11/77. In the main room: Table, *sap* wood, with covering in *indienne* cotton, good condition; table, *sap*, covering in *scamoise*, good condition; large dining table, *sap*, poor condition; small table, poor condition; *bergère, acajou* wood, with cushion, covering in *scamoise*, good condition; *buffet, sap; garde-manger*, very good condition; 11 chairs, 2 in poor condition, plus 2 armchairs, good condition; pottery water container; 2 poor-quality peasant water jars. In the bedroom on the west side: bed, *acajou* wood, with mattress and pallet, cotton bedcurtains; wooden bedstead, *acajou*, pallet, mattress, 2 pillows, bedcurtains and overhead drapery in the Polish style; *bergère*, in very poor condition, *sap*, with pallet and pillows; small table, *acajou*, good condition; trunk mounted on two pillars, *sap*, in which were: 5 handkerchiefs "of Chales"; pair of *culottes* in gingham fabric, new; red and black striped shirt in Indian fabric; another shirt with small red flowers; an *armoire, noyer* wood, w/drawer, poor condition, with following objects: beaver coat lined w/yellow fabric, with gold buttons, matching *culottes;* a uniform, white, with copper buttons, lined in green taffeta; vest and 3 *culottes;* a pair of gray *culottes; culottes*

in taffeta *cramoisy;* grey serge *culottes* with silver buttons; puce *culottes;* 4 sheets; 11 new towels; 9 other towels; 7 towels more used; sheet and 2 towels in *brin;* 6 pieces of cotton cloth; 13 long *culottes* in different cloth; 5 *caterons* in light fabric; 2 *caterons* in good white fabric; 13 vests of different fabric; 12 shirts; 7 handkerchiefs; 5 pillowcases; 3 more towels, 5 [underclothing] in cotton; 4½ sets of sheets and a bedcover in wool; a spool of thread from Rennes; 28 buttons in gilded copper; a new hat and a somewhat used one; a pallet described as *vendé.* The silverware: 3 spoons, 3 forks, knife w/ebony handle, in silver; a pair of pistols in poor condition, decorated w/silver; a pair of shoe buckles in silver; 3 pairs of sleeve-buttons in gold; a razor handle in poor condition with two blades and a strop; a Spanish machete; a sword with copper handle; a Spanish sword; 2 copper chandeliers; a seal in silver; pocketknife covered in silver; another large water container; a hunting musket. In the small room off the hallway: 13 empty demijohns; 8 bottles and 10 half-bottles, empty; 3 pots; 6 pottery plates; 5 china plates; mortar in marble w/pestle in wood; mug in yellow pottery; 2 small soap dishes; a shaving dish and goblet; copper balance; 2 6-pound weights; 4 smaller weights; iron hammer; 2 bricks of soap; 8 *andouilles* of tobacco. In the courtyard: 17 planks from Bordeaux, and lots of other large planks; carpentry tools.

At this point Catherine Auba [daughter of black militia officer Etienne Auba] appeared and claimed that 11 of the planks belong to her as she had loaned them to the deceased.

Continuing the inventory: a lot, located on rue de l'Eglise, bordered by the widow Jolicoeur (free colored), Zabeth *dite* Yonyon (free black), with a *case* [hut] in wood and sun-dried bricks without foundation, with plank walls, 3 bedrooms of which one and the main room have tiled floors, with a hallway on the street and a storage cabinet, roofed in shingles; another building 40 feet long, in very poor condition, shingle roof; and a third building, in poor condition, small, 3 rooms.

Slaves: Louis *dit* Da, Creole, aged 15–16; Olive, Congo, 35; Jeannette, Creole, 35.

Papers: act of manumission for the deceased dated 22/5/45. Liberty given by him to his son Bertrand [the sailor], 20/12/71. Marriage contract between the deceased and Francoise Dorothee in 1749, commission as Ensign in militia, dated 29/10/60, concession of land for the lot his house is located on, no. 193, 63 feet × 124; collection of IOUs from Jean Labadie, 228# [deniers] 10s [sols], 13/3/77; Joseph Baptiste, 33#; 11/3/60; Marie Anne Thilorie [free black], 69#, 22/7/72;. Sinraison [free colored] 36#, 22/4/76; Jean Potanter fils [free colored], 27/2/67, 12 *piastres* 5 *escalins;* Felix [free colored], 29 *piastres,*

15/1/77; the widow Pix, 241#, 19/6/76; the widow Raugaret, 50#, 27/6/76; 61#, Sieur Rolie, 27/9/77; Cochet *dit* Dandin [free colored], 33#, 13/10/76; 66#, 29/1/76, Le Sourd de Dubay; 33#, 1/5/76. A volume of memoirs and other papers that [regrettably] is not further described. Another collection of diverse sales of slaves, animals, etc., not further described. Another set of sale documents in Spanish, [suggesting that he traded across the border, an important activity in Fort Dauphin]. Another file of papers relating to various captains —of ships, one presumes. Another file of merchandise inventories, also not further described. A file of acknowledgments of payments he made to his suppliers, also not further described. LeMoine was the gaurdian [*tuteur*] of the minor children Piot [of whom no other details appear in the sample, perhaps they lived in another parish], and their papers are handed over to their new *tuteur* without further description. Registers and account books, existence noted but contents not described.

Thomany declares that the slave Jean has been *marron* for seven years.[60]

The personal effects, excepting the slaves and real estate, sold on 12 December for 1,185 *livres*, a tidy sum for clothing and furniture.[61] He had accounts receivable for his local business of about 1,100 *livres*, dating back over about a year and a half. We cannot be certain without looking at those account books, but LeMoine must have been making a respectable professional income of several thousand *livres* a year. LeMoine was an urban businessman, who would have been described as a *marchand*, albeit a pretty successful one, had it not been for his immeasurably more prestigious military commission. We can get some idea from the act cited above how important military service was to LeMoine's rise in the world from slave to prominent businessman. He was freed in 1745 and married in 1749. However, his marriage must have been to a slave, as his son Bertrand was a slave (and yet he was described as legitimate in his own will and bears his father's surname).[62] The father, Augustin, was free for fifteen years before becoming a militia officer. It was only after his commissioning, though, that he was able to accumulate enough resources to free his son, who spent twenty years in slavery. *Post hoc* does not always imply *proper hoc,* but it is suggestive that receipt of a military commission, manumission of family members, and then acquisition of a respectable fortune followed each other at about 10-year intervals in the life course of Augustin LeMoine.

Bertrand LeMoine returned to Saint Domingue sometime before 1780, at which time he made his own will, naming Thomany his executor and identifying his illegitimate daughter as his sole heir.[63] It is interesting to note that, perhaps in keeping with the ideal of the navy as the scientific branch of service and thus perhaps more attractive to freethinkers, the two LeMoines, father and son, were the only free blacks in Fort Dauphin not to profess faith in the "holy Catholic, Roman, and Apostolic faith" in their wills.

Some family traditions are more changeable than others, though. LeMoine *père* was a military officer who obviously cherished his status, hanging onto his officer's uniform and sword until his death sixteen years after his commissioning and at least a dozen years after he ceased to exercise the role. LeMoine *fils* served in the navy during the War of American Independence but moved to the civilian merchant marine at the end of that war. In 1782, he gave a power of attorney to the old family friend Thomany to sell the paternal household in the rue de l'Eglise in Fort Dauphin; at the time, he was serving as *maître d'hôtel* on the merchant ship *La Pauline* in Cap harbor.[64] A military career had clearly contributed to the wealth and status of the father; the son found a civilian maritime career more attractive.

Fort Dauphin militia officer Etienne Auba, introduced in chapter 4, served in the militia, like *Capitaine* Vincent Olivier, as an officer of free colored troops. He was sent outside the colony on at least one occasion, embarking on a navy ship for duty in what is now the Dominican Republic. He and his family were part of Le-Moine's social and economic circle, as we can see from the presence of his daughter at the inventory of LeMoine's effects. All three of these officers, as well as their countless descendants, appeared regularly in the notarial archives. Moreau de St. Méry tried to portray Auba as financially strapped in the 1770s to explain his application for financial assistance to the state. The records bear this out; while by no means among the poor, his family did not qualify for inclusion among the economic elite of colored society. Their average notarized transaction was evaluated at 2,150 *livres*, and their largest was for 4,000 *livres*, representing the sale of a one-third interest in the estate as a whole by Auba's son Joseph to his older brother, Etienne. Nonetheless, the Auba family held an important social position in Fort Dauphin. Members of the family, especially Etienne Auba *dit* Bellony, Capitaine Auba's eldest son, appeared frequently as witnesses in marriage contracts, death inventories, and other "family" acts of persons apparently unrelated to them.

Despite coming from an earlier generation and holding the king's commission, these men, along with the noncommissioned officers, can be considered part of the military leadership group. This is primarily because they show the military leaders' habit of building networks of other colored militia officers and noncommissioned officers. Auba's daughter, Catherine, for example, married Guillaume Manigat, a *lieutenant* of the black militia. Auba and Vincent Olivier were former colleagues and business partners. Olivier's sons (or grandsons, more likely), one named René and another possibly Maturin, served in the Chasseurs-Volontaires. His grandson Pierre, most prominent member of the clan in the 1780s after the death of the patriarch, included militia leaders Jean-Baptiste Leveille and his son Jean-François

Edouard Leveille *dit* Riché in his circle, joining them on four "family" acts, as witnesses to their family baptisms or funerals or they as witnesses to his.

Whereas in theory every free adult male in the colony was a militiaman, it is only among coloreds that one sees militia noncommissioned officers citing their rank in official documents as a point of pride. Thirty-two such individuals appear in the sample, with another 7 who identified themselves in a notarial act as noncommissioned officers in one of the overseas expeditionary corps but who probably also held rank in the militia, out of a theoretical maximum establishment of 374 (probably less in practice) in the parishes studied. The "Etat Général des Milices" for 1777 revealed the existence of 5 black or mulatto companies in Cap, 4 in Limonade, 4 in Fort Dauphin, 9 in Port-au-Prince, 6 in Croix des Bouquets, and 6 in Mirebalais. A 1769 survey, which broke down numbers by private soldier, noncommissioned officer, and officer, revealed that free colored companies had a median of 11 noncommissioned slots per company—typically 3 sergeants, a drummer or trumpeter, and 9 corporals—slots that all would have been filled by free coloreds. Cavalry units also contained a farrier sergeant responsible for the horses.[65]

Among free coloreds, especially the poorer or less well connected ones, these militia noncommissioned officers occupied a social position in many ways similar to that of the white militia officers. For those free coloreds with close personal ties to whites, the white militia officer was the source of patronage and judge of local quarrels, as he was, in general, for whites. The colored militia officer in the pre-1765 period also seems to have filled this role for the colored community, as witness the remarks of Moreau de St. Méry on Capitaine Vincent, above. Part of the justification for studying the free colored military noncommissioned officers was the way in which they took up this unofficial community leadership role in the years after 1765. There was a relative dearth of acts made by military leaders that included whites, and instead a large proportion of deals were made with each other. Most of their remaining acts, including many of the family acts, were performed with lower-class free coloreds.

Although military leaders were sometimes the recipients of patronage, as with Fabien Gentil, they were more likely to be the patron than the *protegé*. In fact, their social position depended on the network of *protégés* they built up, not only by sharing their prestige through family acts but also through more concrete acts of support.

Military leaders were somewhat less likely than the free colored population as a whole to be participants in acts of donation: 4.2 percent of their notarial acts in the sample were donations, as opposed to 5.9 percent for free coloreds as a whole. However, donations by elites in general total only 4.6 percent of all their acts. Military leaders were much more likely than other elites to be the donors in these acts of donation. Military leaders and members of their families made donations to non-military families in 56 percent of the acts and were recipients in 13 percent; in 31 percent of the acts, both parties were from military families. In planter group families, in only 36 percent of the acts of donation did the group member give something to a nongroup member. Similarly, 36 percent of the planter group donations were from a person outside their group (typically a presumed but not acknowledged white relative) to the elite individual, whereas 28 percent of their donations were between group members.

In addition to patronage expressed through donations to nonfamily members, free colored military leaders also acted as patrons by making credit available to protégés. Sales contracts reported in the notarial archives as being performed for cash payment were often in fact on some form of credit terms. Therefore, it is difficult to quantify the superior credit terms offered by free colored military leaders, much less to relate them to the social class of buyer and seller. The most common form of credit, especially at the lower social levels, was the sale with "right of recovery," or pawn. Military leaders were as likely to pawn their possessions (implying both an entrepreneurial desire to liquidate assets for reinvestment and also a shortage of those same assets) and to loan money against a pawn: in 36 percent of their pawns, they were the seller, and in 36 percent, the buyer; 28 percent of the transactions were between two military members.

It is difficult to argue that loaning money against a pawn represents patronage, however. It is to the unsecured credit sale that we must look for examples of free colored military leaders extending credit on concessionary terms as a form of patronage. In this area, considering only those sales in which credit terms were specified in the notarial act, free colored military leaders were the lenders to nonmilitary persons in 55 percent of the sales, while they borrowed from nonmilitary lenders in 33 percent; 12 percent of the transactions were between military leaders. Moreover, for these credit sales free colored military leaders made to nonmilitary free coloreds, the average duration of the loan was 10 months, and the average down payment was 34 percent. For credit transactions where free colored military leaders loaned to whites, where patronage can be assumed not to have been a factor, the average duration of the loan was a little longer at just over 13 months, but the average payment up front was over 50 percent. For free coloreds' land sales as a whole, anything under half of the purchase price up front must be considered a concessionary deal, except in the case of large sales of land and slaves where the production of the plantation was to be used to pay off the debt. In those cases, we can assume that the sale price was inflated proportionately to reflect the interest that sellers were legally prohibited from charging. The duration of most credit contracts, again with the exception of very large loans, was in the area of one year.

Thus, we can see that free colored military leaders tended to give a somewhat better deal in credit sales to their fellow free coloreds, both military and nonmilitary, than to whites, suggesting that they were expecting some sort of nonfinancial, social return on their investment.

Jean-Baptiste Malic

We have already met a few of the noncommissioned officers, such as Joseph la Bastide, the *maréchaussée* leader in Croix des Bouquets, and his colleague Pierre Pellerin. Perhaps the best-documented example of this group is Sergent Jean-Baptiste Malic *dit* Mali. He and members of his family appeared in the notarial archives on 48 occasions. The average value of the Malic family's transactions was 7,692 *livres*, and he had three transactions over 10,000 *livres* (meeting the criterion used in this work for identifying a member of the economic elite).

It is interesting to speculate about the source of Malic's name. It does not appear to have been a modified version of a European name. It could be a version of Ti Malice, "little nasty," a trickster character in Haitian folktales. It could refer to the Kingdom of Mali in west Africa (which by this time was defunct), although Malic himself was born in the colony. It could be from the Arabic *Al-Malik* (perhaps Malic's parents were Muslims). It was not a name given routinely to manumitted slaves. In any case, Malic was an example of a prominent free colored who apparently never tried to take on a French or French-sounding surname. While it would be going too far to call this a declaration of independence from white society, it does fit in well with his general independence from white patronage.

A free black with no hint of white relatives, Sergeant Malic was the legitimate son of a free black couple in the town of Cap Français. His first appearance in the archives was in the 1776 cadastral survey of Cap, at which time he owned one piece of property, at number 16, rue des Trois Chandelliers. This was a predominantly free colored neighborhood, and the house was not very valuable—the cadastral assessors described it as a *barraque* and evaluated it at a rental value of 150 *livres* per year.[66] This appears to have been his home, from which he operated a general retail business.

In the following year, Malic married very successfully. His bride, Marie Coeflin, was the recognized but illegitimate daughter of a free black planter in Limbé, a few miles from Cap. Although she was not her father's heir, like the illegitimate mulatto children of white planters, she was not left penniless. In their marriage contract, Malic's property was said to include his house, 2 slaves, merchandise, his personal property, clothing, arms, furniture, tools, utensils, and an enormous list of very small accounts receivable totaling over 10,000 *livres*. The bride, on the other hand, owned three lots in town, one of them with a quite substantial building on it (described in the act as a *maison*).[67] Her houses appear in the notarial record later as renting for up to 1,016 *livres* a year apiece.[68]

It is interesting to compare Malic's wedding with those of the wealthy free colored planter group members. In what would have been a very unusual step for the very "bourgeois" Chavannes or Laportes, Malic and his bride legitimized a 3-year-old prenuptial child, Etienne. In addition, Malic took the even more unusual step of recognizing an illegitimate child by another relationship, a girl named Marguerite, aged 8. He reserved enough from the mutual donation that established the community of property in the marriage contract to purchase and free the little girl, currently the slave of fellow militiaman Pierre Amoune. He purchased and freed the little girl the next year.[69] Both of these steps were clear violations of the code of bourgeois morality that governed the lives of the mulatto elite—not that the man would have extramarital and premarital sexual relationships, but that he would marry the mother of a child that he had fathered through such a relationship. Having done so, it would have been inconceivable for any planter group man to announce to the world in his marriage contract that he had an illegitimate child, especially one who was still a slave. The planter elite very occasionally found a minor place in their kin group for their illegitimate slave children, but it was not in their marriage contracts.

With his marriage, Malic's career began a spectacular climb. As a militia sergeant, he already had a respectable role in free colored society. After his marriage, he became a regular fixture in the Cap parish registers as godfather and witness at marriages and burials. This is an indication of the respect in which he was held in the Cap free colored community. He also seems to have used the concrete benefits of the wealth coming to him through his marriage to build his economic position. His father-in-law may have intended his daughter to live comfortably on the rents of her places in town; such a *rentier* strategy would have fit into the conservative approach to capital and wealth common among the free colored planter group (to which Marie's father apparently belonged, although there is little on him in the sample aside from the marriage contract). Malic liquidated some of her assets and plunged deeply into real estate speculation in Cap.[70]

Malic's most profitable and durable economic connections seem to have been with other prominent free blacks, many of them also military leaders. One example is his long association with Pierre Attila and their joint management of the resources of the Desrouleaux heirs. Attila was most likely Malic's cousin or nephew —as is common in these cases, precise relationships are hard to pin down—and was certainly an important business contact. Attila was chosen as the tutor, or guardian, of the children of Madelaine Desrouleaux, *negresse libre,* upon her death sometime in the spring of 1775, and Malic was named their curator. The children, Madelaine and Louis, were *mulâtres,* but there does not seem to have been any white Sieur Desrouleaux in the offing. Whoever he was, though, his children seem to have been well taken care of. There is no record of the mother's will or death inventory, since the death took place before the start of systematic notarial record-keeping in the North province. However, we can get a good picture of the size of her estate from later notarial entries.

On 12 November 1775, Attila rented Malic a building belonging to the Desrouleaux heirs that was described as a *maison* on the Place de Clugny, at the corner of the rue Royalle, a very prestigious address. Transactions involving the property of an orphan were very carefully supervised by the state. The local court had to agree to the nomination of a tutor for the children, and the tutor's work was usually overseen by a curator whose signature was required for any major transaction. The minors themselves could take action on their own account, with the approval of the court and their curator, but any act of sale they performed was provisional, conditional on their ratification upon majority. Attila, as tutor, and Malic, as curator, seem to have negotiated this minefield of regulations successfully.

The house was not further described in the act, but it rented for 3,600 *livres* a year.[71] This is a truly massive sum—only 16 rental contracts in the sample were more valuable, and 3 of those were performed by Vincent Ogé, by far the wealthiest free colored in the North province. Malic did not rent this palace as a residence. He sublet it to (mostly white) businesspeople, at a handsome profit. As is common in these cases, we have no documentation to demonstrate the scale of the profits he made, unfortunately. We do have indications of what property in this area would rent for on a month-to-month basis. The ubiquitous Vincent Ogé rented a two-room apartment in a building he managed at the corner of the rues Vaudreuil and St. Simon, in the same general neighborhood, on a 36-month lease, in 1785, for 198 *livres* a month.[72] The *marchande* Elisabeth *dite* Jolicoeur sublet a one-room retail space somewhat down the rue Royalle, in a mixed neighborhood, to a Victoire Arelise in 1784 for 1,650 *livres* a year.[73] A single room in a building on the rue Royalle at the rue du Chantier, again somewhat at the edge of the downtown wealthy neighborhood where the house Malic rented was located, went for 50 *livres* a month in 1777.[74] A *maison* like the Desrouleaux's must have had at least six or seven rooms that could have been rented out in this way.

Malic apparently rented two other residences from the *mineurs* Desrouleaux at about this time. The cadastral survey of 1776 shows them owning two other buildings in Cap, in a new area on the edge of town heading up toward the hill that overlooks the harbor. One of the buildings was later sublet by Malic to Jean Baptiste Petit, for a rent equal to that estimated in the cadastral survey at 500 *livres* a year.[75] All these transactions are rather odd considering that the curator was supposed to be an outside, disinterested advocate for the children, while the tutor was typically a family member or close friend of the deceased parents who might be expected to have family interests in mind. The two were supposed to watch each other and balance their powers; instead, here we have a case of the curator gaining a financial interest in the estate.

It is unclear how this cozy relationship between managers and renters of the Desrouleaux estate affected the children's net worth. This was a time of economic boom in Cap, especially after the end of the War of American Independence. Almost nobody who owned urban real estate could have failed to make money. The *mineurs* Desrouleaux certainly made princely sums from their holdings, and those sums were locked into long-term contracts that required little management either from them directly or from their guardians. Perhaps this was the preferable situation, all in all.

One final datum gives me pause, though. On the last day of 1781, Attila and Jacques Sing, a tailor, inked a contract of apprenticeship for young Louis Desrouleaux. The boy was to spend three years as an apprentice tailor working for Sing, at a cost of 1,500 *livres* to the estate.[76] Not only was this a rather high price for an apprenticeship, the median value being 1,166 *livres,* but one questions the necessity for a boy with such resources in land alone to be taught a manual trade. Now, as we have seen, free coloreds from all economic levels, aside from the planter elites, frequently described themselves as practitioners of a trade. This was true even when it is clear that their other economic activities made actually practicing that trade unnecessary. However, one questions the expenditure of the price of a slave on teaching the young man a trade that his wealth made it unlikely, looking from the perspective of 1781, that he would ever need to exercise—unless, in Attila's opinion, that wealth was somehow at risk. Perhaps, given the events of 1791 and the aftermath, young Louis, if he was lucky enough to survive them, found a use for his hard-won and expensive skills. One doubts that even the far-seeing Attila anticipated that development, though.

Malic died relatively young, in 1781, and his property and social position were taken by his determined and energetic wife, Marie Coeflin, now "the widow Malic." She continued to build their fortune and play an important role in Cap free colored society, benefiting from Malic's network of military colleagues. As late as 1786, she rented an apartment to the mother of militiaman Pierre Augustin, managing thereafter to collect her money and resolve a number of ticklish points of law with Augustin without needing to resort to a lawsuit.[77]

The relationships between Prévôt Leprestre and Brigadier la Bastide, between Captain Dupetithouars and Fabien Gentil, between milita officers Olivier, Le-

Moine, and Auba, and between Sergeant Malic and his underlings Zogo and Augustin were all examples of the combined social and financial benefits that military service offered to free coloreds. Holding a commission made one a gentleman even if one's skin was the wrong color. When the governor of the colony invited Vincent Olivier to sit at his table, and Olivier displayed the king's sword, whites were more likely to consider him trustworthy. Even without the commission, simply being the protégé of a white militia officer made the lucky free colored serviceman more trustworthy in the eyes of other whites, made it easier for him to obtain government services for himself and his family, and probably put him in the way of greater income from his military service (as we have seen in the repeated complaints that white officers distributed *maréchaussée* pay and rewards to their favorites). Even having the more humble official role of noncommissioned officer was sufficient to build a network of free colored colleagues that provided a significant advantage in business.

Financial and social advancement, then, went together in this society. Wealth could provide a start toward gentility, and good social connections could help obtain wealth. Free coloreds realized this, and families used the military service of one family member to advance the whole group.

Joseph La Bastide

One family that did this was that of Joseph la Bastide, of Croix des Bouquets and Port-au-Prince, who assisted André Leprestre in getting his inheritance. He was a *brigadier,* or noncommissioned officer, of the *maréchaussée.* His higher rank made him an important local figure. He was the younger of two brothers, and in line with traditional French family strategies, his older brother, Pierre, owned most of the family's assets.

The family's name appears 12 times in the notarial records of Croix des Bouquets, Mirebalais, and Port-au-Prince. Pierre owned at different times three lots in the village of Mirebalais, including one right alongside the municipal sewer that he gave to his former mistress and presumed illegitimate children in 1788.[78] Her predecessor got a better deal in 1782: she received 128 *carreaux* of pastureland and a young female slave off a slave ship.[79] Pierre also owned a quarry and concrete mill in the hills to the north of Croix des Bouquets, more than 150 *carreaux* of low-quality land on the hills overlooking the Plaine de la Cul de Sac north of Port-au-Prince, and various other properties.

The contribution that Joseph made to the la Bastide family was intangible but nonetheless crucial. Perhaps most importantly, he provided a vital conduit to local elites. Sieur Leprestre, *prévôt* of the *maréchaussée* of the region, was an essential contact for any landowner attempting to run cattle and keep slaves in the mountains of the West province. The security situation in this area was very poor in the 1750s and 1760s, at precisely the time that the la Bastide family fortune was being built. Even in the 1780s, after the maroons of the Forêt des Pins had made their peace with the colony and the Spanish had agreed to hinder maroon bands operating out of their territory, planters in the area continued to complain of the depredations of runaway slaves. A landowner attempting to do business in this area would certainly benefit from having a top noncommissioned officer in the rural police in his family and a close patronage relationship to the white police commander. This would be more strikingly true of a landowner without important white kin, like Pierre la Bastide.

Moreover, the family's connection to the white elite through their *maréchaussée* member gave them status in the free colored world. The original white la Bastide was not present during the period the sample covered; it is even unclear if there was an identifiable white progenitor. This would have been a social handicap—in measures of status such as declared ability to sign one's name, what one calls one's house, and so forth, families with identifiable white relatives generally scored higher. However, the la Bastides of Croix des Bouquets scored fairly high on these measures as well. Pierre only began to sign his name during the period under study, signing only one of the 15 acts in which he appeared.[80] Joseph was apparently literate, signing his name to both of the documents in which he was a principal actor. Pierre's son-in-law, Jean Charles Benjamin *dit* Gueyin, could sign to accept a donation from Pierre in the name of his wife, while Pierre's son, Jean Pierre *dit* Bois Clair, did not sign the same act. Gueyin's wife was apparently not called upon to sign and may not have been present for the donation.[81]

Joseph acted as tutor ad hoc and gave away the bride at the wedding of Marie Magdaleine Barbancourt to Pierre Dieudonné Repussard on 7 June 1778. This is significant because the surname that the bride bears is that of a prominent white sugar-planting family that still has an important role today in Haiti's rum production. No members of that family signed the register at the wedding, however. Nevertheless, if the bride could use the surname in her marriage contract, this implies a connection with the family that it did not dispute too emphatically. The presumed father of the groom, who was present at the wedding and gave a substantial present to the couple, was Sieur Joseph Repussard, a reasonably prominent white landowner, if not quite from the rarefied heights of the Barbancourts. Even this early in his career, Joseph was moving in high circles and strengthening his ties with important free colored families.[82]

ENTREPRENEURSHIP

The la Bastide family also serves as an example of the more entrepreneurial attitude free colored military leaders adopted toward their wealth. La Bastide traded freely in land. On several occasions, he developed properties and resold them, sometimes at several times their price. So, for example, in June of 1778, he went into partnership with a white neighbor, Sieur Baillif, to jointly operate two adjacent parcels of land, described as "small," that they owned on the border between Mirebalais and Croix des Bouquets.[83] The land, mostly pasture at the time, was to be developed in indigo cultivation during a 7-year renewable partnership. When la Bastide sold his share of the land in 1784, it was described as an *habitation* in indigo and was worth 2,000 *livres*.[84] Neither act specified the size of the piece of land in question, and the total value of the first partnership agreement included the value of several slaves la Bastide committed to the project, so we cannot know the precise percentage by which the value of the land increased under his stewardship. However, it is clear that he took a piece of pastureland, worth 10 to 20 *livres* a *carreau*, and turned it into an *habitation*, with all that implies socially as well as financially. A "small" piece of land, in Mirebalais context, could not be more than 25 to 30 *carreaux*, so the land was worth, in 1784, in round terms, four to five times its value in 1778.

Planter group members did not experience this sort of growth in their properties. The widow Turgeau and her son, for example, made steady profits on their plantation, but their income did not vary more than 40 percent over the nine years for which we have records.[85] Maximum and minimum incomes during that time were 8,975 *livres* 10 *sols* in 1786 and 5,634 *livres* 12 *sols* 6 *deniers* in 1778. Of course, the Turgeau family did not sell land, as this was something that was considerably less common among the planter group than among the military leaders, so we do not have the market's assessment of the value of their property, but the income figures give us a good picture of a safe investment producing a regular income.

Pierre Zogo

Another military leader who was active in the urban sphere rather than the rural, where the la Bastide wealth was located, was Cap entrepreneur, craftsman, and militia sergeant Pierre Simon Zogo (sometimes Joqui). We have already had cause to notice Zogo for his many manumissions of his slaves. Here again is an example of a military leader who went by an "African" name—in this case, a fairly common one that was given to freed slaves and that Zogo, unusually, hung onto throughout his career. His act of manumission was not in the sample, but from this datum it seems that it took place no earlier than 1773, when free coloreds were forbidden to take the names of whites by government edict and were required to use a surname "drawn from the African idiom." [86] Acts of manumission consistently made ritual obeisance to this regulation by attaching an African-sounding name to the newly freed slave. Most freedmen dropped the "African" name in favor of that of a French relative or at the very least of a French-sounding handle. By sticking to *Zogo* throughout his life, Pierre Simon underlined his lack of white connections.

As was common with militia noncommissioned officers who identified themselves as such in the notarial record, Zogo had little business or personal contact with whites. His name appeared 26 times in the notarial archives; in only 10 of those instances was a white a principal actor (38.6 percent, as opposed to 49.9 percent for the population as a whole). The only hint of a relationship more profound than that of buyer and seller was the two acts in which Sieur Pierre Risteau freed Zogo's godson, Ulisse, and picked up the cost of the liberty tax. [87] Godparenthood was a very important relationship, especially to these men without influential kin of their own. Risteau, by freeing Zogo's godson, must have verged on some sort of a quasi-kin relationship to Zogo, but the relationship seemingly went no further.

Zogo was not a member of the economic elite of the colony. He made no acts evaluated at over 10,000 *livres*. His most valuable act was the sale of a boat on Christmas Eve, 1781, for 7,920 *livres*, and the mean value of the 26 acts in which he appears is 2,629 *livres*. [88] His economic role was as a skilled worker, a boatman, who became an entrepreneur and small-scale merchant. He owned several small sailing vessels which plied routes from Cap Français to nearby towns such as l'Embarquadaire de Limonade and Fort Dauphin. The largest of these boats that was mentioned in the notarial archives was about 30 feet long and was described in the act as a *chaloupe*, or dinghy. Apparently, Zogo transported cargo and people for a fee, rented his boats to clients by the voyage, and carried cargo on his own account. Boat rental from Fort Dauphin to Cap in 1782 cost 150 *livres* a trip for a 14-ton schooner evaluated at around 7,000 *livres* total value—more or less similar to Zogo's largest boat. [89] There is no direct evidence on freight or passenger rates, but they can be estimated: A 30-foot sailboat in Haitian waters today might carry 50 people or 10 tons of cargo. Those passengers traveling from Fort Dauphin to Cap in 1782 would have to pay about 30 *sols* plus the operator's profit margin; a ton of cargo would start at about 7 *livres* 10 *sols*.

The intra-island shipping business, although small-scale, was nonetheless crucial to the economy. Especially given the difficulties of overland transport and the bulky nature of a lot of the produce, the ability to move cargoes to and from plantations by sea was essential. This business seems to have been quite profitable. Cap *négociant* and future rebel Vincent Ogé was heavily involved in short-haul shipping as well as the trans-Atlantic trade. At one point, he formed a partnership with a white merchant and a white captain to operate a schooner evaluated at 10,000 *livres;* later he appeared in the notarial archives issuing a notarized order to the captain of another short-haul sailboat to bring a cargo from Cayes to Cap Français for transshipment to France instead of carrying it directly to North America. Perhaps the vessel was not as "short-haul" as he had thought, or perhaps he was covering himself against accusations of violating the *exclusif* mercantilist trade regulations.[90] By its very nature, seagoing cargo hauling was a risky business, as a result both of the natural perils of the sea and the manmade danger of the British Navy in wartime. It was, therefore, the perfect field for entrepreneurship: high risk, high gain, requiring technical skill but limited initial investment, and providing an essential service to the core industry of the plantation economy. Zogo's role in this trade was riskier than Ogé's, because he had more of his eggs in one basket, whereas Ogé, a wealthier man, was better diversified.

So Zogo, like many of his militia noncommissioned officer colleagues, was an entrepreneur. Few were willing to sit on peasant holdings, no matter how comfortable. Although many had nominal trades such as carpenter or mason, few seemed willing to work for hire any more than they had to, preferring the status of independent businessman. The nature of the job of military noncommissioned officer almost required a take-charge attitude that would not be comfortable in a humdrum, workaday world. It also suits our vision of these men as rising from slavery more or less as a result of their own initiative that they would be willing to take risks for further economic success once free and self-supporting.

CONCLUSION

In conclusion, then, free colored military leaders were a distinct group within free colored society. This group was significantly wealthier than the mass of free coloreds. Some members of this group approached the planter group in wealth, although, in the aggregate, they fell below them in raw financial terms. Many families who were members of this group had had significant wealth for some decades, in some cases as long as the established families of the planter group, though, like their rivals, the military leadership group was recruiting new members throughout the period under study.

The military leadership group was not, however, a transitional middle class whose members would eventually achieve planter group status with enough financial or social success or passage of enough time. Instead, they pursued different strategies and rose along a different path than their neighbors. They were markedly more aggressive in their entrepreneurship than the planter group, seeking financial gain at the expense of the aristocratic values that were the goals of the planter group. Their social success was not the result of acquisition of and protection of landed estates and manipulation of traditional markers of status such as prestige possessions, literacy, or surnames. Instead, the central component in their social success was the network of patronage relationships that they built up among themselves, with their white officers and, especially, with lower-class free coloreds. These relationships were established through both participation in family acts of unrelated persons, creating pseudo-kin relations between the parties to smooth the way for future business dealings, and through actual business transactions. Military leaders were much more likely to do business with people in their "circle," so defined, and also granted and received financial concessions from the members of these networks. Their patronage of lower-class people of color even extended to slaves, as they were the most active manumittors of any group in the colony. This fact is especially striking given their relatively small slaveholdings when compared to to those of free coloreds or white planters.

The distinctiveness of the military leaders gave them a special place in society. They were in a much better position, given their relationship with the lower classes, to lead the society through the trauma of the Revolution.

CHAPTER TWELVE

Conclusion

This author, like many other newly minted Ph.D.s in history, has spent some time teaching part-time in a community college. On the first day of class, I always mention my research, as a way of showing students that we all write research papers—just before I assign them theirs. Questions about my research often include the unspoken question—sometimes it is a spoken one, depending on the tact of the questioner—of why someone would spend five years studying this group of people.

It is a question that any reader should have the right to ask any author, and one that might be especially pointed in this case. Free people of color in Saint Domingue were not very numerous, and they suffered from enormous social and legal handicaps in this society. Granted, they owned land and slaves, something not permitted them in some other plantation colonies. Research for this book has demonstrated that free coloreds owned as much as a third of all slaves. It has been known for some time that they owned significant chunks of the backcountry land that was most useful for growing coffee, as well as a few sugar plantations. Still, white planters owned more of both capital goods. The largest plantations were almost all in the hands of white sugar barons. Whites filled all the niches in free society, from planter plutocrat to starving beggar. Does looking at the free coloreds advance our understanding of the society if they produced only a small minority of its goods?

In addition, it has been argued that free coloreds were little different from their white neighbors, except for the smaller size of their land- and slaveholdings. They clearly aspired to be like whites, and some were so much like whites that they "passed" into whiteness, as many a legal case attests. A Marxist analysis of the free colored planter, at least, would say that his class interests were the same as those of his white neighbor, and any difference in attitude based on race was a false consciousness.

Still, when the crunch of the Revolution came, many free coloreds saw their interests as distinct from those of the white plantocracy, although not necessarily identical with the slave *lumpenproletariat*. They formed a separate political force in the events of 1790–1804, allying with French revolutionaries, royalists, British invaders, or slave rebels as they saw their interests advanced. Even before the Revolution, free colored planters, represented by Julien Raimond, tried to assert their own distinctiveness from the African-descended masses and their right to be treated the same as white planters. After the Revolution, in the first half of the nineteenth century, they tried to continue as a rural landholding elite. The social history of that period is marked by a collision between their interests and those of the newly enfranchised blacks, who, like new freedmen elsewhere in the Caribbean, overwhelmingly wanted to become small farmers rather than landless agricultural laborers. Frustrated as planters, many of the old free colored families migrated to the port towns and became a commercial elite, wielding state power for the interests of their class just as would any bourgeois ruling class. As a self-aware class with an important role to play in future events, they deserve our study.

Moreover, former free coloreds did not form a unitary group in any of these transformations. Scholars of the period have generally ignored the existence of several different groups within the blanket designation "free people of color." During the Revolution, while Rigaud and his forces represented the interests of former free colored planters, another former free colored, Toussaint Louverture, led the other great revolutionary faction, the slave rebels. Toussaint's army contained many prewar freedmen. Before the Revolution, Toussaint and his peers formed a group whose attitudes and values were sharply different from those of Raimond and his folk. The two groups practiced some mutual segregation and were mutually hostile to some extent, although it is easy to exaggerate this tendency. After the Revolution, groups of similar characteristics continued to play out similar roles on the Haitian scene, with generally darker-skinned military leaders competing with, or cooperating with under the *politique de doublure*, the former free colored plantocracy. As the forerunners of a significant divide in Haitian society in the national period, these groups also deserve our attention.

Finally, the role of free people of color in a slave society, like that of a catalyst in a chemical reaction, may be disproportionate to their numbers and their economic role. Like any "intermediate class," free coloreds served as a handy auxiliary for the ruling class, doing jobs that were too dirty for them but too threatening or demanding too much initiative to be entrusted to slaves. The military role of the free coloreds of Saint Domingue is a prime example of this role, while the mixed-race children and African-Dominguan mistresses of the white plantocracy might serve as plantation managers. Perhaps even more important, though, the mere existence of the free coloreds was an important escape valve for pressure on the system by slaves. Slaves could look at the free coloreds and hope that they, too, might some-day achieve that status if they worked hard and conformed to what the society expected of them. This would not be a realistic hope for the majority of slaves, doomed to a short and unpleasant life in the fields. However, for the aristocracy of slavery, the technical experts, domestic servants, and leadership types, hope for manumission was realistic. It was these slaves whose cooperation was necessary for a slave uprising to succeed. In addition, these slaves were the most expensive and difficult to obtain on the plantations. The easier manumission seemed to be to obtain and the better the conditions for the free colored group, the happier these key individuals would be with the system. As a "leaven" for the slave society, then, the free people of color deserve our study in order to better understand that society on its own terms.

This book has been written for the purpose of studying the slave society of Saint Domingue. From the perspective of the twenty-first century, we look at Saint Domingue as the ancestor of Haiti and look for the roots of Haiti's society in Saint Domingue's. This is not an inappropriate task for a historian, but this work prefers to look at Saint Domingue on its own merits, without considering what happened later. Saint Domingue was the most prosperous of the Caribbean slave societies in the 1780s. It was responsible for French sugar displacing English in the continental trade in the mid-eighteenth century. It experienced the coffee revolution earlier than most of the Caribbean and had one of the most productive coffee industries in the region after 1750. It was the destination of the majority of slaves carried by the French and an important market for English slave traders, as witness the success of Zabeau Bellanton. The slave trade aside, Saint Domingue was a very important trading partner for France and, as such, was responsible for the growth of the French bourgeoisie, to play such an important role in the history of the next hundred years. The colony was the first among the Greater Antilles to experience the sweeping effects of the transition to full-scale plantation agriculture, blazing a course for Jamaica and Cuba to follow. It had an enormous effect on the economic and social history of its neighbor, Spanish Santo Domingo, as indeed it continues to do to this day. It also affected the development of French Louisiana, along with the other small French plantation colonies in the Caribbean. Finally, as a market for goods from North America, it was an important engine in the development of the commerce of New England and of the commercial pressure for autonomy in that region.

The free coloreds were important players out of proportion to their numbers in a colony that was important out of proportion to its size during this period. Thus, a study of them is relevant to an understanding of the history of the Atlantic world in the late eighteenth century.

This study of the free coloreds of Saint Domingue shows that there were important differences within the racial caste. Free colored society in colonial Saint Domingue produced two groups of high-status individuals, the planter elite and the military leadership group. These groups were similar in that they were both wealthier and at a higher social level than the mass of free coloreds. The planter elite was the wealthiest group, but the military leaders also outstripped their humbler fellow free coloreds in the financial realm. The military leadership added to their considerable wealth significant social advantages accruing to them from their official positions and from the fictive kin networks that they built up among lower-class coloreds.

These groups differed in many ways. The book has looked at two principal areas of difference between the two. The first is the degree of entrepreneurship in their attitude toward capital goods, that is, to what extent were they were willing to use land and slaves for purely financial advancement and to what extent did they seek to maximize non-economic values. The planter elite's quest for status as landholders and slave owners often tempered their entrepreneurship. They looked on themselves, seemingly, and acted almost as an indigenous class of landed aristocrats. For them, the fact of being a landowner and an *habitant* was as important or more important than the revenue available from agricultural entrepreneurship. They demonstrated this *mentalité* through a marked tendency to engage in financial strategies that stressed conservation of capital over maximization of revenue. They kept both land and slaves off the market longer than white owners or military leadership group owners, and they sold smaller units of both categories of capital goods when they did sell. They were generally unwilling to risk capital to obtain credit to finance business expansion. Free coloreds as a whole were risk-averse. Failure for them carried a higher social price than it did for whites, who always had the option of returning home to France. White planters routinely borrowed upwards of 60 percent of the cost of agricultural capital, whereas for free coloreds as a whole the figure was closer to 20 percent. The free colored planter elite carried the general conservatism of free coloreds to great extremes, rarely leveraging any significant portion of major purchases. Free coloreds of the military leadership group were often in business in urban areas, and these businesses give evidence of their more aggressively entrepreneurial attitude toward capital. Some free colored military leadership group *commerçants* who appear in chapters 5, 6, and 7, like Zabeau Bellanton and Jacques Coidavy, were as aggressive, both as speculative traders and as consumers of credit, as any land-hungry young white immigrant.

The relative youth of the free colored population of the cities gives rise to an alternate explanation for this difference in aggressiveness between the two groups. Young people went to the cities to seek their fortunes and used aggressive tactics in their search. Once having achieved respectable wealth, they were expected to retire to the countryside and seek respectability by adhering to the traditional values and practices of the planter elite, progressively joining this class. This turns out not to be the case, though, as seen in chapter 11. Members of the military leadership group who scored financial gains in urban business did reinvest in the countryside and attempt to become *habitants*. They also often sought other, non-economic markers of high status such as impressive possessions, legitimate marriage, and even "whitening" strategies in rare cases. However, the examples of Brigadier Joseph la Bastide in the West province and Capitaine Vincent Olivier in the North show us that the attitudes of these successful military leadership group members toward capital did not markedly change. Even second-generation members of military leadership group families, like the children and grandchildren of Capitaine Vincent, did not transform into planter group members in their attitudes.

On the other hand, *parvenu* members of the planter elite, like the *menagères* and their children, did not seemingly pass through much of an aggressively entrepreneurial stage before adopting the conservative strategies of their group. Even the counterexample of Julie Dahey's abortive pottery shop is the exception that proves the rule. She failed rather quickly at an entrepreneurial business. She was partner with a white in this business. He provided the "sweat equity"—already a conservative element. Following that, she invested the rest of her funds in conservative, agricultural enterprises that would have left her a major sugar planter had the Revolution not intervened. The other matriarchs of illegitimate mixed-race families whom the reader has met, like Nanette Pincemaille or the widow Turgeau, for example, were careful to stick to the agricultural enterprises that were more conventional for their group.

Another major area of difference between these two groups, and perhaps the key distinguishing factor between them, was their connections to the rest of society. The planter elite was principally connected to wealthy white society. In many cases, they had family members who were influential whites. Even in those cases where the white progenitor of a planter elite family was so distant in time that few close relatives were around, as in the case of the Laportes of Limonade, these families still invited unrelated white neighbors to participate in notarial acts dealing with the most intimate family issues. Moreover, they were overwhelmingly likely to do business with whites or members of their own group. The Laportes, for example, transacted 50 percent of their sales and rental contracts exclusively with free coloreds of their own group. An additional 42 percent of these acts included white partners.

Only 8 percent of their business transactions were with free coloreds not of their group. Thus, they had relatively few dealings with other free coloreds, either the military class or the masses. With the exception of a few anomalous individuals, the planter elite almost never shared family acts with free coloreds not of their social group. Not for these people, except for Jean-Baptiste Chavanne, Michel-François Pincemaille, and a few other less notable exceptions, was the military leaders' practice of acting as godfather or marriage witness for unrelated free coloreds of lower social standing.

They also had seemingly cold relations with their slaves. They freed fewer slaves than either the military leadership group or whites. They clearly owned fewer slaves in total than the whites. An estimated 30 percent of the slave population of the island was in the hands of free coloreds by 1786. Of those, more than half must have been in the hands of the planter elite, given their greater total slaveholdings and greater overall wealth as compared with both the military leadership and the mass of free coloreds. Thus, the bulk of slaves remained in the hands of whites, and so the lower raw number of manumissions by free coloreds of the planter elite group does not suggest that they were less likely than whites, in proportion, to free their slaves. The greater stability of free colored families, especially true among the planter elite, would make it less likely that planter elite members would be freeing their illegitimate children and their slave mistresses, an important motive for manumissions by whites. However, it would be reasonable to suspect that at least a few of these individuals, especially among the new recruits to the group, might have had family members still in servitude. Thus, it seems, in the absence of solid evidence, that the free colored planter elite freed their slaves at more or less the same rate, proportionally to their smaller overall slaveholdings, as did whites.

In contrast, warm relations with the rest of colored society distinguished the military leadership group. In place of the kinship networks, both within the group and with whites, upon which the planter elite relied, the military leadership group built networks of fictive kin through godfathering of unrelated children, serving as witnesses at marriages, and other family acts. Although many of the participants in these networks were also members of the military leadership group, a significant number of those receiving patronage from military leaders were lower-class free coloreds.

The free colored military leadership group had contacts with whites, although those contacts were of considerably lesser importance to them both socially and economically than were such contacts to the planter group. These relations were also more businesslike and at arm's length than the warm personal contacts between the planters and their white relatives. Even when members of the military leadership group had a white relative, and it was not uncommon to find persons of mixed race in this group, that family member would not be such an important part of their lives as would be the case for the planter group.

Moreover, the military leadership group enlarged their circle of clients, and the population of free coloreds as a whole, by freeing slaves at a rate unsurpassed by any other group. In addition, as discussed in chapter 5, their behavior toward their slaves may betray a persistence of African cultural values. The military leadership owned more African-born slaves, valued them more highly, and bought and sold them more freely. In contrast, they were more likely to free their creole slaves, generally the children of their African-born slaves, than was the free colored population as a whole. This may betray the persistence of the African tradition of treating slaves purchased (or captured in war) as "trade" slaves subject to sale or direct employment. Meanwhile, slaves born to the master's household were often accorded certain rights, such as to work the land or enjoy possessions, and were not subject to sale except in dire circumstances. The whole issue of the relationship between slaves and free coloreds is one that calls for further research. This work attempts to place some preliminary road signs for future investigation with the comparison of white and free colored slave populations in chapter 5.

Another issue that this book raises and that will require further study is the relationship between the different groups of the military. The differences between the groups are noted, but this analysis has treated all their leaders as one undivided group. They all demonstrated the characteristics described here, but the differing conditions of their service would reward further analysis.

The Chasseurs-Volontaires, as an ad hoc organization raised in a climate of patriotic fervor, attracted a wide variety of men to its ranks. Its junior leaders were serving militia noncommissioned officers for the most part, but what led one militia sergeant, like Pierre Augustin, to sign up, while a colleague, like Jean-Baptiste Malic, stayed home?

The *maréchaussée* was another very different organization. Its supposed lowest rank, the *archer*, was almost a noncommissioned officer in his own right, as he oversaw the activities of a number of supernumeraries. The analysis presented here does not include the *archers* in the ranks of the military leaders, although some were quite prominent men in their communities, because officially they were designated as private soldiers. However, the *maréchaussée* was strikingly different from the other organizations in that it was never "at peace." *Maréchaussée* supernumeraries received tax-free manumission at all times, peace or war. The *maréchaussée* was always active and regularly confronting the important enemy, from the point of view of the white plantocracy, anyway. This made *maréchaussée* men more likely to receive patronage from whites. In fact, 51 percent of all notarial acts executed by *maréchaussée* men and their families included a white participant, while for militiamen, the figure is 33 percent.

The final avenue for further study, and perhaps the most fruitful, is the connection between the military of the colony, the revolutionary military, and the Haitian armed forces of the independence period. It seems reasonable to assume that the soldiers, and especially the leaders, of the free colored armed forces in the colonial period would have been an important asset to any leader trying to form an army during the Revolution. Generals are notoriously willing to use trained men regardless of ideological differences. If Cromwell could form his New Model Army out of Royalist prisoners, and Trotsky his Red Army out of Czarist officers, it seems reasonable to assume that slave rebels in Haiti could find a place in their army for trained free colored leaders. In fact, they did just this as early as 1791, when Toussaint Louverture was employed as secretary to the slave leaders of the insurrection. How important was their contribution? To what extent did they retain control of the army as an institution in the early national period? Aix-en-Provence does not contain the materials necessary to answer this question. It is to be hoped that Haitian archives will provide the answers that will shape the successor to this work.

Finally, in a few places the book attempts to make comparisons between the situation described in Saint Domingue and that in other plantation colonies. This work does not pretend to be a comparative study, but the broad mechanism of group formation outlined here might be considered in the context of other slave societies. Saint Domingue has a reputation for uniqueness because of its great slave rebellion, the only wholly successful one in the plantation colonies of the Americas. However, many of the conditions found in the pre-revolutionary society of Saint Domingue resemble those in other colonies. Free coloreds in Puerto Rico owned an enormous percentage of the agricultural land, much more than in Saint Domingue, perhaps even more than in the coffee highland areas like Limonade. While Puerto Rico was far from the core of the plantation complex, it still produced export crops during this period, and free colored farmers there had some connection with the market. Was there a "planter elite" in Puerto Rico? Might their presence explain attitudes and behaviors of free coloreds in that colony? Free coloreds in Cuba, Jamaica, and elsewhere made important contributions to the defense of their colonies. In many cases, society rewarded these contributions with military rank and responsibility, even while racist discrimination against free coloreds was growing worse. Did these military leaders form a distinct "military leadership group" in their colonies?

In sum, then, this book demonstrates that slave societies were not as simple as they might seem on the surface. History is complex and is carried out by individuals. Saint Domingue's free coloreds were individuals. They had distinct interests, or perceived interests, or prejudices, that led them into courses of action that make a hash of racially based or class-based analysis. This work looks at them in the aggregate and tentatively discerns some commonalties. Until we have a science of human behavior that works as rigorously as the physical sciences, this is the best that can be done.

Appendix One

FAMILY TREE OF THE LAPORTES OF LIMONADE

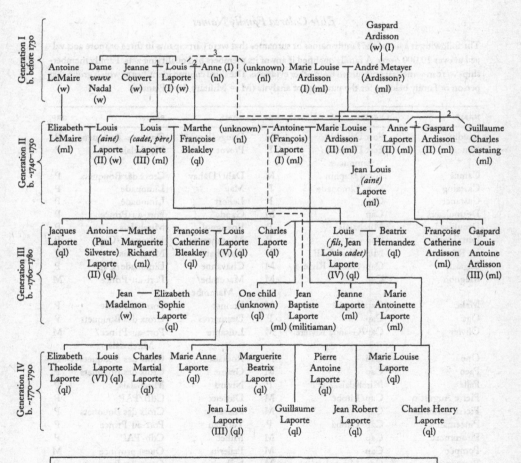

Legend: ml = free mulatto   nl = free black   ql = free quarteron   w = white   – – – = illegitimate
Note: women are generally identified by their maiden names, as was normal practice in notarial acts.

Appendix Two

Elite Colored Family Names

The following is a list of the family names or surnames that were participants in three or more acts valued at over 10,000 *livres*. A family qualified if any of its members had qualifying acts. Family memberships were in some cases presumed from other evidence. The third column identifies to which group that person or family belongs for the purposes of analysis (M = Military, P = Planter).

NAME	PARISH	GRP.	NAME	PARISH	GRP.
Baudin	Fort Dauphin	M	Daugé/Baugé	Croix des Bouquets	P
Blot	Fort Dauphin/ Limonade	P	Prevot	Mirebalais	P
Camus	Fort Dauphin	M	Dahi/Dahay	Croix des Bouquets	P
Castaing	Cap/Limonade	P	May	Limonade	P
Castanet	Cap	P	LeFort	Limonade	P
Desrouleaux	Cap	M	Gaudé	Port-au-Prince	P
Droulliard	Mirebalais	P	Rossignol	Mirebalais	P
Juin/Houin	Cap	P	Mommereau	Limonade/Cap	P
La Racointe	Mirebalais/CdB	P	Blanchard	Mirebalais	P
Lagarde	Cap/Grande Riviere	M	Chavanne	Limonade/Cap	P
Magnon	Cap	M	Macombe/ Marombe	Port-au-Prince	M
Malic	Cap/Limbé	M	Bonnet	Port-au-Prince	P
Ogé	Cap	P	Desmarres	Croix des Bouquets	P
Olivier	Cap/Grande Riviere	M	Luisante	Port-au-Prince/ Mirebalais	M
Oné	Cap	M	Rousseau	Croix des Bouquets	P
Paco	Cap	M	Graine	Croix des Bouquets	P
Pellé	Mirebalais/PaP	P	Nivard	Mirebalais	P
Pierre Augustin	Cap/Limbé	M	Durieux	CdB/PAP	P
Pierre Antoine	Cap	M	Plaisance	Croix des Bouquets	P
Pincemaille	Cap/Limbé	P	Turgeau	Port-au-Prince	P
Pirommeau	Cap	M	Millet	Cdb/PAP	P
Pompée	Cap	M	Pellerin	Ouest province	M
Provoyeur	Cap/Mirebalais	M	la Buxiere	Croix des Bouquets	P
Riché/L'Eveille	Cap	M	Bleakley	Limonade	P
Viau	Cap	P	Laporte	Limonade	P
Zabeau Bellanton	Cap	M	Ardisson	Limonade	P

Military Leaders' Names

The following persons identified themselves in notarial acts as leaders in the free colored units of the colonial armed forces. All these persons have been treated in the text as members of the military leadership group, even though some did not have the wealth necessary to define them as economic elites. In the column for branch of service, C-V = Chasseurs Volontaires de Saint Domingue (1779–81) and C-R = Chasseurs-Royaux de l'Amérique (Seven Years' War).

NAME	PARISH	BRANCH	RANK
Alloun	Cap Français	Militia and C-V	*Caporal*
Augustin, Pierre	Cap Français	C-V and Militia	unknown NCO
Baudin, Jean-Baptiste	Fort Dauphin	Militia	*Maréchal de Logis*
Bellony (*dit*), Etienne Auba	Limonade	Militia	*Capitaine*
Belly, Jean-Baptiste	Cap Français	Milita	unknown NCO
Bertole (*dit*), Barthelemy Ibar	Petite Rivière de l'Artibonite	Militia	*Capitaine*
Blaise, Mathieu	Cap Français	Militia and C-V	*Sergent*
Blanchet, Bruno	Fort Dauphin	Militia	*Caporal*
Camus, François	Fort Dauphin	Militia	*Sergent*
Cassagne, Jean-Louis	Cap Français	Militia and C-V	*Caporal*
Cezar, Joseph	Cap Français	Militia	*Maitre de Musique*
Coidavid (Coidavy), Jacques	Port-au-Prince	Militia	*Tambour-major*
Doué, Paul	North Prov.	C-V (militia?)	*Sergent*
Dubreuil, (fnu)	Cap Français	*Maréchaussée*	*Brigadier*
Eustache, Jean Marie	Limbé	Militia	*Caporal*
Favrel, Pierre	Mirebalais	*Maréchaussée*	*Brigadier*
Felix, François	North Prov.	C-V (militia?)	*Caporal*
Foutand, Pierre	Cap Français	Militia	*Caporal*
Gautier, Jacques Le Roy	North Prov.	C-V (militia?)	*Sergent*
Gentil, Fabien	Limbé and Limonade	C-V and probably militia	*Caporal*
Gestier (Gestieu), Antoine	Port-au-Prince	Militia	*Tambour-major*
Guyot, François Charles	Croix des Bouquets	*Maréchaussée*	*Brigadier*
Hulla, Jean	Cap Français	Militia	*Tambour-major*
Jupiter, François	Cap Français	Militia	*Capitaine*
L'Eveille (*dit*), Jean-François Edouard	Cap Français	Militia and C-V	*Sergent*
La Bastide (Bastille), Joseph	Croix des Bouquets	*Maréchaussée*	*Brigadier*
Lagarde, Jean-Baptiste	Cap Français	Militia and C-V	*Sergent Fourrier*
LaRiviere, Etienne	Cap Français	C-V (militia?)	*Sergent*
LaRondière, Louis	Fort Dauphin	C-R (1760s)	*Sergent*
LeMoine, Augustin	Fort Dauphin	Militia	*Ensigne*
Lepine, Louis (aka Marc Laviolette)	Fort Dauphin	Militia	unknown NCO
Malic (*dit*), Jean-Baptiste Magny	Cap Français	Militia	*Sergent*
Manigat, Guillaume	Fort Dauphin	Militia	*Lieutenant*
Milloy, Laurent	Cap Français	Militia	*Capitaine*
Monteil, Nicolas	Cap Français	Militia	*Sergent*
Olivier, Vincent	Cap Français	Militia	*Capitaine*
Oné, Jean	l'Acul du Nord	C-V (militia?)	*Sergent*
Pellerin, Joseph	North Prov.	C-V (militia?)	*Caporal*

Military Leaders' Names (continued)

NAME	PARISH	BRANCH	RANK
Pyracmour, Joseph	Cap Français	C-V	*Caporal*
Riché (*dit*), Jean-Baptiste L'Eveille	Cap Français	Militia and C-V	*Sergent*
Roussame, Manuel Louis	Cap Français	Militia	unknown NCO
Titus (*dit*) Jacques Brisetous	Mirebalais	Militia	*Caporal*
Yari (*dit*), Pierre L'Eveille Marion	Cap Français	Militia	unknown NCO
Zogo, Pierre Simon	Cap Français	Militia	unknown NCO

Notarial Acts Reporting Militia Membership by Parish

It is very important to note a striking regional difference in self-identification of militia rank in the notarial archives. Free colored militia noncommissioned officers in the West province were much less likely to identify themselves by their rank in notarials than their colleagues in the North. The following table suggests the scale of this difference:

PROVINCE	PARISH	NUMBER OF ACTS BY MILITIAMEN	TOTAL ACTS BY FREE COLOREDS	MILITIA ACTS AS % OF TOTAL
Total		437	4252	10.3
North	Cap	229	1635	14.0
	Limonade	103	761	13.5
	Fort Dauphin	66	373	17.7
West	Port au Prince	6	543	1.1
	Croix des Bouquets	10	310	3.2
	Mirebalais	13	536	2.4

The column for number of acts by militiamen includes all acts by militiamen, whether identified as leaders or not. It is difficult to account for this difference by reference to standards of free colored society. Almost no free colored identified himself as a militiaman in the West province, although there is plenty of evidence that colored militia companies existed there and that free coloreds held noncommissioned rank in them. This difference can only be explained in terms of data collection. Each notary, and each provincial *Conseil Supérieur,* which oversaw the notaries, had its own standards of correct usage. All notarial acts had to be approved by the *Conseil Supérieur* and registered at the *Greffe,* or secretariat, of the local court. Notaries in the West province were much more punctilious than their northern colleagues, for example, about including the proof of free status of people of color who performed notarial acts. Northerners were more likely to refer to free coloreds as *Sieur* or *Demoiselle* if their social status allowed it. Westerners were generally more likely to include the ownership history of a piece of land (the most striking example being Michel of Port-au-

Prince). All these bespeak a greater formalism on the part of the Port-au-Prince authorities that perhaps also led them to be unwilling to permit persons to identify themselves through reference to militia noncommissioned rank. There do not seem to be any examples in the West of a white militia noncommissioned officer identified by his title either. There were, on the other hand, plenty of western militia officers, including some free coloreds, who identified themselves as such in the notarial archives, commissioned rank in the militia being a very important social cachet. Most of the few examples of colored militiamen from the West province are people who gained their liberties as a result of militia service. Thus, their militia status was germane to the particular act. These cases were a small minority in the North.

It remains an open question whether those in the free colored group who identified themselves as military noncommissioned officers were truly representative of the group as a whole. Perhaps those colored military leaders who had more extensive contacts with whites chose other ways to give themselves social status through self-identification of their "condition." Perhaps only those leaders who were "self-made" men would lay explicit claim to their military rank. Perhaps they were stressing their connections with the white militia officers precisely because they had no other whites with whom to identify.

In the case of the militia, however, those noncommissioned officers who identified themselves by their military rank were laying claim to that rank for social advantage, vis-à-vis other free coloreds for the most part but also toward whites, in a way very much similar to the white militia officers who did the same thing. These were men who formed, with their families, a separate elite, distinct both from white society and from the mulatto plantocracy. Their militia status served to validate their membership in that elite.

Marchande Names

The following is a list of names of women identified as *marchandes,* or shopkeepers, in at least one notarial act.

NAME	PARISH	NAME	PARISH
Bonne Femme *veuve* Jolicoeur	Cap	Marie Jeanne	Cap
Bréthoux	Port-au-Prince	Marie Jacques	Fort Dauphin
Cadiagnon/Kadijatou	Cap	Victoire Fontaine	Port-au-Prince
Dupré	Port-au-Prince	Concongnan	Fort Dauphin
Elisabeth	Cap	Sarazin	Cap
Marie Barra	Port-au-Prince	Rozette	Cap
Zanguoe/Zanquoe	Cap	Bellanton	Cap
Zulica	North Province	Dougé/Daugin	Port-au-Prince

Menagère Names

The following women were identified in notarial acts as being employed as *menagères*, or housekeepers. Names identified with an asterisk (*) were employed by free coloreds.

NAME	PARISH	NAME	PARISH
Catin Romeus	Cap	Marie Louise à Traitte*	Borgne
Grasse *dite* Balanquin	Limonade		
Hélène*	Cap	Jeannette Canibon	Cap
Laurence	Mirebalais	Marie Marguerite Zubin	Mirebalais
Louise	Croix des Bouquets	Julie Dahey	Croix des Bouquets
Marie Anne Lefèvre	Mirebalais	Marie Geneviève	Mirebalais
Marie Richard	Mirebalais	Marguerite l'Hermite	Mirebalais
Marie Zabeth	Port-au-Prince	Sanitte l'Islet	Mirebalais
Nannette à Savie	Cap	Rose Merza	Cap
Nicolle Collette	Fort Dauphin	Marie Jeanne	Port-au-Prince
Rose	Croix des Bouquets	Marie Magdeleine Garrette*	Cap
Zabelle Bayeux	Cap	Manon Quila	Port-au-Prince

INCORPORATION PAPERS OF THE *GRASSERIE* MARIE JOSEPHE

This account of the starting stock of the store owned by Marie Josephe and Sieur Guillemet is drawn from the Archives Nationales Françaises, Section Outremer, Notariat de Saint Domingue 1298n, 12/7/85. The symbols for *livres, sols,* and *deniers* are, respectively, #, s, and d.

Contribution of Marie Josephe: a barrel of wine containing 10½ demi-johns, 66#; 3 full demi-johns, 24# 15s; 25 pounds of *morne* @ 61# 17s 6d the quintal, 15# 8s 3d; 25 pounds of cheese @ 20s/pound, 25#; a pound of pepper, 3#; 12 large plates @ 25s, 15#; 4 large oval plates @ 25s, 5#; 2 goblets, 15#; 1 *entomier*, 4# 2s 6d; 12 pots of cooking oil @ 20s, 12#; 5 pounds of candle wax @ 25s, 7# 10s; one *duedane* of grease, 3#; 50 empty bottles @ 7s 6d, 18# 15s; 17 empty demi-johns @ 12#, 204#; 7 *echelles* (shelf units?) @ 6# 5s, 57# 15s; 4 boards 9 feet long @ 15s the French foot, 25# 15s; 52 feet of planks @ 7s 6d, 19# 10s; 10 others of *halle* for *garniture,* @ 1# 10s, 15#; two tables, one missing its legs, with two empty barrels, 18#; a pint measure, 1# 10s; 3 pots of olive oil, 4# 10s; pair of scales in iron, 8# 5s; 11 pounds of weights, 8# 5s; 1 cabbage (pound? barrel of sauerkraut? or is it chalk?), 3#; 1 large jar, 49# 10s; 1 *terrine de France,* 4# 2s; 2 chairs, 8# 5s; 1 wicker cover for jar, 1# 10s; 1 large scale in wood with two platforms, 6#; 2 demi-johns of vinegar, 30#; total contribution of Marie Josephe: 838#.

Contribution of Sieur Guillemet: 84 feet of wood at 7s 6d, 41#; 1 table and two barrels, 8#; 1 pair of scales and 14 pounds of weights, 44# 15s; 4 chairs @ 4# 2s 6d, 16# 10s; 50 empty bottles @ 7s 6d, 18# 15s; 11 demi-johns, some empty, some full, 15#, 165#; 1 small *entommier,* 1 *gaudet,* 1 *pinte,* 6#; 1 jar , 27#; 1 small *jarre de Provence,* for butter, 12#; 1 coffee mill, 16#; 1 block of sugar, 42 pounds @ 20s, 42#; 7 (illeg.) @ 3#, 21#; 9 oval plates @ 25s, 10#; 3 small plates @ 20s, 3#; 8 plates @ 10s, 4#; 55 pots of grease @ 25s, 67# 10s; 7 pots of fine oil @ 1# 10s, 10# 10s; 18 pots of (illeg.), 9#; 17 bottles of fine oil @ 33# the doz., 45#; 4 *sirzaim de Casthe* @ 3# 10s, 14#; ½ a ream of paper, 6#; 1 (illeg.) 85#; 4½ bts. of thread @ 16# 1s, 74# 5s; 8 demi-johns of Taffia, 66#; 1 barrel of Taffia, 92#; 1 small table, 12#; 4 shelves @ 8# 5s, 33#; 2 pieces of *macoute* @ 5# 5s, 10# 10s; 1 sack of lentils, 8# 5s; 3 panniers of *pomponilles* 4# 10s; some rice, 12#; total contribution of Sieur Guillemet: 1062# 10s.

Marie Josephe also put in 232# in cash to make immediate purchases and loaned the society, or partnership, 230# more in cash, to be returned to her at the first accounting.

Conditions of society: Sieur Guillemet will manage. To do business in the *magasin* rented by Marie Josephe, rent 5 *gourdes* (= 100#) per month. There is a kitchen, small room, and street-front gallery that the two associates will share. Starting now, the society will pay the rent. Merchandise will be bought in Cap, and bill must be signed by both associates before it can be paid. Sieur Guillemet is forbidden to give credit to anyone. Monthly accountings. The society will rent a slave.

Appendix Four

The following is a notarized act of sale for a house in Port-au-Prince. The contract is quite typical of the sources used for this book and contains several important features that have been indicated by footnotes. The text used is the "second minute," the copy kept by the notary and sent to the national archives. It is reproduced in a large folio volume and was probably written at the time the contract was made, although this copy was not signed by the principals as was the case with some second minutes. This contract was copied out by the notary, an educated man. By this time, French grammar, spelling, word usage, and handwriting had been standardized among the educated elite, so translation posed little difficulty. Some notarized acts were written out by the principals and merely formalized and archived by the notary, and these offer a greater challenge to the non-Francophone reader.

Before the notary general of the Conseil Supérieur of Port au Prince, island and French coast of Saint Domingue, and his colleague, notary in the *senéchausée* of the said town, undersigned

Were present: the *nommée*[1] Elisabeth Dougé, wife of Daguin, *marchande*[2] living in this town, parish Notre Dame de l'Assomption, in the name of and acting with the ad hoc power of the *nommé* Daguin, her son, *habitant* in Nippes, dated last March 12th, which she showed us and which we attached to the first minute of this act,[3] for the record, after we certified it as true and correctly signed. The said [Dougé] in this capacity declares that this day she has sold, ceded, given up, let go, and transported in full property, in perpetuity, and for ever, with promise and all guarantees of law,

to the *nommée* Luce, known as Rasteau, free *quarteronne*, living in this town, here present and accepting in her own name, for her own, and for her creditors,[4]

To wit: half of a lot located in the new town of Port-au-Prince, number 274 on the plan [of the redeveloped section of town], containing, the half sold, 60 feet wide by 120 deep, bordered on the east by Sieur Chatele, on the south by the rue de Provence, on the west by Sieur Gaudé, and on the north by Sieur Pierroux.[5]

On the said half of a lot there is a *case*,[6] composed of two chambers, equipped with doors and windows that latch, roofed in shingles, in the courtyard of which is a small building, also of two chambers, of which one is used as a kitchen, and a well to be shared with the seller, and the *nommée* Marie Therese, free black, owner of the other half of the lot; the whole in the state in which it is found, with its circumstances and dependencies. The lot belonging to the said Daguin for having acquired it from the said Luce Rasteau, purchaser here present, in an act made before *Maître* Poul and his colleague, notaries in this jurisdiction, the 23rd of March, 1776, the said Luce having acquired it from the *nommée* Marthe known as Marthonne, free black, by act made before *Maître* Poul and his colleague, notaries in this jurisdiction, the 9th of August, 1774, who had it from Sieur Augustin Etienne, Royal Surveyor, by act passed before *Maître* Fillegue, notary in this jurisdiction, the 30th of July, 1763, to whom the entire lot belonged by virtue of a concession accorded by MM. Bart and [indecipherable] General and *Commisaire Ordonnateur* of this colony to Sieur Alemand, the 5th of February, 1760, who transferred the concession to the said Sieur Augustin Etienne by private act of sale written on the back of the said concession and dated the 14th of August, 1761. The said Louis Daguin sold the property in an act before us on the 25th of March, 1776, to Sieur Perotte, *negociant*[7] in this town, who returned the property to Daguin this day in an act before us in return for the sum of 3300 *livres*, which was counted out to him before us, the said notaries.[8]

All of which the buyer declares that she knows well, and is content and satisfied with the said portion of a lot, buildings, circumstances, and dependencies, from having seen, visited, and examined them, and being this day in good and real possession and tenancy.

The present sale is thus made at the will and with the consent of the parties, for the price and sum of 6000 *livres*, which the said seller declares having this day received in cash[9] from the said buyer in specie of Spanish gold and coins having value in this colony of which sum she gives her in the said name good and valuable discharge.

By means of which payment the said seller in the said name lets go, releases, and renounces property and tenancy rights and any other pretensions that the said Louis Daguin has to the said portion of land, buildings, circumstances and dependencies, in favor of the said purchaser, who for her part will enjoy, use, and dispose of it as her own property properly acquired.

And in order to justify property rights to the said portion of a lot the said seller has at this instant given the said purchaser before us, the said notaries:[10]

1. A copy of an act of sale between the *nommée* Marthonne and Sieur Augustin Etienne drawn from the files of *Maître* Fillegue and his colleague, notaries in this jurisdiction, the 31st of July, 1763,

2. Of the sale made by the *nommée* Marthonne to the *nommée* Luce known as Rasteau from the files of *Maître* Poul, and his colleague, notaries in this jurisdiction, the 9th of April, 1774, of the half of the lot hereby sold,

3. Of that made by the said Luce to the *nommée* Louis Daguin fils in an act before the same notary the 23rd of March, 1776,

4. And finally, the act of sale made by the said Louis Daguin to Sieur Perotte, businessman in this town, of the same piece of land, in an act from the files of these notaries, the 25th of the same month, for the price of 3300 *livres*, with the possibility of repurchase, following which is the act of return made by the said Sieur Perotte of the

said piece of land in return for the sum of 3300 *livres* which was paid to him by Claude Deroux.[11] The said return made before us, notary general, undersigned on this day.

All of which titles of property the said purchaser acknowledges being in due and proper possession and of which she discharges the said seller.

Performed and passed in the study of the aforementioned notary general and his colleague, the 23rd of June, 1777. The said purchaser signed with us, the said seller declared that she did not know how to sign and the document was interpreted to her in accordance with the ordinance.[12]

Signed, Luce Rasteau, DeGrandpré, Michel

NOTES

1. The *nommée*, or the "so-called," was a formulaic title generally reserved for free coloreds.

2. The *marchande*, or merchant, was a term suggesting retail trade and a lower order than the haughty *négociant*, a term that appears later in the document.

3. The copy in the register in the AN SOM is the second minute, so unfortunately many of the supporting documents are unavailable, seemingly having been retained by the parties.

4. This is a boilerplate expression, not necessarily indicating that there are creditors seeking the property. Note also that Luce is "known as" Rasteau while Elisabeth is "wife of" Daugin. Free coloreds were not supposed to use the surnames of their white parents if they were illegitimate, but they often got around the rule with this official phrasing (while, one presumes, remaining plain Luce Rasteau outside the pages of the notary's journal), although Elisabeth's marriage is a social plus, possibly outweighing Rasteau's superior racial title.

5. Despite the reputation of Port-au-Prince as "a vast Tartar camp," there had been considerable effort to plan the city, and many of the neighborhoods were surveyed. Titles sometimes appear clearer here than in the older Cap Français.

6. A *case*, or hut, is a term used very broadly for places of considerable luxury (as this one appears to be) as well as for tiny shacks with straw roofs. To term one's residence a *maison*, or house, is to make a claim to wealth and social status.

7. The term *negociant*, or businessman, signifies a higher status than a lowly merchant. It denotes someone involved in wholesale trade and land speculation and frequently serving as an agent for an important French trading house.

8. A frequent means of establishing credit, especially in the towns, was to sell property "with right of repurchase," in essence, to pawn. As in this case, the cash paid out on the pawn was often considerably less than the market value of the property, and the lender had the use of the property during the period of the loan. Often the property would be rented back to its original owner, the borrower, although there is no evidence that this occurred in this case.

9. This statement is not necessarily true, even though clearly enough stated. The sample contained several examples of people trying to collect debts in which the money supposedly

paid in cash according to the original act of sale was in fact a promise to pay. If the act says "counted out before the notaries," as with Daguin's redemption of the pawn of the land in this case, then it appears very likely that the sum was actually paid in cash. In general, cash payment was rare; most acts of sale were settled by exchange of personal paper containing promises to pay.

10. This notary was exceptionally careful to detail the ownership history of land in all his acts of sale. Note that more than half of the act details former owners. Most other notaries would satisfy themselves by noting the name of the immediately preceding owner and the act by which it was originally conceded by the government.

11. Who is Claude Deroux? Probably somebody who owed Dauguin or his mother money or maybe their new creditor. This act does not say, but according to the formula, since Deroux is an important secondary participant, his quality, estate, obligations vis-à-vis the other parties, etc., should have been spelled out.

12. Literacy, or at least the ability to sign one's name, was an important marker of social status. Note that it was the socially climbing *quarteronne* who signed this act while the plebian *marchande* at least claimed to be unable to read and write.

Notes

ABBREVIATIONS

The following abbreviations are used throughout the notes.

AN SOM   Archives Nationales Françaises, Section Outremer
DFC   Depot des Fortifications des Colonies
E.C.   Etat Civil de Saint-Domingue
Not.   Notariat de Saint-Domingue

INTRODUCTION

1. AN SOM Not. vol. 693, dated 9/8/80 (all dates are dd/mm/yy).

2. AN SOM G1 495a.

3. For example, he was chief mourner at the burial of fellow militia noncommissioned officer (NCO) Joseph Pyracmour's wife (AN SOM E.C. 20, 20/5/83), stood as godfather to a young *griffe*, Robert Sicart (E.C. 20, 29/1/83), was principal witness at the marriage of fellow militia NCO Jean-Baptiste Mali's ward (Not. 174n, 29/1/78), and guaranteed a transaction by the Desrouleaux minor children, for whom the tutor was his militia colleague Pierre Attila and the curator, Mali (Not. 1532, 23/7/78).

4. The Laportes appear almost ninety times in the set of documents that forms the basis of this book. The average cash value of their notarized transactions was 21,098 *livres*, more than three times the average for the entire sample.

5. Not. 1402n, 24/1/85.

6. Pertinent scholarship began some time ago with the seminal work of Frank Tannenbaum, *Slave and Citizen: The Negro in the Americas,* and continues more recently with David Cohen and Jack Greene, eds., *Neither Slave nor Free: The Freedman of African Descent in the Slave Societies of the New World.* John Garrigus's dissertation, "A Struggle for Respect: The Free Coloreds of Pre-Revolutionary Saint Domingue, 1760–1769," deals specifically with the situation of Saint Domingue's free coloreds, especially those of the South province. A more recent general work is Jane Landers, ed., *Against the Odds: Free Blacks in the Slave Societies of the Americas.* The subject is treated more peripherally in many general studies of slave societies such as Franklin Knight, *Slave Society in Cuba during the Nineteenth Century.*

7. Douglas Hall, in his piece entitled "Jamaica" in Cohen and Greene, *Neither Slave nor Free,* 201–203, attributed this to a conscious strategy to distinguish themselves from the slaves, who were predominantly rural agricultural laborers.

8. Edward Cox, *Free Coloreds in the Slave Societies of St. Kitts and Grenada, 1763–1833,* 30–31, 60 (figures from table 4–1).

9. A. J. R. Russell-Wood, "Colonial Brazil," in Cohen and Greene, *Neither Slave nor Free,* 98–108.

10. See Franklin Knight's article "Cuba," in Cohen and Greene, *Neither Slave nor Free,* 278–308.

11. See the introduction to Cohen and Greene, *Neither Slave nor Free,* 1–18.

12. See Theophilous G. Steward, "How the Black St. Domingo Legion Saved the Patriot Army in the Siege of Savannah, 1779," or, more recently, David Geggus, "The Haitian Revolution," in *The Modern Caribbean,* ed. Franklin Knight, 25, in which he says the "muster roll [of the Chasseurs-Volontaires] reads like a roll call of future revolutionaries." Unfortunately, I was unable to find this muster roll in AN SOM.

13. AN SOM D2C 41.

14. "Extrait du Recensement Général de la Colonie de S. Domingue pour l'année 1788 en ce qui concerne les blancs et les gens de couleur libres," AN SOM G1 509, 38.

15. John Garrigus has noted that the general census figures consistently underreported the population of free persons of color. In his example, for the parish of Nippes in 1753, the census figure was almost 30 percent less than figures compiled for local use by the militia commander. Garrigus, "Struggle for Respect," 63–65.

16. For more background on this class, see, for example, Gabriel Debien, *Une plantation à Saint-Domingue: La Sucrerie Galbaud du Fort, 1690–1802,* and Robert Forster, "A Sugar Plantation on Saint Domingue."

17. The adult white male population of the colony increased from 4,452 in 1752 to 7,912 in 1775, an increase of 77 percent, while the adult male free colored population increased from 1,332 to 1,976, an increase of 48 percent. AN SOM G1 509 pieces 28 and 31.

18. Not. 82n, 1/2/79. This and all other French or Haitian creole translations contained in this work are my own, unless otherwise stated. The cause of death was more likely to have been some gastrointestinal tract infection than simple starvation, but the doctor's diagnosis that his death was due to poverty can be reinforced by the fact that he died alone by the roadside and no kin could be found.

19. On the French regulations, see Sue Peabody, "Race, Slavery, and French Law: The Legal Concept of the *Police des Noirs.*"

20. The "Edit servant de Réglement pour le Gouvernement et l'Administration de la Justice, Police, Discipline et le Commerce des Esclaves Nègres dans la province et Colonie de la Louisiane" in Médéric Louis Moreau de St. Méry, *Loix et constitutions des colonies françaises de l'Amérique sous le vent,* 3:88–95, holds this is Article 52. The Louisiana law, claimed by Moreau de St. Méry to be customary law for Saint Domingue as well, was cited in a few court cases, which he cites to buttress his claim. This particular provision was clearly not observed there.

21. I owe the expression *tache ineffaçable* in this context to Michel Réné Hilliard d'Auberteuil, *Considerations sur l'état présent de la colonie française de Saint-Domingue,* 1:74.

22. "Code Noir ou Edit servant de Réglement pour le Gouvernement et l'Administration de la Justice et de la Police des Isles Françoises de l'Amérique, et pour la Discipline et

le Commerce des Negres et Esclaves dans l'edit Pays," March 1685, in Moreau de St. Méry, *Loix et constitutions*, 1:417.

23. See Tannenbaum, *Slave and Citizen*.

24. See, for example, C. L. R. James, *Black Jacobins: Toussaint L'Ouverture and the San Domingo Revolution*, which treats the free people of color as a relatively undifferentiated middle class in a strongly Marxist analysis.

25. This is the attitude, for example, of Médéric Louis Moreau de St. Méry in his *Description topographique, physique, civile, politique et historique de la partie française de l'Isle de Saint-Domingue*. Julien Raimond, in his *Réponse aux considérations de M. Moreau dit St. Méry, député à l'Assemblée national sur les colonies par M. Raimond, citoyen de couleur de Saint-Domingue*, starts from an unspoken assumption of the superiority of the mixed race.

26. Philip Curtin, *The Atlantic Slave Trade: A Census*, 268.

27. Robert Stein, *The French Slave Trade in the Eighteenth Century: An Old Regime Business*, 32, 38.

CHAPTER ONE. THE NOTARIAL RECORD AND FREE COLOREDS

1. Moreau de St. Méry states in his *Loix et constitutions* that the authorized notarial fee scale for 1775 was the following: for a marriage contract taken in the notary's office, 66 *livres*; for a will, 8 *livres*/hour; for a sales contract, 12 *livres*; for travel per diem, 60 *livres*/day; for a "simple act," 12 *livres*; for research, 3 *livres* if the year of the act was known, 6 *livres*/hour if the year was not known (5:619–39). Given the wide variation of prices for acts in which the notary's fee was written in the margin of the copy in the register, it is reasonable to conclude that what Moreau de St. Méry has cited were guidelines only, and the fee depended, like all professional fees then and now, on the client's ability to pay.

2. A *carreau* is a piece of land 100 paces (each pace being about 1.5 meters) on a side; it is enough for comfortable subsistence farming for a family if the land is well watered and flat.

3. Garrigus, "Struggle for Respect."

4. Claude de Ferrière, *La science parfaite des notaires ou le parfait notaire*.

5. Jean-Paul Poisson, *Notaires et société: Travaux d'histoire et de sociologie notariales*, 297–302.

6. Not. 87n, 8/7/87.

7. Moreau de St. Méry, *Loix et constitutions*, 5:448–49.

8. Garrigus, "Struggle for Respect," 139.

9. AN SOM G1 509 piece 31, "Recensement de la paroisse de Cap Français 1775."

10. Not. 1396n, 14/4/80, and Not. 1394n, 8/4/78.

11. AN SOM G1 509 piece 32, "Recensement General . . . pour l'année 1780."

12. Not. 1383n item 34, 15/2/78.

13. Moreau de St. Méry, *Loix et constitutions*, 1:422.

14. No examples of colored *priests* appear in the records, although no royal or papal rule appears to have forbidden it.

15. These are included under the notarial acts in table 1. There were 16 in the sample.

CHAPTER TWO. THE LAND

1. Garrigus, "Struggle for Respect," which discusses the wealthy free colored family of political activist Julien Raimond, residents of Aquin on the southern peninsula of the colony.

2. Paul Butel, "L'Essor Antillais au XVIIIe siècle," in Pierre Pluchon, ed., *Histoire des Antilles et de la Guyane*, 113.

3. Michel-Rolph Trouillot, "Motion in the System: Coffee, Color, and Slavery in Eighteenth-Century Saint Domingue," 331–88.

4. Moreau de St. Méry, *Description de la partie française*, 1:294.

5. Spanish imperial theory in the late fifteenth through seventeenth centuries held that the treaty of Tordesillas granted all land in the New World west of Brazil to Spain. Thus, Spain did not accept the legality of any non-Spanish colonies in the New World until almost the end of the seventeenth century. Nonetheless, the French settled the western part of Hispaniola and adjoining islands starting in the 1620s, and French colonial governors were regularly assigned to the "Isle et Côte Française de Saint-Domingue" starting in November of 1641, when Levasseur was named to this title. Spain made several unsuccessful attempts to evict the French settlers from Isle de la Tortue and the main island of Saint Domingue during the seventeenth century before accepting their presence, and fixing borders between their territories, in the Treaty of Ryswick, 1697.

6. The capsule economic history of the colony that follows is drawn from a number of sources, principally Moreau de St. Méry, *Description de la partie française*, in which he describes the economies of the various parishes and, in the chapter on Cap Français, the North province in general, and Pluchon, ed., *Histoire des Antilles*.

7. Moreau de St. Méry, *Description de la partie française*, 1:294–95.

8. Baron Alexandre-Stanislas de Wimpffen, *Voyage à Saint-Domingue*, in *Haiti au XVIIIe siècle: Richesse et esclavage dans une colonie française*, ed. Pluchon, 239–40.

9. Baudry des Lozières quoted in James E. McClellan III, *Colonialism and Science: Saint Domingue in the Old Regime*, 83.

10. Moreau de St. Méry, *Description de la partie française*, 300.

11. Moreau de St. Méry, *Description de la partie française*, 333–34, bemoans the bastard construction of the sanctuary.

12. Moreau de St. Méry, *Description de la partie française*, 481, citing an ordinance of 24/3/61.

13. Moreau de St. Méry, *Description de la partie française*, 1002.

14. The notarial registers total 106 for Port-au-Prince and 95 for Cap. Port-au-Prince produced lots of notarial activity after 1789, when the insurgency in the countryside and in the North concentrated activity there, while very few notarial registers from the North dating from after 1789 have survived. As a result, Port-au-Prince has many more total registers than Cap, although we are only concerned here with the period 1776–89.

15. Moreau de St. Méry, *Description de la partie française*, 357.

16. Moreau de St. Méry, *Description de la partie française*, 345. One *piastre* equaled 8.25 *livres*.

17. McClellan, *Colonialism and Science*, especially part 3.

18. Jean Fouchard, *The Haitian Maroons: Liberty or Death*.

19. The cadastral survey is AN SOM G1 495a. The race of the owner was usually noted in the cadastral survey, and in many cases, so was the race of the occupant.

20. AN SOM G1 495a (cadastral survey of Cap Français, 1776). That is approximately the price of one slave each year, pretty substantial by any standards.

21. AN SOM G1 509 piece 32, "Récapitulation du recensement général . . . 1780."

22. Moreau de St. Méry, *Description de la partie française*, 213–15, and Samuel M. Wilson, *Hispaniola: Caribbean Chiefdoms in the Age of Columbus*, 69–71.

23. Moreau de St. Méry, *Description de la partie française*, 222.

24. AN SOM G1 509 piece 32, 1780 Census Compilation. This source combines census data by *quartiers*, which were administrative divisions consisting of one or more parishes under the jurisdiction of a single *sénéchaussée* court. Of the parishes studied for this work, Cap and Mirebalais were the only parishes in their *quartier*, Limonade was combined with l'Acul du Nord, a parish of similar size and economic profile, Fort Dauphin was combined with Ouanaminthe, a small rural area on the Spanish border, and Port-au-Prince and Croix des Bouquets formed a *quartier*.

25. Moreau de St. Méry, *Description de la partie française*, 125.

26. Moreau de St. Méry, *Description de la partie française*, 132.

27. AN SOM G1 509 piece 38. Slave populations are difficult to estimate since many slaves, for tax purposes, would be listed as resident on a rural *habitation* when in fact they worked as domestics in the *habitant*'s urban residence.

28. Moreau de St. Méry, *Description de la partie française*, 133.

29. Moreau de St. Méry, *Description de la partie française*, 136.

30. AN SOM G1 509 piece 32.

31. Moreau de St. Méry, *Description de la partie française*, 980–81.

32. Wimpffen, *Voyage à Saint-Domingue*, in Pluchon, *Haiti au XVIIIe siècle*, 175.

33. Moreau de St. Méry, *Description de la partie française*, 980.

34. Moreau de St. Méry gives a tragicomic description of the embezzlement scandal at the *Comédie*, *Description de la partie française*, 988–89.

35. Moreau de St. Méry, *Description de la partie française*, 962.

36. AN SOM G1 509 piece 32.

37. Not. 1538n. 3/8/31.

38. Census figures from AN SOM G1 509 piece 38.

39. See John Garrigus, "Blue and Brown: Contraband Indigo and the Rise of a Free Colored Planter Class in French Saint Domingue," for a discussion of the part the interloper trade played in the economic viability of indigo planting in the South province.

40. AN SOM G1 509 piece 32.

41. Not. 1177n, 22/8/81.

CHAPTER THREE. THE PEOPLE

1. AN SOM G1 509 piece 31. Note that the sum at the bottom of the "Recapitulation" for adult free colored women is 1,000 fewer than the total of the figures for the different regions. I have used the regional figures.

2. AN SOM G1 509 piece 32.

3. AN SOM G1 509 piece 38.

4. Garrigus, "Struggle for Respect, 63–65.

5. AN SOM G1 509 pieces 31 (1775), 32 (1780), and 38 (1788).

6. AN SOM G1 509 31, 33, 38. These figures represent the socially adult, excluding *garçons portant arms,* or boys capable of bearing arms, and *filles à marier,* or marriageable girls.

7. AN SOM Etat Civil, Saint Domingue (E.C.) registers 17–21. Population statistics from census figures for 1775, 1780, and 1788 from AN SOM G1 509 31, 33, 38.

8. This phenomenon is reported by virtually all the contributors to David Cohen and Jack Greene, eds., *Neither Slave nor Free,* and in the introduction, 4.

9. AN SOM G1 509 31, 33, 38.

10. See, for example, Carolyn Fick, *The Making of Haiti: The Saint Domingue Revolution from Below,* 92.

11. Fouchard, *Haitian Maroons.*

12. Based on estimated population numbers obtained by linear progression from the 1775 and 1780 figures cited above and on E.C. 17 (for Cap) and E.C. 119 (for Limonade). Baptisms are problematic as records of births because many children were not baptized at birth but months or years later, disguising some infant mortality, and also because some, especially white, children were baptized not in their native parishes in Saint Domingue but in France. Free colored children, on the other hand, especially if their fathers were powerful white men, might be baptized in the regional center even if born in the countryside in order to provide an opportunity for a status-enhancing large public ceremony.

13. This was the case with the burial of Charles Ducatel, a reasonably well-off farmer who died in Sainte-Suzanne on 5 December 1779 and whose burial was reported to the *curé,* Father Michaud, on 16 December. E.C. 119, 16/12/79.

14. E.C. 119 and 120.

15. The units used to report population of Fort Dauphin vary between the three census tables used. The figures presented here include the population of the parishes of Fort Dauphin and Ounanaminthe (a very isolated rural parish inland along the Spanish border).

CHAPTER FOUR. FREE COLOREDS IN THE COLONIAL ARMED FORCES

1. Governor de Fayet of Saint Domingue letter to Minister of Marine Maurepas, 16/5/1733, transcript in state correspondence received, AN SOM C9A no. 37.

2. Not. 1402n 11/3/85.

3. Herbert S. Klein, "The Colored Militia of Cuba, 1568–1868," 17–27.

4. Peter M. Voelz, *Slave and Soldier: The Military Impact of Blacks in the Colonial Americas,* 44–45. The subtitle suggests a broad study, but this book deals almost exclusively with the British colonies and the United States. Mention is occasionally made of conditions in Saint Domingue, especially during the Revolution, but the weakness of Voelz's work as regards Saint Domingue is one thing I attempt to address in this book.

5. Moreau de St. Méry, *Description de la partie française,* 229.

6. AN SOM Not. 1533, 21/6/79.

7. Voelz, *Slave and Soldier*, 41–42.

8. Moreau de St. Méry, *Loix et constitutions*, 1:416.

9. Not. 848, 28/10/79.

10. Moreau de St. Méry, *Description de la partie française*, 85. The data bear him out as to the high numbers of manumissions, but taxed as well as tax-free acts increased rapidly throughout this period.

11. "Ordonnance du Commandant en Chef par interim, concernans l'établissement de cinq Compagnies de Chasseurs-Royaux, tirés des Compagnies de Milices des Gens de Couleur," 5/16/1780, in Moreau de St. Méry, *Loix et constitutions*, 6:22–29.

12. "Arrêt de Réglement du conseil de Léogane . . . ," 16/3/1705, in Moreau de St. Méry, *Loix et constitutions*, 2:25–27.

13. A Spanish custom, generally imposed by gubernatorial fiat rather than edict from the Council of the Indies, was that slaves who fled to Spanish territory would be freed if they became Catholics. Occasionally, Spain would agree by treaty that runaways would be returned, but in the Caribbean such agreements were hard to enforce.

14. "Ordonnance des Administrateurs pour l'établissement d'une maréchaussée," 27/3/1721, in Moreau de St. Méry, *Loix et constitutions*, 2:726–33.

15. The private soldier of the *maréchaussée* was called in most sources an archer, although he was to be equipped with musket, two pistols, machete, saber, cartridge box, and bayonet —a veritable walking arsenal, but not a bow or arrow in sight. Clearly another term borrowed from the metropolitan *maréchausée* and suggesting the venerability of the institution.

16. Moreau de St. Méry, *Loix et constitutions*, 2:726–33.

17. "Arrêt du Conseil du Port-au-Prince sur la composition et la distribution des Brigades de Maréchaussée," 21/7/1767, in Moreau de St. Méry, *Loix et constitutions*, 5:119–21.

18. Marquis de Fayet and Duclos, general and intendant of Saint Domingue, "Ordonnance portant re-etablissement de la *maréchaussée*" in Moreau de St. Méry, *Loix et constitutions*, 6:344–49.

19. There were 219,698 slaves in 1771 according to the census in that year. AN SOM G1 509 piece 30.

20. Julien Raimond, "Troisième Mémoire à Monseigneur le Maréchal de Castries Ministre et Secrétaire d'État au Département de la Marine," AN SOM F/3/91 190–92.

21. Not. 1289n 6/5/77.

22. As described in Charles Frostin, *Les Révoltes blanches à Saint-Domingue aux XVIIe–XVIIIe siècles*.

23. This practice was regularized in an act by the *Conseil Supérieur du Cap* in 1790, in Moreau de St. Méry, *Loix et constitutions*, 6:546.

24. "Arrêt du Conseil . . . touchant les jeux defendus," in Moreau de St. Méry, *Loix et constitutions*, 6:632.

25. AN SOM F/3/91, 145–54. The entire story appears in chapter 6 of this book.

26. The term "slaves of the state" and the general disrespect for servicemen are discussed in John Garrigus, "Catalyst or Catastrophe? Saint Domingue's Free Men of Color and the Battle of Savannah, 1779–1782," 112.

27. Moreau de St. Méry, *Loix et constitutions*, describes a local militia commander who

is reprimanded for having taken jurisdiction over a disputed inheritance when such cases were to have gone to the court (2:275) and a similar case (3:395).

28. Pierre de Vaissière, *Saint-Domingue: La Société et la Vie créoles sous l'ancien régime, 1629–1789*, 112–14.

29. M. le Comte de Nolivos, "Instructions . . . sur quelques objects du service des états majors des colonies, des troupes, et des milices," 2/12/70, manuscript in AN SOM DFC, carton 1, no. 58.

30. "Ordonnance générale des Milices," 15/1/1765, in Moreau de St. Méry, *Loix et constitutions*, 4:812–24.

31. M. de Carnage de Mailhert complains in his *memoire* of 28/9/39 about this phenomenon. AN SOM F/3/91 folio 19.

32. White resistance to militia reforms is a consistent theme in discussions of prerevolutionary society in Saint Domingue, ranging from Pierre de Vaissière, *Saint-Domingue*, to John Garrigus, "Catalyst or Catastrophe." Frostin, *Les Révoltes blanches*, is the classic source on this topic. The government's plan for reorganization is laid out in "Ordonnance générale des Milices," 15/1/1765, in Moreau de St. Méry, *Loix et constitutions*, 4:812–24.

33. See especially Garrigus's account of free colored participation in the anti-militia uprising in the South province in "Catalyst or Catastrophe"; also see Frostin, *Les Révoltes blanches*.

34. Moreau de St. Méry, *Description de la partie française*, 1:451. Population figures are from census data, AN SOM G1 509 piece 38.

35. Nolivos, "Instructions," DFC Saint Domingue, 1/58, 2/12/70.

36. M. le Baron de Castellane, two letters to the general commanding French troops on the island, dated 6/3/86 and 10/3/86, manuscripts in Collection Moreau de St. Méry, AN SOM F/3/91, 163–65.

37. Raimond, "Troisième Mémoire à Monseigneur le Maréchal," AN SOM F/3/91, 192.

38. AN SOM F/3/91, 167, undated but sometime in 1786.

39. Roger Norman Buckley, ed., *The Haitian Journal of Lieutenant Howard, of the York Hussars, 1796–1798*, 123.

40. Moreau de St. Méry, *Description de la partie française*, 1:92.

41. Numbers vary depending on sources: In "Controle des Forces," July–Aug. 1779, AN SOM D2C/41, 765; all ranks are listed as detached for service in Savannah. In "Etat de troupes embarqués sur l'expedition de M. le Comte d'Estaing," 14 Aug. 1779, there are 772 Chasseurs listed as leaving for Savannah. The second document states that in addition, 195 Chasseurs-Grenadiers were among those in the expedition.

42. The Régiments du Cap and de Port-au-Prince were regular "colonial" troops, recruited in France especially for service in the colonies. About one-quarter of their strength was detached for the Savannah expedition. The other troops came from the Régiments de Gatinois, d'Agenois, and de Cambresis and the Royal Artillery.

43. Statement of Colonel Laurent François Le Noir de Rouvray, commander of the Chasseurs-Volontaires, letter to Minister of Marine, 12/12/79, AN SOM E278, without listing the names. The expedition commander's report has apparently not survived.

44. The original law is D'Argout, Governor-General, "Ordonnance et Règlement sur les Grenadiers-Volontaires et les Chasseurs-Volontaires de St. Domingue" in Moreau de St. Méry, *Loix et constitutions*, 5:860–69.

45. D'Argout, "Ordonnance et Règlement," in Moreau de St. Méry, *Loix et constitutions*, 3/12/79 and 21/4/79, 5:860–69.

46. Le Noir de Rouvray letter, 12/12/79, AN SOM E278.

47. Lettres-Patent du Roi 5/22/1775 in Moreau de St. Méry, *Loix et constitutions*, 5:587; administrative structures established in Ordonnance des Administrateurs concernant les Libertés, 10/23/1775, 5:610–13.

48. Not. 850, 10/7/79.

49. Not. 176 n, 4/8/79.

50. Not. 1616, 14/4/80, promotion to captain AN SOM D2C 114 (3 Comp. An V [1794]).

51. Appendix 2 contains a list of 55 surnames or family names for which there were more than three transactions over 10,000 *livres* in the sample. Six of these families included militia noncommissioned officers, 11 had members who joined the Chasseurs-Volontaires (2 of whom also had militiamen in the family, and the remaining 9 were planter elites), 2 included *maréchaussée* men, 5 were female-headed households, 4 of which joined the elite during the time under study thanks to donations from white elite men to their colored lovers, and the remaining 33 were older free colored families, of the planter elite, without military connections.

52. "Ordonnance et Règlement," Moreau de St. Méry, *Loix et constitutions*, 5:861.

53. Out of 26 Chasseurs-Volontaires for whom both parish of residence and company are known, 14 served in companies headed by officers from other parishes.

54. John Garrigus, "Sons of the Same Father: Gender, Race, and Citizenship in French Saint Domingue, 1760–1789."

55. Rouvray letter to Minister of Marine, 12/12/79, AN SOM E278.

56. "Ordonnance générale des Milices," 15/1/65, in Moreau de St. Méry, *Loix et constitutions*, 4:813.

57. Moreau de St. Méry, *Loix et constitutions*, 4:825–31.

58. John Garrigus discusses the appeal to free colored patriotism in "Catalyst or Catastrophe." He comes to the conclusion that the expedition was a catastrophe for free coloreds' dreams of social advancement.

59. Moreau de St. Méry, *Description de la partie française*, 230. René was one of the Vincent family members who participated in the Savannah expedition; he is almost certainly Vincent's grandson. The other Chasseur-Volontaire to whom Moreau de St. Méry refers remains unidentified in the notarial records.

60. Pluchon, *Histoire des Antilles*, 104.

61. Pluchon, *Histoire des Antilles*, 106.

62. Voelz, *Slave and Soldier*, 44–45.

63. Moreau de St. Méry, *Description de la partie française*, 186–87.

64. Moreau de St. Méry, *Description de la partie française*, 229–30.

65. Moreau de St. Méry, *Description de la partie française*, 186–87.

66. The construction of their camp is detailed in Moreau de St. Méry, *Description de la partie française*, 180–81.

67. Parish Register for Cap Français, AN SOM E.C. 17, burial, 27/10/78.

68. M. le Comte d'Argout, "lettre à M. le Ministre sur les Chasseurs Mulâtres," 28/7/79, manuscript in Collection Moreau de St. Méry, AN SOM F/3/91, piece 139. The requirement of eight years of service was reduced to one in the actual regulation; it still encountered considerable opposition.

69. "Ordonnance du Commandant en Chef par interim, concernans l'établissement de cinq compagnies de Chasseurs-Royaux, tirés des compagnies de milice des gens de couleur," 16/5/1780, in Moreau de St. Méry, *Loix et constitutions*, 7:22–29.

70. Not. 1616, 6/8/80.

71. Not. 1616, 27/9/80.

72. He is described as such in Not. 1619, 14/12/82.

73. AN SOM F/3/91 142, 3/7/81.

74. Not. 1394n, 28/9/78.

75. Their act of manumission, Not. 1615, 1/9/79, was tax-exempt because of their service.

76. As, for example, in his first memoire to the Minister of Marine in 1786, AN SOM F/3/91, where he cites both the pursuit of runaways and the defense of the coast against English raiders as tasks best suited to free coloreds.

77. *Affiches Américaines*, 30/3/79, Bibliothèque Nationale Française, 4, 1c 12 20/20.

78. Cited in Garrigus, "Sons of the Same Father," 15–16.

79. AN SOM F3/188.

80. Garrigus, "Catalyst or Catastrophe," 120–23.

81. Moreau de St. Méry, *Loix et constitutions*, 5:246–47.

CHAPTER FIVE. SLAVEHOLDING PRACTICES

1. AN SOM Not. 181n, 29/8/82.

2. Not. 181n, 29/8/82.

3. Purchase of a lot and nine-room house, plus outbuildings, on the rue Penthièvre, from M. le Vicomte de la Belinaye, through his agent in the colony, Stanislas Foäche, for 9,900 *livres* in cash, 2,400 *livres* in a six-month note on the large merchant house of Faurier *frères*, 1,500 *livres* in a one-year note on Sieur Guignard (a smaller merchant), 2,400 *livres* in a fifteen-day note on Sieur Bertrand (apparently he was a planter), and 1,800 *livres* in five-month paper on Sieur Gobert (unidentified). Not. 175n, 9/12/78.

4. Not. 176n, 7/2/80.

5. Not. 181n, 10/8/82.

6. Not. 1403n, 26/6/86.

7. Garrigus, "Struggle for Respect," especially chapter 2.

8. Gabriel Debien, *Les Esclaves aux Antilles françaises, XVIIe–XVIIIe siècles*.

9. Pluchon, *Histoire des Antilles*.

10. David Patrick Geggus, *Slavery, War and Revolution: The British Occupation of Saint-Domingue, 1793–1798*. Geggus's bibliography, 467–80, among 54 documentary sources for

his work, cites ten French sources, the most important of which seem to be AN SOM "Saint-Domingue: Administration Anglaise," 15 volumes recording management of lands owned by mainly white, although not exclusively so, absentees in the part of the colony controlled by the British during the Revolutionary War and AN SOM Saint Domingue: Dossiers "de l'indemnité" relating to claims by (again mostly white) landlords who were driven out by the independent Haitian government after 1804 and who were seeking redress in the 1830s out of the indemnity funds paid by Haiti as the price of its recognition by France. His notes for chapter 1, on the pre-revolutionary situation, reveal extensive reliance on Moreau de St. Méry's *Description de la partie française,* an important source, but one that, as we have seen, tends to ignore smaller operations regardless of the color of their proprietors. Debien's extensive work is widely cited here as well.

11. Newer sources are Michel-Rolph Trouillot, "Coffee Planters and Coffee Slaves in the Antilles: The Impact of a Secondary Crop," 124–37, and David P. Geggus, "Sugar and Coffee Cultivation in Saint Domingue and the Shaping of the Slave Labor Force," 73–100. The general survey by David Geggus is "The Slaves of British-Occupied Saint Domingue: An Analysis of the Workforces of 197 Absentee Plantations, 1796–97," 5–41.

12. Richard Sheridan, *Sugar and Slavery: An Economic History of the British West Indies, 1623–1775,* 231.

13. E. Bradford Burns, *A History of Brazil,* 65.

14. Knight, *Slave Society in Cuba,* 134, citing Antonio C. Gallenga, *The Pearl of the Antilles,* 100–102.

15. Curtin, *Atlantic Slave Trade,* 90–93.

16. Imports from Curtin, *Atlantic Slave Trade,* 88; slave numbers from Knight, *Slave Society in Cuba,* 22. Slave populations seem to have declined from 1841 (with the end of the legal trade), reaching 287,620 in 1871: Knight, *Slave Society in Cuba,* 63.

17. Geggus, "Sugar and Coffee Cultivation," 74, 76.

18. Debien, *Les Esclaves,* 58–66.

19. Geggus, "Sugar and Coffee Cultivation," 79, 81.

20. Debien, *Les Esclaves,* 342–43.

21. Debien, *Les Esclaves,* 353.

22. Geggus, "Sugar and Coffee Cultivation," 79.

23. See, for example, David P. Geggus, "Sex Ratio, Age, and Ethnicity in the Atlantic Slave Trade: Data from French Shipping and Plantation Records," 23–44.

24. Debien, *Les Esclaves,* 138.

25. Debien, *Les Esclaves,* 348.

26. Debien, *Les Esclaves,* 347.

27. Geggus, "Sugar and Coffee Cultivation," 91.

28. Debien, *Les Esclaves,* 345, citing Médéric Louis Elie Moreau de St. Méry, *Description de la Partie Espagnole de Saint-Domingue,* 214.

29. Debien, *Les Esclaves,* 344.

30. Gabriel Debien, *Plantations et esclaves à Saint-Domingue: La sucrerie Foäche,* 53.

31. Geggus, "Sugar and Coffee Cultivation", 87.

32. AN SOM Not. 1535n, 25/5/77.

33. Fick, *Making of Haiti*.

34. Geggus, "Sugar and Coffee Cultivation," 87.

35. Not. 1391n III, October 1785 (date illeg.).

36. Not. 179n, 26/11/81. A wigmaker and hairdresser would need lots of clean linen but not be of the economic status to be able to afford a private domestic servant. La Combe apparently possessed no other slave besides Rosalie.

37. Not. 1403n, 9/8/86.

38. Not. 1395n, 3/12/79, and 1404n, 21/8/87.

39. Debien, *Les Esclaves*, 64–65.

40. Geggus, "Sugar and Coffee Cultivation," 79.

41. Debien, *Les Esclaves*, 65.

42. Geggus, "Sugar and Coffee Cultivation," 79.

43. All the stereotypes that follow are drawn from Moreau de St. Méry, *Description de la partie française*, 49–59.

44. Not. 1382n 152, 15/12/77.

45. Not. 1178n, 6/1/82. He also says that he is a native of "Guinée," which was a general term applied to black Africa or to west Africa at the time. One wonders if he knew Lucrèce.

46. Some authorities have suggested that Timbo could be a synonym for the Jalonka, a tribe related to the Fula.

47. John Thornton, "'I Am a Subject of the King of Congo': African Political Ideology and the Haitian Revolution," 181–214.

48. John Thornton, *Africa and Africans in the Making of the Atlantic World, 1400–1680*, especially chapters 5–10.

49. David Geggus, "Haitian Voodoo in the Eighteenth Century: Language, Culture, Resistance," 1–31.

50. For the Moreau de St. Méry fragment, see Moreau de St. Méry, *Description de la partie française*, n. 67.

51. See Debien, *Les Esclaves*, tables on pages 56–65.

52. Geggus, "Sugar and Coffee Cultivation," 86.

53. Debien, *Les Esclaves*, 59–68.

54. Moreau de St. Méry considers creoles to have been at least 25 percent more valuable than *bossales*; see *Description de la partie française*, 59.

55. Laird Bergad, Fe Iglesias Garcia, and Maria del Carmen Barcia, *The Cuban Slave Market, 1790–1880*, 67–71.

56. The concept can be found explained in much greater detail in Martin Klein and Paul Lovejoy, "Slavery in West Africa," and in its specific application to the Senegambian region, source of many slaves who came to Saint Domingue in the early days of the colony's existence, in Philip Curtin, *Economic Change in Precolonial Africa: Senegambia in the Era of the Slave Trade*.

57. Debien, *Les Esclaves*, 65–66.

58. Geggus, "Sugar and Coffee Cultivation," 82.

59. Debien, *Les Esclaves*, 61.

60. Debien, *Les Esclaves*, 345.

61. The "comparable" group value is a weighted average taking into account gender, age, and ethnic composition of the occupational group.

62. Gender ratios in the slave trade are extensively discussed in David Eltis and Stanley Engerman, "Fluctuations in Sex and Age Ratios in the Transatlantic Slave Trade, 1663–1864," 308–23, and in Geggus, "Sex Ratio, Age, and Ethnicity."

63. Bergad et al., *Cuban Slave Market,* 111–12.

64. Geggus, "Sugar and Coffee Cultivation," 79.

65. The *habitation* Baugé in Croix des Bouquets employed 32 males and 14 females (30 percent) on 3 July 1778 (Not. 1536n) and the *habitation* Poisson in Belair, Port-au-Prince, employed 20 males and 8 females (29 percent) on 1 May 1785 (Not. 1391n 59). The former was owned by the Baugés but operated by a partnership between two of the Baugé brothers and a woman; some of the slaves belonged to her.

66. Bergad et al., *Cuban Slave Market,* 62.

67. Debien, *Les Esclaves,* 66–69.

68. John Thornton, "Sexual Demography: The Impact of the Slave Trade on Family Structure," 39–48, suggests this line of reasoning while not committing to it wholly, whereas David Eltis, in his *Europe and the Rise of African Slavery in the Americas: The English Experience in Comparative Perspective,* chapter 4, page 16 of manuscript, argues that it was the preferences of European slave traders for males that led to the large numbers of male slaves in the Atlantic trade.

69. Geggus, "Sugar and Coffee Cultivation," 91.

70. Robert Fogel and Stanley Engerman, *Time on the Cross: The Economics of American Negro Slavery,* 218.

71. Not. 1298n, 12/7/85, contract establishing a partnership to operate a small retail general store in Fort Dauphin between Marie Josephe, *negresse libre,* and Sieur Guillemet. For complete text, see appendix 3.

72. *Code Noir,* Art. 22, in Moreau de St. Méry, *Loix et constitutions,* 1:418.

73. Debien, *Les Eesclaves,* 213.

74. Marie appears on one occasion, as debtor in the amount of 1,200 *livres* to her son, Not. 1297n, 20/3/83. Godin appears three times as a principal in sales contracts, Not. 1294n, 27/5/80, 5/3/80, and Not. 1293n, 11/9/79.

75. Admission of family relationship between slave and master was sometimes made in other notarial acts with the same participants. Family relationship was presumed, as previously explained, when the newly freed person received a donation "in lieu of subsistence allowance," or through other actions by the presumed father suggestive of a family relationship.

76. "Lettres-Patent du Roi," 5/22/1775 in Moreau de St. Méry, *Loix et constitutions,* 5:587, included in Saint Domingue official legal practice in "Ordonnance des Administrateurs concernant les Libertés," 10/23/1775, in Moreau de St. Méry, *Loix et constitutions,* 5:610–13.

77. Debien, *Les Esclaves,* 374.

78. Moreau de St. Méry, *Considerations sur l'état présent des colonies.*

79. Figures on slave sales from "Etat de la Colonie de Saint-Domingue, Année 1786," AN SOM G509 Piece 36. Julien Raimond, *Réponse aux considérations de M. Moreau dit St. Méry,* 56.

80. Not. 524n, 16/7/78.

81. Not. 524n, 2/5/78.

82. Not. 1294n, 22/1/80.

83. Not. 524n, 1/3/78. The liberty does not, in fact, appear in the sample, although it could easily have been performed before another notary in Cap or else in Grand Rivière where Malic had his *habitation*.

84. Not. 524n, 20/2/77.

85. Forster, "Sugar Plantation on Saint Domingue," 18–20.

86. Not. 1390n 18, 4/3/84.

87. Not. 200n, 29/2/88.

88. Moreau de St. Méry, *Loix et constitutions*, 5:767–68.

89. Interestingly, the most striking work on runaway slaves in the colony, Jean Fouchard's *The Haitian Maroons*, is also written from indirect sources—in his case, announcements of runaway slaves in the provincial newspaper *Affiches Américaines*.

90. Not. 194n 14/3/86. The official manumission of Pierre did not appear in the sample, but it may have been executed in Port de Paix.

91. Not. 1401n, 16/9/84.

92. Three appear as adults in an act in 1788 in which they recover some of their mother's property at the expiration of a long lease, along with a tutor speaking for the "minor children Poupart," Not. 1405n, 2/6/88.

93. Burial was E.C. 120, 6/3/83, at Sainte-Suzanne; inventory was Not. 1399n, 23/5/83.

94. As described in the act of rental, Not. 1395n, 12/5/79.

95. Charles's will is Not. 525n 90, 4/8/79, Laurent's is Not. 175n, 18/3/79.

96. Payment of the first three years' rent is Not. 1405n, 1/12/88.

97. Trouillot, "Motion in the System," 331–88, and Garrigus, "Blue and Brown," 233–63.

98. Curtin, *Atlantic Slave Trade*, 179–80.

99. AN SOM G509 piece 36.

100. Debien, *Plantations et esclaves*.

101. Not. 196n, 3/10/86. Twelve years old, no sign of parents, and working in a bar (Coidavy was an innkeeper as well as a slave dealer, and, possibly, Henry Christophe's master).

102. See, for example, Julien Raimond, *Réclamations addressées à l'Assemblée Nationale par les citoyens de couleur de l'Isle de Saint-Domingue*.

103. See, for example, Suzanne Miers and Igor Kopytoff, "African Slavery as an Institution of Marginality" in *Slavery in Africa: Historical and Anthropological Perspectives*, Miers and Kopytoff eds., which demonstrates the overwhelming importance of social promotion to African masters, while the free colored masters were competing in a capitalist system and needed to make profits.

CHAPTER SIX. LANDHOLDING PRACTICES

1. AN SOM Not. 1538n, 4/2/82.

2. The five younger siblings of the Nivard family rented their interests in the family

habitation in Mirebalais, 77 *carreaux* in indigo, along with livestock and 35 slaves, to their oldest brother, Michel Michel Apollon, for 11,000 *livres* a year, Not. 1168n, 2/3/77. The *habitation*, expanded and improved, rented to Louis Datte in 1786, after the end of the Revolutionary War for 20,000 *livres*, Not. 86n, 4/4/86. The Baugé *habitation* in Croix des Bouquets, 23 slaves, water rights, and as much land as could be brought under irrigation, rented for 12,000 *livres* plus the requirement to build a number of structures and plant 24 *carreaux* of sugar, in 1781, in the middle of the war. The *habitation* Peignanan seems to have been in the same league as these other large plantations, although, since Peignanan did not die during the period under study, his possessions were never inventoried.

3. Not. 1538, 23/11/82.

4. Not. 1537n, 30/3/81.

5. Not. 1536n, 25/6/79.

6. Not. 1538n, 15/3/82.

7. Chapter 3 of this work discusses the comparative context. In sum, Saint Domingue was a highly developed sugar-producing colony during the third quarter of the eighteenth century. French sugar production, led by Saint Domingue, exceeded even that of Jamaica (see Sidney Mintz, *Sweetness and Power,* 39). Saint Domingue was at the heart of the "plantation complex" during this period, passing its mantle to Jamaica only after 1791.

8. Free coloreds had reached 22 percent of the free population in 1752 (3,819 out of a total free population of 17,745), rising to 6,897 out of 26,335 (26 percent) in 1775, despite the rapid growth of the white population through immigration during that period, and thereafter meteorically to more or less half of the free population by 1788. The 1752 population figures are from AN SOM G1 509 piece 24.

9. The conquest of the highlands of the colony by coffee is detailed in Trouillot, "Motion in the System," 331–88. In his alternate explanation for the beginning of the coffee boom, Trouillot points out that Debien found that the very earliest experimenters with coffee in the 1750s and 1760s were white professionals, craftsmen, and public functionaries who left the trade when prices declined in response to rapidly increasing production and were replaced by the freedmen (Trouillot cites Debien, *Les colons de Saint-Domingue,* 350). Debien's sources might be more likely to describe the experience of the white participants in the coffee business, who were, as all sources acknowledge, in the minority in the industry by the end of the 1760s. Trouillot continues with the argument that has been outlined above, that free coloreds were already present in the coffee-growing areas when coffee became an important crop, giving them an advantage over late-coming whites (352–53).

10. Trouillot, "Coffee Planters and Coffee Slaves," 127.

11. AN SOM G1 509 piece 32. This figure is obviously a rough estimate, based on the assumptions that all pieces of land in coffee production had an equal chance of appearing in the notarial record, that the census data is accurate, and that the free coloreds in the sample are representative of the free colored population as a whole. Still, it gives some indication of the importance of free coloreds in the coffee industry in the colony.

12. AN SOM Not. 1536n, 7/6/79.

13. Not. 1540n, 1/3/85.

14. Not. 1536n, 1/3/78.

15. Not. 86n, 23/1/86.

16. Not 525n 86, 19/7/79 for the North province sale, Not. 1178n, 7/4/82, for the Mirebalais sale.

17. Not. 1540n, 27/3/85. Notaries would commonly copy descriptions of land verbatim from earlier acts unless the owners had made some significant improvements.

18. Not. 201n, 15/6/88.

19. Not 1535n, 16/10/77.

20. Not. 1536n, 3/2/79.

21. The geography and urbanization history of these cities and towns is described in Moreau de St. Méry, *Description de la partie française*, 1:12–149 (Fort Dauphin), 1:294–607 (Cap Français), 2:902–19 (Mirebalais), 2:936–72 (Croix des Bouquets), and 2:973–1084 (Port-au-Prince). The preceding paragraphs summarize this extensive primary source, to which the interested reader is referred.

22. Not. 1399n, 23/5/83.

23. Not. 191n, 26/7/85.

24. Archives Départementales E-1715 (Saulx-Tavanes), in Robert and Elborg Forster, eds., *European Society in the 18th Century*, 299.

25. Of course, a good deal of Saint Domingue's food supply was imported, much of it from the northern colonies of North America.

26. AN SOM G1 509 piece 32. Pastureland in this calculation probably includes fallow.

27. Moreau de St. Méry, *Loix et constitutions*, 3:94, Article 52 of the Louisiana *Code Noir*, corresponding to Art. 57 of the old code.

28. "Arrêt du Conseil," 5/10/75, in Moreau de St. Méry, *Loix et constitutions*, 4:609. Moreau de St. Méry chose this example because of its size and because of the celebrated nature of the case. Most white heirs gave up somewhat more gracefully than the cousins in this case—but then, most others gave up less.

29. Not. 174n, 7/5/78.

30. Not. 177n, 22/8/80, rental of a six-room house in the rue St. Joseph (a new area at the south end of the town where property values were generally moderate) evaluated at 14,760 *livres;* Not. 175n, 9/12/78, sale of a six-room house in the rue de Penthievre (a somewhat tonier neighborhood) for 18,000 *livres;* Not. 177n, 31/3/81, sale of a large eight-room house in the rue St. Pierre (a mixed neighborhood) for 45,500 *livres.*

31. AN SOM Greffe de Port-au-Prince (Gr2) 118, 28/2/82 and 677–78 29/9/84.

32. Not. 178n, 8/8/81.

33. Not. 1537n, 12/3/81.

34. Not. 1538n, 18/12/82. Both acts were quite clear in describing her as a free person. By claiming that she was required to serve him for the remainder of his time in the colony, he was alleging that he had made advance payment of wages that she was required to repay through her labor.

35. Not. 1399n, 23/5/83.

36. Not. 1394n, 11/11/79.

37. AN SOM F/3/91, 143.

38. The rental was Not. 1395n, 3/12/79, and one or the other sister appears as *habitant* several times, the latest in Not. 1405n, 31/3/88.

39. Not. 1168n, 11/5/77.

40. Not. 200n, 11/4/88.

41. As, for example, AN SOM G1 495, entry "Milla" on the rue St. Laurent no. 7, or entry "Marcon *ci-devant* la Fleur" on the rue de la Providence no. 7.

42. Not. 191n, 14/7/85, 15/7/85, and 15/9/85.

43. The 64,000 *livre* house appears in Not. 186n, 8/4/84, and was located in the rue Espagnolle, at no. 733. It rented for 7,200 *livres* a year on a long-term contract.

44. Not. 1381n 33 29/3/85.

45. Not. 1402n, 20/10/85.

46. Not. 1403n, 9/2/86.

47. Wimpffen, *Voyage à Saint-Domingue*, in Pluchon, *Haiti au XVIIIe siècle*, 243–49.

48. Not. 86n, 20/5/87.

49. Not. 1397n, 23/1/81.

50. Found in AN SOM F/3/91, Collection Moreau de St. Méry, 145–55.

CHAPTER SEVEN. ENTREPRENEURSHIP

1. The land is mentioned in Not. 1170n, 14/6/78.

2. Not. 1170n, 14/6/78.

3. Not. 87n, 1/11/87, for the coffee plantation; Not. 1388n 31, 9/3/82, for the pastureland in Port-au-Prince; Not. 1387n 127, 13/11/81, for a developed urban property in Port-au-Prince; and Not. 87n, 23/7/87, for an urban lot (very low rent, next to the municipal sewer) in Mirebalais.

4. Wimpffen, *Voyage à Saint-Domingue*, in Pluchon, *Haiti au XVIIIe Siècle*, 134–38, 237–42; quote, 138.

5. F. G. Brueys d'Aigalliers, "De l'emploi que les habitants de Saint-Domingue font de leur revenus, année 1764," from *Oeuvres choisies de F. G. Brueys d'Aigalliers*, 55–58, reproduced in Pluchon, *Haiti au XVIIIe siècle*, 291–92.

6. Robert Forster, *Merchants, Landlords, Magistrates: The Depont Family in Eighteenth-Century France*, especially chapter 1.

7. Butel, "L'Essor Antillais," in Pluchon, *Histoire des Antilles*, 132.

8. Such as a parcel of 100 *carreaux* in Plaisance involved in a disputed inheritance in Not. 1399n, 15/5/83.

9. AN SOM F/3/91, 148.

10. Based on 562 acts of sale of land from 1776–91. Credit was occasionally extended but not officially noted in the notarial act; the extent of this phenomenon cannot be measured here but may be assumed to follow the pattern of regular and overt credit.

11. Pierre Pluchon, "Le Spectacle Colonial" in Pluchon, ed., *Histoire des Antilles*, 203–4.

12. In chapter 5 of this work, see the section dealing with slave demography.

13. AN SOM F/3/91 folio 19, 28/9/39.

14. AN SOM G1 509 piece 32.

15. Wimpffen, *Voyage à Saint-Domingue*, in Pluchon, *Haiti au XVIIIe Siècle*, 122–27.

16. Not. 1535n, 10/8/77.

17. Not. 203n, 26/12/88.

18. Renewals in Not. 1384n 174, 4/11/78; 1389n 105, 21/11/83; 1392n 84, 9/11/86.

19. Not. 1399n, 5/3/83. He is sometimes referred to as "formerly known as Cochet," although he got to be fairly well known as Pavie as his plantations made money.

20. See Wimpffen, in his chapter on the establishment of a new plantation, *Voyage à Saint-Domingue*, in Pluchon, *Haiti au XVIIIe siècle*, 243–49.

21. Forster, *Merchants, Landlords, Magistrates*, 62.

22. Wimpffen, *Voyage à Saint-Domingue*, in Pluchon, *Haiti au XVIIIe siècle*, 244.

23. N = 211 sales of slaves by free coloreds to whites, 140 sales by whites to free coloreds, and 268 sales between free coloreds. Sales described as *comptant*, or on account, were defined as noncredit sales, as they were, in principle anyway, repayments of old debts instead of creation of new ones. Pawns were defined as credit sales for the proportion of the estimated market value of the slave that was not paid out at the time of the pawn. If final payment was promised within fifteen days or on the day the purchaser took possession, the acts were considered cash sales.

24. Cornelius de Pauw, "The White Creoles," in Pluchon, *Haiti au XVIIIe siècle*, 292–94.

25. Peabody, "Race, Slavery and French Law," 4.

26. Among them Julien Raimond, in his *mémoires* to the Minister of Marine, AN SOM F/3/91 190–92.

27. AN SOM G1 509 pieces 31 and 38.

28. Not. 187n, 1/7/84.

29. Not. 1298n, 12/7/85; see appendix 3.

30. Not. 1538n, 15/3/82.

31. In his will, and at the beginning of the last chapter: Not. 1538n, 4/2/82.

32. Not. 199n, 4/12/87.

33. Jacques Ménétra, *Journal de ma vie*, is the life story of one such *compagnon* that casts great light on the institution as a whole.

34. Not. 186n, 8/5/84. This slave cost 3,000 *livres*, at least 50 percent over the going price for female slaves without special talents.

35. Not. 693, 9/8/80.

36. Out of 11 *sociétés* in my sample that were founded during the period under study, 5 were dissolved during this period, 4 of these before their originally stated renewal date.

37. Not. 525n 106, 17/6/79.

38. Not. 178n, 25/5/81.

39. Not. 524n, 14/11/78. The house was to be solidly constructed of hardwood on a masonry foundation with a tile roof. However, it was rather small, with one large room and a kitchen. It seemingly was of respectable value although no specific figure was stated; other small houses in Cap rented for 400–1000 *livres* a year, e.g., Not. 1617, 30/11/81, two *cabi-*

nets for 400 *livres*/yr.; Not. 1532, 11/7/78, one *chambre* in masonry, repairs required, for 500 *livres*/yr.; Not. 176n, 3/11/79, *chambre* and *cabinet* in masonry for 1,044 *livres*/yr.

40. Not. 1616, 14/5/80.

41. Not. 182n, 9/2/83.

CHAPTER EIGHT. NON-ECONOMIC COMPONENTS OF SOCIAL STATUS

1. Especially Julien Raimond, second and third memoirs to the Minister of Marine, ca. 1783, AN SOM F/3/91 nos. 185 and 186, *Réclamations addressées à l'Assemblée Nationale* (Paris: n.p., 1790), and his *Observations sur l'origine et les progrés du préjugé* (Paris: n.p., 1791).

2. Raimond, third memoir to the Minister of Marine.

3. Members of the Chambre de l'Agriculture limited themselves to *legitimate* quarterons born free. AN SOM F/3/125 44.

4. Moreau de St. Méry, *Description de la partie française*, 83–101.

5. Moreau de St. Méry, *Description de la partie française*, 91.

6. Hilliard d'Auberteuil, *Considerations sur l'état*, 1:74.

7. This case and the whole phenomenon are discussed (and condemned) in Hilliard d'Auberteuil, *Considerations sur l'état*, 1:82–83.

8. R. P. Jean-Baptiste Labat, *Nouveau voyage aux Isles de l'Amérique* (Paris: n.p., 1742), 114–15.

9. Yvan Debbasch, *Couleur et liberté: Le jeu du critère ethnique dans un ordre juridique esclavagiste*, 48.

10. Moreau de St. Méry, *Description de la partie française*, 1:100.

11. "Arrêt du Conseil Superieur du Cap," 2/1/1779, and "Arrêt du Conseil d'Etat," 4/13/1784, in Moreau de St. Méry, *Loix et constitutions*, 5:879–82 and 6:500–501.

12. James, *Black Jacobins*, 38–43.

13. AN SOM Not. 1404n, 14/2/87.

14. White women in Saint Domingue, the reader can be sure, absolutely never had children of color, legitimate or otherwise, or at least not children that were identified as such in the records. Moreau de St. Méry did not even consider the possibility. In the section on the various shadings of free coloreds, he describes the various outcomes of the coupling of white men (using the masculine pronoun and adjective) with women of color and between various shades of people of color of both genders (using both grammatical forms) but never between white women and men of color.

15. Not. 525n 90, 4/8/79.

16. As in Not. 782, 6/4/89.

17. Not. 1626, 3/5/88.

18. The family of Alexis Duchemin appear in Not. 86n, 8/1/86, 3/2/86, 13/2/86, 1/3/86, 4/5/86, 21/6/86, 2/12/86, 11/6/87; Not. 87n, 23/11/88, 9/2/88.

19. Verse by Gabriel-François de Brueys d'Aigalliers in 1763, cited in Frostin, *Les Révoltes blanches*, 319.

20. See, for example, Not. 1398n, 17/8/82, in which Marthe Castaing's brother Guillaume received a gift of slaves from their mother.

21. Guillaume rented an apartment under that title in Cap in Not. 1616, 14/5/80.

22. See, for example, Not. 178n, 17/7/81.

23. AN SOM E.C. 120, Marriage, 31/10/85.

24. Once again to the outrage of Julien Raimond, in his *Réclamations*, 3–4, and his *Observations*, 8. He cites the names of two *gens de couleur* who were surgeons before the 1764 regulation. The regulation appears as "Ordonnance du Roi Concernant la Chirugerie aux Colonies," in Moreau de St. Méry, *Loix et constitutions*, 4:724.

25. Not. 525n 74 (date illeg.). The son joined the Chasseurs-Volontaires, and perhaps the father anticipated that the military position would be sufficient to support him and his mother.

26. "Reglement des Administrateurs concernant le Gens de Couleur Libres," 24/6/1773 and 16/7/1773, in Moreau de St. Méry, *Loix et constitutions*, 5:448–50.

27. Not. 86n, 24/4/86.

28. Not. 86n, 4/5/86.

29. Garrigus, "Struggle for Respect," 139.

30. Not. 525n 74.

31. Not. 190n, 23/6/85.

32. Peabody, "Race, Slavery, and French Law."

33. Not. 1391n 67, 15/5/85.

34. "Règlement Provisoire des Administrateurs concernant le Luxe des Gens de Couleur," in Moreau de St. Méry, *Loix et constitutions*, 5:855–57.

35. The prohibition on coaches was a very sore point with Julien Raimond, who might have been expected to be able to afford one; he mentions it both in his *Réclamations*, 3–4, and his *Observations*, 10.

36. Not. 1403n, 26/6/86.

37. Not. 1402n, 21/7/85.

38. Not. 1290n, 1/12/77.

39. The First Lady of Haiti during the 1970s to 1984, Michelle Bennett Duvalier, owned a large collection of fur coats, kept in her "summer house" in the (somewhat cooler) heights overlooking Port-au-Prince. An urban legend holds that she and her friends used to turn up the air conditioning as high as it would go, light a fire in the fireplace, and wear the coats. Unfortunately for LeMoine and the other inhabitants of the island, the eighteenth century had not yet developed air conditioning. LeMoine's son traveled widely, as a noncommissioned officer in the French Navy and Merchant Marine, and possibly Augustin had done some voyaging in his youth to places where he would need a warm coat.

40. Moreau de St. Méry, *Description de la partie française*, 105–6.

41. Not. 1401n, 16/9/84.

42. Not. 1299n, 1/2/87.

43. Not. 1300n, 29/9/88.

44. Not. 1399n, 12/4/83. The parenthesized roman numerals distinguish individuals in the Laporte extended family who share the same name. Young Gaspard was the third-oldest member of the clan to hold that name. See appendix 1.

45. Not. 176n, 12/8/79.

46. Not. 1635n, 15/7/78.

47. Not. 1299n, 31/3/87.

48. "Ordonnance des Administrateurs pour l'établissement d'une maréchaussée," Art. 25, 3/27/1721, in Moreau de St. Méry, *Loix et constitutions*, 2:731.

49. "Ordonnance des Administrateurs pour l'établissement d'une maréchaussée," Art. 32, 3/27/1721, in Moreau de St. Méry, *Loix et constitutions*, 2:732.

50. "Arrêt du Conseil du Cap touchant la Porte d'armes et qui l'interdit expressément aux Negres et Mulâtres libres," 2/3/1761, Moreau de St. Méry, *Loix et constitutions*, 4:342–43.

51. Moreau de St. Méry, *Description de la partie française*, 229–30 (Vincent) and 186–87 (Auba).

52. Not. 1290n, 1/12/77.

53. The phenomenon is discussed in Garrigus, "Sons of the Same Father."

54. Not. 1399n, 14/2/83.

55. Moreau de St. Méry, *Description de la partie française*, 103.

56. Not. 694, 1/9/81.

57. Not. 1536n, 2/3/78.

58. Not. 1399n, 12/4/83.

59. Not. 1536n, 3/2/79.

60. Not. 86n, 11/5/86.

61. Not. 1394, 6/2/86.

62. Not. 196n, 17/10/86.

63. Not. 1178n, 29/3/82.

64. Not. 177n, 31/3/81.

65. Art. 3, Moreau de St. Méry, *Loix et constitutions*, 1:415.

66. Moreau de St. Méry, *Description de la partie française*, 339.

67. Wimpffen, *Voyage à Saint-Domingue*, in Pluchon, *Haiti au XVIIIe siècle*, 222.

68. Not. 1175n, 13/10/80.

69. See, for example, in Not. 1289n, 17/12/76, the will of one Dame Marie Anne Charlotte Dèpe, a white woman.

70. The wills—Not. 1290n, 18/9/77, for Augustin and Not. 1295n, 25/10/80, for Bertrand —were both notarized by the good Catholic Leprestre.

71. Toussaint appeared as principal actor in the following notarial acts: Not. 525n 106, 17/8/79; Not. 178n, 25/5/81; Not. 178n, 31/7/81; Not. 694, 9/2/81; Not. 525n 109, 18/8/79.

72. Not. 189n, 24/3/85.

73. Not. 194n, 6/4/86.

74. Not. 525n 26, 24/2/79.

75. Not. 525n 52, 30/4/79.

76. Not. 525n 132, 7/11/79.
77. E.C. 19, 9/1/81.
78. E.C. 20, 4/4/82.

CHAPTER NINE. FAMILY RELATIONSHIPS AND SOCIAL ADVANCEMENT

1. Not. 1168n, 4/1/77.

2. Moreau de St. Méry, *Description de la partie française,* 101, 104. Raimond, *Réponse aux considérations.*

3. *Code Noir,* Art. 11, in Moreau de St. Méry, *Loix et constitutions,* 1:416.

4. Alexis Phaeton and Marie Angelique Angerone, recently freed in 1779, purchased their two legitimate children from their former master; Not. 1293n, 9/7/79. Ladouceur and Therese, noted in the record as legitimately married, but no date given, were sold, possibly to a relative, in Cap in 1781; Not. 178n, 21/8/81. Boue and Toinette, still slaves in 1786, authorized their free, minor, legitimate son Joseph Manda's marriage to his slave, Marianne Quinque in Cap; Not. 195n, 9/6/86. Philippe and Fanchon's legitimate son Jacques, a free carpenter living in Petite Anse, married Marie Jeanne Negre Zelimé in 1787, his parents having died in slavery some years before; Not. 198n, 15/8/87.

5. Art. 9, Moreau de St. Méry, *Loix et constitutions,* 1:416.

6. Francois Bernard, native of the Spanish colony of Santo Domingo, married his slave Catin, a black Creole, in Mirebalais in 1788, Not. 87n, 9/11/88.

7. Jean *dit* Lafortune, slave of "nation" Arada, married his mistress, Magdelaine, of "nation" Congo, on 12 July 1784, legitimizing their children Michel, Magdelaine, Marie Noelle, Nicolas, Toussaint, and Modeste. The children's ages do not appear in the act, but the bride was aged 40 and the groom 50. E.C. 120, 12/7/84.

8. *Code Noir,* Moreau de St. Méry, *Loix et constitutions,* 1:416, "Ordonnance des Administrateurs concernant le concubinage avec les esclaves," 18/12/13, in Moreau de St. Méry, *Loix et constitutions,* 2:406.

9. "Lettre du Ministre," in Moreau de St. Méry, *Loix et constitutions,* 4:520. "Alliance" may mean matrimonial alliance; this is unclear from context. No evidence exists that it was ever enforced in either sense.

10. See, for example, James, *Black Jacobins,* 32.

11. See, for example, Alex Haley, *Roots,* 427–28, in which the author's ancestor Kissy is raped by her master, contributing a white admixture to the heritage of the Haley family. Although described by its author as "not history, but a legend for my people," *Roots* represents attitudes of the general public, especially the African American public, toward the question of miscegenation under slavery.

12. Hilliard d'Auberteuil, *Considerations sur l'état,* 2:94.

13. The average age of the freed children was 11.9 years, whereas the average age of all slave children was 7.9.

14. Not. 1396n, 3/8/80.

15. Not. 200n, 27/3/88.

16. "Arrêt du Conseil," 5/10/75, in Moreau de St. Méry, *Loix et constitutions*, 4:609.

17. Not. 1300n, 13/10/88.

18. Not. 1396n, 15/7/80.

19. Garrigus, "Sons of the Same Father," 14, citing his notarial sample from the 1760s in the South province. The sources for this work do not include acts in which only whites participated, but white women made up only about 6 percent (22 out of 383) of the white participants in sales of land with both white and free colored participants.

20. AN SOM G1 495a.

21. AN SOM G1495a.

22. Not. 195n, 21/8/86.

23. Not. 195n, 31/8/86.

24. Not. 188n, 27/12/84.

25. AN SOM Greffe 2, 254–55.

26. Moreau de St. Méry, *Description de la partie française*, 107.

27. James, *Black Jacobins*, 32. Not even the population figures were right.

28. Not. 197n, 18/1/87.

29. Not. 182n, 27/2/83.

30. Not. 1396n, 6/3/80 (will) and 10/3/80 (inventory).

31. Not. 195n, 3/8/86.

32. Not. 200n, 28/1/88.

33. Not. 1391n 134, (date illeg.) December 1785.

34. Raimond, *Observations sur l'origine*.

35. Not. 1388n 47, 2/4/82.

36. Not. 1168n, 2/3/77.

37. Not. 1168n, 1/6/77.

38. Not. 87n, 7/7/88.

39. Not. 1171n, 2/7/78.

40. Value of contribution was estimated by reducing the value of gifts promised with a delay of more than a year by 10 percent per year, by evaluating land at the average value for that parish and description of land if not evaluated in the act, and by evaluating slaves at 2,000 *livres* each. Contracts were deemed substantially equal in their terms if estimated value of one party's contribution did not exceed the other's by more than 25 percent. Only amounts entering into a community of property were taken into account.

41. Not. 190n, 21/5/85.

42. Not. 1401n, 16/9/84.

CHAPTER TEN. PLANTER ELITES

1. Not. 1535n, 16/10/77.

2. Not. 1537n, 31/3/81.

3. Rentals of land: Not. 1535n, 16/2/78, and Not. 1535n, 22/12/77.

4. "Arrêt du Conseil," 5/10/75, in Moreau de St. Méry, *Loix et constitutions*, 4:609.

5. Rental contracts found in AN SOM Not. 1535n, 22/12/77, for 200 *carreaux* and 1535n, 16/10/77, for at least 24 *carreaux* of sugar cane fields.

6. Not. 1537, 6/7/84.

7. Not. 1616, 14/5/80.

8. The Foäche sugar plantation is the subject of Gabriel Debien's *Plantations et esclaves*.

9. AN SOM G1 495a.

10. Not. 191n, 26/7/85.

11. Not. 1537n, 30/3/81.

12. Not. 1538n, 4/2/82, in which he gives the plantation, and codicil, 23/11/82, in which he substitutes the slaves, 12,000 *livres*, and a collection of high-status household goods.

13. Society formed in Not. 1536n, 20/7/79, and dissolved in Not. 1538n, 15/3/82.

14. Not. 1538n, 15/3/82.

15. Not. 1537n, 30/3/81.

16. Not. 1394n, 25/9/78.

17. Not. 1536n, 3/2/79.

18. Letter from Commandant Mailly de la Bannière, Limbé, to M. le Commandant du Quartier (Paul Cairou), AN SOM F/3/91 156.

19. See, for example, Not. 1/12/81, where he was a witness at the marriage of former Chasseur-Volontaire Jean-Baptiste Lagarde.

20. Pincemaille appeared as witness, for example, at the marriage of Pierre *dit* Franjou, mason, to his slave Marie Therèse *dite* Colette, *nation* Mandingue, Not. 1624, 2/5/87, or at the marriage of Jean Baptiste Balazar to his slave Françoise, AN SOM E.C. 119, 24/11/78.

21. This figure of 21 includes such things as the two marriages cited in the previous note, where a member of the planter and merchant group, Jean-Baptiste Chavanne, was present at and witnessed the manumission of a slave through marriage to her master—hardly playing a key role in the process although indicative of his personal and somewhat peculiar (for the planter and merchant elite) interest in building bridges to lower-class free coloreds.

22. The document under which he transferred the land and slaves has not survived and is not properly cited in the act in which the family wealth is revealed, Not. 1400n, 22/10/83, where they trade the land they got from him to a white neighbor for 28 *carreaux* with 10,000 growing coffee trees.

23. Garrigus, "Struggle for Respect," and also his paper titled "Some Background to Free Colored Political Activism: Julien Raimond in Saint Domingue, 1744–1784."

24. Forster, *Merchants, Landlords, Magistrates*. Forster focuses on the Deponts, who over a period of three generations went from merchants trading between La Rochelle and the colonies to robe nobles in the *parlement* of Paris, by way of extensive landholdings in the hinterland of La Rochelle and local officeholding in that city.

25. This figure for average tenure is based on analysis of 222 sales, donations, and other transfers of land where the date the seller or donor obtained the land was given.

26. Baron de Wimpffen, *Voyage à Saint-Domingue*, 131–42, and Brueys d'Aigalliers, "De l'emploi que les habitants," 55–58, both reproduced in Pluchon (ed.), *Haiti au XVIIIe siècle*.

27. Not. 1535n, 16/10/77.

28. Not. 1536n, 3/7/78.

29. Not. 1537n, 31/3/81.

30. Not. 1394, 6/2/86.

31. See the marriage contract of Achile Chavanne, Not. 1537, 6/7/84.

32. Not. 1393n, 7/9/77.

33. Raimond, third memoir to the Minister of Marine, AN SOM F/3/91 no. 186, and Chambre de l'Agriculture du Cap memorandum, AN SOM F/3/125 no. 44.

34. The Turgeau house sold in Not. 1388n 162, 16/12/82, for 17,000 *livres*, the 100 *carreaux* appear in Not. 86n, 11/6/87, the 96 *carreaux* in Not. 1390n 69, 20/6/84.

35. The contract was renewed in Not. 1384n 174, 4/11/78; 1389n 105, 21/11/83; 1392n 84, 9/11/86. Annual accountings were performed in Not. 1388n 141, 13/11/82; 1382n 146, 9/11/77; 1385n 128, 11/11/79; 1386n 107, 9/11/80; 1390n 153, 21/11/84; 1391n 117, 9/11/85.

CHAPTER ELEVEN. THE MILITARY LEADERSHIP GROUP

1. Moreau de St. Méry, *Description de la partie française,* 229–30.

2. AN SOM Not. 524n, 16/5/78.

3. AN SOM G1 495a, cadastral survey of 27/6/76.

4. AN SOM E.C. 17, 16/1/79.

5. Not. 1396n, 1/5/80, an act of sale by the chevalier that mentions the adjacency. No notarial act during the period under study deals with the *habitation* itself.

6. Not. 524n, 11/12/78.

7. Pluchon, *Histoire des Antilles et de la Guyane,* 95–106.

8. Planter elites were part of vibrant families, whereas many individuals in the military leadership group had little or no formal family ties at all. This is one of the most interesting characteristics of the group.

9. See chapter 8. Among these acts were many by Michel François Pincemaille, a Chasseurs-Volontaires noncommissioned veteran who came from a prominent planting family but who shared many of the social behaviors of the military leadership group.

10. Marriages: AN SOM Not. 177n, 8/7/80; Not. 174n, 29/1/78; E. C. 17, 24/2/78; Not. 524n, 6/3/78; burial: E. C. 17, 18/3/78; baptisms: AN SOM E.C. 17, 5/1/79; E. C. 19, 16/1/81; and E. C. 17, 15/5/77.

11. Not. 525n 1, 5/1/79.

12. Not. 178n, 3/7/81.

13. Not. 189n, 31/3/85, for the procuration, and Not. 202n, 13/9/88, for the final act.

14. Not. 203n, 23/10/88.

15. Not. 176n, 25/4/80.

16. See Not. 187n, 6/7/84 for the second will.

17. Not. 178n, 6/7/81.

18. The concept can be found explained in much greater detail in Martin Klein and Paul

Lovejoy, "Slavery in West Africa," and in its specific application to the Senegambian region, source of many slaves who came to Saint Domingue in the early days of the colony's existence, in Philip Curtin, *Economic Change in Precolonial Africa.*

19. Moreau de St. Méry, *Loix et constitutions,* 3:828.

20. Moreau de St. Méry, *Loix et constitutions,* 4:864.

21. Moreau de St. Méry, *Loix et constitutions,* 5:25–26.

22. Moreau de St. Méry, *Loix et constitutions,* 5:246–47.

23. Not. 1384n 186, 26/11/78.

24. Not. 1295n, 19/11/80.

25. Not. 24/4/82.

26. Moreau de St. Méry, *Loix et constitutions,* 3:244–46.

27. Moreau de St. Méry, *Loix et constitutions,* 4:119.

28. Moreau de St. Méry, *Loix et constitutions,* 6:344–49.

29. Not. 1398n, 19/10/82.

30. "Ordonnance Portant Reestablissement . . . ," Moreau de St. Méry, *Loix et constitutions* 6:344–49. This is the only reference to an *ecu* in the records. It is a seventeenth-century term for a money of account worth, depending on the source, either 3 *livres* or 3.33 *livres.* It is unclear what this would mean in a late-eighteenth-century context.

31. Moreau de St. Mery, *Loix et constitutions* 6:344–49. This distribution system is not so unfair as it seems, in the context of the times. Prize money paid for captured ships or other enemy property in the British Navy at the time was distributed according to a similar system; enlisted sailors shared about one-fourth of the value of the prize. The *maréchaussée* men actually seem to have gotten a better deal than the British sailors, most of whom were white.

32. Conseil Supérieur de Cap, "Arrêt qui defend . . . ," 1790, in Moreau de St. Méry, *Loix et constitutions,* 6:546.

33. Not. 1290n, 13/12/77. The beaver coat was much more valuable: 33 *livres.*

34. Not. 1399n, 12/4/83.

35. Not. 1402n, 25/7/85. His musket went for only 3 *livres,* though, and was described in poor repair.

36. M. de Carnage de Mailhert, "Memoire sur les *maréchaussées* et les piquets de gens de couleur," 28/9/1739, manuscript in AN SOM Collection Moreau de St. Méry, F/3/91 folio 19.

37. Chambre de l'Agriculture du Cap Français, "Memoire sur les defauts de la police des negres," 2/6/85, manuscript in AN SOM Collection Moreau de St. Méry, F/3/126 folio 80.

38. Moreau de St. Méry, *Loix et constitutions,* 2:756.

39. M. le Baron de Castellane, two letters to the general commanding French troops on the island, dated 6/3/86 and 10/3/86, manuscripts in Collection Moreau de St. Méry, AN SOM F/3/91, 163–65. The outcome of this case is unfortunately not recorded, but Captain Audige appears on a 1789 list of militia officers in Port-de-Paix.

40. Conseil Supérieur du Cap Français, "Arrêt . . . touchant le paiement des appointemens . . . des maréchausée," *Loix et constitutions,* 6:134–35, 141. Of course, all this became academic shortly thereafter, but the regulation illustrates a preexisting problem.

41. "Arrêt du Conseil . . . touchant les jeux defendus," in Moreau de St. Méry, *Loix et constitutions,* 6:632.

42. Collection Moreau de St. Méry, F/3/91, folio 154.

43. "Ordonnance portant re-etablissement . . . ," Moreau de St. Méry, *Loix et constitutions,* 3:344–49. This was also a common complaint against slave catchers in the American South.

44. Moreau de St. Méry, *Loix et constitutions,* 6:718.

45. "Arrêt du Conseil du Cap touchant les excès commis sur un habitant . . . ," 14/12/80, in Moreau de St. Méry, *Loix et constitutions,* 6:86–90. Furthermore, note that this case took place under the jurisdiction of the Conseil du Cap—that is, in the North province where *gens de couleur* were less numerous and less well-organized. In addition, the dead man was described as an *habitant,* that is, a landowner. Nonetheless, the police role of the free coloreds was obviously crucial.

46. Michel Réné Hilliard d'Auberteuil, *Considerations sur l'état,* 2:74, where he stated that if a free colored struck a white, colonial custom required that the sentence was amputation of the hand or death.

47. Not. 1665, 19/9/80.

48. Not. 1388n 158, 12/12/82.

49. Not. 1537n, 7/4/80.

50. Not. 1538n, 8/6/82.

51. Moreau de St. Méry, *Loix et constitutions,* 3:244–46.

52. Not. 850, 7/8/79.

53. Not. 1616, 10/5/80. Interestingly, the original request to the government for permission to free the slave Jean was made while Gentil was himself still a slave. So much for the legal incompetence of slaves to perform notarial acts.

54. Not. 1396n, 30/11/80.

55. Not. 1404n, 9/6/86.

56. Not. 1401n, 11/12/84.

57. Not. 1402n, 9/3/85; recovery of pawn, Not. 1404n, 9/6/87. The sale of the land is in a separate, private act, dated 9/3/85 and placed in the archives 24/5/85. This latter act marks the first appearance of Elisabeth Petrouille *épouse* Gentil.

58. With the exception, of course, of Augustin LeMoine's beaver coat.

59. Not. 194n 14/3/86. The official manumission of Pierre does not appear in the sample, but it may have been executed in Port-de-Paix.

60. Not. 1290n, 1/12/77. It is worth noting that no merchandise is listed, although it is clear from the papers that LeMoine was a merchant and seemingly traded overseas. It appears that LeMoine had a place of business or warehouse distinct from his residence that was not inventoried.

61. Not. 1290n, 13/12/77.

62. Not. 1295n, 25/10/80.

63. Not. 1295n, 25/10/80.

64. Not. 1297n, 12/8/82.

65. The names and ranks of identified military leaders in the sample are listed in appendix 2.

66. AN SOM G1495a. *Barraque* means "shed" with connotations of ruin and disorder.

67. Not. 524n, 20/2/77.

68. Not. 178n, 20/6/81.

69. Not. 524n, 1/3/78.

70. Lots of his speculations were done on credit. He rented places and sublet them. He may have sold his grocery business or at least collected on some of those endless lists of outstanding debts. Such information is lost without an account book.

71. Not. 178n, 17/7/81, act in which the lease was resolved and back rent paid.

72. Not. 191n, 14/7/85.

73. Not. 188n, 27/12/84.

74. Not. 174n, 20/5/78.

75. Not. 178n, 17/7/81.

76. Not. 179n, 31/12/81.

77. Not. 195n, 22/9/86.

78. Not. 87n, 28/5/88. It was worth only 660 *livres,* the smallest and least desirable of his lots, so one might suppose that Pierre had had a fight with his former mistress and was pensioning her off.

79. Not. 1388n no. 31, 9/3/82. This was not the best land in the colony, but 128 *carreaux* of anything is a lot of land.

80. A sale of land, in 1787. Not. 87n, 1/11/87.

81. Not. 87n, 28/5/88.

82. Not. 1536n, 6/7/78.

83. Not. 1170n, 14/6/78.

84. Not. 84n, 11/9/84.

85. Partnership between the two renewed in Not. 1384n 174, 4/11/78; 1389n 105, 21/11/83; 1392n 84, 9/11/86. Intermediate accountings made in Not. 1388n 141, 13/11/82; 1382n 145, 9/11/77; 1385n 128, 11/11/79; 1386n 107, 9/11/80; 1390n 153, 21/11/84; 1391n 117, 9/11/85.

86. "Règlement des Administrateurs concernant le Gens de Couleur Libres," 24/6/1773 and 16/7/1773, in Moreau de St. Méry, *Loix et constitutions,* 5:448–50.

87. Not. 202n, 13/9/88, and Not. 203n, 23/10/88.

88. Not. 179n, 24/12/81.

89. Not. 1081, 21/4/82. That would be 14 *displacement* tons. Such a vessel would not hold 14 tons of cargo.

90. Not. 184n, 2/12/83, for the partnership and Not. 187n, 1/7/84, for the procuration containing the orders to the captain.

Works Cited

MANUSCRIPT PRIMARY SOURCES

Archives Nationales Françaises. Archives Départementales de Loire Maritime. Private archives (Section E). Saulx-Tavanes, E-1715. Cited in Robert Forster and Elborg Forster, eds. *European Society in the 18th Century.* New York: Harper and Row, 1969.

Archives Nationales Françaises. Section Outre-Mer. Censuses and Cadastral Surveys (Section G). Cadastral survey of Cap Français, 1776, G1 495a.

Archives Nationales Françaises. Section Outre-Mer. Censuses and Cadastral Surveys (Section G). Census tables for 1754, 1777, 1780, and 1788, G1 509, pieces 28, 31, 36, and 38.

Archives Nationales Françaises. Section Outre-Mer. Collection Moreau de St. Méry (Section F). M. de Carnage de Mailhert, "Memoire sur les maréchaussées et les piquets de gens de couleur," F/3/91 piece 19. M. le Comte d'Argout, "Lettre a M. le Ministre sur les Chasseurs Mulatres," F/3/91 piece 139. M. le Baron de Castellan, two letters to the general commanding French troops on the island, dated 6/3/86 and 10/3/86, F/3/91, pieces 163–65. Julien Raimond, "Troisième mémoire a Monseigneur le Maréchal de Castries Ministre et Secrétaire d'État au Département de la Marine," F/3/91 pieces 190–92. Chambre de l'Agriculture du Cap Français, Memorandum, F/3/125 piece 44. Chambre de l'Agriculture du Cap Français, "Memoire sur les defauts de la police des negres," F/3/126 piece 80.

Archives Nationales Françaises. Section Outre-Mer. Colonial military personnel records (Section D2C). Volumes: 41, Savannah expedition; 114, Armée de Saint-Domingue (Leclerc expedition and Santo Domingo garrison); 115, Militia.

Archives Nationales Françaises. Section Outre-Mer. Colonial personnel records, individual files (Section E). *Colonel* Laurent Francois Le Noir de Rouvray, commander of the Chasseurs-Volontaires de Saint-Domingue, E278.

Archives Nationales Françaises. Section Outre-Mer. Dépôt des Fortifications des Colonies. Saint Domingue. M. le Comte de Nolivos. "Instructions sur quelques objects du service des etats majors de la colonies, des troupes, et des milices," 2/12/70, carton 1.

Archives Nationales Françaises. Section Outre-Mer. Dépôt des Papiers Publiques des Colonies. État Civil de Saint-Domingue. Volumes: 16–21, Cap Français; 120, Limonade; 121, Sainte-Suzanne.

Archives Nationales Françaises. Section Outre-Mer. Dépôt des Papiers Publiques des Colonies. Greffe de Saint-Domingue. Volumes: 2–4, Conseil Supérieur de Port-au-Prince; 21, Sénéchausée de Port-au-Prince.

Archives Nationales Françaises. Section Outre-Mer. Dépôt des Papiers Publiques des Colonies. Notariat de Saint-Domingue. Volumes: 82–87, Beaudoulx, Mirebalais, 1777–92; 173–203, Bordier Jeune, Cap Français, 1776–78; 524–25, Doré, Cap Français, 1755–80; 1168–79, Lamauve, Mirebalais, 1777–97; 1289–1301, Leprestre, Fort Dauphin, 1776–96; 1382–92, Michel, Port-au-Prince, 1777–86; 1393–1405, Michel, Limonade, 1777–1801; 1535–40, Renaudot, Croix des Bouquets, 1777–85. In addition, selected acts are cited from the following: 361–72, Cassanet, Cap Français, 1780–87; 405–14, Cormeaux de la Chapelle, Cap Français, 1776–An X; 659–60, Fromentin, Cap Français, 1777–86; 782–90, Gerard, Cap Français, 1776–1800; 851–70, Grimperel, Cap Français, 1776–88; 1084–1107, Hourclatx, Cap Français, 1777–87; 1083, Haumont, Le Borgne, 1781; 1165–67, Lamarre, Cap, 1779–87; 1268, Lemay, Plaisance, 1778–88; 1407–8, Minée, l'Acul, 1778–87; 1450–55, Mouttet, Cap Français, 1778–82; 1545–54, Rivery, Cap Français, 1772–88; 1622–37, Tach, Cap Français, 1776–88; 1658–81, Thomin, Port-au-Prince, 1777–90.

Archives Nationales Françaises. Section Outre-Mer. Incoming state correspondence, pre-revolutionary, Saint Domingue (Section C9A). Governor de Fayet of Saint Domingue letter to Minister of Marine Maurepas, 16/5/1733, C9A no. 37.

PRINTED PRIMARY SOURCES

Affiches Américaines. Cap Français, Saint Domingue, 30/3/79.

Brueys d'Aigalliers, F. G. "De l'Emploi que les habitants de Saint-Domingue font de leur revenus, année 1764." In *Oeuvres choisies de F. G. Brueys d'Aigalliers,* 55–58. Nimes, 1805. Reprinted in *Haiti au XVIIIe siècle: Richesse et esclavage dans une colonie française,* ed. Pierre Pluchon. Paris: Karthala, 1993.

Ferrière, Claude de. *La Science parfaite des notaires ou le parfait notaire.* Paris, 1771.

Hilliard d'Auberteuil, Michel Réné. *Considerations sur l'état présent de la colonie française de Saint-Domingue.* Paris, 1777.

Labat, R. P. Jean-Baptiste. *Nouveau Voyage aux isles de l'Amérique.* Paris, 1742.

Ménétra, Jacques. *Journal de ma vie.* Paris, 1805.

Moreau de St. Méry, Médéric Louis Elie. *Considerations sur l'état présent des colonies.* Paris, 1791.

———. *Description de la partie espagnole de Saint-Domingue.* Philadelphia, 1796.

———. *Description topographique, physique civile, politique et historique de la partie française de l'isle de Saint-Domingue.* Paris, 2d ed., 1797; reprint, ed. Blanche Maurel and Etienne Taillemite, Paris: Société de l'Histoire des Colonies Françaises, 1958.

———. *Loix et constitutions des colonies françaises de l'Amérique sous le vent.* Paris, 1784–90.

Pauw, Cornelius de. "The White Creoles." In *Philosophical Research on the Americans, or Interesting Notes to Serve as a History of the Human Species.* Vol. 2:140–42. Berlin, 1774. Quoted in *Haiti au XVIIIe siècle: Richesse et esclavage dans une colonie francaise,* ed. Pierre Pluchon. Paris: Karthala, 1993, 292–94.

Raimond, Julien. *Observations sur l'origine et les progrés du préjugé contre les hommes de couleur.* Paris, 1791.

————. *Réclamations addressées à l'Assemblée nationale par les citoyens de couleur de l'Isle de Saint-Domingue.* Paris, 1790.

————. *Réponse aux considérations de M. Moreau dit St. Méry, député à l'Assemblée national sur les colonies par M. Raimond, citoyen de couleur de Saint-Domingue.* Paris, 1791.

Wimpffen, Alexandre-Stanislas (Baron) de. *Voyage à Saint-Domingue pendant les années 1788, 1789, 1790.* Paris, 1797. In *Haiti au XVIIIe siècle: Richesse et esclavage dans une colonie française,* ed. Pierre Pluchon. Paris: Karthala, 1993.

SECONDARY SOURCES

Bergad, Laird, Fe Iglesias Garcia, and Maria del Carmen Barcia. *The Cuban Slave Market, 1790–1880.* Cambridge Latin American Studies Series. Cambridge: Cambridge Univ. Press, 1995.

Buckley, Roger Norman, ed. *The Haitian Journal of Lieutenant Howard, of the York Hussars, 1796–1798.* Knoxville: Univ. of Tennessee Press, 1985.

Burns, E. Bradford. *A History of Brazil.* New York: Columbia Univ. Press, 1993.

Cohen, David, and Jack Greene, eds. *Neither Slave nor Free: The Freedman of African Descent in the Slave Societies of the New World.* Baltimore: Johns Hopkins Univ. Press, 1972.

Cox, Edward. *Free Coloreds in the Slave Societies of St. Kitts and Grenada, 1763–1833.* Knoxville: Univ. of Tennessee Press, 1984.

Curtin, Philip. *The Atlantic Slave Trade: A Census.* Madison: Univ. of Wisconsin Press, 1969.

————. *Economic Change in Precolonial Africa: Senegambia in the Era of the Slave Trade.* Madison: Univ. of Wisconsin Press, 1975.

————. *Rise and Fall of the Plantation Complex: Essays in Atlantic History.* Cambridge: Cambridge Univ. Press, 1990.

————. *Two Jamaicas: The Role of Ideas in a Tropical Colony, 1830–1865.* New York: Atheneum, 1970.

Debbasch, Yvan. *Couleur et liberté: Le Jeu du critère ethnique dans un ordre juridique esclavagiste.* Université de Strasbourg, Annales de la Faculté de Droit et des Sciences Politiques et Economiques de Strasbourg, no. 16. Paris: Presses Universitaires, 1967.

Debien, Gabriel. *Les Colons de Saint-Domingue et la Revolution: Etudes antillaises.* Paris: Colin, 1956.

————. *Les Esclaves aux Antilles françaises, XVIIe–XVIIIe siècles.* Basse-Terre and Fort-de-France: Société d'Histoire de la Guadeloupe and Société d'Histoire de la Martinique, 1974.

———— *Une Plantation à Saint-Domingue: La Sucrerie Galbard du fort, 1690–1802.* Cairo, 1941.

————. *Plantations et esclaves à Saint-Domingue: La Sucrerie Foäche.* Dakar, 1962.

————. "Toussaint Louverture avant 1789: Legendes et réalités." *Conjonction* 134 (June/July 1977).

Eltis, David. *Europe and the Rise of African Slavery in the Americas: The English Experience in Comparative Perspective.* Forthcoming.

Eltis, David, and Stanley Engerman. "Fluctuations in Sex and Age Ratios in the Transatlantic Slave Trade, 1663–1864." *Economic History Review,* 46:2 (May 1993), 308–23.

Fick, Carolyn. *The Making of Haiti: The Saint Domingue Revolution from Below.* Knoxville: Univ. of Tennessee Press, 1990.

Fogel, Robert, and Stanley Engerman. *Time on the Cross: The Economics of American Negro Slavery.* Boston: Little, Brown, 1974.

Forster, Robert. *Merchants, Landlords, Magistrates: The Depont Family in Eighteenth-Century France.* Baltimore: Johns Hopkins Univ. Press, 1980.

———. "A Sugar Plantation on Saint Domingue." Paper presented to the General Seminar in History at Johns Hopkins University, n.d.

Forster, Robert, and Elborg Forster, eds. *European Society in the 18th Century.* New York: Harper and Row, 1969.

Fouchard, Jean. *The Haitian Maroons: Liberty or Death.* Trans. A. Faulkner Watts. New York: Blyden Press, 1981.

Frostin, Charles. *Les Révoltes blanches à Saint-Domingue aux XVIIe–XVIIIe siècles.* Paris: L'École, 1975.

Gallenga, Antonio C. *The Pearl of the Antilles.* London: Chapman and Hall, 1873.

Garrigus, John. "Blue and Brown: Contraband Indigo and the Rise of a Free Colored Planter Class in French Saint Domingue." *Americas* 50, no. 2 (October 1993): 233–63.

———. "Catalyst or Catastrophe?: Saint Domingue's Free Men of Color and the Battle of Savannah, 1779–1782." *Revista/Review Interamericana* 22:1–2 (spring/summer 1992), 109–125.

———. "Colour, Class and Identity on the Eve of the Haitian Revolution: Saint Domingue's Free Colored Elite as *Colons Américains.*" In *Against the Odds: Free Blacks in the Slave Societies of the Americas,* ed. Jane Landers, 20–43. Portland OR: Frank Cass, 1996.

———. "Some Background to Free Colored Political Activism: Julien Raimond in Saint Domingue, 1744–1784." Paper presented to the Association of Caribbean Historians, Martinique, April 13–17, 1987.

———. "Sons of the Same Father: Gender, Race, and Citizenship in French Saint Domingue, 1760–1789." In *Society, Politics and Culture in Eighteenth-Century France: Papers of a Conference in French History to Honor Dr. Robert Forster,* ed. Jack Censer. College Station: Pennsylvania State Univ. Press, 1997.

———. "A Struggle for Respect: The Free Coloreds of Pre-Revolutionary Saint Domingue, 1760–1769." Ph.D. diss., Johns Hopkins University, 1988.

Geggus, David P. "The Haitian Revolution." In *The Modern Caribbean,* ed. Franklin Knight. Chapel Hill: Univ. of North Carolina Press, 1989.

———. "Haitian Voodoo in the Eighteenth Century: Language, Culture, Resistance." *Jahrbuch für Geschichte von Staat, Windschaft und Geschelschaft Weinamerikas* 28 (1991): 1–31.

———. "Sex Ratio, Age, and Ethnicity in the Atlantic Slave Trade: Data from French Shipping and Plantation Records." *Journal of African History* 30 (1989): 23–44.

———. "Slave and Free Colored Women in Saint Domingue." In David B. Gaspar and Darlene C. Hine, eds. *More than Chattel: Black Women and Slavery in the Americas,* 259–78. Bloomington: Indiana Univ. Press, 1996.

————. *Slavery, War and Revolution: The British Occupation of Saint Domingue, 1793–1798.* Oxford: Clarendon, 1982.

————. "The Slaves of British-Occupied Saint Domingue: An Analysis of the Workforces of 197 Absentee Plantations, 1796–97." *Caribbean Studies* 18 (1978): 5–41.

————. "Sugar and Coffee Cultivation in Saint Domingue and the Shaping of the Slave Labor Force." In *Cultivation and Culture: Labor and the Shaping of Slave Life in the Americas*, ed. Ira Berlin and Philip Morgan, 73–97. Charlottesville: Univ. Press of Virginia, 1993.

————. "Urban Development in 18th Century Saint Domingue." *Bulletin du Centre d'Histoire des Espaces Atlantiques* 5 (1990), 197–228.

Haley, Alex. *Roots.* Garden City NY: Doubleday, 1976.

Hall, Douglas. "Jamaica." In *Neither Slave nor Free: The Freedman of African Descent in the Slave Societies of the New World*, ed. David Cohen and Jack Greene, 201–3. Baltimore: Johns Hopkins Univ. Press, 1972.

James, C. L. R. *Black Jacobins: Toussaint L'Ouverture and the Santo Domingo Revolution.* New York: Knopf, 1963.

King, Stewart. "Blue Coat or Lace Collar? Military and Civilian Free Coloreds in the Colonial Society of Saint Domingue, 1776–1791." Ph.D diss., Johns Hopkins University, 1997.

————. "Discrimination and the Growth of an Intermediate Class: *Gens de Couleur* in Colonial Saint Domingue (1629–1790)." Paper presented to the Johns Hopkins Seminar in History, 2 March 1993.

Klein, Herbert S. "The Colored Militia of Cuba, 1568–1868." *Caribbean Studies* 6 (1966): 17–27.

Klein, Martin, and Paul Lovejoy. "Slavery in West Africa." In *The Uncommon Market: Essays in the Economic History of the Atlantic Slave Trade*, ed. Henry Gemery and Jan Hogendorn, 181–212. New York: Academic Press, 1979.

Knight, Franklin. "Cuba." In *Neither Slave nor Free: The Freedman of African Descent in the Slave Societies of the New World*, ed. David Cohen and Jack Greene, 278–308. Baltimore: Johns Hopkins Univ. Press, 1972.

————. *Slave Society in Cuba during the Nineteenth Century.* Madison: Univ. of Wisconsin Press, 1970.

Landers, Jane, ed. *Against the Odds: Free Blacks in the Slave Societies of the Americas.* Portland OR: Frank Cass, 1996.

McClellan, James E., III. *Colonialism and Science: Saint Domingue in the Old Regime.* Baltimore: Johns Hopkins Univ. Press, 1992.

Miers, Suzanne, and Igor Kopytoff. "African Slavery as an Institution of Marginality." In *Slavery in Africa: Historical and Anthropological Perspectives*, ed. Suzanne Miers and Igor Kopytoff. Madison: University of Wisconsin Press, 1977.

Mintz, Sidney. *Sweetness and Power: The Place of Sugar in Modern History.* Baltimore: Johns Hopkins Univ. Press, 1990.

Parker, Geoffrey. *The Military Revolution.* Cambridge: Cambridge Univ. Press, 1988.

Peabody, Sue. "Race, Slavery, and French Law: The Legal Concept of the *Police des Noirs*." Paper presented to the American Historical Association, 29 December 1992.

Pluchon, Pierre, ed. *Histoire des Antilles et de la Guyane.* Univers de la France et des Pays Francophones, vol. 48. Paris: Privat, 1982.

Poisson, Jean-Paul. *Notaires et société: Travaux d'histoire et de sociologie notariales.* Paris: Economica, 1985.

Russell-Wood, A. J. R. "Colonial Brazil." In *Neither Slave nor Free: The Freedman of African Descent in the Slave Societies of the New World,* ed. David Cohen and Jack Greene, 84–133. Baltimore: Johns Hopkins Univ. Press, 1972.

Sheridan, Richard. *Sugar and Slavery: An Economic History of the British West Indies, 1623–1775.* Baltimore: Johns Hopkins Univ. Press, 1974.

Socolow, Susan. "Economic Roles of the Free Women of Color of Cap Francais." In *More than Chattel: Black Women and Slavery in the Americas,* ed. David Gaspar and Darlene Hine, 279–97. Bloomington: Indiana Univ. Press, 1996.

Stein, Robert. *The French Slave Trade in the Eighteenth Century: An Old Regime Business.* Madison: Univ. of Wisconsin Press, 1979.

Steward, Theophilous G. "How the Black St. Domingo Legion Saved the Patriot Army in the Siege of Savannah, 1779." Occasional Paper no. 5. Washington: American Negro Academy, 1899.

Tannenbaum, Frank. *Slave and Citizen: The Negro in the Americas.* New York: Random House, 1945.

Thornton, John. *Africa and Africans in the Making of the Atlantic World, 1400–1680.* Cambridge: Cambridge Univ. Press, 1992.

———. "'I Am a Subject of the King of Congo': African Political Ideology and the Haitian Revolution." *Journal of World History* 4, no. 2 (1993): 181–214.

———. "Sexual Demography: The Impact of the Slave Trade on Family Structure." In *Women and Slavery in Africa,* ed. Martin Klein and Claire Robertson, 39–48. Madison: Univ. of Wisconsin Press, 1983.

Trouillot, Michel-Rolph. "Coffee Planters and Coffee Slaves in the Antilles: The Impact of a Secondary Crop." In *Cultivation and Culture: Labor and the Shaping of Slave Life in the Americas,* ed. Ira Berlin and Philip Morgan, 124–37. Charlottesville: Univ. Press of Virginia, 1993.

———. "Motion in the System: Coffee, Color, and Slavery in Eighteenth-Century Saint Domingue." *Review* 3 (winter 1982): 331–88.

Vaissière, Pierre de. *Saint-Domingue: La Société et la vie créoles sous l'ancien régieme, 1629–1789.* Paris: Perrin et Cie, 1909.

Voelz, Peter M. *Slave and Soldier: The Military Impact of Blacks in the Colonial Americas.* Studies in African American History and Culture. New York: Garland, 1993.

Wilson, Samuel M. *Hispaniola: Caribbean Chiefdoms in the Age of Columbus.* Tuscaloosa: University of Alabama, 1990.

Index

The modifiers fnu (first name unknown), nln (no last name), lnu (last name unknown), and *fils* (son) are used in this index.